THE
AMERICAN ALPINE
JOURNAL

1992

THE AMERICAN ALPINE CLUB
NEW YORK

COVER PHOTO: Kangchenjunga from the west. *Photo by Vanja Furlan.*

ISSN 0065-6925
ISBN 0-930410-51-3

Manufactured in the United States of America

Articles and notes submitted for publication
and other communications relating to

THE AMERICAN ALPINE JOURNAL

should be sent to

THE AMERICAN ALPINE CLUB
113 EAST 90th STREET
NEW YORK, NEW YORK 10128-1589 USA
(212) 722-1628

FRIENDS OF
THE AMERICAN ALPINE JOURNAL

THE FOLLOWING PERSONS HAVE MADE CONTRIBUTIONS
IN SUPPORT OF THE CONTINUED PUBLICATION OF
THE AMERICAN ALPINE JOURNAL

JOHN M. BOYLE

NEW YORK SECTION OF THE A.A.C.

WILLIAM LOWELL PUTNAM

MARION & VERNE READ

VINCENT & MILDRED STARZINGER

HORST VON HENNIG

THE AMERICAN ALPINE CLUB

OFFICIALS FOR THE YEAR 1992

THE AMERICAN ALPINE JOURNAL

VOLUME 34   •   ISSUE 66   •   1992

CONTENTS

COLOR PLATE 1

Photo by Andrej Štremfelj

**Prezelj in the Icefall on the lower part
of the Southwest Ridge of
KANGCHENJUNGA SOUTH.**

Slovene Kangchenjunga Expedition

Tone Škarja *and* Marko Prezelj, *Planinska zveza Slovenije*

Škarja begins:

The OBJECTIVES OF OUR EXPEDI-
TION were three-pronged. We hoped to ascend several of the summits of
Kangchenjunga from the west primarily by already explored routes, we wanted
to make the first ascent of the east face of Kumbhakarna (Jannu) East, but above
all we wished to climb a new and difficult route on the southwest ridge of
Kangchenjunga, alpine-style. We came close to achieving all three goals and
also completed the second ascent of Talung by a new route. The success of our
climbers is reflected by our being awarded the prestigious *Piolet d'Or,* which is
given to the most successful expedition of the year. Tragically, however, two of
our number remain forever on Kangchenjunga's frozen slopes.

Our expedition was composed of eleven Slovene men, a Slovene woman, a
Croat man and two Polish women. We were assisted by a Tamang and three
Sherpa high-altitude porters. After leaving Kathmandu on March 25, our first
climbers arrived at Base Camp at Pache's Grave below the western side of
Kangchenjunga on April 12.

I shall first describe our success on the western flank of the great mountain.
Viktor Grošelj and Stipe Božić established Camps I and II at 6200 and 6750
meters on April 15 and 20. On April 22, Marija Frantar, Uroš Rupar, Robert
Držan, and Jože Rozman set up Camp III at 7250 meters. After a rest at Base
Camp, Grošelj and Božić left Base Camp on April 25, intending to climb to the
main summit of Kangchenjunga by the 1953 British route. They halted at Camp
III during poor weather, awaiting Sherpa help, and finally established Camp IV
at 7600 meters on April 30. On May 1, this pair followed the British route and
reached the summit of Kangchenjunga Main at 1:25 P.M. This was Grošelj's
ninth 8000er. The weather turned bad and on the descent they missed Camp IV.
They continued on and staggered down to Camp III at eleven P.M. Meanwhile,
Rupar had left Camp III at ten P.M. on April 30 and climbing through the night
got to the summit of Kangchenjunga Central by the Polish route on May 1 at
10.40 A.M. He descended also in fog and falling snow to reach Camp III at 8:30
P.M., where he found Frantar and Rozman. I shall describe their sad tale later.
The four summit climbers were back in Base Camp on May 2.

1

PLATE 2

Photo by Jiří Novák

KUMBHAKARNA EAST, showing Furlan-Počkar attempt. Solid line shows ascent (Bivouacs 1 and 2 = △) and dotted line shows descent (Bivouacs 3 and 4 = O).

The second objective was the east face of Kumbakharna East. Vanja Furlan and Bojan Počkar acclimatized, helping with the stocking of camps on Kangchenjunga. On April 28, they left Base Camp and moved close to the bottom of Kumbhakarna's east face, where they spent the night. The next day, they crossed Kumbhakarna's east glacier. At four P.M., they started up the wall at 5530 meters. By midnight, they had climbed 400 meters of 60° to 85° ice, UIAA Grade V rock and mixed climbing. They continued on through the night and at five A.M. reached the biggest sérac in the center of the face. The next 50 meters took them four hours to climb: two rope-lengths of VII, one of VII−, 90° ice and A1. There, at 6380 meters, they rested for six hours because of avalanches. They set out again at three P.M. and at eleven P.M. bivouacked at 6750 meters, having climbed one pitch of VII− and ice of 65° to 70°.

On May 1, they departed from their bivouac at eight A.M. At ten A.M., they left their bivouac equipment behind at 6900 meters to lighten their loads on 70° to 85° ice. Just below 7000 meters, they climbed in two hours the most difficult pitch: VII, 90° to 95° ice. The brittle ice was discouraging enough, but it began to snow furiously. This was their high point at 7050 meters, still 400 meters from the summit. The next 80 meters of rock were deluged with continuous avalanches. They waited there for nine hours, half sitting, half hanging on a tiny shelf. When it cleared a bit at eleven P.M., they rappelled 150 meters to their bivouac gear. Both got frostbitten fingers and toes. They were in the bivouac for eight hours and on the morning of May 2 decided to continue the descent. They were becoming seriously dehydrated and had had little to eat. Avalanches forced a halt at one P.M. but after three hours they took advantage of a quiet interlude between avalanches to escape to a snow cave in the sérac and a fourth bivouac. The next morning, in clearing weather, they climbed and rappelled down the rest of the face and finally reached Base Camp in the evening.

Prezelj continues: (Translation by Maja Košak Bučar.)

Kangchenjunga! At first it meant nothing to me. Now, it means a colossal heap of rocks and ice, which took a lot from me but gave me back even more.

An organized expedition seemed to provide the best solution. Andrej Štremfelj and I understood each other perfectly all the time. We had no worries over porters, food, Sherpas and other "minor" matters, which would have taken all our energy and nerves. All we had to be concerned with was the climbing. Thank you, Tone Škarja, for all your help, which sometimes seemed beyond reason.

Acclimatization was quick and pleasant. Two days before getting to Base Camp, we had climbed Boktoh in six hours, and a week later Talung, from a bivouac at 6600 meters, in only two days from Base Camp and back, a second ascent by a new route. Andrej, who had been suffering from a touch of flu, had to turn back 50 meters from the top, but I got there in a hurricane gale. This climb also served wonderfully as a reconnaissance for our main objective, the unclimbed southwest ridge of Kangchenjunga, which was in full view.

After five days of rest, repacking and uneasy thinking, we start early on the morning of April 26 with Damijan Meško and Tone Škarja who help us transport

PLATE 3

Photo by Tone Škarja

**Southwest Ridge of
KANGCHENJUNGA SOUTH.
Štremfelj-Prezelj route is marked.**

equipment to the beginning of the climb. We finally leave our friends and shoulder impossibly heavy loads. Soon we have to rope up. I climb a 35-meter-high vertical tongue of ice and haul my pack up. Andrej joins me quickly. The change then from ice to rock is a real treat. With difficulty, Andrej climbs to the first expanding flake, where he places a piton and takes his crampons off. It will go faster when we get to the cracks, I find myself thinking. I am cold and impatient. Finally, Andrej calls on me to climb. I don't remove my crampons. Halfway up the pitch, I am ashamed of having urged Andrej to hurry on this extremely difficult pitch. I get help from the rope several times and join Andrej with due respect. We have spent three hours on this one pitch! After ten hours, having belayed only three pitches, we have climbed the first 650 meters of the wall, which we grade at VI, A1, with ice averaging from 60° to 90°. It clouds up and starts to snow. Despite our original plan to climb all night, we set up a bivouac at 6200 meters. Thunder and lightning, unusual in these parts, confirm our decision.

In the morning only the sun could invite us out of the tent. New snow had made the climbing more difficult, covering steep, smooth rock slabs. Not being able to move up the ridge itself, we switch onto its eastern side. In turn, we search for a better route. After a lot of difficulty, we reach "easier" ground. The points of our crampons find meager support on the slabs and we stick ice axes into minor cracks. We manage to regain the crest of the ridge and easier going. We proceed more quickly until the evening. Only in the dark, after eleven hours of climbing, do we find a sufficiently safe place at 7250 meters in the bottom of a crevasse for a bivouac.

The furious winds the next morning nearly blow away my enthusiasm for going on. We reach the shallow col between the hogback peak and the main ridge. Andrej leads ahead while I seek shelter from the blast. He is back soon. There is no way to continue along the ridge; the ridge is too corniced and the winds of hurricane strength. We could traverse along the Great Shelf towards the left to Camp III on the southwest face. We move along the shelf toward an alternative we had spotted from Base Camp. I try as hard as I can to catch up to Andrej so that I can suggest completing the traverse to Camp III. When I reach him, we abandon the plan to continue up the normal route. From the Great Shelf, we ascend a couloir leading back to the ridge crest, where we make our third bivouac at 7600 meters.

While looking for the bivouac, we notice a rock ramp, leading over an overhang. In the morning we find the ramp is easier than we had expected and there are ways around the overhangs. We emerge on snow slopes under the last shoulder of the rib, where we bivouac at 7900 meters after only seven hours of climbing. To our far left, we spot Russian fixed rope.

In the morning, we decide to leave the tent and unnecessary equipment to pick up on the way down. Surprisingly fast, we reach the ridge, but we cannot stay on the crest and continue along on the east side, already lit by the sun. I belay Andrej as he crosses a potential avalanche section. We plow through deep snow, feeling hot despite being at 8000 meters. At 8100 meters, we join

BC

C1

C2

C4

C3

PLATE 4

Photo: Marko Prezelj

YALUNG KANG, KANGCHENJUNGA MAIN CENTRAL and SOUTH from the west. Ascents marked with solid line, descent from Kangchenjunga South with dotted line.

the Russian route, helped in places by the remains of their fixed ropes. The climbing is demanding until we reach the junction of the Russian and Polish routes 250 meters below the summit of Kangchenjunga South. Andrej goes ahead. When I reach a snowfield, just below the summit, I see him again. I can almost touch it but have to fight back a strange wish to quit and turn back. Somehow, at 4:45 P.M., I reach the top!

The top! The top of what? Dead, cold rocks, chained together by ice. The only joy is the end of a tiresome climb. For a moment, I have a feeling of relaxation; and then emptiness. We take pictures. We talk, but I don't know about what. Slowly, we set out for a descent of the Polish route. Andrej cuts some of the old fixed rope to take along for rappels. I am in no particular hurry and enjoy the solitude around me. The sunset is magnificent.

Soon it is black night. By chance or by luck, we find old fixed ropes. These and not being able to see where we are going speed us on our way. We call Uroš in Camp III on the radio. He urges us to follow a steep couloir to the left, but the batteries are so worn out that we can't ask him if he means to our left or his. At 7900 meters, we leave the Polish route and descend the couloir between the central and south summits. I drop my ice axe. It falls down a steep gully. Luckily, I find it where it stuck just before pitching over into the void. We now have to climb down since we have no rope left to rappel. Our only headlamp gives no more light. At the end of the rock, we find hard ice.

Exhausted, I sit down on a snow ledge and watch Andrej. Slowly, I try to follow. We have no hope of finding our bivouac equipment. I know I must not sit down, but here I sit and watch Andrej disappear. Behind a ridge I see five red tents. I close my eyes and they are still there. Hallucinations! I drag myself over the ridge. There I see Andrej, who is resting often too. I stumble after him. I lost the trail long ago as well as any feeling of danger or fear. Then I'm sure I see Tone and Damijan, waiting for us with tea and beer. I can even smell those drinks. I try to decide which I prefer. Then I realize it is again an hallucination. I shake my head and spot a tent. But this time it is for real. I climb in and fall fast asleep. After twenty hours of continuous exertion, my fondest dream was for that warm sleeping bag.

Andrej made it to Base Camp the next day. I took another one. After a day of rest, we have to face the tragic truth that Jože and Marija have left us forever.

How can I learn from what happened to them if in a year's time I'll want to hear the gusting of wind, the thunder of avalanches, the hissing of drifting snow, the crackling of ice in an icefall, the striking of crampons onto the slope, the dripping of water into a crevasse? Am I any wiser? There is so much that I experienced that I don't understand: daring, desire, fear, climbing, wind, snow, doubts, hope, risks, uncertainty, the summit, the moment of freedom, descent, relaxation, falling, hallucinations, sleep, dreams about Marija and Jože, stumbling in the mist, joy, anxiety, death, indifference, confusion, sadness. Why all this chaos of thoughts? What did Andrej and I achieve in those six days? Only a line on a photograph of the mountain. But all this I experienced so intensely that I will never be able to forget or repeat.

Škarja concludes:

Marija Frantar and Jože Rozman left Base Camp early on April 30 and climbed to Camp II. On May 1, they continued on to Camp III, taking only one bottle of oxygen with them; Marija wanted to climb Kangchenjunga without bottled oxygen. They spent the night with Rupar, Grošelj and Božić. On the 2nd, they climbed to Camp IV, hoping to set out for the summit at ten P.M. We don't know just when they left because they did not use their radio before they got to the high point. May 3 was the coldest and windiest day of the expedition. The pair began at a fast pace, but their progress became slower hour by hour. The stormy west wind picked up speed all day. At three P.M., they finally called Base Camp on the radio and reported that they were 150 meters from the main summit. They were weak, their oxygen bottle was empty and they were in disagreement about continuing. Marija wanted to go on, but Jože was for descent. At Base Camp, we recommended that they return. Ten minutes later, they decided to descend. Two hours later, at six P.M., they called with tired voices and were having difficulty handling the walkie-talkies. The last radio contact was at seven P.M. when we heard broken voices saying that they didn't know where they were or where the route down was. The weather was clear but the wind still strong. They obviously must have fallen to their deaths from exhaustion.

Wanda Rutkiewicz found Jože Rozman's body at 7400 meters on May 4. On May 5, Robert Držan and Dare Juhant found Marija Frantar's body at 7500 meters. They buried both dear dead friends in a big crevasse. The accident stopped all further climbing activity.

Summary of Statistics:

AREA: Kangchenjunga Himal, Nepal.

ASCENTS: Boktoh East, 6142 meters, 20,150 feet, April 10, 1991 (Štremfelj, Prezelj, Rupar).

Talung, 7349 meters, 24,112 feet, Second Ascent via a new route, the West Face, April 20 (Prezelj).

Kangchenjunga South, 8476 meters, 27,809 feet, via new route, Southwest Ridge, April 30, 1991 (Štremfelj, Prezelj).

Kangchenjunga Central, 8482 meters, 27,828 feet, via Polish Route, May 1, 1991 (Rupar).

Kangchenjunga Main, 8586 meters, 28,170 feet, via First-Ascent Route, (Grošelj, Božić).

ATTEMPT: Kumbhakarna (Jannu) East, 7468 meters, 24,502 feet, via East Face, to 7050 meters, May, 1991 (Furlan, Počkar).

PERSONNEL: Tone Škarja, leader, Jože Rozman, Robert Držan, Marija Frantar (f), Bojan Počkar, Vanja Furlan, Marko Prezelj, Uroš Rupar, Dare Jahant, Viktor Grošelj, Andrej Štremfelj, Damijan Meško, *Slovenes*; Stipe Božić, *Croat*; Wanda Rutkiewicz (f) and Ewa Panejko-Pankiewicz (f), *Poles*.

Sherpa Everest Expedition

PETER ATHANS

ON MAY 8, THREE MEMBERS of the 1991 Sherpa Everest Expedition attained the wind-scoured summit of Mount Everest or Sagarmatha, the peak's Nepalese name. I accompanied the trio of Sherpa mountaineers. Just one year before almost to the day, I had reached the world's highest summit for the first time. I later wrote this about my second ascent to the roof-top of the world.

"As Apa, Ang Temba and Sonam Dendu traversed the tightwire of the southeast ridge above the south summit, I stopped to change oxygen cylinders and take a moment's break. Throughout the morning, the wind's ferocity seemed only to gain momentum and render every motion the more precarious. Watching the three steadily ascend the short, though abruptly precipitous Hillary Step, I was filled with an even greater admiration and respect for the Sherpas than I had possessed before this, our fourth and last summit attempt. While Sonan Dendu fixed the new 7mm rope over the step for our descent an hour later, I began moving again with the renewed vigor which rest and oxygen bring at 28,700 feet. The three Sherpas climbed out of sight above the step and I was left alone to get on with the business of ascending the exposed, steep summit ridge. The wind rendered the climbing more difficult than I remembered from the previous year and I found myself concentrating on the pick of my ice axe and crampon front-points. To the southwest, the sky had perfect clarity and 15,000 feet below I could faintly perceive the clearing in the wooded hillside near the Tengboche Monastery. Yet to the east, toward the summit of Makalu and into Tibet, the wind from the north flooded the air with the whiteness of driven, dispossessed snow.

"Reaching the bottom of the Hillary Step, I attached my ascender to the new green rope that Sonam had left and began climbing the final obstacle before the summit. Halfway up the 40-foot-high step, I could only marvel at what Sir Edmund Hillary, whose name now graces this climbing problem, accomplished in 1953. Once at the end of the fixed rope and on easier ground, I was relieved that the summit was a scant ten minutes away.

"In short order, I could see Sonam, Apa and Ang Temba taking photographs and tying fluttering white prayer scarves (called *Kata* in Sherpa culture) on an abandoned yellow oxygen cylinder. As I reached the Sherpas, I could hear Temba radioing Lopsang in Base Camp, passing the news of our success. While Lopsang returned the congratulations and gave a cautionary word about descending carefully, I photographed our little group on the summit. Throughout the day, beginning with our 2:30 A.M. start, I thought we would certainly return unsuccessful to Camp IV on the South Col. The extreme cold and relentless wind seemed insuperable problems. A team composed of anyone other than Sherpas certainly would have chosen descent rather than continuing in the maelstrom of stinging, blinding snow. Only through their strength, determination and commitment did the team succeed in placing the first team organized by Sherpas on the summit."

We four climbers then descended together to the last camp at 26,000 feet, rested for about half an hour and then continued down to Camp II at 21,300 feet. The ascent was Ang Temba's first time on Everest's summit, Apa's second and Sonam Dendu's third . . . but their May 8 ascent had significance beyond the accomplishment of three individuals. Their climb was a tribute to the Sherpa people, honoring the efforts of Sherpas from the past, commemorating 70 years of climbing on the world's highest mountain. From the British pre-war attempts on Everest from Tibet, to the success of Sherpa Tenzing Norgay and Sir Edmund Hillary in 1953 and up to the present, the Sherpas have made an indelible impression on the history of Himalayan mountaineering. Now, with the success of the *1991 Sherpa Everest Expedition*, the Sherpa team had contributed significantly to the identity and pride of their culture.

Everest had not posed the optimum of climbing conditions in the pre-monsoon period of 1991. Fierce high winds, snowfall and extreme cold had forced back three previous summit attempts of some of the strongest living Sherpas. April 20, 26 and May 3 were the team's earlier dates of attempting the summit, but only one of those bids even left the tenuous security of the last camp on the South Col.

The expedition was a collaboration between Sherpa ways and American means and organization. The germination of the idea began with 36-year-old Lobsang Sherpa, who resides in Kathmandu, has worked in the trekking/mountaineering industry since the age of 11 and has participated in no less than two dozen expeditions to 8000-meter peaks. With the assistance of Americans Steven Matous, Ron Crotzer, William Lane, Dr. Charles Jones and me, Lobsang organized the complete expedition from our February 25 arrival in Lukla to our departure from there on May 18. The team arrived in Base Camp at 17,600 feet on March 8. The route through the Khumbu Icefall was completed by March 24 and Camp I at 19,800 feet was inhabited on March 25. The route below Camp I was abnormally tortuous as a result of an extremely dry winter and required several extra days in fixing bridges of aluminum ladders over dozens of crevasses occupying the usually moderately angled glacier. Camp I was established on April 2 and, enjoying good weather but icy conditions on the Lhotse Face, the team of Sherpas established Camps III and IV on April 7 and 14. Excellent collaboration between the Sherpa expedition and the New England Everest team rendered the establishment of the route easier.

Summary of Statistics:

AREA: Mahalangur Himal, Nepal.

ASCENT: Mount Everest, 8488 meters, 29,028 feet, by South Col route. First expedition organized by Sherpas. Summit reached May 8, 1991 (Apa, Ang Temba, Sonam Dendu, Peter Athans).

PERSONNEL: Lopsang Sherpa, leader; Tenzing Tashi, climbing leader; Sonam Dendu, Ang Temba, Ang Pasang, Ang Chumbi, Apa, Rinzing, Nima Tashi, Gyalzen, Lhakpa Gyalu, Ang Nima, climbing team; Onchu and Karma, Base Camp cooks and support; Americans Peter Athans, Steven Matous, Ron Crotzer, William Lane, Dr. Charles Jones.

PLATE 5

Photo by Peter Athans

Sherpas Api, Sendrup and Ang Temba on the summit of EVEREST.

The West Buttress of Lobuje East

ERIC BRAND

AN EARTH-SHAKING CRACK told me I was in trouble. Giant slabs of snow swirled around me as my world fell into chaos. Slow motion became fast forward, which became slow motion again as I began to fall. With feet desperately trying to find purchase on the disintegrating slab, I knew there was only one direction for me to go. I heard two voices, one saying, "Be cool, stay on top, stay upright!" and the other, that of a madman, screaming obscenities.

I was in the Ganesh Himal, on Paldor, where I had gone to acclimatize before getting to the main project of my three-month stay in Nepal. An inexperienced Sherpa had triggered a slab avalanche above me and sent me on a 500-foot plunge which stopped just short of a cliff. During the next three days of walking, sliding and crawling to Base Camp with torn knee ligaments, I had time to reflect on my luck. I hobbled back to Kathmandu where I spent three weeks healing and waiting for my climbing partner, Pemba Norbu Sherpa, to return from guiding a party on the south ridge of Lobuje East.

The late Mike Cheney called Pemba "the best Sherpa climber in Nepal." Pemba leads 5.10 rock, overhanging ice and snow-covered fifth-class rock in double boots and is an exceptional climber by any standard. His accomplishments include Annapurna via a new route, guiding Himalchuli and climbing to 8400 meters in winter on the Bonington route on the southwest face of Everest. In 1984, he received an award for heroism from the Himalayan Research Association for saving a porter's life. He diagnosed high-altitude pulmonary edema, carried the man on his back over the 16,770-foot Yalung La, leading and safeguarding the descent of the rest of the party. Pemba was climbing with me out of friendship, not for money. For Sherpas, small expeditions are not nearly as lucrative as big ones.

The approach to the Lobuje Base Camp was slow but uneventful. En route, I realized I had giardia and with a dose of Tinaba still in my system, I felt less than well. Base Camp was placed at 5100 meters between two beautiful hidden lakes at the base of the west face.

After a rest, Pemba and I spent some time teaching Sarke and Beamen, our two Sherpa helpers, the basics of rock climbing, jümaring and rappelling. As we

13

PLATE 6

Photo by Eric Brand

LOBUJE EAST.

were top-roping a 5.10 face problem, we heard a big rockfall very close. Above the talus approach to our route, there was a huge granite slab with a giant dirt-and-boulder "sérac" clinging to it. Unfortunately, only part of it had cut loose. Every day, it sent down little reminders of its presence. Carrying loads across the fresh debris was always a humbling experience. The lower part of the route was developing a personality.

We had attempted the route the previous year, following an obvious ridge to the crux pillar, where a lack of time, sickness and foul weather turned us back. This year, Pemba did all the route finding to our first camp. Dry conditions on the ridge led him to find a faster but more dangerous alternative on the right side of the ridge.

Our route from Base Camp off the talus above the southern lake went up the fifth-class rightmost chimney which cleaved a cliff band. This led to a long easy ledge trending up and right and to a big cliff with an obvious ledge-ramp system. On my birthday, April 26, I led a section of hard water-washed rock through steep and sometimes loose 5.6 rock. This is what I had come for, virgin rock in a wild spot. Pemba fired off the easy ramp. We left a rope and rappelled off as it began to snow. This introduced us to a soon-to-be familiar pattern.

Camp I was under an overhang. We called it "Paradise City," being the safest place next door to Hell. We were across from a gully that was freeway for the nastiest séracs on the mountain and 200 feet away there was a chimney that regularly spewed hundreds of pounds of rocks right next to home. All but the biggest sérac-fall would have missed us, but in any case we were out of there as soon as possible.

All of Camp I was moved to Camp II. Our first trip to Camp II was mostly unroped; we wore rock shoes and carried most of the climbing gear. We swung "leads" up fourth-and fifth-class rock with occasional patches of snow and ice and soon intersected the previous year's route. Our campsite at 18,500 feet had been the high point of our last year's attempt. It was perched on two rock platforms on the side of the obvious col beneath the steep final pillar. Pemba wanted to get one pitch fixed below the pillar. He got to lead 165 feet on snow-and-ice-covered loose blocks topped off by a short section of easy fifth-class rock.

It was four pitches to the base of the pillar from Camp II. The first pitch was already fixed. After that, we went across a fifty-foot section of class 2 to a series of A1 and A2 overhangs. I led through the overhangs quickly and then ran it out along a long, easy fifth-class ramp to a good belay. Sitting at the belay with a panoramic view of Tibet and Rolwaling in one direction and all the way to Chamlang in the other convinced me why I was there. As I soaked up the sun, I didn't realize how cold I would be later that afternoon and on every successive foray up our route. At the moment, it was bliss beyond compare.

Pemba followed up over the overhangs with one Jümar, a prusik, both packs and a lot of swearing. He led a short pitch to a big snow-covered ledge where we had to decide where and what kind of route we wanted to climb. To the right of the ledge, two possible routes led over giant flakes toward the summit of Lobuje

East. The lower route would have been very easy, the upper more stable. I preferred a third option: straight up the pillar. The direct line would involve hard fifth- and sixth-class climbing. This was our choice. Pemba took the next lead up a crack and face with Tuolomne-like knobs, ending in 5.10 R ceilings at the top. The fourth pitch above Camp II was the first difficult aid. After a miserable chimney section in a bergschrund, a couple of slippery free moves led to a short string of tied-off knifeblades. A rivet took me into a flake-choked chimney.

Free climbing up the main pillar above was fun but cold. Here I pendulumed into steep crack systems just left of the pillar to avoid drilling. I continued upward, nutting and nailing. A week before, the pillar would have gone mostly free on steep friable rock crystals.

As the weather pattern deteriorated into daily snowfalls and cold wind, our progress up the pillar slowed to a crawl. A pitch a day of steep technical climbing was usually limited by the ability of the belayer to stay warm. We crawled up the pillar fixing rope as we went, usually getting stormed off by early afternoon. By then, I was leading most of the steep rock. The crux aid pitch was just below the summit ice ridge, a 110° overhang at the top and A3, mainly nailing and nutting a flake system. As I hung from a doubtful nut at the lip, it began to snow like hell. As the snow from the upper face funneled onto me, I decided to bag any fair tactics and went for the bolt kit. I managed to get a rivet in and groveled over the lip into the continually avalanching gully, breathing snow and eating it. After negotiating the short gully, I reached a big ledge where I stumbled around looking for non-existent anchors. Finally, I sank in a bolt, equalized it to a dubious #2 Friend and rappelled down my haul line to a frigid Pemba, ready for the now familiar descent down icy ropes and slippery rock.

With all but one pitch on the pillar fixed, we were ready to go for the top. At four A.M., I awoke feeling good and looking at clear skies. Not hearing Pemba's alarm, I rolled over "to rest my eyes" for a minute or two. The next moment it was 5:30. I called Pemba, "Hey, we're a little late but let's go for it." His mumbled response announced, "We're not going today . . . I didn't sleep all night. My tooth is killing me." A couple of years before, Pemba had cracked his incisor during some martial arts exercises and now he sports a gold cap over the tooth. The tooth was beginning to abcess. His face was drawn from pain and lack of sleep. We were low on food and fuel. The weather had been getting worse; there were fewer and shorter windows in the weather, less time for the rock and fixed lines to dry and thaw.

A year ago nearly to the day, we had been in the same kind of situation, with the roles reversed. We'd had to bail out when I fell sick. Now, after several false starts and as the snow began to fall, Pemba headed down for Base Camp for Ampicillin and a needle to lance the abcess. After nearly ten days, we were tired of our talus pile camp and wanted to get it over with.

The snow started coming down hard, sticking to the rock immediately instead of melting as is more typical in spring weather. My spirits were low, but I said to myself, "I don't care if I have to sit here for another week. I'm not going

PLATE 7

Photo by Eric Brand

**Pemba beginning the crux ice pitch on
LOBUJE EAST.**

until I have the summit!" Patience isn't a virtue on long technical routes; it's a necessity.

Pemba came back the next day, somewhat improved. We decided to go for it no matter what the next morning. Jümaring up the snow- and ice-encrusted lines was a nightmare, especially for Pemba, who had left one Jümar in Base Camp. The weather stayed clear until we reached the ice ridge when it whited out. So much for a summit view!

Pemba has a disinclination toward protection, and Sherpa lungs make him go fast on ice. He got to lead the ridge that worked out to be seven pitches of mostly easy climbing along the now desiccated ice ridge. After four pitches, we came to a dead end. Choice A was to rappel into what looked like an artist's twisted idea of Purgatory in ice. Choice B was to step up the north side of the ridge onto honey-combed ice. Choice B it was and the crux pitch went with a one-screw belay at a good stance. Two more straightforward pitches followed. Upon reaching the last "belay" before the top, I found Pemba standing on his axe and an ice screw. I bent down and plucked the screw out with two fingers. The ice was frozen on the outside, but hollow on the inside. The next lead brought us to the summit. My belay was a joke; if Pemba had fallen off one side, I'd simply have pitched off the opposite one. I was mildly concerned when, as I watched him, one of his crampons sheared. Pemba had taken our only snow deadman with him on this pitch and so the summit belay was an improvement over the last. We reached the unclimbed northwest summit of Lobuje East and looked over at the main summit. It was 150 feet away, at most some 30 feet higher and split by a giant crevasse creating an overhang in the rotten ice. We decided that this was it. We had been prepared for it, having seen the summit on our approach. Pemba, too, had seen it up close a month before when he guided a party to the far east summit.

We were happy with our climb. It was five P.M. and we had a lot of descending to do or a cold bivouac. We reached our high camp at ten P.M., sixteen hours after leaving. The next day, loaded down with 70 pounds of gear, I was too tired to feel much satisfaction; just relief it was over. Satisfaction came when we were both safely in Base Camp and on our way home.

Summary of Statistics:

AREA: Mahalangur Himal, Khumbu Subsection, Nepal.

FIRST ASCENT: Lobuje East's Northwest Summit, 6110 meters, 20,045 feet, via the West Buttress, May 20, 1991, VI, 5.10, A3 (Eric Brand, Pemba Norbu Sherpa).

Solitude on K2

PIERRE BEGHIN, *Groupe de Haute Montagne*

IT WAS ON THE SOUTH FACE OF Lhotse that I really got to know Christophe Profit. In October of 1990, we lived together on that forbidding wall during an adventure of the kind we both love: a simple rope-team for days and days without logistical support striving with incertitude towards a summit, a goal with real meaning. What is the purpose of setting out with ten or fifteen climbers on that kind of objective while uncoiling kilometers of fixed rope? Today, when our technology lets us explore space, the conquest of the great walls of our planet is interesting only if done "by fair means."

* * * * *

Last June, the two of us were there on the Baltoro Glacier, that loveliest glacial avenue in the world, accompanied by two doctor friends, Alain Perard and Raphael Briot. They were not climbers, but their company might be more than welcome in tight moments.

Most of the expeditions that planned to attempt K2 in 1991 cancelled because of the Gulf War. What a privilege to have the "Mountain of Mountains" to one's self! A real luxury which you dream about in the uproar at Everest Base Camp. Moreover, it is certain that K2 is much more difficult than its "older brother."

At the end of the inevitable period of acclimatization during July, our adventure really began on August 8. In the middle of the night, we left our bivouac tent at 6900 meters on a hump of the northwest ridge of K2. We were anxious to join that point to another at 8611 meters of elevation.

Alas! Towards the west, the glittering stars disappeared. A black hole, more worrying than the night itself, was devouring the sky and advancing over the mountains of the Karakoram. Along the horizon, a still ill-defined storm was unfurling. Suddenly, lightning flashes pierced the darkness over Nanga Parbat, 150 kilometers at our backs. The needle of our altimeter began a crazy climb and let us guess what a terrible barometric depression was digging itself into our region. Without a moment's hesitation, we returned to our shelter.

Just before dawn, the southwest wind struck. With extraordinary violence, it lashed the mountain, enveloped it and whirled furiously along its flanks. We sat in our sleeping bags, completely dressed and even shod and gloved in case we might have to make a precipitous departure. The gusts became so powerful that we feared for our tent. Although solidly guyed to the slope, it threatened to fly

19

COLOR PLATE 2

Photo by Pierre Beghin

North Face of K2.

off at any instant. The wind squalls became more and more frequent and more and more brutal. The tent swelled and flapped, sounding like gunfire. To counteract the formidable pressure from the outside and to keep from being crushed, we propped ourselves on the windward side of the tent, vaguely in panic, with muscles aching from the cramped position.

At dawn on the second morning, after folding up our tent, we left our camp without the slightest regret. The visibility was so limited that we wandered about for some moments before finding where to descend. While climbing down, I remembered that from the beginning of July we had already made six round trips to 7000 meters. Each time, the weather had blocked us there. The result was a certain lassitude and not an inconsiderable loss of weight. This adventure was turning into a war of attrition. We agreed that we had only until the end of August to set foot on the summit. "We can't spend the winter here!" said Christophe.

On August 14, two days after the new moon, we finally again crossed the 7000 meter barrier. It seemed that the weather had stabilized. A light north wind, a few lazy clouds and a hazy horizon were encouraging signs. In about ten hours we had gained 1000 meters. We climbed simultaneously, mostly with the rope in the bottom of the pack; it took too long to belay. In places the rock was so rotten that it seemed like a vertical scree slope. Towards 7800 meters, the climbing became harder; airier too! From there, our northwest ridge merged into the north spur of K2, the only one that is entirely in Chinese territory. This has been trodden only four times, as evidenced by old ropes rotting, faded by the sun, gnawed by the wind and rockfall and some of them no longer anchored to anything.

Toward noon, we reached a kind of eagle's nest, blown clear of snow. The summit was still very distant, separated from us by slopes overloaded with snow. During the morning, with the gain of altitude our panorama had grown, letting us see to the north the ragged relief of Chinese Tartary.

The next morning around seven o'clock, we had a leisurely get-away. We carried little in our rucksacks: a headlamp each, down mittens, extra goggles, a survival blanket and a stove. At 8100 meters we were faced with a long traverse of 200 meters before reaching the right side of the great couloir that stretches up to the summit. Over broad stretches, there was breakable crust, indicating windslab. We had no choice: cross them or kiss K2 goodbye. I went ahead. Each of my steps plunged deeply into the slope and added to the dotted line of my tracks. This exhausted me mentally, fearing that at any moment the whole slope might avalanche. Christophe followed, treading exactly in my tracks, hoping not to dislodge the fragile cover. We spent a crazy amount of time. Towards noon, I crossed the bergschrund that marks the beginning of the couloir, which rose at 50° to 55°.

I headed for the rocks at the edge of the couloir, but the higher I got, the deeper the snow became. I was thigh-deep and had to stop every two paces. Some meters lower, Christophe tried his chances in the center of the couloir, where the ice gleamed in places. He progressed at a good pace, halting only every ten steps. He had found the key. However, after 200 meters, the snow

PLATE 8

Photo by Pierre Beghin

**K2 from the north, showing
Beghin-Profit route with 6900-meter
camp and 7950-meter bivouac.**

improved and the windslab disappeared. At two P.M., we had half the couloir below our feet. But then the situation took a turn for the worse. An icy shadow crept over the slope. Our feet rapidly numbed. A greater worry was that my fingers began to lose their mobility. We hesitated, discouraged. With the risk of frostbite, the summit receded into an improbable future.

I extracted my down mittens and pulled them over my under-gloves. In a few minutes, enough warmth returned to let me continue. At 8500 meters the slope lessened and Christophe plowed a trench in the bottomless snow. Under it lay hard, blue ice, into which our crampons barely bit. Breathless, completely groggy from oxygen lack, I climbed by instinct. Suddenly, I saw Christophe ten meters higher astride a sunny ridge at the top of the couloir. It was six P.M. when I emerged at his side.

From that moment on, we were drawn on toward the summit as by a magnet. That meant that we would go on, come what might. Everything became simple: nothing more existed but that point at 8611 meters, us and immense, painful fatigue. To keep up my morale, I didn't look more than two meters ahead. Suddenly, instead of snow ahead of me, there was dark emptiness, the other slope down K2. It was hard to believe. My watch showed ten minutes to seven. Christophe turned and we fell into each other's arms.

While the powerful shapes of the Karakoram were sinking from sight, drowned in the night, a glimmer of light clung around us. Way below, the Baltoro Glacier wound through a forest of confused mountains. This twilight stage-setting took on a planetary dimension. It was hard to understand. Despite the uncertainty of the descent, I felt a moment of rare bliss. We stood there, oblivious of ourselves. Then the routine tasks: a radio message to Alain and Rafael, the summit photos, the headlamps to put on and the parkas to adjust.

A curious thing happened just then at Concordia on the Baltoro Glacier. French trekkers were admiring K2 in the failing light. Suddenly, they noticed on the summit, ten miles distant, several flashes of light. No! It was not a question of extra-terrestrials from Outer Space. They had seen the flashes of our cameras. Several days later, it was they who announced news of our success to the Pakistani authorities.

Twenty minutes passed. The biting cold—it was −35°—pushed us to flee, to lose altitude fast.

Guided by the flickering of our headlamps, we found the couloir again. We plunged into the black, bottomless hole. Hour added onto hour. No halts, no incidents, no sudden difficulties; we trudged insensible to the cold, fatigue and unconscious of time and space.

In the great traverse, our tracks had completely disappeared. Only a few guiding marks; that was enough. Again, we had to break trail in that deep, treacherous snow. A little before midnight, we crouched before the tent. The buckle had been buckled! For 16 hours we had eaten nothing and drunk almost nothing.

The next morning, seated on the boulder field, I savored the moment. Thanks to our physical condition, we had made only a brief incursion into the

PLATE 9

Photo by Christian Profit

**Beghin high on K2's North Face.
Bivouac was in rocks at left.**

domain of "rare oxygen." The doors of altitude had not had time to slam upon us. I had an intuition: the mountain gods would let us escape and two days later we would be back in Base Camp. The psychological tension which had grown ever stronger on the slopes of the mountain disappeared as if by magic. The magic of the summit! In its place, I felt again a new spiritual equilibrium, a sort of euphoria. I knew that it would last for some time. Until we were caught up in the daily agitation, back there in France . . . Happily, we shall construct other dreams.

Summary of Statistics:

AREA: Karakoram, Pakistan.

ASCENT: K2, 8611 meters, 28,250 feet, via the Northwest Ridge and North Face, Summit reached August 15, 1991 (Pierre Beghin, Christophe Profit).

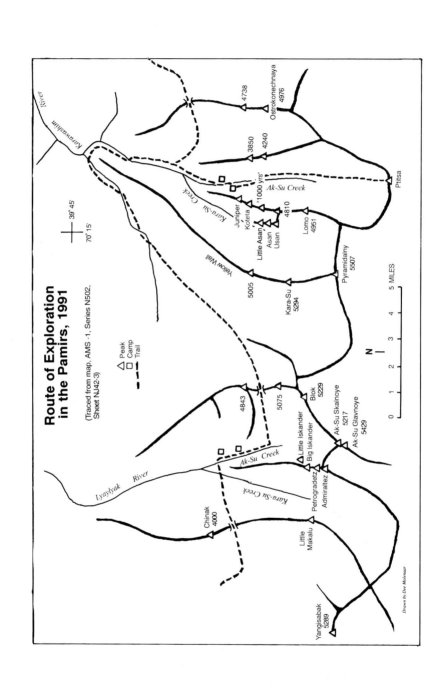

Route of Exploration
in the Pamirs, 1991

(Traced from map, AMS - 1, Series N502,
Sheet NJ42-3)

△ Peak
▢ Camp
▬ ▬ Trail

39° 45'
70° 15'

N

0   1   2   3   4   5 MILES

Karawashim River

Kara-Su Creek

Ak-Su Creek

4738
Ostrokonechnaya 4976
3850
4240
Pititsa

Juniper
Kotela
"1000 yrs"
Little Asan
Asan
Usan
4810
Lomo 4951

Yellow Wall

5005
Kara-Su 5294
Pyramidalny 5507

4843
5075
Blok 5229
Ak-Su Skalnoye 5217
Ak-Su Glavnoye 5429

Little Iskander
Big Iskander
Petrogradetz
Admiraltez

Ak-Su Creek

Lyaylyak River

Kara-Su Creek

Chinak 4000
Little Makalu

Yangisabak 5289

Drawn by Dee Molenaar

Granitic Peaks of Kirgizia

MARK BEBIE *and* TOM HARGIS *with* IGOR TSARUK, *St. Petersburg*

Michael GRABER WROTE in *Ascent* of 1980, "God went nuts when He created the Cathedral Spires," and halfway around the world from Alaska, this statement applies equally well to a recently discovered climbing paradise in central Asia. Located on the Kirghiz side of the border with Tadzhikistan, these stunning granitic peaks form a narrow east-west spine about 15 miles long among the usual shale and limestone peaks of the Pamir Alai. In the quality of their rock and their sheer and massive shapes, they resemble their granitic cousins in Patagonia, Pakistan and Alaska, yet with much less severe weather.

The moderate altitude combined with moderate climate makes climbing here a pleasure. The climate is so dry that couloirs are best climbed early in the season since they can be snowless or composed of old, hard ice late in the season. Permanent snowfields and glaciers are generally found above 4000 meters, although many rock routes have stagnant snow and ice to cross on the approach. As on all high mountains, storms can coat the peaks with a healthy layer of snow, but here it disappears quickly. The long rock routes on the lower peaks are usually free of snow, but sometimes the cracks can be filled with ice. What is the best way to characterize the region? Patagonia without the weather? A Yosemite-scale Wind River Range? Analogies never tell the real story, but most people returning from this region can't stop talking.

For centuries, shepherds and their sheep, goats, cows and horses were the only visitors to the lush alpine meadows at the headwaters of the Lyaylyak and Karavashim rivers. Early in this century, the Asan-Usan valley was a site for mica, tin and beryllium mining, and some abandoned mines can be found there today. In 1933, the General Staff of the Red Army produced a map of this region. In 1942, the German General Staff also mapped the area, and the U.S. Army produced its map in 1952[1]. These maps are now out of print, and since they are difficult to read, we hope that the accompanying sketch map illustrates the topography well enough.

One will quickly notice that the names Ak-Su ("white water") and Kora-Su ("red water") are used quite freely, especially when it comes to creeks. Fortunately that is not the case for mountains. A nameless peak is identified by a number that is the peak's height in meters. Also, as a reference for climbs described here, the length of the Nose Route on El Capitan is 900 meters, the height of the northwest face of Half Dome is 600 meters and the altitude of Mount Whitney in the Sierra Nevada is 4418 meters.

PLATE 10

Photo by James McCarthy

The West Face of BLOK, Ak-Su Group, Kirgizia. The West Ridge is on the right skyline and the North Face appears just over the northwest prow.

COLOR PLATE 3

Photo by James Dockery

**AK-SU SKALNOYE. Behind is
AK-SU GLAVNOYE, Kirgizia.**

Unfortunately, our information is less than complete for many of the routes described, but we hope that this article sheds light on the history, potential and development of climbing here. It will quite clearly illustrate the tremendous skill of the Soviet climbers, skills which have been developed, for the most part, isolated from the West.

An apology is also made for the use of "Soviet" and "Leningrad." Although they are no longer appropriate, they indicated the currently used names at the time when the described events took place.

The Ak-Su valley was first discovered by Soviet climbers in the winter of 1982. At the head of the valley stands the namesake Ak-Su, a beautiful double-summited peak. The granitic Ak-Su Skalnoye ("Rocky Ak-Su;" 5217 meters, 17,116 feet) lies just north of the crumbling, snow-covered Ak-Su Glavnoye ("Main Ak-Su;" 5429 meters, 17,812 feet). A few climbers from Leningrad (now St. Petersburg) took a chance on the fantastical stories emanating from central Asia, and that summer Big Iskander ("Alexander the Great") was climbed. Currently, Big Iskander has been climbed by its west face, a mid-fifth-class mixed route, a 19-pitch grade V. Suddenly interest in the region blossomed, and in 1983, the 1500-meter-high face of Ak-Su Skalnoye was the scene of two teams competing for the National Championship. Both the right-hand buttress route of 41 pitches and the left-hand one were ascended over a period of eight days, involving aid, free- and mixed-climbing. Also on Ak-Su Skalnoye is the very alpine northeast ridge (30 pitches, V, 5.10d) and in 1991, the very obvious central couloir was climbed by the Krasnoyarsk Club. Other notable ascents were done in the 1980s. On Blok (5229 meters, 17,156 feet), the classic west ridge (IV, 5.10b) was climbed as well as two routes on the 1000-meter west face. Both of these are grade VI aid climbs, one of which gains the northwest prow, where it steepens. The popular east face of Little Iskander (14 pitches, III, 5.10b) was climbed, and Little Makalu is reported to have a mostly snow mixed route. Above the Base Camp area at 2700 meters is the rare solid limestone peak Domashnyaya ("House"). Its popular northwest face has more variations than routes, so it is better to choose a line and go. After four years of development by Soviets, the reputation of the climbs in the Ak-Su valley spread to western Europe, and starting in 1986, the first outsiders, a Czech team, visited the valley[2]. The first Americans followed in 1987[3,4].

In the mid-1980s, geologists, using helicopters, saw with climbers' eyes the Asan-Usan peaks, which are above two valleys, and 14 hours on foot, to the east of the Ak-Su valley. Asan and Usan are Kirgiz names given to twins. Viewing them from the cirque between them and P 4810, one can easily see why. Thus, in 1986, three teams from the cities of Dnepropetrovsk, Odessa and Rostov made the first climbing visit to the Asan-Usan valley, expressly for competing for the National Championship on the 900-meter-high west face of Asan (4230 meters, 13,878 feet). In addition to three grade VI west-face routes, the southwest pillar ("Alperian Route;" 26 pitches, the top ten of which are scrambling, V, 5.11b, A1) was climbed. Typical of peaks in this region, the descent off Asan is involved. Opinions differ, but the descent requires at least 16 rappels.

PLATE 11

Photo by James McCarthy

The 1500-meter-high North Face of
AK-SU SKALNOYE, showing the
Northeast Ridge on the left skyline.

The north ridge of P 4810 (15,781 feet; 45 pitches, VI, 5.11) was also climbed; the approach couloir is best done early in the season.

Interest waned in 1987, but two teams from Odessa and Leningrad used mules to transport their food and gear to the 2700-meter Base Camp. They climbed the remote north face of Pyramidalny Peak (5507 meters, 18,068 feet; grade VI), and the 16-pitch diagonal route on the Yellow Wall (IV, 5.10b/c), which has become a popular climb. The southeast pillar of Usan (IV, 5.10b, grade IV) was climbed, and further south, a 15-pitch, grade III, 5.8 route was also put up on Usan which starts from the col with P 4810. Finally, a small dent (12 pitches) in the huge west face of P 4810 (15,781 feet) tentatively set the stage for the following year.

In 1988, eight teams showed up to compete for the National Championships on the smooth, steep, 1200-meter-high west face of P 4810. Four grade-VI routes were completed, and three more have been added since. These are certainly of the highest standard of alpine rock climbing in what used to be the Soviet Union, since they are comprised of 60% aid and free climbing up to 5.11. Our co-author, Igor Tsaruk, moaned about the lack of ledges on the winning climb he was on: a 38-pitch, eight-day route. It took two days to descend. The nature of the rock on this face lends itself to much hooking, but the difficulty (A3, A4 or A5?) has not been translated into its Yosemite equivalent. Nevertheless, these climbs could probably be grouped with the moderate-to-hard nailing routes on El Capitan.

Igor claims that the Soviet method of aid-climbing is superior to the Western style. Instead of multiple étriers, the Soviets have a single strap to which equally spaced rings are attached with two rings at the top. To use this ladder of rings, they attach hooks to a point just below the kneecap by straps running around the upper calf and around the arch of the foot. One ascends by means of "knee-hooking" (literal translation) to the top rings and once established, it is claimed to be a more secure stance than top-stepping in étriers. Igor also claims that one has a longer reach from this position of greater support and stability.

Also in 1988 on P 4810, a route on the south ridge was added, a mostly free climb (26 pitches, 5.10+). The peak just north of P 4810 is named "One Thousand Years of Christianity in Russia" (4507 meters, 14,787 feet). The striking south ridge was climbed in 30 pitches over a period of three days. Due to its extremely narrow profile, the descent was a very difficult series of rappels, including 50 rappels down a couloir after the descent off the rock! A difficult, although unfortunately dangerous, route was put up on the 1000-meter-high west face. Asan saw more activity with three new routes, two of which are on the west face. Also in that year, yet another valley to the east was visited. An aid route on the 700-meter north face of P 3850 (12,631 feet) was done, as well as a free route on the northwest ridge (V, 5.11 o.w.). Two routes were climbed on the 900-meter-high face of P 4240 (13,911 feet). Other peaks climbed were the snow peak Kara-Su (5294 meters, 17,379 feet), located behind the Yellow Wall, Shaitan Khanna (c. 5000 meters, 16,404 feet), which is just east of Pyramidalny, and the unattractive shale peak Lomo (4700 meters, 15,420 feet),

PLATE 12

Photo by Giacomo Baroni

West Face of P 4810.

climbed from the pass between it and P 4810. A lot can happen in one year when 250 climbers spend their summer vacation in one valley.

In 1989, the central pillar of the north face of Ptitsa ("The Bird") was climbed. This striking 20-pitch, grade-V, 5.9 line with 60 feet of aid is a five-hour hike south of the P 3850-P 4810 Base Camp. Two routes were done on the 1100-meter-high east face of P 4810. The first visit by foreigners, Americans, was made to the Asan-Usan valley. Since then, the two valleys have become increasingly popular with foreigners[5,6,7,8,9].

A word on the National Championship. Climbing teams of, say, three people come from clubs located in the cities. More than three from a club may attend, but they climb as their own ability and interest dictates. A "meet" is not held. Climbers just show up at a place of their own choosing to do a climb and then submit a report of their efforts to a committee which reviews the year's climbs. These judges choose the winners and runners-up. Coincidentally, other teams may choose the same route at the same time. Apparently, only coins (not fists) have been tossed and the losers of the toss have chosen another line. Of course, to submit a report on a first ascent carries more weight than the repeat of an already completed route. When the Soviet system existed, a prominent climber would gain respect and encouragement from the State and thus be able to climb more. There is a National Championship for alpine climbing on technical peaks such as Ak-Su Skalnoye or P 4810 and one for big peaks, such as Pik Pobedy. This championship has nothing to do with crag-oriented speed climbing.

These reports contain photographs, pitch-by-pitch descriptions, and anything else you can think of. For example, the report for the north face, right, of Ak-Su Skalnoye is 27 pages long. These reports are not kept in any central location, nor published annually in something like the *American Alpine Journal*. However, new route information is easily exchanged among the clubs since they all know each other. These reports are personal property and are carried back and forth by the owners.

The climbing season is June through August, and most Soviets climb in June, tapering off during the season. Visiting climbers looking for route information may be out of luck if they are there in the latter part of the Soviet high season.

Access to the Ak-Su valley can be made by truck, although helicopters are used. One can approach the Asan-Usan valley on foot, but for the purposes of climbing, helicopters are almost essential. The Tadzhikistan (south) side of the border is much more rugged, steep and barren than the gently rising valley bottoms on the north side.

Since foreign currency and foreign gear are highly desired by the Soviet climbers, outsiders are welcome. That is not to say that Soviet climbers are purely mercenary, but most of their equipment (even Friends) is home-made and they really want access to Western products. Since Soviet hospitality is second to none, no reason, not even a language barrier, should prevent anyone from visiting this region. Only the biggest and most significant routes have been reported here. There are many smaller half-day and one-day routes available,

PLATE 13

Photo by Giacomo Baroni

**Piramidalny's North Face. Italian
Paolo Tamagnini's solo is marked.**

and much potential exists for new crag climbs on cliffs south of the Yellow Wall. At the time of this writing, very few organizations in the West are communicating with the Soviet clubs, although a little digging can uncover a Western liaison to obtain the prerequisite "invitation" for a sports visa.

Except for the arrival of climbers in the last ten years, not much had changed in these high valleys. The Kirgiz shepherds still live in the same stone, wood and canvas huts they used to and they still walk or ride their horses (although an occasional motorcycle is seen). They dye their wool and make their cheese as they always have, and their flocks still graze the meadows in abundance. Keeping this last fact in mind, visiting climbers should not neglect water purifiers and antibiotics.

REFERENCES

[1]U.S. Army Mapping Service, NJ 42-3, series N502, 1952, scale 1:250,000.
[2]Note by Vladimir Weigner, *AAJ, 1987*, pages 312-3.
[3]"Ak-Su Adventure" by Sibylle Hechtel, *Mountain* #122, July/August 1988, pages 32-37.
[4]Note by Sibylle Hechtel, *AAJ, 1988,* page 289.
[5]"Back in the USSR" by Mick Fowler, *Mountain* #136, November/December 1990, pages 32-7.
[6]"Asan Acquaintance" by Brian Swales, *Mountain* #137, January/February 1991, pages 26-31.
[7]Note by Darko Podgornik, *AAJ, 1989*, page 295.
[8]Note by Michael Fowler, *AAJ, 1991*, pages 305-7.
[9]"Back in the USSR" by Jim Dockery, *Rock and Ice* #44, July/August 1991, pages 20-27.

Jeff Lowe on the Eiger

DAVID ROBERTS*

CLIMBING HARD ALL DAY, Jeff Lowe had forced an intensely complicated route through a wilderness of false leads and deadends, but darkness caught him short of the ledge he had hoped to reach. He had no choice but to carve a makeshift cave in the steep fan of snow where he was stranded, then crawl inside. Stupified with weariness, he fired up his balky stove and turned pot after pot of packed snow to water. *Hydrate, hydrate*, his brain cajoled his listless body. In the middle of the night the storm came in. The wind was moderate, but a heavy snowfall poured out of the black sky.

By morning, Lowe was in a perilous situation. It was Thursday, February 28, his ninth day on the north face of the Eiger. He was 4500 feet up, but in the 1500 feet of frozen limestone that still hung above him, he was sure to find the hardest passages of all. He was running out of food. He could not stay warm at night. And he was on the verge of exhaustion.

A little after noon, the snow let up. With a tight rope to his anchoring pitons, Lowe cautiously climbed out of his cave to survey his blizzard-struck surroundings. He peered into the void below his feet, still blank with clouds, as he remembered the nine days of agonizing work that had brought him to his stance three-quarters of the way up the Nordwand. Then he craned his neck to look upward, toward the ledge, plastered now with rime, that he had failed to reach the night before. He kicked his right foot into the snow and stepped up. He kicked his left foot: another step.

Seven hours later, in darkness, Lowe settled once more into his soaked sleeping bag. He would have to spend another night in the hated snow cave. He got out his two-way radio and warmed the batteries. Rousing his support team, Jon Krakauer and me, at the hotel far below, Lowe spoke slowly, his voice seamed with fatigue, "I've got a decision to make, whether to go up or down. It's a tough one." There was a long pause. "I don't know how hard it would be to get down from here. I figure it'll take three days minimum to reach the summit if I go up. And that's only if the weather's good tomorrow and Saturday."

* * * * *

On February 19, his first day on the Nordwand, Lowe had cruised up 2000 feet in only two hours. The going was easy but dangerous, a matter of planting

---

*Excerpted with the publisher's permission from an article which has recently appeared in *Men's Journal*.

PLATE 14

Photo by Bradford Washburn

The EIGER'S NORTH FACE. Jeff Lowe's route is marked.

COLOR PLATE 4

Helicopter Photo by Jon Krakauer

Jeff Lowe on difficult mixed climbing on the headwall of the NORTH FACE of the EIGER.

the picks of his ice axes in a steady rhythm, of stabbing the crampon points into the brittle ice overlying steep rock. He soloed without a rope: if he slipped, he would die. But Lowe was in his element. The speed and precision that had made his technique famous among a generation of American climbers spoke in every swing of his axes. It was still winter, and this was the Eiger. Over the past six decades, it was the easy start that had seduced so many alpinists. Between 50 and 60 of the best climbers of the world had died here, in a variety of gruesome ways.

At the foot of a sheer 350-foot rock cliff called the First Band, the climbing turned abruptly hard. As Lowe used his rope for the first time, his pace slowed to a vertical crawl. In 3½ hours, he gained only 110 vertical feet. On the second day, a dogged and ingenious struggle over nine hours won him a mere 80 feet more.

On other great mountain faces, clean vertical cracks, good ledges and solid rock abound. The Eiger, however, is notorious for limestone knobs that crumble as you seize them, for downsloping ledges covered with ice and for a scarcity of good cracks. The severity of the terrain brought out the best in Lowe as he "hooked" his way upward.

But already there were problems. Lowe had what he called "fumble fingers," dropping three or four of his most valuable nuts and pitons. The adjustable pick on one of his ice axes had worked loose. When he searched his gear bag for the tiny wrenches to tighten the pick, he realized he had left them behind, down at the hotel. He had climbed on, which meant he could really never swing the axe hard and plant the blade. It was a bad compromise, like driving at 30 miles per hour on a flat tire.

On the third day, ignoring the malaise that had troubled his snow-cave sleep, Lowe pushed on. By 2:30 P.M., he had almost beaten the First Band, but the storms of the last few weeks had plastered snow and ice into dead-plumb rock. He had to shift back and forth between rock and snow, from spidering with bulky plastic boots and gloved hands among the limestone nubbins to crabbing his way up the hollow snow with crampons and axes. When he could, he placed protection.

At 2:50, he clung to a flimsy patch of rotten snow. He doubted that he could reverse the moves he had made above his last protection eight feet below. He had no idea if he could place any above or climb through the looming overhang that blocked his view of the rest of the gigantic wall. He seized a tiny nut and began to place it in a good crack. Suddenly, the snow broke loose beneath his feet. He was falling.

Solo self-belaying is far more awkward, and far less reliable, than the kind offered by a human partner. He carried a new kind of self-belay device he had never used. Before his first hard pitch, he had not even taken the contraption out of the plastic bag it was sold in. The question now, as he fell through the air, was whether the device would work.

An abrupt jolt gave him the answer; the rig had done its job. Lowe was unhurt. He edged his way back to the high point, where he found another plate of snow to try. Gingerly, he moved up it, anticipating another fall with each step, until he stood beneath the rock overhang. He made a series of delicate moves, angling left through a weakness in the browing cliff, until he could plant the picks of his axes on snow above. The left pick wobbled in disturbing fashion. But the snow was worthless, sloughing loose under the slightest touch. For a full hour, he struggled in place. At last, he found a small patch of more reliable snow. He planted both ice axes, moved his feet up and stabbed the front points. The snow held. He moved a few feet higher, then surged upward.

He had put the First Band behind him, but it was getting dark. After placing three ice screws, he rappelled all the way back to his snow cave and crawled into his thin sleeping bag. Tired though he was, sleep escaped him. The loose pick on his ice axe nagged at him. At the rate he was burning fuel, he would run out long before he could reach the summit. And he needed those nuts and pitons he had dropped.

The boldness of his choice to go without a bolt kit was now manifest. On the First Band, he had been stymied by blank rock. With bolts, you can drill the rock and build a ladder through the blankest impasse. Every other new route on the Eiger in the last thirty years had employed bolts; the Japanese, who had pioneered the excellent line just to the right of Lowe's, had placed 250 of them. As he struggled to relax in his snow cave, his problems of unhappiness of the last year danced mockingly in his mind. In the morning, he turned on his radio and called Krakauer and me, down at the Kleine Scheidegg. "Guys," he said in a slow, gravelly voice, "I'm thinking about a slight change of plans." He paused. "I'm going to come down."

*   *   *   *   *

After the snowstorm on the morning of his descent, the weather had stabilized with high overcast. But the temperatures were strangely warm. There were plenty of reasons to give up the climb; alibis were lying around ready to be seized. However, with minutes to spare, he caught the first train to the Eiger Gletscher station the next morning. By 12:20, he was back at his bivouac site at the lower end of the ropes he had left in place. It was warm, but perfectly clear with a forecast for more of the same.

One of the bugaboos of solo climbing is the weight of one's gear. On his first day back on the face, it took him 4½ hours to wrestle the gear up to his previous high point. Then, boldly, he led on into the dusk. It was not until 9:55 P.M.—three hours after dark—that he got established in a good bivouac site. He was halfway up the Nordwand.

The next morning, for a couple of pitches his route coincided with the classic 1938 line. The Ice Hose had been a formidable test to more than one party of experts over the years. For Lowe, with his impeccable ice technique, it was almost like hiking. He surged up the Hose and across the Second Icefield and at the day's end bivouacked at the base of the summit headwall. Only a little more than 2000 feet of climbing remained, but it promised to be severe and unrelenting. As he inched his way up into the dark, concave headwall, it would be increasingly hard to retreat.

It was Monday night, February 25. The forecast from Zürich was for continued good weather through Wednesday, then snow for Thursday and

Friday. A fiendish scenario began to propose itself. With two days' steady climbing, Lowe might well find himself at the point of no return, only to get socked in by a storm.

By pushing into each evening, he had gotten stuck with a late start every morning. On Tuesday, the 26th, he didn't get going until 10:55. That night as Krakauer and I looked up, we caught sight of a pinpoint of light three-fifths of the way up the wall: Lowe's headlamp as he dug his bivouac site.

On the night of the 27th, the storm came in hard while Lowe was in his claustrophobic snow cave, not a good place at all. "I've never been so pummeled in my life," he radioed in the morning. "There's a big avalanche coming down every five minutes. I couldn't move if I wanted to." Yet, a moment later he said, "I'm going to have to muscle my way out of here and get a better bivy site." The forecast was mixed. The snow was supposed to stop later in the day. Friday and Saturday would be better, but another storm was due on Sunday.

At noon, he broadcast again. He had managed to get out of his snow hole, but the search for a better bivouac site had been fruitless. The avalanches were still pouring down, his clothes were wet and he was cold. To our surprise, he said, "I'm going to sign off and try to get something done. If I can get my act together, I think I can get to the Central Band today. If the next storm is bad, I really need to get to the top before Sunday."

Because of the storm, Krakauer and I hadn't been able to see him since the previous afternoon. At 2:30, the clouds broke for a few minutes. I ran to the telescope. The face was plastered with rime, coating even vertical slabs beneath overhangs. I found Lowe, climbing almost 300 feet above his snow hole. The Central Band, a long horizontal ledge that divided the headwall, lay less than a rope-length above him. The clouds moved back in, and we did not see him again that day.

Wrapped once more in the blank mist, Lowe plugged on upward. It was imperative that he reach the security of the Central Band. With spindrift spilling over cliffs all around him, he seemed to be stopped cold by a rotten overhang until he found a way to bypass it. Then, with daylight waning, he just managed to gain the Central Band. But it was too late to haul his gear; he had to rappel down and camp one more night in the miserable snow cave.

Friday, March 1 marked the sixth day of Lowe's second push on the Nordwand, his tenth overall. A south wind sent hazy wreaths of fog over the mountain, but the weather was basically good. By noon, he had hauled all his gear up to the Central Band. Only 1200 feet of climbing remained. Here the wall was scored by ice-caked ramps leading up and to the left, most of which ended nowhere. The protection was minimal, the climbing nasty. He was aiming for the Fly, a small icefield 500 feet above. He had to move fast with the threat of Sunday's storm hanging over him, but he was slowed drastically by what turned out to be the most difficult climbing yet.

Through the telescope, I could gauge how steep the cliff was when I saw loose chunks of snow plunge forty feet before striking rock again. At one point, it took him an hour to gain 25 feet. The rock was loose and rotten. Stone towers,

PLATE 15

Helicopter Photo by Jon Krakauer

First day of Jeff Lowe's winter solo of the EIGER'S NORTH FACE.

like gargoyles, sat waiting to collapse at the touch of a boot. Pitons, instead of ringing home as he pounded them, splintered the flaky limestone and refused to hold. Bolts would have been a godsend. When he set up an anchor from which to rappel back for his loads, the anxiety peaked. For his shakiest anchor, he strung nylon webbing to equalize forces among eight different nuts and pitons, each of them almost worthless by itself.

On Saturday, March 2, Krakauer started up the west ridge, the easiest route on the Eiger, hoping to camp near the top to greet Jeff and, if need be, help him down, but it soon became apparent that because of soft, wet snow, he could never make it. When Lowe next radioed, I had to tell him about Krakauer's retreat from the west ridge. He took the news calmly, even though it raised the specter of serious danger for his own descent. For the first time, we talked about the possibility of a helicopter's picking him up on the summit.

Lowe climbed on. Pushing himself beyond fatigue, again well into the night, he managed an uncomfortable but secure bivouac just below the Fly. His two-day push from the Central Band had been a brilliant piece of work, but the Sunday storm was coming in early and 700 feet lay between him and the summit.

That evening, he settled into his bivouac and tried to sleep. He had two gas cartridges left to melt snow, but his food was down to several candy bars. His hands were in terrible shape. Each morning, his fingers were so sore and puffy that he had a hard time tying his shoelaces. Worse, his sleeping bag, thin to begin with, was soaked like a dishrag. For 14 hours he shivered, waited for dawn, as the snow fell outside his cave.

By noon on Sunday, he had not moved. At two o'clock, through a break in the clouds, we saw him climbing slowly above the Fly. As he started to climb, he grew deeply alarmed. Something was wrong. He felt weak all over. He had been going on too little food, he had spent a sleepless night, and he had not drunk enough fluid. He could do no more that day than advance two pitches and string the ropes. He would then devote himself to resting and drinking and trying to get warm.

Once more, sleep was impossible. He shivered through the night, even though he lit the stove and burned precious fuel in an effort to heat his frigid cavern.

At 7:30 A.M. on Monday, March 4, we received Jeff's morning call. For us, the night had been filled with premonitions of disaster. It was astonishing to hear him say cheerily, "Right now, I'm just watching beautiful spindrift going by." At 8:30, he started climbing. A perfect day had dawned, of which he would need every moment. Another storm was due on the morrow. We called REGA, the government-run rescue service, and alerted them to a possible need for a summit helicopter pickup. Then we watched Lowe climb. At 9:15, he turned a corner and disappeared into a hidden couloir.

Lowe had hoped that above the Fly the going would get easier, but in icy chimneys broken by bands of brittle rock, he was forced onto some of the hardest climbing yet. He felt less weak than the day before, but a sense of struggling to meet a terrible deadline oppressed his efforts. It was hard to place good protection. He found himself hooking with front-points and axe-picks on rounded rock wrinkles that he had to stab through the snow to locate. And then, just before it happened, he knew he was going to fall.

The picks scraped loose. He was in midair, turning. Twenty-five feet lower, he crashed back-first into the rock. The self-belay held, but he was hurt. He felt as if someone had slammed a baseball bat into his kidneys. He pulled himself together, started up again and found a way through the dicey hooking sequences, despite the pain. At last he surmounted a good ledge only 400 feet below the summit.

But here he faced a problem. The warm sun had loosened the summit snowfields. Every chute and runnel became an avalanche track. One swept over him, buffeting his body as it tried to knock him off the wall. For two hours he climbed doggedly on. Three more avalanches engulfed him. One knocked his feet loose, but he hung on with his axes.

REGA was waiting in Grindelwald, ready to fly the moment Lowe emerged on the west ridge. A stiff wind had begun to blow a steady plume off the summit. The wind could defeat the helicopter's maneuvers, or even cause it to crash.

As we prepared to call REGA, we watched in distress as Lowe halted at a mottled band of rock and snow, only 20 feet below the ridge, pitching stones down the cliff. He found the band was only a skin of ice holding together rocks that were as loose as a pile of children's blocks. When he flung stones aside and dug below, he found only more of the same. He could get no protection in—neither piton, nut nor ice screw.

Lowe got on the radio. Krakauer asked, "Jeff, if you just dropped the rope and went for it, could you solo the last twenty feet?"

"No problem," said Lowe. "But are you sure the helicopter can get me?" He untied his rope, abandoning all the gear that he had fought for nine days to haul up the 6000-foot cliff, and without it, deserting his own last refuge. We called REGA and the helicopter took off from Grindelwald. He seemed to sprint up the last twenty feet.

The helicopter spiraled upwards toward him. It would lower a cable, which he was to clip into his waist harness. Now it was just above him, hovering in the stiff wind. Suddenly, it peeled away and flew toward the Jungfraujoch. Lowe wailed.

The chopper, we later learned, was carrying three passengers: a co-pilot, a winch operator and a doctor. Appraising the tricky situation, the pilot decided to drop two of his colleagues at the Jungfraujoch so that he could fly as light as possible when he made the pickup.

The helicopter hovered again, its rotors straining against the wind. The steel cable dangled from its belly. We saw Lowe swipe for its lower end, miss once and then seize it. He clipped in and the helicopter swept him into the sky. He was off the Eiger! The cable wound upward as he rode it toward the open door. The winch man reached out his hand. Lowe climbed through the door and crawled back into the conundrum of his life.

Summary of Statistics:

AREA: Berner Oberland, Switzerland.

SOLO WINTER ASCENT: Eiger, 3970 meters, 13,025 feet, A 60% New Direct
Route on the North Face; Summit reached on March 4, 1991 after nine days
on the final push; VII, 5.10, A5, 60 pitches (Jeff Lowe).

PLATE 16

Helicopter Photo by Jon Krakauer

**Jeff Lowe on difficult mixed ground
on the final day, 300 feet below the
summit of the EIGER.**

Stortind's Unclimbed Southwest Ridge

PAUL RICHINS, JR.

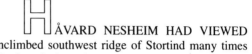ÅVARD NESHEIM HAD VIEWED
with awe the impressive, unclimbed southwest ridge of Stortind many times
from the Ullsfjorden ferry. The ferry is the main transportation link between the
quaint village of Lyngseidet and Tromsø, the closest major city in northern
Norway. He had been itching to challenge the unclimbed ridge for a number of
years but conditions and circumstances had kept him away until now.

Little was known of the spectacular ridge. From the maps and viewing the
ridge from the nearby ferry, Håvard knew that it would not be your typical climb.
The southwest ridge is long, challenging and exposed, jutting up more than 3000
feet above the glaciated valley floor. In places the ridge narrows to a knife edge
with nearly vertical drops on both sides.

Håvard knew all this, but Dick Ratliff, my climbing companion from
California, and I did not. I had been in Norway for just ten days and had not seen
the route. Dick was under the false impression that we would be climbing a
different, less difficult route on Stortind. All we knew was what Håvard told us
the night before the climb as we sorted through our equipment in his lovely home
near Lyngseidet. The home is surrounded by grandeur. The back looks out over
Kjosen Fjord and from the front one looks straight up at the Lyngen Alps.
Håvard was tight-lipped when we clamored for information. All I could pry out
of Håvard was that it would be a long route and that I should bring a little extra
food.

What in the world did that mean? Should I bring an extra apple or plan for a
multi-day epic? Since I had just met Håvard only hours earlier, I had no idea how
long was "long." What was "long" to him might be considered routine or
conversely an epic marathon to me. However, I did know that he had successfully climbed Everest in 1985 and had done many extreme routes in Norway and
around the world. With this in mind, I doubled my lunch to last me a full two
days, if necessary.

In retrospect, it was clear that he played down the severity of the route in
order not to alarm us or his wife. As it was, she was very apprehensive about the
climb. She knew of the reports from the earlier unsuccessful attempt in which
several of Håvard's friends had attempted the ridge but turned back early in the

climb. They reported that it was a very long and technically demanding ridge requiring an estimated 13 to 15 hours to complete.

At 5:30 the next morning, with much apprehension I saw the imposing route for the first time as we skied to the base of the peak and the snow couloir leading up to the ridge. I wondered why Håvard, a mountaineer of considerable reputation, was taking on such a difficult ascent with two climbers from California, whom he hardly knew. What about his local buddies? Why wasn't he climbing the route with one of them? Had they all turned him down?

I would start the climb, but I reasoned that while in the snow couloir I could back down at any time and let Dick and Håvard continue on. What I didn't realize was that the couloir was much longer and steeper than it appeared from below. It took us nearly five hours in the couloir to reach the ridge. As it steepened from 40° to 55° near the half point, we roped up. Once roped, I was committed. I now could not go down without taking the other two down with me. We reached the ridge just in time for lunch. I was glad I had brought extra food, as Håvard had suggested, as we had been skiing and climbing for six-and-a-half hours and hadn't even started the real part of the climb.

The ridge was plastered with snow, ice and rime, driven by high winds from the north and south. This sculptured rime characterized the entire southwest ridge as well as the descent down the north ridge. It built up in frothy, feathery layers that exaggerated the size of the rock it encrusted, resulting in grotesque, overhanging heaps of crud. It was beautiful to look at, but tough to climb. These granular ice tufts were more air than ice and snow, rendering our ice axes nearly useless. We resorted to digging out hand, finger and arm holds in the rime in place of more conventional ice-axe techniques.

We started up the ridge with running belays as the lower part was less severe than higher up. In four to five pitches we came to a place which could not be climbed or avoided by traversing left onto the northwest face. We rappelled 70 feet down the right side and traversed left across steep snow for half a pitch. From this belay point, we continued to traverse steep rock, snow and ice for 80 feet and then went left up into a difficult 70° mixed gully. After a pitch in the gully, we regained the ridge.

From here on, the climbing became harder with the ridge narrowing and the obstacles becoming more numerous and larger. We continued up the ridge by staying, where we could, directly on the crest. Many times we had to drop down to the left, traverse across and up the northwest face back to the ridge to avoid difficult, if not impossible, obstacles that lay right on the crest. This continued for ten or fifteen pitches.

We passed over two false summits before reaching the true one. Beyond each, the climbing became more and more difficult. After moving over and down from the second false summit, we encountered the most difficult climbing of the route on the four leads which culminated in the true summit. Three rime-encrusted rock steps had to be surmounted. They were not big, some 20 to 25 feet high, but they were vertical or nearly so and covered by fragile frost feathers. As we struggled upwards, the thin cover of snow and rime would unpredictably break off the smooth rock face. These three steps were the crux of the ascent.

To climb the first step directly would have been difficult as the smooth, exposed rock face offered no opportunities for protection. Håvard tried in vain to find a route by moving left onto the northwest face. Finally we found a very obscure route on the right side. We dropped fifteen precipitous feet and then climbed straight up a nearly vertical gully back to the ridge. The next step was not so hard and was climbed direct. The final step was the most difficult and there was no way around it. Håvard did a masterful job on the vertical ground, which put us right on the summit.

Håvard summited at 11:30 P.M., I at 11:40 and Dick at 11:50. As I belayed Dick up this last desperate step, I urged him to hurry if he wanted to complete the climb today; in ten minutes it would be tomorrow.

In very low light, I was able to get a picture of Dick and Håvard on the summit. At this time of the year, northern Norway has 24-hour daylight, although it is faint around midnight. We had been climbing on the ridge for twelve hours, plus the five in the couloir.

We descended the north ridge to a prominent saddle and continued down to the west, returning to our skis and finally to the road and car at 6:30 A.M. after 25 hours of continuous climbing.

In all, we climbed about 25 or 30 pitches with one short rappel. The ridge became more difficult and exposed with the obstacles getting larger and more frequent as we approached the summit. There are no escape routes down either side of the ridge. The best way down lay on the other side of the mountain. Once on the ridge, the prospect of retracing our steps was unthinkable. The descent would have been as difficult and as time-consuming as the ascent.

Håvard led the entire route and did a masterful job of route-finding and climbing. Without his strong leadership and climbing skill, Dick and I would not have completed the route. It was a great challenge and a wonderful experience that I am ready to repeat!

Summary of Statistics:

AREA: Lyngen Peninsula, Northern Norway.

NEW ROUTE: Stortind, 1512 meters, 4960 feet, Southwest Ridge, April 27, 1991 (Håvard Nesheim, Dick Ratliff, Paul Richins). (Vertical elevation gain = 4960 feet from sea level.)

EQUIPMENT: A small assortment of Friends, chocks, pitons and 3 snow flukes.

Huntington's Phantom Wall

JAY SMITH

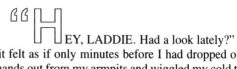EY, LADDIE. Had a look lately?"

"Huh?" I moaned, as it felt as if only minutes before I had dropped off to sleep. I pulled my gloved hands out from my armpits and wiggled my cold toes. Then turning to the right, my anchor rope pulled tight and I suddenly remembered where I was. I popped my head out of the bivy sack at once.

Peal Teare was sitting up half out of his sack pointing toward Mount Hunter, an immense cloud now obscuring its summit plateau.

"Hell, doesn't look too promising now, does it?" I asked.

"Nope," he said as he fired up the MSR stove.

Our meager accommodations for the night, what there was of them in the Alaska Range during early May, 1990, had been a 3x10-foot slot carved into an exposed snow fin. We were perched 4000 feet above a narrow fork of the Tokositna Glacier on Mount Huntington's southwest face, attempting a new route on the mountain's largest and last unclimbed wall. The night, although only five hours long, had been a cold one without the comforts of a sleeping bag and had dragged on with the cold and discomfort seeping into our bones. Before I finally dropped off to sleep, my last memory was of Paul's toes clicking together as he tried to keep the circulation moving while waiting for the Grabbers to kick in. (These were the chemical heat packs we inserted into our inner boots for warmth. The old lighter-than-sleeping-bag theory! Nice try!)

Within an hour, we had eaten, packed and started the next lead, a 5.10 crack that was packed with ice and now A2. Before I got twenty feet up, it was snowing. By the end of the pitch, the visibility was down to forty feet with the flakes growing in size and volume. One more free pitch on thinly iced rock slabs and Paul had us on the large snowfield at two-thirds height. I continued the next lead without even stopping at the belay and headed for a large rock outcrop for a full rope-length. Small powder sloughs passed to the right and left as I dashed for the security of the stone abutment. Slamming in a knife-blade, I sat on the snow and brought Paul up.

"I think it's going to get serious here really fast. What do you think?" he asked as we both turned and stared at the route ahead.

The next section involved traversing the snowfield to the right for several hundred feet before following a 1500-foot fluting which provided drainage for the entire summit snowfield. Just then a powder avalanche shot airborne off an overhang midway across the traverse. We turned to each other and graciously

COLOR PLATE 5

Photo by Jay Smith

Paul Teare on SOUTHWEST FACE of MOUNT HUNTINGTON.

PLATE 17

Photo by Bradford Washburn

**MOUNT HUNTINGTON's Southwest
Face on the right. The upper
three-quarters of the route are
marked.**

declined the next lead. We gazed leftward to check the options when another slough swept just ten feet beyond us and began to creep our way. Soon we were buried under six inches of spindrift and it was clear this was no place to admire the view. We simul-climbed *muy rápido* to a larger outcrop in hopes of finding shelter, giving the storm one last chance to stop.

Five minutes of studying the Washburn photo identified the quickest line of descent to Base Camp. To retreat down our line of ascent would be long and dangerous in a storm and place us 2000 feet below and several miles away from camp. No, our best bet was to try to traverse, down-climb and rappel a ramp system which led to the top of the Stegosaurus on the Harvard route. From there it would be about six rappels into the basin we called home. As we discussed, a thunderous roar disrupted our conversation as the largest avalanche yet swept around both sides of our fortification.

"I think we best beat feet out of here while we still can," suggested Paul.

We began the 2500-foot descent as the storm grew in intensity.

* * * * *

A year later, as we heaped our eight huge mule bags onto the tarmac in Talkeetna, a man carrying a small white poodle strolled out of the Hudson Air Service hangar and stared at our immense pile.

"You boys fly'n into the Kahiltna?" he asked.

"No, we're going into the Tokositna, Mount Huntington."

"Well, if ya were goin' into the Kahiltna, I could fly ya right now, but the Tokositna. Well that's a bit tricky. Yeh, it's kinda socked in at the moment. Many of ya?" he asked, eyeing the mountain of gear.

"Just the two of us."

"Shore have a lot of stuff," he stated, eyebrows raised.

"We like to travel light. Only the bare essentials."

Cliff Hudson just shook his head, smiled and said his son Jay would have to fly us in with the more powerful turbo-prop 206 Cessna.

"Come back in the morning and we'll see what we can do."

The wings tipped at a dizzying angle before leveling out on the final approach. The view ahead was all rock and ice of the towering walls of Huntington's west face. No aborted landings here. The narrow cirque left no room for error.

Jay Hudson set us down on the glacier as if he were simply pulling his cab to the side of the curb. Quickly, we unloaded the aircraft and he sped away into rapidly enclosing clouds. We dragged our hefty pile an entire thirty feet before erecting Base Camp. Then, we introduced ourselves to our new neighbors, who were also trying a new route on the hill.

Our previous year's two attempts on the route had given us much insight as to the snow conditions needed for a successful ascent. Since it had been snowing relentlessly for nearly a month, there was little need to hurry. Avalanches poured down every conceivable path as the sun struck the face for the first time in a week.

PLATE 19

Photo by Paul Teare

Jay Smith on steep ice on HUNTINGTON.

Eight days after our arrival in Base Camp, Huntington appeared to be coming into fine form. Yesterday, it had cleared in the morning and we prepared for the route while avalanches rocked the region. By late afternoon, the walls grew silent and we knew that our route had shed its new coat.

The "Phantom Wall," due to its hidden nature in the confines of a lower fork of the Tokositna, had been overlooked completely, not easily visible from any vantage point. Or perhaps it was because of the approach required to reach its start, 2000 feet *below* Base Camp, the closest available landing strip. But most likely, its immense size and committing nature had been the greatest deterrent. The 6000-foot funnel-like face would be a death trap if you were caught in its belly during a storm.

We knew that the key to success was to be fast and light, though this time we opted for sleeping bags since the morning air temperature was dipping below $-15°$ C.

At one A.M., we cached our skis after an exciting high-speed chase by headlamp on crusty snow and a crevasse-strewn glacier. Ahead, our track from previous days had been covered by avalanche debris. We tumbled through, made a rappel into a couloir and down-climbed into "Death Valley." God, what a place! Monstrous cornices perched thousands of feet over this tiny area not much wider than a football field. This was no place to dawdle. We broke out the rope and quickly made for the schrund across thousands of tons of fresh rocks and debris.

The first hard bit had changed radically from a year before. Instead of easy ice to the right of the hanging glacier guarding the entrance to the face, we now had to climb its flank. I swung my picks at the rock-filled, fractured and overhanging ice. With feet scraping on verglas-covered slabs, I wished I had grabbed the screws from Paul before embarking on the "easy" wake-up pitch. My feet popped only four times before the sidewall eased to vertical. I tied off my tools and belayed Paul up. A few delicate moves and he had us on easier ground. Now was our chance to make up for lost time. We simul-climbed unroped up huge gouged grooves in the ice face till our calves screamed for relief.

By ten A.M., we had surmounted one more difficult ice pitch and climbed together across the second snow band to the start of the large rock face at just over mid-height. This section could become a shooting gallery with us being the clay pigeons. We were glad the sun had still not hit its top.

Paul climbed quickly up the black diorite vein which formed the route amongst steep, smooth walls, one tool in ice and the other hand laybacking on some dubious flake. Crampons on edges, then snow, then ice. This was mixed climbing at its best. It was never too desperate, but never with much protection. It called for techniques one could never learn from books. Simply great and all free!

We passed our old bivouac site just after midday. Up a short aid section and then we continued up more mixed ground. Paul shot past and we were soon climbing together again above our previous high point to the wall's only safe

PLATE 20

Photo by Jay Smith

**Paul Teare rappelling on
HUNTINGTON's Southeast Face.**

bivouac. Basking in the evening sun on a perfectly sheltered platform, we stretched out, brewed up and feasted on Raman. Just one more day! We weren't asking for much, just another 24 hours and we'd be done with this mountain.

Crrrack! The sound of cannons popped our bubble. "Bloody hell! Check it out!" Paul screamed as he jumped up for a better view.

"Whoooa!" was all I could manage as we watched truck-sized granite blocks roar down from high off the south ridge. They dislodged all in their path and then terrifyingly engulfed the bottom-most section of our route. It was the only thing, other than us and the sun, that had moved all day. But it presented a convincing argument that Death Valley was no place to gawk.

The dawn was crystaline. Our prayers answered, we were climbing by eight A.M. No packs, no water, a skeleton rack and one Powerbar each. We again climbed 50 meters apart. Protecting only occasionally, we had unquestioned confidence in each other's judgement and ability. We were a good team, having endured many alpine faces together before.

Miles above, the ice hardened. Our dull crampons and tools forced us to belay. Three more leads up the final flutings placed us on top with a vista for a king. For hundreds of miles peaks rose in the distance and not a single cloud was to be seen. We rejoiced at our luck and the excellent climbing we had enjoyed. Basking in the sun and our glory, we remained thirty minutes before starting down.

The descent went smoothly till a wee landslide missed us by several feet and swept down our next rappel. Increasing our speed tenfold, we were back in camp for supper and our last two beers.

Summary of Statistics:

AREA: Alaska Range

NEW ROUTE: Mount Huntington, 3731 meters, 12,240 feet, Southwest Face, May 20-21, 1991 (Jay Smith, Paul Teare).

"Snake-Bit" in the Alaska Range

JACK TACKLE

T HE EAST FACE OF MOUNT BARRILLE is the size of Half Dome and yet it is dwarfed by its neighbor, Mount Dickey. The center of the face had only one route, that done by Austrians in 1988 (*AAJ, 1989,* pages 74-82). This face has one major feature which stands out—a pillar shaped like a cobra standing on end and ready to strike, the "Cobra" Pillar. It is on the right of this pillar that the Austrian route follows a major right-facing corner system. From down-glacier, we could see another major system on its left side.

On June 10, 1989, Jim Donini and I had just survived the worst descent epic of our collective 35 years in the mountains. Nearby Mount Wake, almost too aptly named, was to have been a "warm-up" for more climbing on Mount Foraker. Even though I had been on more than a dozen previous Alaskan trips, three of them with Jim, we once again learned that there are no first ascents in the Alaska Range that are warm-ups.

Our initial attempts on Barrille took place only after sitting on the glacier in bad weather. We had then intended to go on over to Foraker, but the weather was so bad that we could not get there and were flown out to Talkeetna. There was no time left that year for Foraker and we returned again to Barrille. Four separate attempts were foiled by repeated storms. We flew out at the beginning of what turned out to be the most bombproof high pressure of the entire season. The sky was blue from there to Siberia for ten days after we left. That was round one.

Round two took place in June of 1990. I was unable to go, but Jim Donini and another partner got seventeen pitches up, only to be stopped by a blank headwall that needed to be drilled. They ended by doing another route on the face to the right, but the main line still remained undone.

The final round found Jim and me back in the Ruth Gorge in June of 1991, bound and determined to get up the wall this time. We came equipped with plenty of "tricks" in our bag, so as not to be repulsed another time. I was able to fly from my home in Montana to the landing site in the Ruth Amphitheater in less than fourteen hours.

The very next morning, Jim and I fixed four ropes on the first six pitches in perfect weather. We returned the following morning and went up on the wall for

PLATE 21

Photo by Bradford Washburn

**Upper two-thirds of BARRILLE's
Cobra Pillar. B = bivouac.**

good. We had learned in earlier attempts that taking enough gear to be "comfortable" is too much. We took no tent, just bivouac sacks, lightweight bags, one Northwall hammer each, a lightweight stove and hardware for a long free climb. For the upper part of the face were crampons, onesport presles and gaiters. The heavy metal selection consisted of a generous bolt kit and a healthy pin rack.

The rock is very good for the most part, especially for the Ruth Gorge. We encountered only short sections of bad rock, the wonderful crackerjack variety, but they were not major obstacles, just temporary inconveniences. The rock climbing consisted of 23 pitches, with seven mixed pitches of snow and ice. A long section of snow up high allowed us to move together for a considerable distance. The final pitch involved aid off of ice tools shoved into unstable snow which repeatedly gave way.

The weather pattern was unstable, but not horrible. It would be good for 12 to 36 hours and then snow for 12 to 16 hours. Once it cleared, we could be climbing on dry rock in very little time.

Eight pitches up was a ledge where we had spent a lot of time in 1989. This was home for the first two of the four nights we spent on the face. The other bivouac was at Pitch 17, also a two-night affair.

Above the first bivouac, both in 1989 and 1990, we had followed the left side of the pillar in a big corner system. This had led Jim in 1990 to the blank headwall which turned them back. Since we had the gear to deal with a temporary lack of crack systems, we focused undaunted on the headwall, but after hours of drilling and hooking, I lost my enthusiasm for the line. It was not only because of the bad esthetics, but also because the route up to now had gone all free except for 40 feet.

Just before starting up the wall for good, I had seen from the base a series of cracks in the middle of the pillar. While still lower down, we had attempted to get into these cracks, but at that point the rock was too friable. We decided to rappel down two rope-lengths and try to gain access to the cracks out in the middle of the pillar. A 5.9 traverse with one bolt for added protection got us to the system in the center of the "Cobra." This was the key to the route and provided some of the best and most spectacular climbing on the face. Being out there in the middle of this beautiful rock, following a single crack for hundreds of feet and peering down onto the Ruth Glacier flowing below us was as good as it gets.

The second bivouac site was at the top of the initial section of the pillar, 17 pitches up. We occupied this veranda for two nights. Again, as had been the case below, we were driven back to this retreat temporarily because of storms. But the site was spacious and had a good supply of snow for water. We could see the Austrian route off to the right. It was wet with snow melting up high; and we wanted to continue our line if possible.

Two pitches straight above the bivouac we could see another gorgeous corner system heading on up our pillar. Once into that, we were sure it would lead us on up to the top. For three rope-lengths it was classic crack climbing. All of a sudden, the cracks ended in a totally blank 60-foot-high headwall at the top of which the rock climbing ended. The snow was so close I could smell it. We tried either side but no cracks were to be found. A classic Alaskan situation, especially in the Ruth Gorge. Out came the drill. Jim hooked and bolted the headwall in an horrendously cold wind. We placed only three bolts for protection, hooking in between. The rock was so hard that it took 30 minutes to place each bolt. In typical Ruth Gorge fashion, as soon as the rock leaned back at the top of this headwall, it turned to the rottenest of the entire wall. In ten feet, it went from being marble-hard to decomposed garbage that you could use your ice tools in.

It was late on the fifth day when we stepped into the snow that led us to the summit of Barrille. The climbing above the rock was easy with the exception of the summit cornice. The view from the top was absolutely stunning. The only major peak we couldn't see was Foraker, our next objective. The descent off the back side was just a matter of following steps to our tent in the twilight.

* * * * *

After a day and a half of rest and relaxation at the Mountain House landing site, we flew to our other objective, a new route on Foraker. So much for the fun-in-the-sun rock climbing! Jim Okonek landed us on the southwest fork of the Kahiltna Glacier, a short 30-minute hop from the Ruth.

A few years back, Jim Donini and I had unsuccessfully tried to make the second ascent of the Infinite Spur. Bad weather forced us off after we had sat out storms for three days. I had always wanted to climb Foraker. It is so massive and imposing. From the Kahiltna it looks more ominous and impressive than Denali. I had always dreamed of doing a new route on all three of the major peaks in the range. Denali and Hunter were out of the way, but Foraker remained.

Some years ago, Chip Farrow had shown me this major unclimbed rib on the south side of the mountain. The ridge runs for 6000 feet straight up to the southeast ridge, joining it at 13,500 feet. It bypasses the dangerous terrain which has killed climbers through the years. The ridge looked straightforward except near the top where an ice cliff hung over the ridge. This had been responsible for making climbers think the ridge was dangerous, when in actuality it is not only safe but safer by a long shot than the southeast ridge.

We spent seven days on this ridge, calling it "Viper Ridge." The ice cliff looks like the head of a viper peering over the rock buttress high up.

The ridge has three distinct sections. The first segment was easy snow climbing to around 9500 feet. The middle section was a spectacular 14-pitch, knife-edged traverse of a corniced ridge. Above that lay the crux, a 1000-foot rock buttress with the ice cliff on top of it. The hard part ended at 12,500 feet.

We actually spent only three-and-a-half days climbing on the ridge. Bad weather was hammering Foraker. We had to bivouac three nights in a row only a few hundred feet apart in the middle of the climb. The mixed-climbing crux in the rock section took place during a full-fledged storm. We just wanted to get up the ridge and be done with it. After we were past the difficulties, we were faced with going to the summit in poor conditions with few supplies or with bailing out before the weather caught us high and pinned us. And two or three feet of snow

PLATE 22

Photo by Bradford Washburn

Viper Ridge on MOUNT FORAKER.

had already fallen. We bailed out. What had taken us seven *days* total to ascend took only five *hours* to rappel and down-climb. We did bypass the ice-ridge traverse and just down-climbed a gully system to the east of the ridge.

This ended my personal goal of routes on Denali, Hunter and Foraker. It does not end my interest and love of climbing in Alaska.

Summary of Statistics:

AREA: Alaska Range.

NEW ROUTES: Mount Barrille, 2332 meters, 7650 feet, "Cobra Pillar" on the East Face; 5.10+, A3, 100 feet of aid, 23 pitches and 7 pitches of ice and snow; June 5-10, 1991.

Mount Foraker, 5303 meters, 17,400 feet, "Viper Ridge," South Spur of Southeast Ridge; June 11-17, 1991.

PERSONNEL: Jim Donini, Jack Tackle.

Mount Dickey's South Face

FABIO LEONI, *Club Alpino Italiano*

$\mathbb{A}$FTER LEAVING ITALY, we first vis-
ited for some training climbs the Yosemite, where the weather was bad: snowy
and cold. Manica, Zampiccoli and I did manage to climb El Capitan by the Triple
Direct: a combination of the Salathé, Muir and Nose routes. We then traveled to
the hospitality of the city of Anchorage on May 16 and took several days to
complete our arrangements.

On May 14, we were flown from Talkeetna to the Ruth Glacier and landed
below the imposing east face of Mount Dickey. During unsettled weather, which
lasted several days, we reconnoitered to judge what would be the best route on
the face. When the weather seemed to improve, we immediately decided to
attack. Our route rises at the right side of the south face and follows a nearly
direct line. It seemed to be protected from rockfall.

By taking turns, we kept climbing continuously, thanks to the lack of
darkness at that latitude. After four days, we had fixed 700 meters of rope. The
difficulties were extreme, whether in free climbing or artificial aid. The fright-
fully bad quality of the rock made the climb more difficult and exhausting. The
cracks appeared to shatter literally as they were touched. Placing protection
often required numerous attempts. Every so often at our rest halts, we preferred
to place bolts.

We returned to Base Camp for several days of rest and then, on June 5, all
seven of us set out in calm weather for the final attack. We ascended the fixed
ropes and began climbing again. While two led and another two supported them,
the other three, having found a proper bivouac site, stopped and prepared the
spot. At midnight, we descended to the ledge and all of us slept a few hours.

The weather deteriorated some the next day, but we continued the climb
anyhow. The temperature was not too severe and so, shod in rock-climbing
shoes, we forced our way up some very difficult pitches. After half a day,
however, we lost several hours on a very dangerous pitch, which we overcame
entirely on aid. Toward evening, the first ice-covered pitches obliged us to put on
our mountain boots. The face was no longer quite vertical and we encountered
many mixed pitches covered by unstable snow.

We climbed through the whole night but at a much slower pace because of
fatigue.

A heavy snowstorm transformed the face into a gigantic white plaster cast.
Unfortunately, during the last rock pitch, Danny Zampiccoli took a leader fall

PLATE 23

Photo by Bradford Washburn

South Face of MOUNT DICKEY.

because of unstable snow and rotten rock. He injured his right hand. By good luck, the summit was near and the climbing progressively easier. On a single rope, all seven of us safely ascended the final mixed and snow pitches.

At eleven A.M. on June 7, we were on the summit of Mount Dickey. The glorious weather let us admire the full panorama, especially Mount McKinley, our next objective.

We descended and after a few days transferred to the McKinley Base Camp. In June 21, Bagatolli and Defrancesco completed the ascent of Denali by the West Buttress. Manica and De Donà meanwhile made a very difficult new route on the Throne in Little Switzerland. Then De Donà returned to McKinley and made the round trip to the summit and back in only four days. With my wife Paola Fanton and Corrado Coser, I reached McKinley's summit via the West Buttress on June 20.

Summary of Statistics:

AREA: Alaska Range, south of Mount McKinley.

NEW ROUTES: Mount Dickey, 2909 meters, 9545 feet, via the right side of the South Face, June 5-7, 1991 (Fabio Leoni, leader, Mario Manica, Giuseppe Bagatolli, Danny Zampiccoli, Fabrizio Defrancesco, Bruno De Donà, Paolo Borgonovo).

The Throne, Little Switzerland, via Harmonica Crack, UIAA VI, A3, June 15, 1991 (Manica, De Donà).

Many climbers will be interested in subscribing to **IWA TO YUKI,** Japan's foremost mountain magazine, which has six regular issues and one special mountaineering annual issue per year. Articles in Japanese about climbing in all parts of the world are summarized in English. It contains numerous photographs, many in color, valuable maps, diagrams and topos with English captions. Annual subscription is 7700 yen. **IWA TO YUKI,** Yama To Keikoku Sha Co., Ltd., 1-1-33 Shiba Daimon, Minato-ku, Tokyo 105, Japan.

Northwest Face of Denali's West Buttress

THOMAS WALTER, *Unaffiliated*

Y EARS AGO, I FIRST BECAME aware of the face, the perfect hard Denali route: no hanging ice above, too steep and windswept to collect snow and with easy access to the West Buttress highway. On the West Buttress proper, it starts from the lower Peters Glacier and rises 7000 feet to the top of the buttress at 16,200 feet. The climbing looked pretty straightforward, mostly ice slabs and mixed climbing, but the rock band in the middle looked interesting.

I set about researching the route and pestering friends for slides that might show the face. I was not in a hurry until I saw, to my horror, that Jon Waterman's new book *High Alaska* had a dashed line, signifying "unclimbed," running up the face. I imagined a throng at the base of the route, books in hand, queuing up for the route.

Determined at least to be near the head of the line, I geared up for an attempt in early May of 1990 with a friend from Anchorage, John Tuckey. We acclimatized at 14,000 feet on the West Buttress route until we felt confident with the weather. When we got a close-up view, we were disheartened—it was bitterly cold, windswept and the ice was a glistening brittle blue. We abandoned the attempt.

In late June of 1991, I returned with the "Wyoming hired guns," Greg Collins and Phil Powers. They were good friends with whom I had shared many climbs although I had not seen them for years. Both Phil and I were due to get married later in the summer and so the trip turned out to be a good reacquaintance/bachelor party.

Two days after flying in, we were at the 14,000-foot West Buttress camp. At the top of Motorcycle Hill, I again got a view across the face. This time, to my relief, temperatures were much warmer and the ice had a more hospitable, whiter look. We waited a day at 14,000 feet before Greg and Phil, fit after guiding in the Rockies, went to the summit via the West Rib in a ten-hour round trip.

After another rest day, confident with the weather, we headed down over Kahiltna Pass to the base of the route, carrying only a two-person bivouac tent and food for three days. Much to our surprise, a big thunderhead rolled in that

PLATE 24

Photo by Bradford Washburn

Northwest Face of McKinley's West Buttress.

evening and it poured rain for most of the night. With three of us tangled up in the tiny tent, we got little sleep. The next night, we headed up the face. We wanted to get up and off the climb before the weather broke. It was no place to be caught in the high southerly winds that commonly scour the face.

And that, essentially, is how it turned out. Conditions were as perfect as they could be. Temperatures never dipped below 25°, the ice was reasonably soft and the winds remained calm during the 39 hours we were on the face. Most of the climbing was either about 55° ice or moderate mixed climbing where we could climb quickly with running belays. The six pitches of fifth-class climbing on the rock band slowed us, but it was so warm that we could climb comfortably without gloves.

After twenty hours without a remotely hospitable bivouac spot, we were forced to hack ledges in the ice, where we stole seven hours of sleep. When we topped out the next morning, we were all almost too exhausted to move. Greg and Phil remembered what they had experienced after a summit attempt on K2 the year before. When we reached the fixed ropes at 16,200 feet on the West Buttress route, we decided on descent. We had all been to the summit before—Greg and Phil just a few days earlier. The next evening, we were back in Talkeetna, a mere ten days after we had flown in.

I strongly suspect that the conventional wisdom about climbing Denali—that earlier is better—is suspect. In my experience, the weather pattern is always hit-or-miss between April and July. You might as well go late when the temperatures approach the livable. Our climb would have been much more difficult in colder weather.

In honor of Bradford Washburn's contributions to American mountaineering—his routes, his aerial photographs and beautiful maps—we suggest that at some time Denali's west face be known as the Washburn Face.

Summary of Statistics:

AREA: Alaska Range.

NEW ROUTE: Mount McKinley, Northwest Face of the West Buttress from 7000 feet on the Peters Glacier to the West Buttress at 16,200 feet, June 22-July 1, 1991 (Gregory Collins, Philip Powers, Thomas Walter).

Neacola

JAMES GARRETT

T HE NEACOLA RANGE, neatly tucked into the Lake Clark National Park in Alaska, has effortlessly kept climbers from converting it into a mountaineering goal. Neacola, its highest peak at 9426 feet, had spurned two previous attempts. The only published report was in the 1980 *American Alpine Journal* and described a try on the 4500-foot-high shattered northeast face in 1979. Fred Beckey had, however, visited the area in the early 1970s, but Neacola had repelled his efforts as well. Almost twenty years passed before he shared the secret. His photos and enthusiasm were intoxicating and plans were laid for May of 1991.

I easily recruited Lorne Glick and Kennan Harvey. Though neophytes to Alaska, they were hungry for adventure. Uneventfully, we arrived in Kenai to bland and cloudy weather with only occasional glimpses of Iliamna and Mount Spurr across the sound. Our young, though experienced pilot, Doug Brewer, had never landed in the Neacola Mountains and wanted to wait for a bluebird weather day. He and Fred shared an affinity for lengthy weather discussions. While Doug busied himself with the routine flying of fishermen, oilmen and firefighters, we camped in his hangar. We lounged in the local library by day and crawled through the haunt at night. For eleven days, we were an enigma to the towns-people of Kenai. Most had met few, if any, climbers. Kennan and Lorne, with the impatience of youth, were like whinnying thoroughbreds quivering in the starting gate, salivating and bucking to get on with it. Fred held the reins taut, repeating accounts of his many epic waits and approaches to climbs throughout Alaska. He told us, "When the weather is good, we'll know it."

Hardly too soon, and just before spending our last coins, Doug deftly landed us on the unnamed glacier below the east face of Neacola. Our sullen mood tranformed chameleon-like with the dramatic change of scenery. Unbridled, we skied with heavy loads up the Lobsterclaw Glacier to cache the first of the gear at Advance Base Camp. The next day, we set out with a final load to Advance Base. Fred, frustrated by the ineffectiveness of his snowshoes through the icefall, bowed out and remained at the landing strip.

Four days of poor weather ensued. An occasional glimpse of the western flanks of Neacola showed an enticing slash ending on a saddle just below the summit. Avalanches scoured the face, but a sense of comradery developed amongst us. We held little doubt about if, only when.

Early on the morning of May 20, I was tossing and turning as gusts pounded the flapping tent. I mentally prepared myself for another day in the waiting

71

PLATE 25

Photo by James Garrett

NEACOLA.

game. Lorne ventured a look outside. A sea of clouds swirled and splashed up, obscuring the view, but Lorne's bit had long since been chomped through. We held a vote and democracy ruled. Within two hours, we were uncoiling two 100-meters ropes. We frontpointed and banged our tools up the smooth, icy gash. The winds abated, sunshine crept up the adjacent walls and Lorne smiled about the decision.

On unconsolidated snow over bulletproof ice, we worked our way up the right edge along the rock. The hard ice provided secure belays, although it was a wrenching effort to get the anchors in. Rock placements yielded little protection in rock unlike so much of the beautiful granite on surrounding peaks. The angle steepened to 65° as evening neared. We hacked our way up. Even when rockfall started, a certain tranquility enveloped us. In accord with each other, we knew we would not be trampled.

Ice clogged many of the screws and they became difficult to place; long runouts followed. Kennan led the last pitch through the ice bulges below the saddle. Three hundred feet, two ice screws! Lorne and I cheered him on. He was in his own private Hell. Having underestimated the route when he looked at photos in Utah, he had brought a dull, old, 80cm ice axe to complement his ice hammer.

By eleven P.M., in the sinking alpenglow, we marveled at the spectacular Kichatnas, the Revelations, the seaside volcanoes and the immense Denali massif. During our first real pause of the day, we wolfed down salami, cheese, bread and tepid tea. Two quick, dreamlike pitches later, we straddled the narrow, snowy summit. Hoarsely, we yelped greetings to Fred, warmly ensconced in his tent 5000 feet below in the dark shadows of the east face. It was futile—we barely could hear each other.

After rappelling back to the saddle, we shivered and drank more tea in a makeshift snow shelter, organizing anchors for the descent and waiting for morning light. With long ropes and a slick surface, we were back at Advance Base by ten A.M. Sleeping bag to sleeping bag in 36 hours! If not for good friends, Neacola would have been a lonely and desolate place.

Summary of Statistics:

AREA: Neacola Range, Lake Clark National Park, Alaska.

FIRST ASCENTS: Neacola, 2873 meters, 9426 feet, via the West Face Couloir, May 20, 1991 (Garrett, Glick, Harvey).

P 7020, 2140 meters, via the 55° West Face, May 24, 1991 (Garrett).

P 6920, 2109 meters, via the clean granite of the West Ridge, May 25, 1991 (Garrett, Glick, Harvey).

PERSONNEL: Fred Beckey, spiritual leader; James Garrett, Lorne Glick, Kennan Harvey.

Under Pressure on the Devil's Thumb

MARK BEBIE

Put all thine eggs in one basket, and—watch that basket. —Mark Twain

NUMEROUS SNOW-AND-ICE PEAKS come to mind in the 1000-mile chain of summits that make up the "panhandle" of southeast Alaska. One rock peak particularly captures the attention of pilots and climbers: Devil's Thumb. Although easily visible from the coastal town of Petersburg, this massive spine of granite is thoroughly locked into the white wilderness of the vast Stikine Icecap. This peak, among many others nearby, will provide opportunities for wilderness alpinism well into the next century.

Near the end of April, Bill Pilling and I board the Alaska Ferry in Bellingham and two days later disembark in Petersburg. The slow pace of the journey impresses upon us the great distance to Alaska, and the extent and beauty of the region we are about to visit. Clearcuts remind us that "progress" reaches even these remote shores. Will these hillsides ever be less scarred than they are now?

Proverbial Alaskan hospitality greets us at the ferry terminal. Dieter Klose and his wife Kay share their roof with us for the night along with large helpings of pie and ice cream. Dieter has summited on the Thumb twice, and being the only climber in Petersburg, he is especially starved for conversation and eager to listen to our plans.

Despite rain during the night, Devil's Thumb is clearly visible in the morning. Our frenzied dash to the waiting helicopter is momentarily interrupted by Kay's adding five pounds of halibut to our supplies. That will taste good! All our gear and food are somehow squashed into Temsco Helicopter's Hughes 500. We could never figure out whether our pilot, "Doc," loved flying more or keeping us off balance with his constant clowning and joking. We were glad to see that he is all business when it comes to flying.

As we approach the Thumb, I am surprised by the lack of snow on the peak. Jon Krakauer's slides showed much more when he made his solo trip here in 1977. "Doc" leaves us on the large plateau southeast of the Thumb, and we spend the first days ski touring, gazing up the peaks and down into the swirling mists of the witches' caldron.

Among the many routes to choose, we decide on the northeast face, and by climbing it, we'll feel out the conditions expected on other routes. After viewing the route through binoculars, we spend a day resting and packing.

74

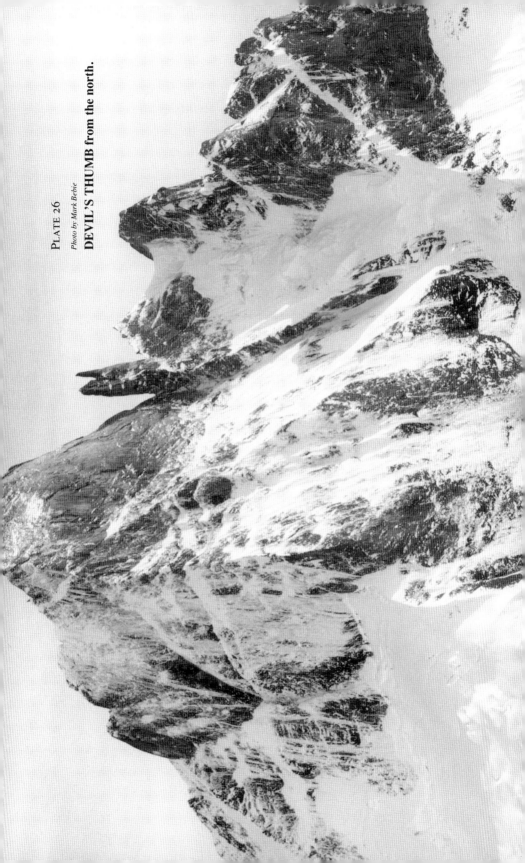

PLATE 26

Photo by Mark Bebie

DEVIL'S THUMB from the north.

At midnight, we rise as the northern lights glow dimly in the northeast. By the time we are ready to leave camp, the entire sky in all directions is bright green. As clouds sometimes become familiar objects in the mind's eye, I pick out an eagle with a 100-mile wingspan in the shafts and curtains of this fantastic display.

By four A.M., Bill is leading the first pitch in the couloir that was the scene of Jon Krakauer's second attempt on the face. The obnoxious spindrift seems to be a feature of this initial couloir. However, we are lucky to have less of it than Jon did. On the fifth pitch, Bill leads onto the right-trending ramp. Here the ice becomes spotty, but this only increases the quality of the climbing. As one moves between holds on a rock climb, we move about as the ice patches dictate. It is also comforting to be placing rock gear at regular intervals. The ramp ends too soon, and we move horizontally trying to find a way through the steep headwall above us. On my next lead upwards, I have to down-climb half a rope-length to the last good cracks to set a belay. Bill's lead ends at a poor belay, and, as Murphy's law would have it, my next lead is the crux pitch. I methodically clear snow off the rock, uncovering edges for my front points, and I inspect everywhere for cracks. I must not fall, so progress is slow. The pitch ends in a small pocket of hard snow, and I take great pleasure in the effort required to force a picket in halfway. Bill easily gains the hanging ice face and, as darkness falls, we top out onto the east ridge. The wind chills us. We debate an unplanned bivouac versus rappelling down the southeast face toward camp. Once we are in our warm sleeping bags, we are glad we made the effort to descend.

The weather remains fair, and despite protests of rest for the weary, we set out to finish our climb to the summit. We quickly ascend the 1946 route to the crest of the east ridge, which coincides with our descent route, and we pick up our rappel stations along the way. On this upper east ridge, the rock is excellent. We climb on knobby faces, around towers, up zig-zag cracks and across a horizontal knife-edged section to a notch. The higher we go, the more the snow covers the rock and rock shoes give way to boots. With ideal conditions, the climbing would be about 5.6, but we feel it is 5.8. In a gathering storm, we quickly move across the nearly horizontal summit ridge and remain on the tiny summit only long enough for a few photos. Three rope-lengths back along the summit ridge is the notch where we begin eight rappels down to the snow shoulder. Occasionally we find a rappel station, but mostly we set them ourselves. By the time we reach camp, the storm is furious.

The next 36 hours are Hell. In 50 miles-per-hour winds, we struggle to keep a roof over our heads. We are hardly in control. The tent fly rips; the tent collapses under the weight of the snow; there is too much digging and running around. Climbing is trivial compared to this. The morning of the second day brings a break in the storm. We shovel snow, dry everything and shovel some more. For eight more days, we are tent-bound in "moderate" winds and falling snow. Every break in the storm has us bounding outside to exercise, get more food and work on the tent area. But most of our time is spent reading books and

COLOR PLATE 6

Photo by Mark Bebie

Pilling following on the Quartz Pitch on the SOUTH PILLAR of the DEVIL'S THUMB.

listening to the local radio station KFSK, where we learn more than we could ever imagine about the cultural activities and economic issues of Petersburg and the State of Alaska.

At long last, the weather forecast is for four days of good weather. In two hours we are on the rock of the approach spur to the south pillar. The climbing is easy with a few fifth-class pitches at the end. On this spur grows an unbelievable collection of lichens, mosses and flowers—an alpine tidepool. We fix rope on the pillar and then spend an hour stomping out snow at the base of the rock only to find more rock. We finally make a bivouac site out of a snow arête 100 feet down from the crest. In the morning, clouds begin to form as we ascend, and we abandon the climb as clouds thicken. The Petersburg forecasters maintain their optimism as snow begins to fall.

After hiding for two days in Base Camp, the forecast is now for five days of good weather. Should we trust them? Retreat has proven easy, and so we hope for the best and begin our second attempt. We use the same tactics as before and happily settle into the bivouac site early. The next day dawns clear. Generally on the buttress crest, we meander up the coarse-grained and well-fractured rock. After their 1973 climb, Chris Jones and George Lowe wrote about the Chamonix-like granite. They couldn't have been more accurate. With a couple of hours of daylight remaining, we arrive at the biggest ledge on the route so far. I try to fix a rope above, but all cracks blank out and I descend. One obviously large, pointed rock ruins an otherwise perfect sitting bivouac. But that is a small concern since the skies stay clear and windless. Frederick Sound and the lights of Petersburg are visible to the west, and the Stikine Icecap with its many horn-like peaks spreads out at our feet in the moonlight. Such a vista I promise never to forget.

In the morning, we choose a "quartz" ramp leading east. The next pitch looks hard. Bill does a good job leading up and back west to the crest of the pillar, but the gear is spotty and he has tied-off pitons on the traverse. How am I going to follow this with a pack on? And clean the pitons? Bill eventually hauls the pack after I spend too much time dealing with it. Fatigued, I begin aiding the next pitch, but a few tentative free moves reveal the best pitch of the climb—corners, cracks and edges everywhere I need them. The angle lessens. Three easier pitches of dihedrals, ramps and mixed ground put us on the top of the pillar. We spend a few minutes unwinding, opening our senses to more than the next few feet of rock. Climbing any peak in southeastern Alaska, as well as any other big alpine route, has to be done on its own terms, not on some artificial time frame of our making. We feel really fortunate and satisfied to have had enough time and luck with the weather to make this long climb in the most likely ideal conditions.

We marvel at the slow flight of the helicopter, showing us the great scale of the landscape below us. "Doc" is bringing in three from Sitka to attempt the 1946 route. We had stamped out a pickup date and time on the snow, but our hearts sink when he lands right on top of it. He pauses to hover when he takes off and so we hope that he sees it after all. We break the solitude of the newcomers by hollering, and, surprised, they holler back. We pull out the plastic boots and ice

PLATE 27

Photo by Austin Post

South Pillar Route on the DEVIL'S THUMB follows the line between the light and shade on the right.

axes and ascend easy snow to the summit area. In two minutes, we have an excellent bivouac site instead of the two hours the night before for a mediocre one.

Clouds build in the morning as we traverse the summit ridge and go down our rappel route to Base Camp, passing the three from Sitka on their way up. We pack quickly, and, as our pickup time passes, we watch the clouds close in. The weather seems too rough for flying now, but more likely, "Doc" never saw our message. Dejected, we smooth out a tent platform since we shall be needing one imminently. Just as we finish, we hear the helicopter. The storm obscures the Thumb as we fly towards Petersburg.

Summary of Statistics:

AREA: Stikine Icecap, Southeast Alaska.

NEW ROUTES: Devil's Thumb, 2767 meters, 9077 feet, via a new route on the Northeast Face, 500 meters, IV, AI4, 5.7, May 3, 1991.

Devil's Thumb, via a new route on the South Pillar, 970 meters, V, 5.10, A2, May 22-24, 1991.

PERSONNEL: Mark Bebie, William Pilling.

Kayak-Mountaineering: Mount Abbe

WALTER R. GOVE *and* WILLIAM PILLING

Gove begins:

/A\S A MOUNTAINEER, I have come to aspire to the goals I associate with an earlier era. Besides a hard and good line to an unclimbed summit, I want unexplored and difficult terrain, a practical self-sufficiency and an environment undisturbed by humans. To my continuing amazement, such climbs not only exist but some are readily accessible to any competent mountaineer with a little imagination and a willingness to seek out the unknown. The north face of Mount Abbe is such a climb.

Mount Abbe is at the head of the Johns Hopkins Inlet in Alaska's Glacier Bay, perhaps the most striking fiord in North America. Its cliffs descend directly to the sea. Abutting one side of these cliffs is active Johns Hopkins Glacier, whose 300-foot face is constantly calving. Abutting the other side is the Gilman Glacier, also with an active calving face. When large chunks of ice plunge into the water, disconcertingly huge waves ripple down the fiord. In winter and early spring the fiord is frozen; in late spring and early summer, the pack-ice is impenetrable. And until the first of July, the fiord is closed to boat travel as seals congregate there to pup on the ice.

I first saw Abbe in September of 1987, an improbable time for climbing but a good time for getting into Johns Hopkins Inlet. Loren Adkins and I had come from Juneau by skiff, an open work-boat, despite strong winds and high waves, a trip of 150 miles. In the inlet, we landed at the only plausible place, a large rounded promontory on the north side of the fiord, two miles from its head. As the take-out point was on large boulders, we had to use chunks of glacier ice that were larger than basketballs for rollers in order to drag the 35-foot skiff high enough to avoid the 26-foot tides and stray waves caused by the calving glaciers. Mostly, it rained, or, above 2000 feet, it snowed. The closest rain gauge at Yakutat recorded an even 100 inches of rain that September and October. In partial clearings, we would get glimpses of the storm-shrouded summit of Abbe. Abbe rises sharply out of the sea in an unbroken line to 8300 feet, a pointed granitic peak, draped with hanging glaciers.

Back in civilization, a quick check verified what we already knew. The north or main peak of Abbe was unclimbed. The south peak, of comparable height on the topo maps, had been climbed in 1977 by Wickwire and Jagersky who, having

81

failed in their attempt to negotiate the ice in Johns Hopkins Inlet, had approached Abbe via the icefields that lay to the south. (*AAJ, 1978,* pages 392-396.) The two summits are half a mile apart, connected by a very deeply notched, knife-edged, gendarmed ridge.

The challenge was irresistible for Loren and me. Kayak-mountaineering is particularly aesthetic, for you are truly independent and are immersed in the diverse world of ocean, rock and ice. And for Abbe, a kayak provides the only practical approach. On July 7, 1988, we were dropped off in mid-morning at Ptarmigan Creek by the Glacier Bay tour boat. As we approached Johns Hopkins Inlet, we met two kayakers who had failed to push their way through the ice at the mouth of the inlet. However, after a long and tedious day, we reached the promontory on which we had camped the previous September. After a day of reorganization and packing, we set off in heavy ice.

In many places the ice was so densely packed it was impenetrable and we were constantly searching for partially open leads. At times, we had to back-track. Sharp-edged smaller pieces discernibly damaged the kayak's fabric. (Hard-shell kayaks are problematic because of their limited storage space.) We kept away from the larger icebergs, for they can roll unexpectedly, easily flipping a kayak; survival time in these cold waters is very short. Also of concern is the occasional swell caused by calving glaciers, for they can turn the ice-pack into a gyrating grinding machine.

The only possible, though difficult, take-out on an approach to Abbe is on the down-bay side of the Gilman Glacier, where the talus, at the angle of repose, merges into a 1000-foot cliff, which gives way in turn to the face of the Gilman. The large tidal zone means a rapidly changing waterline, and we would be landing a heavily loaded kayak on steep ledges or loose talus which would be slippery with seaweed and slime. And there always were random six-foot swells caused by calving ice. Although the cliff blocks a view of the glaciers, the loud boom from the Johns Hopkins gave a two- to four-minute warning. The Gilman, however, was nearer. We prayed that a mammoth chunk would not let go. The actual take-out went reasonably well, although we were forced to adjust our position as rocks of various sizes skittered down the steep snow above.

Having stashed the kayak, we set out with food for nine days. We were concerned about the steep slope above. Viewed head-on, it looked difficult, but it was reasonable. We camped on a bench at 1100 feet, which provided a grand view of the calving glaciers and the constantly changing ice patterns in the fiord. Abbe was mostly in the clouds but occasionally we would get a view of the upper slopes.

Our next task was to get across the Gilman. The lower Gilman, an impressive jumble of séracs and crevasses, was clearly uncrossable. The only possible crossing was a point, up-glacier and out of sight, where the map indicated a slight flattening. Our attempt to traverse along the margin of the glacier was quickly stopped by an unclimbable array of unstable rock, snow and ice cliffs. We eventually pieced together a devious high-angle traverse well above the glacier. The terrain alternated between very hard dirt and unstable rock, always

PLATE 28

Photo by Walter Gove

MOUNT ABBE's North Face seen from Johns Hopkins Inlet.

with the cliffs below. On the dirt, we wore crampons and in places belayed. After a day and a half of hard, tense effort, we had moved a full pack-load one mile up the Gilman and had made our way through the lower rotten rock cliff to the glacier. Compared to the rest of the glacier, this section was unbroken. Nevertheless, it took us six hours to work our way through the maze of crevasses to the other side, a distance of a half mile.

We were now under the north face of Abbe, which towered 7000 feet above us. The upper face has three hanging glaciers. The left one descends from the summit and its face is very active. The far right one is the next most active. Our goal was to ascend the snow rib between the left and the center glaciers, bypass a striking granite buttress on the right and then climb a line of snow that angled to the right. We hoped there would be a steep ramp through the rock band which would give access to the north ridge at 7200 feet. The immediate problem was getting onto the face.

The lower part of the face was a band of smooth, wet, overhanging rock. The one plausible line was an hourglass cone of partially snow-covered talus that breached much but not all of the lower rock band. On the right side of the cone, the snow merged into a jumble of séracs of a low hanging glacier that appeared inactive. At the top of the cone was a short, wet, vertical rock pitch that would give access to the lower snowfields. That evening, with a sense of dismay, we watched a substantial slab of snow break loose and fall to the Gilman.

In the morning, concerned with rockfall, we moved rapidly up the talus, but the route would not go. The critical rock pitch was being barraged by boulders. We turned to the icefall. The day was spent climbing around and over séracs, mostly on hard ice where two ice tools were essential. At mid-evening, we exited the icefall only to find ourselves in a deep avalanche trough. We quickly moved left and camped in the first secure spot.

From there, the route went as we had hoped, but the snow was atrocious and the weather marginal. The next day, in a whiteout, we moved up the snow rib and camped slightly below and to the left of the center hanging glacier. After a second day of intermittent rain, we continued up the snow rib, moved onto the hanging glacier and then angled to the right across mushy snow flutings, using plates for protection. We camped on the one secure spot on the face, a tiny snow saddle leading to a rock spire. That night it snowed and we spent the following day in a whiteout, listening to wet snow avalanches, one of which split around the saddle on which we were camped.

The next day was our last chance for a summit attempt, for it was our eighth day out and food was short. We were off at 2:45 A.M. It was 33° F temperature, with limited visibility and light rain. To avoid avalanches, we climbed a snow-covered rock rib on the right, wallowing up extremely steep mush. Finally at 7000 feet, just below the north ridge, we acquiesced to the inevitable and turned around. It was impossible to down-climb the mush; nor could we rappel as we had only three plates and snow bollards were out of the question. However, the visibility improved and we could see the closest snow flutings were free of avalanche danger. We down-climbed them, moving on the hard ice between the snow. Three tough days later, we were back at the kayak.

The next year, Loren and I explored some attractive peaks above Wright Glacier Lake, south of Juneau, and in 1990 we walked into the northern Fairweather Range from the ocean. In 1991, I had a strong urge to get back to Abbe while Loren was looking forward to a mellow summer. Loren had done most of the leading and I needed someone stronger and technically more proficient than I. In 1984, I had been frostbitten on the south face of St. Elias (*AAJ, 1985,* pages 20-29), and the loss of fingers and toes as well as the sensitivity to cold was having an effect on my climbing. Particularly bothersome was my right foot where I still had only a badly damaged little toe. On my right hand, I had lost all or part of three fingers. I had also lost the big toe of my left foot and one digit from the little finger of my left hand. At 53, I was slowing down. Fortunately, I had met Bill Pilling in Yakutat the past summer just after his Augusta climb (*AAJ, 1991,* pages 111-117), and he was easily enticed into an attempt on Abbe.

On the afternoon of July 7, 1991, Bill and I were dropped off by the Glacier Bay tour boat near the Gilbert Peninsula. A short paddle took us to Reid Inlet, where we camped. The next day, there was surprisingly little ice and we easily made it into the head of Johns Hopkins Inlet. At first, I was disoriented, for I was unable to locate the large promontory on which we had previously camped. I finally accepted the fact that it was now buried under ice. Not visible in 1988, the Tyeen Glacier had surged two miles, dropped 2500 feet and become a tidewater glacier. We were just able to squeeze out a landing and a campsite. The next day, we paddled across the fiord. As there was relatively little ice, we were able to get close to some of the adult seals and pups lying on the larger icebergs; according to the Park Service census, there were 3700 seals in the fiord at the time. After storing the kayak, we made two carries to the bench at 1100 feet.

Pilling continues:

Our bench camp was the most impressive sounding spot in which I have ever spent a night. Even inside the tent, I could make out the vast, articulated shape of Abbe's north face from the clonk of tumbling chunks of ice and rock. Just beneath the camp, we could hear the clank and wham from the nearby crevasses of the Gilman, and the upper Gilman valley funneled down to us the thuds of the higher icefalls. Far below, the ice fronts of the Gilman and Johns Hopkins Glaciers gave cannon-like reports.

The northern margin of the glacier looked as if it might go and we spent a day exploring the edge. After a mile of traversing compact moraine slopes, teetering on shifty debris and squeezing through moats, we stopped to rest in a protected spot. A steep ice pitch put us at the beginning of the ice-bridge system leading to the middle of the Gilman Glacier. We cached a light load of food as it began to rain and headed back to camp. Traveling on the edge of the glacier was dusty, gritty, muddy work, but it gave us a wonderful feeling for the way the glacier worked. Two and a half rainy days later, all our gear was on the south side of the Gilman, beneath the north face of Abbe. At noon on July 14, with seven days of food, we headed down glacier, angling slightly up to the start of the climb.

The debris cone Walt and Loren climbed on the earlier attempt was completely bare of snow and was either compact morainal concrete or treacherously loose rock. After a few rock moves at the top of the cone, we headed left along a debris-covered ledge. To the west, rocks of all sizes cartwheeled down the slabs to the Gilman. Here was the surprise: the icefall and séracs had disappeared during the last three years! We cut right across the smooth, low-angled ice and then swung left to a protected bivouac spot.

The next day, we climbed a snow rib leading to the upper hanging glacier. As we ascended the thin ribbon of wet snow lying against the steep bank granite, we were aware that the snow rib was quickly becoming a rock rib. The climbing was not technically hard, but each move required knowing just how to do it, as an injudicious move might knock off all the snow, leaving us with slow, belayed climbing on rock. Just above its bottom face, the hanging glacier provided a safe campsite, and we stopped there.

The next day, we climbed to the top of the hanging glacier and then traversed to the right through remnants of snow flutings where we used snow flukes for anchors. Following a late lunch at the high camp of the previous attempt, we headed up the right side of a funnel-like slope leading to the summit ridge. After several tricky slab pitches on solid brown granite, we went straight up the middle of the funnel on snow and ice, using ice screws for anchors. On the north ridge we finally stood together in the golden evening light. We watched the clouds play over every peak from Mount Wilbur to the summits above the Grand Plateau Glacier and saw the shadows fall on the deep blue-green inlet. Across the Johns Hopkins Glacier, the north face of Crillon was aglow. We set up our tent in an excellent, protected spot and fell asleep.

In the morning, we awoke to find the peak socked in. We did not need perfect visibility and started out anyway. Most of the ridge was exciting snow climbing along the side of the sinuous, corniced arête. Where we could climb directly along the crest, we scrambled on rock, some of it excellent granite. We belayed several short pitches of moderate fifth-class on our way to a deep notch. Each of us had anxious moments when we were stuck trying to squeeze through a cannon hole. The climb out of the notch involved loose scrambling. This was followed by more snow climbing along the ridge. From the last snow saddle, the ridge rises sharply to the summit. Abbe's summit is a rock battlement cleft in the middle by a large hanging glacier with an active face. The only feasible route was along our ridge and then up a steep, dark rock tower that would enable us to pass the ice cliff. We had examined the rock tower from below with misgivings, but an easy fifth-class route took us to its top and onto the summit snow dome. We waited for the clouds to clear, but saw little.

As the wind turned gusty and snow flurries came and went, we started the descent. It had taken six hours to get up and we would not be much quicker on the return. After exhausting hours on our ridge traverse, we topped the rise

PLATE 29

Photo by William Pilling

Walter Gove on the third day on MOUNT ABBE. Johns Hopkins Inlet below.

above camp to find that the wind had broken every pole in my Wild Country tent. This was the low point of the climb. Walt stood in the snow exhausted as I conducted a panicky tent-pole clinic involving spoons, tent pegs and all the tape in our first-aid kit.

We spent another day in High Camp in poor weather and then descended to our lowest bivouac site in a long day. On the way down, we passed through a zone of very wet snow. Walt's feet became wet and the constant thrusting of his feet into the toe of his boots was painful. That night, he warmed his numb feet, using a bottle filled with hot water. His right foot was twice as thick as the left and the solitary little toe had a very deep blister. On the final day of the descent, we did a long rappel to avoid being exposed to rockfall coming down off the lowest hanging glacier, and then descended to the moraine-covered ledge. Banging down the morainal cobbles that day was hard on Walt's feet. By the time we had reached the side of the Gilman, he flinched in pain whenever his right foot was jarred.

Picking up our cache, we crossed the Gilman. When we got to the other side, we were astounded by the change in the glacier and its margin. Giant snow slopes had disappeared without a trace and debris slopes had collapsed into huge unstable piles. We had to work out a new route for the one we had taken no longer existed. As it got dark, I wondered if we could get to camp that night. Suddenly, there was a loud boom from the face of Abbe; a massive block of rock had melted out, knocking loose a continuous fanning barrage of large rocks all over the talus cone we had descended not five hours earlier. As we labored up the slope to the bench camp, I could hear Walt gasp with pain when his foot hit a rock, but he just kept on going.

Gove continues:

Following a leisurely morning, we had an uneventful, although for me a painful, descent to the inlet. After reassembling the kayak and experiencing the stress of launching, we decided to spend some time among the seals before the long paddle to Reid Inlet. We were able to get close to some of the adult seals and pups lying on icebergs by using the wind to propel us while we remainded motionless. As we got near, the seals would slide into the water, sometimes all at once, but frequently a particular seal would lag behind, apparently reluctant to take our intrusion seriously. Upon entering the water, many of the seals would swim closer and stare at us with their nearly human faces.

By the following afternoon, we had made 28 miles to the Gilbert Peninsula, where we were picked up by the Glacier Bay tour boat. Because of the prior tissue damage caused by frostbite, my blistered toe refused to heal and three weeks later, I had the toe amputated. I admit it is a rather unusual way to take care of a blister, but I did obtain a somewhat more functional foot.

Of all the mountains I have known, Abbe has the most distinct personality. In its unique and aesthetic setting, it mixes elegant granite buttresses, steep snow and ice, complex glaciation, unadulterated crud and incredible volatility. I have been on Abbe four times (twice up and twice down). I have never seen a mountain so active or one that changed so much. Abbe does not have a crux pitch and does not need one. From fiord to summit, Abbe is always alive, difficult and well defended.

Summary of Statistics:

AREA: Fairweather Range, Southeast Alaska.

ATTEMPT AND FIRST ASCENT: Mount Abbe, 2499 meters, 8200+ feet, attempted July 12-17, 1988 (Loren Adkins, Walter Gove); ascended July 14-17, 1991 (Walter Gove, William Pilling).

Patagonia—Dreams and Reality

TOMMY BONAPACE, *Österreichischer Alpenverein*

FOR SOME WEEKS, we had been enjoying our existence in a hut near the waters of Laguna Torre. We sat in front of the warming fire, alternately whittling on a stick of wood, reading a few pages of a cheap thriller or recording our thoughts on paper and drinking such colossal quantities of tea that each hour our bladders threatened to burst. Discussions about the weather met with complete apathy. We had been sitting here for weeks, waiting for the next fine spell. Outside, a wild snowstorm raged. We had been occupied for days trying to repair the roof and the smoke hole of the hut.

Both of us had had the idea of invading the Patagonian winter in order to reach long-sought goals. It is well known that it is easy to forge plans but carrying them out when you are on the spot is quite a different matter. My partner Toni Ponholzer and I were no greenhorns in Patagonian matters. We had already been here and could accomplish great routes "by fair means." It was our fervent wish to climb without fixed ropes new routes or repeats in big-wall fashion or alpine-style. That was for us the only acceptable manner in which to climb.

From August of 1990 to March of 1991 we dwelt in the Laguna Torre hut, hoping to carry out the objective of our expedition. We had not really planned to spend so many months there. Our real goal was to make the second ascent of the much disputed Egger-Maestri route on the Cerro Torre. We were waiting with great hopes for a long period of favorable weather to carry it out. We set out dozens of times, but we never succeeded in reaching the summit. Foul weather forced us to retreat. Time and again we started off and in the end we were never further ahead than when we had started, but we fixed no ropes.

On September 2, 1990, we did succeed in making the first winter ascent and the third overall climb of the Bridwell route of Cerro Stanhardt. The chief difficulties lay in a 250-meter-high chimney, the interior of which was defended by a thick armor of ice. On a snow pulpit at the bottom end of the chimney, we carved a meter-deep bench in order to have a little shelter from the frigid wind during the long winter night. Crouched in his bivouac sack, Toni played on his harmonica some fragments of lullabies to coax us to sleep. Interrupted by periodic warm-up sessions, we put our thoughts on hold for short periods and dozed off.

In our rucksacks we had only the essentials to let us move quickly and save strength. I jümared to the point where darkness the night before had turned me around and I attacked the overhanging ice bulge. The water ice was brittle and as hard as glass. You can imagine how the plate-sized ice projectiles shot into the abyss as I placed protection. Before they shattered, they whizzed past the stance where Toni cowered, trying to ward them off with the limply filled rucksack. My arms and calves turned to lead as I attempted to insert an ice screw into the ice. That was the belay where I could extract Toni from his sparsely shielded perch and where fresh blood could force its way into my rigid muscles. Toni banged his ice gear into a crack and climbed higher with his crampons on tiny rough spots. They screeched on the perpendicular rock as he straddled the ice hose, which was now broader. Delicately balanced, he set an ice screw. It was getting to be a programmed necessity to place protection in order to calm the nerves. Above Toni hung columns of ice, like walrus tusks. We climbed until the early evening hours before the summit area emerged. There, four huge ice mushrooms towered side by side. Neither of us could guess which was the highest. After we had decided on the the next to last one, we saw that the outermost mushroom was a little higher. It lay still another 40 meters from us. We traversed below the snow-white mushrooms the whole summit zone until we could climb up the last one.

Below us lay a dream landscape composed of an endless snow-covered surface of ice out of which glaciated mountain chains rose. In the distant horizon the sun gleamed like a glowing ball lightening the whole region with a reddish orange light. Behind us, the shadows of the Torre group were creeping over the granite needles of the Fitz Roy peaks with their cols, buttresses and gullies. Way beyond, on the edge of the Pampa, lay Lago Viedma. In the yellowish brown landscape, it was being fed by uncounted arteries as they snaked into it blood-red in the sunset. The sun began to sink, losing brilliance but gaining gorgeous color. An ice-cold wind blew up onto us from the Patagonian Icecap and seemed to sweep the evening glow before it and pull the shadows out longer. Suddenly, all the colors flowed away into a monotonous gray-black. We had arrived at the place where we humans without wings can go no higher. Here, where all the rising lines meet at a point was the summit mushroom of ice and snow, high above all rock. We had struggled for a day and a half up the Bridwell route onto the top of Stanhardt in order to experience this drama.

The full moon lighted the way down until we reached the inky blackness of the ice chimney and had to use our headlamps. We still had to endure a frigid bivouac before we got back to our little Paradise, our hut, the next day.

A surprisingly short period of bad weather—only ten days—was followed by a deceptively lovely morning. We hoped to ascend the unclimbed east face of the Cuatro Dedos. The whole day we struggled against a bitterly cold strong wind which late in the afternoon dragged in a cruel snowstorm. When we were just a rope-length from the summit, we were forced to retreat. There was no climbing technique we could use to gain more altitude and the lack of bivouac gear reinforced our decision quickly without second thought. At the foot of the

COLOR PLATE 7

Photo by Tommy Bonapace

Steep ice near the summit of CERRO STANHARDT.

face we sought our bivouac tent. Battered by the wind, it lay in ribbons on the slope of the moraine. The five-hour descent to our camp was out of the question. We were exhausted and staggering in the wind gusts like drunks. We spent an extraordinarily instructive bivouac that night; before we started up a wall, we should dig a snow cave. That is the only real possibility in this unreal desert of ice, snow, storm and wintery cold if you want to survive. All the next day, as a kind of bad-weather therapy, we grubbed out a snow cave, a real snow palace, which served from then on as an Advance Base close to the beginning of the climbs. We spent a total of a month of nights there. We often wondered if we hadn't lost the last spark of human intelligence in this lonesome wilderness.

Some days later, on September 17, we completed the ascent of the east face of the Cuatro Dedos. Climbing up a steep, icy couloir and snow-covered cracks and rock bands, we reached the summit late in the afternoon. In Spanish, Cuatro Dedos means "Four Fingers." The mountain got its name because of the remarkable appearance of the four granite needles. We climbed the highest finger and later got the idea that we should traverse the other three. It was nearly two months later, on December 13, before we could carry out our plan. No human foot had trodden on them and we were impressed by their unusual form, like the wings of a condor extending to the east. The south ridges of the middle two offer steep crack-climbing and with the conditions as we found them could be ascended free with nuts and chalk. On all the other routes we had to climb with ice gear, crampons and plastic boots. For that reason, it was a pleasure to be able to free-climb with nuts and chalk.

From the middle of September until the beginning of December, there was endless bad weather with much precipitation. On one of the many attempts we made on Bifida, which like the Cuatro Dedos lies on the main ridge of the Torre massif, we turned, because the weather suddenly went sour, to the Perfil del Indio. This is the peak to the left of Bifida. The climbing difficulties are not so great but it was challenging enough considering the weather. The date was September 23.

We were not able to ascend Bifida until December 7. From the ice cave at the foot of Stanhardt, we sought the way with headlamps through the labyrinth of crevasses to the foot of the peak. It dawned gray and we counted on a day without a storm, as much as one can do so in Patagonia. Deliberately, we climbed a snow-and-rock couloir to the col between Bifida and Perfil del Indio. A giant dihedral to the right of the south ridge offered a logical route to the head of a buttress from which we reached Bifida's south summit by ascending exposed cracks. The heavy icing of the crack system made this a treacherous and technically difficult mixed climb.

We attempted many other routes. We also spent a number of days on the Southern Patagonian Icecap, ending with a circuit around the Torre massif. And so our seven months in Patagonia came to an end. Despite hideously bad weather, we were happy with our successes.

Summary of Statistics:

AREA: Cerro Torre Region of Patagonia, Argentina.

ASCENTS: Cerro Stanhardt, 2800 meters, 9186 feet, Bridwell Route, V+, First Winter Ascent and Third Ascent of the Route, September 2, 1990.

Aguja Cuatro Dedos Main Peak, 2245 meters, 7366 feet, First Ascent of East Face and Second Ascent of the Peak, September 17, 1990.

Perfil del Indio, Probable First Ascent, September 23, 1990

Bifida South Summit, 2450 meters, 8038 feet, New Route via couloir on southwest face (400 meters) and 350-meter face, December 7, 1990.

Aguja Tres Dedos, Traverse of the Three Lower Fingers, VII−, December 13, 1990.

Circuit of the Cerro Torre Massif via the Southern Patagonian Icecap, Paso Marconi, Lago Viedma, Río Túnel, January 23-27, 1991.

PERSONNEL: Tommy Bonapace, Toni Ponholzer, *Austrians.*

Sea Kayaking and Climbing, Chilean Patagonia

Rick Ridgeway

OR YEARS Yvon Chouinard and I have speculated about journeying into the labyrinth of canals, fjords and islands of the Magellanic archipelago—that remote region of Chilean Patagonia north of the Straits of Magellan. Speculation might have remained just that if Yvon had not happened on a magazine photograph of a rime-crusted cluster of spires with a caption that read, "From the fjords of northwest Tierra del Fuego." He called the magazine and located the photographer, who told Yvon that he had taken the picture from the ferry along the inland passage between Puerto Natales and Puerto Montt. He sent us a map circling the spot where he thought the spires were located. It was in the heart of the area that had long fascinated us.

We organized a trip there in November, 1988. Two more friends were signed on for the adventure: Doug Tomkins and Jim Donini. There was no question but that we would have to approach the peaks by boat. We decided to take collapsible sea kayaks: two single Feathercrafts for Yvon and me, and a double Klepper for Doug and Jim. Research turned up hardly any information about the area. The only climber who had been in the region, Jack Miller, had never seen so much as a break in the low clouds the entire time he was there.

In Punta Arenas we did discover that the locals called the rock spires Grupo La Paz. In the fishing village of Puerto Natales, we hired a local fisherman to take us to the outer archipelago and to drop us off in the area where we thought the spires were located. We would try to climb them and kayak back.

The boat journey took us two days, and the fisherman let us off along the coast of the uninhabited Fiordo de las Montañas, 35 miles southwest of Puerto Natales. There were no mountains to be seen through the rain and sleet, and we could only hope that we were in the right place. The next day brought a five-minute break in the cover. Through a hole in the clouds we glimpsed a rime-crusted spire, possibly 1500 feet of very steep rock on the eastern side of the fjord.

We decided to wait for a day of reasonable weather to be able to pull it off in one long alpine day. We waited . . . and waited. A week, then two. We were all

95

COLOR PLATE 8

Photo by Rick Ridgeway

Leaving Fiordo de las Montañas Base Camp after the climb, heading for Puerto Natales.

PLATE 30

Photo by Rick Ridgeway

Kayaking in the Fiordo de las Montañas.

past the stage in life where we could afford the luxury of waiting out Patagonian weather; schedules were ticking away back home. We decided to try the peak, weather notwithstanding.

There was a short glacier leading to the start of the most likely route, but at the base I thought the wind was blowing too hard to make an attempt feasible. Everyone agreed, except Donini. He convinced us to belay him while he tried a pitch. As he climbed, he had to place protection, not so much in case he fell but to take pressure off the rope that was arcking madly in midair from his waist down to us. Suspended by the wind as though under the spell of a Hindu snake charmer, it threatened to pull him off. When Jim got to the top of the pitch, Yvon decided to follow. Doug and I stayed behind; we didn't think they were really serious. They climbed off into clouds scudding off the summit.

Doug and I waited until dark and felt they must have rappelled off the other side. We returned to our camp on the shores of the fjord, fighting thick beech forest. We got back around midnight. No Yvon or Jim. We wondered if they would ever turn up. Doug and I got desperate, fearing the worst. About daybreak, they got back, exhausted. It had been hard climbing, 5.9 and 5.10 with cold rain, sleet and gale-force winds the entire way. On top, a brief break in the clouds let them see that they were indeed on the highest of the three spires. As night fell, they began to rappel. For the rest of the night, they felt their way down the glacier and crawled through the beech thickets.

The epic was only half over. We paddled north along the Fiordo de las Montañas and portaged to the east to the Fiordo Resi. The paddle home was a thriller. Williwaw gusts capsized Yvon and held him down. He had to bail out of his boat into the frigid water. Another day, we had to raft our boats together to stay upright. Going downwind, without paddling we were doing four to five knots. On edge the whole time, it took five days to paddle back to Puerto Natales. I can still relive every hour. We all made it back in time for our pressing meetings, but if you ask me what they were about, I can give you only the foggiest answer.

Summary of Statistics:

AREA: Patagonia, Chile.

FIRST ASCENT: P 1190, 2904 feet, Grupo La Paz, Cordillera Riesco, First Ascent, November 25, 1988 (Chouinard, Donini).

PERSONNEL: Yvon Chouinard, James Donini, Richard Ridgeway, Douglas Tomkins.

Mount Alberta's North Face and Northeast Ridge

MARK WILFORD

INSPIRATION FOR INVOLVEMENT with this great Canadian peak came early in my climbing career via a photo by Jim Stewart in the 1973 *Ascent*, entitled "Canada in Winter." A two-page spread of Mount Alberta's sinister north face, plastered in snow and ice, held my attention. The isolation and magnitude of the mountain was almost impossible for me to imagine all those years ago. Only a few pages further, there was George Lowe's account of his and Jock Glidden's first ascent of this great north face. Even more inconceivable than the mountain itself was how anyone could climb it. It would be a long time before I fully understood the remoteness and grandeur of Mount Alberta and the significance of Lowe's and Glidden's ascent.

Ascent remained in my library with only a brief perusal during the past decade, lost amongst old *Summits, Climbing* and *Mountain* magazines. Only in 1989 did I pull the journal out with intent. Business would put me in the Canadian Rockies in January. I wanted a project for my visit. Ignorance and arrogance reared their big heads. I managed to have a tremendous epic on the visit but failed to muster more than hot air as far as Alberta was concerned. I limped back home embarrassed by my brashness and attempted to extricate my tail from between my legs with proclamations of returning.

A seed was sown.

*   *   *   *   *

My pride had mended and my head had swollen sufficiently by the summer of 1990 for me to be ready for round two. This episode deserves a little more space than the winter venture, but not much more.

After the marathon drive up from Colorado, I managed the morale-eating approach of river-fording and scree-groveling to the top of Woolley Shoulder to be confronted with the source of my desire. The vision itself, the remoteness and magnificence of it all, were worth whatever was the outcome of the journey. There, a couple of miles distant, rose Alberta from a sea of glaciers and vastness. The valve retaining my motivation leaked a bit. I could feel a subtle loss of psyche as I drank in the improbability of the whole setting. I made it over to the tiny hut, spent from the day's efforts.

The following day, I rested a bit and then took an afternoon stroll to the base of Alberta's northeast ridge. This gave me a view of the north face, as intimate as most would want to get to this widow-maker. I well remembered Tobin Sorenson's death ten years earlier. Tobin's reputation was so strong that we had felt him immortal, but here was the stage of his last act.

At that time, I had intended to head for the northeast ridge. Safety from rockfall and easier terrain rationalized the route. Ease of access also played a role. The north face proper requires a committing rappel, down-climbing and glacier crossing to the start of the route. With blinders on, I set to work on the ridge. Steep, black limestone, solid but almost crackless save for a few knife-blade placements. Over a period of a few hours, I tensioned, freed and balanced my way up 200 feet of overhanging rock. I fixed my lines and hurried back to the hut. Smug in the small amount of success, I kept the shroud of ignorance bound tightly that night as I struggled to sleep.

I set out the next morning and quickly topped the fixed lines. Above, I cruised up an easy snowfield and then hit the crest of the ridge. From here, the mountain began to show its soul. Its façade of beauty and charm from a distance was peeling away with each step. The black tile gave way to a putrid yellow shale which had no visible adherence to anything. Gravity merely held the stacked dinner plates in place precariously. I had the feeling of walking through a tightly packed antique store of china and glass while trying not to crush the eggs covering the floor. And all the while, a neon sign flashed, "You break it, you buy it!" I wove my way through the little towers of teetering plates all too aware of the voids growing on my left and right: 1200 feet down the east face and 2000 down the north face. After what seemed like miles of tight-wire walking, I came to a small spire in a horizontal section of the ridge. It stood there like a sentinel, not so much guarding the mountain from me, but rather questioning my purpose, seaching my soul for intent and my logic for sanity. Leaning next to it, I gazed over the darkness of the north face. A 2000-foot ice face dropped steeply away from the gangrenous yellow bands. I could hear Tobin's whispers. I craned my neck to hear but couldn't. I sucked down air to calm my stomach. It was still early in the day. Up to now, I had been making progress. As I viewed the north face, I felt a lurid sensation. Perched out of sight, I was a voyeur watching the maiden undress. My eyes would burn if I did not turn away. The sentinel put it to me again, "What do you want?" I had no answer. I soon reached the steep, black limestone of the headwall.

I was leery of the apparent solidarity of the black rock. Traversing up the yellow band had spawned a monster of dread in my stomach. Faith in my position had been seriously undermined. I pondered my inability to answer to my purpose. Voices drifted up to me, some from across the north face, some from the east. Voices of men and women. My confidence was being devoured. I set some dubious anchors and started up the headwall. After some reasonable face climbing, I came up under a black roof. I set some protection in a sharp crack and then moved out left and over the bulge. The moves were cool, the rock all right, but my psyche had been bled so low that each move became a major

COLOR PLATE 9

Photo by Gregory Horne

**Northeast Ridge and North Face of
MOUNT ALBERTA.**

effort. It was like pulling against a huge rubber band, pulling harder and harder and waiting for the snap to end it all. I was over the bulge on decent rock, overly suspicious of it. No more protection for quite a way. I looked down into the darkness of the north face, almost 3000 feet down. The void held my eye and slowly sucked out my remaining nerve. Voices again—some from home, some from strangers. I faced the torment of retreat and failure. The nemesis was mightier than the mountain itself—giving up. I backed down the overhanging moves, down to the belay. I swallowed hard. My eyes watered. The climbing wasn't too hard, nor the temperature too cold, nor did I lack gear. It was merely too scary. I wanted to live; that was the answer to the sentinel. It was a long way down.

The seed of Mount Alberta was cultivated.

*   *   *   *   *

August, 1991. I loaded the trusty Isuzu Trooper for another blast north. The strings of home were painfully tight this time. Breaking them to venture on this journey took immense determination and understanding. Twelve-hundred miles of white-line fever, 80-to 90-mph and no smokies. I whizzed past Banff and up the Icefields Parkway. And then I was back. The Columbia Icefields. I had an ugly reception. Rain pounded down and the campsites were full. I waded through the mud. What was I doing back here again? My purpose seemed faint, almost invisible. Maybe Edith Cavell would be drier. I was already thinking of easier objectives. The rain abated and a beam of sunshine broke through the black clouds. My psyche fired up again. I pulled my gear bag into the spot of sun and began the pacifying task of tool-sharpening as the late Canadian sun set.

The next morning was partly cloudy, better than rain but not what I had been banking on. The Rangers gave the classic, "You should have been here last week—the best weather all summer." I signed in. Objective: Mount Alberta, north face. Number in party: one. Estimated return: I hope.

Previous experience lent its hand in loading the sack. Less of this and that, more of these and those. I made one last telephone call home. My Isuzu Trooper motored me down to the river crossing and I climbed out. Goodbye, old buddy. Keep a cold one for me. I donned my Tevas and started the plunge across the frigid Sunwapta River.

The march hadn't shortened and Woolley Shoulder was still a bitch, but somehow it all seemed to go by pretty fast. That afternoon, I was back at the cozy hut. Not alone either. Two fellows from Boulder were just on their way out after a week of pondering the north face—too much rockfall, they determined. It was a nasty, windy, wet night. I was relieved; there is no better excuse to bail out than bad weather.

The next morning, the friends left and I lay about in a quagmire of indecision. Finally, I hiked to the north-face overlook. The weather had cleared, taking with it the main excuse for backing out. I was committed now. With no good excuses at hand, if the next day was clear, I would at least rappel down onto the icefield below and get truly up close and personal with the north face. I didn't spend much time at the overlook. I knew the power of the north face and how it could drain my psyche. Back at the hut that night, I was tormented by nightmares of all sorts and I prayed for bad weather. It didn't come.

The next morning, the sky was clear and so I fulfilled my commitment to venture into the north face's lair. After a quick rappel and some down-climbing, I arrived on the mild glacier below the wall. The snow was dirty and pitted by rockfall. The temperature was above freezing. I scoped the face and wondered where I would breach the headwall, 2500 feet up.

The initial 2000-foot ice face itself looked straightforward, almost casual. I wandered over to the obvious break in the bergschrund which gave access to the wall. It was apparent that the rocks littering the glacier's surface were recent projectiles from above. At the bergschrund, I donned crampons and, with little ceremony, ventured onto the north face.

After the initial ice of the schrund, I came upon some solid and moderate rock slabs. I traversed up and left on them toward the massive ice face. Once I was near it, I saw that I could move just as easily on the rock slabs bordering the face. I quickly gained altitude until the steepness of the slabs increased and forced me onto the ice. Until there, I had been protected relatively well from rockfall by my position on the rock steps. This changed instantly as I committed myself to the ice face. The warmth was freeing numerous rocks that had been tethered by the evening's frost. Initially, the main barrage was to my left, but as I moved higher, I became more exposed and the rockfall came closer.

As the rockfall increased, I quickened my pace, launching myself into the barrage. My lungs were burning, dry heat scorched my throat. The flame flickered down to my calves, licking the life out of them. There was no time or place to rest. A rock the size of a half-gallon milk carton hurtled just over my head. The fluttering of the high-speed rocks sounded as if I were being buzzed by a fleet of helicopters. I was traveling through a corridor of terror.

I aimed for the nearest buttress of yellow rock. By now, my body had taken charge of matters while my electrified brain drank in the surging adrenaline. My pace forced me to take brief intermissions from the horror show. Finally, I arrived at the sanctuary of the yellow buttress, where I regrouped, set up some dubious anchors and fueled up.

It was from this section of shattered yellow shale which it is surmised that Tobin Sorenson met his demise; yellow rock embedded in the pitons attached to Tobin's climbing rope were found with his body. With this in mind, I cautiously made my way up and through the rotten shale. After 300 feet, I came to a band of shattered black tile. Anchors became increasingly difficult to find. Any crack larger than a hairline usually indicated that the surrounding rock was shattered. My belay anchors were now combinations of knifeblades.

I was gaining on the headwall. As this happened, I began to lose my perspective of the route above. Upon reaching the toe of the headwall, I had little idea where Lowe's route had gone. The only sign of previous activity was a single sling 100 feet directly above me. This wasn't convincing evidence and so I traversed a full rope-length to my left and to my right in search of an alternate

PLATE 31

Self-Photo by Mark Wilford

The top of the ice slope on the North Face of MOUNT ALBERTA.

route. None of the other potential lines were convincing either. I returned to my belay and proceeded to climb to the tattered sling. My original speculation was correct: the sling was merely an old retreat anchor. Nevertheless, I pushed through for one more pitch.

The climbing was now vertical and overhanging. The quality of the rock was improving, but I still encountered numerous loose blocks. Eventually, the crack system I was in petered out and I was forced to retreat off the headwall. At this point, the hour was growing late and I decided it best to secure a bivouac spot. From the headwall, I made two diagonaling rappels to the east, back to the yellow band. After a little more traversing, I found a suitable ledge which I cleared to form a decent platform. My position and commitment on the wall was just beginning to sink in. I was still not convinced on how to proceed through the headwall, yet when I peered down the sweeping icefield below, retreat seemed equally improbable. I was in a labyrinth. Spent from the day's efforts, my mind was given a reprieve as I sank into a healthy sleep. That night, the weather moved in and frosted me with a light snow.

In the morning, my position hadn't changed, but the rest had given me new strength to weigh the options. It was still not clear to me where the line up the headwall went. I was also certain that I didn't want to retreat down the ice face. As an alternative, I could make a long traverse to the northeast ridge and, once there, continue on up or escape. This traverse, though, required climbing and rappelling across the terrifying black tile.

After a long deliberation, I opted for the traverse to the left. It was a long, drawn-out process of setting what anchors I could (usually a single A4 knife-blade) and then tensioning or rappelling diagonally until I ran out of rope. I would then climb as high as I could before pulling the ropes. This kept me from losing height along the traverse. It was, needless to say, a most frightening series of maneuvers.

After a short eternity, I finally reached the towers on the northeast ridge, bathed in sunshine. Ironically, it was precisely the point from which I had retreated one year earlier and it gave me a strange feeling of familiarity, a mixture of fear from the year before and relief of being back in the warmth of the sun. I was once again faced with a difficult decision, one that I had made a year ago. Then I opted out. But that was a long time ago. I knew I'd never come to this place again. I also knew that the ridge had been done and that retreat, though involved, would be possible. With nary a blink, I went for it.

The climbing above was steep, yet on relatively solid rock. I was able to move quickly, free-climbing all the moves. In places, the route was actually overhanging. Crack-climbing up to 5.10 was required. I belayed each pitch and so was ensured a relative element of safety. After about eight pitches, the angle began to decrease and I moved into steep gullies. A fixed pin showed signs of earlier passage. By now, I was very tired and dehydrated. To save weight, I had chosen not to bring a stove and the only moisture I had had that day was from sucking melt-water from the rocks. A couple of hundred feet higher, the rocks began to be covered by steep, unconsolidated snow on the east edge of the ridge and disappeared into the dark void on the north side.

At one point, I came across a single bolt on a small island of rock in a sea of rotten snow—a sign of desperation from an earlier ascent. My ropes were coiled and the bolt was of no use to me. I tiptoed along the sharp ridge, leery of the rotten snow on my left and the shattered rock on the right. I finally realized that I had better stop before exhaustion forced a mistake. I cleared a small perch and collected drip-water from a sérac. The view was awesome. I could lie in my bivy and look straight 4000 feet down the north face! To the southeast was the monstrous north face of North Twin. To the south and west was an ocean of peaks as far as I could see. I settled in for a long peaceful night. Again that night, I was dusted with snow.

I awoke in a whiteout. My visibility was now a mere ten meters. Still tired but in grip of my faculties again, I packed up and set myself at the thin, steep snow ridge above. A large cornice loomed on my left and I was forced to drop down onto the north edge of the ridge. Though I couldn't see it, the void of the north face licked at my boots.

Higher up, crevasses intersected the cornice, offering obstacle upon obstacle. Finally, the angle declined and a few yards further I found myself on the summit platform. As if choreographed, the clouds parted and views down the west face showed the Athabasca river valley. I spent little time in celebration, for the weather was threatening and the descent down the long Japanese route was still ahead. A half-mile of ridge scrambling and a dozen rappels later, I was finally out of Mount Alberta's grasp.

The seed was harvested.

Summary of Statistics:

AREA: Canadian Rockies

SOLO ASCENT: Mount Alberta, 3619 meters, 11,874 feet, August, 1991.

The Bar-Headed Goose

Thomas H. Jukes

$\mathbb{M}$ILLIONS OF YEARS before George Leigh Mallory attempted to ascend Everest "because it was there," a remarkable bird had found its way over Everest's summit, thanks to winning a prize in evolution's lottery. The bird was the bar-headed goose, truly a Reinhold Messner of the avian world.

High-altitude climbers depend absolutely on the oxygen supply to their muscles. This, in turn, depends on a substance that is called hemoglobin that is carried by the red blood cells. The evolution of hemoglobin is one of the remarkable stories of biology.

Our human hemoglobin started out about 500 million years ago, long before we appeared on the scene, as a single molecule of a protein containing about 140 amino acids. About 450 million years ago, a great event in evolution took place. This was when the hemoglobin gene duplicated and the two duplicates went in different directions. One of them became alpha hemoglobin and the other beta. Alpha and beta form a pair held loosely together, and this pair joins to another alpha-beta pair. The quartet of these four molecules has remained in the blood of all vertebrates ever since. Transition from a single molecule to a quartet changed the properties of hemoglobin so that it could more efficiently pick up oxygen in the lungs and release it in the tissues where it is needed for the production of energy in the muscular movement. The process was characterized by the Bohr effect. Oxygen combines readily with hemoglobin in the lungs where the acidity, or pH, is slightly higher than average. The oxygenated hemoglobin, abbreviated as HbO_2, travels to the capillaries in the tissues where the acidity is slightly higher, which means that the pH is lower. Under these conditions, the oxygen is readily given up, and the HbO_2 becomes Hb, or reduced hemoglobin, which is why our veins are blue. At high altitudes, oxygen in the air is lessened because of the lower barometric pressure, and the difficulty in obtaining enough oxygen stimulates the bone marrow to make extra quantities of red cells. The stimulus is provided by a hormone called erythropoietin, abbreviated as EPO, which has made a fortune in the stock market for its producer, the AMGEN Corporation, in the last year or two.

The amino acids in the hemoglobin molecule can become changed by mutations in DNA. Hundreds of hemoglobin mutants have been identified and described. Some of them make no difference, and others are harmful, producing genetic diseases.

107

This story is about a hemoglobin mutant that made a goose into a mountaineer several million years ago. I am writing about this because in August 1991 some German scientists reported that they had transformed human hemoglobin to be like the hemoglobin of the bar-headed goose which breeds around lakes in Tibet at an elevation of 4000 to 6000 meters. The goose migrates to the Plains of India, across the Himalaya and flocks have been known to fly over Mount Everest.

The fascinating part of the story is that, although most mutations in hemoglobin in humans and other animals are either harmless or deleterious, the mutations that took place in the bar-headed goose actually improved its hemoglobin as compared with that of its close relative, the non-mountaineering greylag goose, so that the mutant hemoglobin had a greater capacity for oxygen. When this happened to the ancestor of the bar-headed goose, the bird found it could fly higher and further than before, so that it could live in places where ordinary geese could not compete with it. The key mutation was changing from proline to alanine at the 119th position in the alpha hemoglobin chain. Several other mutations took place in other locations, but these had no effect on oxygen transport; they were so-called "neutral" mutations.

This sounds like an unusual and unique event, but, very remarkably, a similar but not identical mutation took place in the Andean goose, thus making it possible for this goose to fly at 9000 meters, far above the usual enemies of geese. This time, the mutation was from leucine to serine at position 55 of the beta chain.

At this stage of our story, the two unusual geese were merely scientific curiosities. Enter a new scientific discovery called site-directed mutations. This remarkable procedure makes it possible to remove an amino acid from its place in a protein and replace it with another. It is carried out through the genetic code. As an example, the sequence CCG in the hemoglobin gene can be replaced by GCG. This changes proline to alanine. The new genetically engineered human hemoglobin artificial mutants have been studied for their oxygen-carrying capacity, and, like those of the high geese, it is greater than regular hemoglobin.

Somewhere down the line, in the future, an expedition of Himalayan climbers will receive tranfusions of the new mutant hemoglobin to prepare them for ascending to 8000 meters, Perhaps, far above them, they will see a wedge-shaped flock of birds. These will be bar-headed geese.

Climbs and Expeditions, 1991

The Editorial Board is extremely grateful to the many people who have done so much to make this section possible. Among those who have been very helpful, we should like to thank in particular Kamal K. Guha, Hari Dang, Harish Kapadia, H.C. Sarin, Józef Nyka, Jerzy Wala, Tsunemichi Ikeda, Sadao Tambe, Hanif Raza, Zafarullah Siddiqui, Trevor Braham, Luciano Ghigo, César Morales Arnao, Vojslav Arko, Franci Savenc, Bernard Newman, Paul Nunn, José Manuel Anglada, Jordi Pons, Josep Paytubi, Carles Capellas, Xavier Eguskitza, Elmar Landes, Robert Renzler, Colin Monteath, Claude Deck, Annie Bertholet, Fridebert Widder, Silvia Metzeltin Buscaini, Zhou Zheng, Ying Dao Shin, Karchung Wangchuk, Dolfi Rotovnik, Robert Seibert, Lloyd Freese and Tom Eliot.

METERS TO FEET

Unfortunately the American public seems still to be resisting the change from feet to meters. To assist readers from the more enlightened countries, where meters are universally used, we give the following conversion chart:

meters	feet	meters	feet	meters	feet	meters	feet
3300	10,827	4700	15,420	6100	20,013	7500	24,607
3400	11,155	4800	15,748	6200	20,342	7600	24,935
3500	11,483	4900	16,076	6300	20,670	7700	25,263
3600	11,811	5000	16,404	6400	20,998	7800	25,591
3700	12,139	5100	16,733	6500	21,326	7900	25,919
3800	12,467	5200	17,061	6600	21,654	8000	26,247
3900	12,795	5300	17,389	6700	21,982	8100	26,575
4000	13,124	5400	17,717	6800	22,310	8200	26,903
4100	13,452	5500	18,045	6900	22,638	8300	27,231
4200	13,780	5600	18,373	7000	22,966	8400	27,560
4300	14,108	5700	18,701	7100	23,294	8500	27,888
4400	14,436	5800	19,029	7200	23,622	8600	28,216
4500	14,764	5900	19,357	7300	23,951	8700	28,544
4600	15,092	6000	19,685	7400	24,279	8800	28,872

NOTE: All dates in this section refer to 1991 unless otherwise stated. Normally, accounts signed by a name alone (no club) indicate membership in the American Alpine Club.

UNITED STATES

Alaska

Denali National Park and Preserve Mountaineering Summary, 1991. The 1991 mountaineering season on Denali began with a rumble as a major earthquake hit the range on April 30. It measured 6.1 on the Richter scale. The epicenter was just south of Mount Foraker. Huge avalanches were triggered throughout the range and there were several close calls among climbers, luckily none with injuries. The 1990-1 winter was another with heavy snow in the Alaska Range. There were no winter attempts on Mount McKinley. The weather in the spring was generally poor. An abundance of cold and stormy weather turned away most summit tries until late May when a stretch of stable weather arrived. Still, the success rate remained low until another stretch of good weather in mid to late June brought the success rate up to normal. This year, in order to maintain safe, reliable and timely air support for high-altitude rescues on McKinley, the National Park Service contracted an Areospatiale Lama helicopter to be stationed in Talkeetna for the mountaineering season. U.S. Army Chinook helicopters were not available as in years past. The Lama was successfully used in five major rescue missions this year. Its worthiness was especially proven after it completed two rescues above 18,000 feet, one of which required four landings on the "Football Field" at 19,500 feet. In addition, for the first time in Alaska, the Park Service implemented "short-haul" rescue using the Lama. This is a technique of inserting rescuers who are clipped into a fixed line suspended beneath the helicopter into rescue sites where it is not possible to land nearby. Once the victims have been stabilized for transport, they are extracted from the rescue site in a similar manner. The Park Service plans to keep the Lama helicopter under contract and stationed in Talkeetna for at least the next two years. Due to the unavailability of air support from the U.S. Army helicopters, the Denali Medical Research Project did not operate this season. However, the Park Service maintained a camp at the 14,000-foot basin on the West Buttress. Mountaineering rangers were able to provide emergency medical care, coordinate rescues and base their patrols from this camp. The Park Service conducted four 24-day patrols on McKinley, plus numerous other patrols in different parts of the Alaska Range. We continue to staff a ranger station in the town of Talkeetna where climbers register for their expeditions. Registration is required for all expeditions on McKinley and Foraker. Climbers headed to other areas in the South District of Denali National Park and Preserve are encouraged to register. A strong emphasis is placed on the importance of environmentally sound expeditionary climbing and sanitation practices. Additionally, mountaineers must remain self-sufficient and conduct their own rescues whenever possible.

Interesting statistics: *Number of climbers on Mount McKinley:* In 1991, 935 climbers attempted to climb McKinley. This is 63 fewer persons than in 1990. Although this is a drop of 6.3%, it still represents a vast increase over the previous two decades: 1972=181; 1973=203; 1974=282; 1975=362; 1976=508; 1977=360; 1978=459; 1979=533; 1980=659; 1981=612; 1982=696; 1983=709; 1984=695; 1985=645; 1986=755; 1987=817; 1988=916; 1989=1009; 1990=998; 1991=935. *Success rate:* 557 (59%) of those attempting McKinley reached the summit. Ten expeditions attempted six different routes on Foraker. Four out of 28 climbers (14%) reached the summit. Nine expeditions attempted Hunter via five different routes. Five out of 24 climbers (21%) reached the summit. *Acute mountain sickness:* 79 (8%) reported symptoms. Of these, 60 (76%) were mild, 16 (20%) were moderate, 3 (4%) were severe. *Frostbite:* 43 (5%) reported some degree of frostbite. Of these 26 (60%) were mild, 11 (26%) required physician care, 6 (14%) required hospitalization. *West Buttress Route:* 680 (73%) climbers on McKinley attempted the West Buttress, by far the most popular route. It is interesting to note, however, that the percentage on the West Buttress has dropped during the past two years. Typically, 80% to 85% of the climbers on McKinley attempt the West Buttress. *Soloists:* 14 (1.5%) persons attempted a solo climb of McKinley. Eight reached the summit, including two on the Cassin Ridge. *Mountain Guiding:* 265 (28%) persons climbed with one of the seven authorized guide services. The success rate for the guided groups was 67%. They attempted the West Buttress, West Rib, Muldrow Glacier and West Buttress-Muldrow Traverse. *Nationalities:* 531 (57%) of those on McKinley were Americans and 404 (43%) from foreign countries. This is a large increase in foreign climbers. The average for the past ten years is 30%. A total of 28 nationalities was represented: Argentina=5; Australia=14; Austria=29; Barbados=1; Canada=25; Czechoslovakia=13; England=47; Finland=3; France=21; Germany=51; Hong Kong=1; India=1; Italy=21; Japan=29; Korea=50; Mexico=13; New Zealand=2; Norway=4; Poland=2; Puerto Rico=1; Scotland=9; Spain=13; Switzerland=42; USA=531; USSR=1; Yugoslavia=2. *New Routes and Interesting Activities:* On Mount McKinley, new routes were made on the start of the Cassin ridge, on the northwest face, on the southeast face above Thayer Basin and on the south face between the Orient Express and the Messner couloir. New routes were climbed on the south face of Foraker, the west face of Huntington, the south face of Dickey, the southeast face of Barrille and on P 6800 above the Ruth Gorge. [These are described in articles or in the "Climbs and Expeditions" section.] **Accidents:** The National Park Service conducted five major rescues on McKinley in 1991, resulting in the evacuation of nine climbers by helicopter. An additional nine incidents were reported to the climbing rangers. Of these, two climbers were evacuated by helicopter coincidental to other rescue operations that were in process. The remainder of climbers were able to conduct their own self-rescues without assistance from the Park Service. For the first time since 1982 there were no mountaineering related fatalities in the Park. Following are the more significant accidents and incidents that occurred in 1991. *Avalanche, Multiple Injuries, Self-Rescue:* On April 25, Klass Wierenga, Frank De Vos, Frank Kleinbekman and Matthijs Wiggers of the Dutch Mount Foraker Expedition were climbing at 8000 feet on the 1974 variation of the southeast ridge of

Foraker. Just a few feet below the ridge crest, the group triggered a large slab avalanche with a five-foot crown and running about 1600 feet. All four climbers were swept to the base of the ridge. Kleinbekman and Wiggers received minor injuries and were able to dig out Wierenga, who was unconscious and suffered a pneumothorax. De Vos was semi-conscious, suffering a pneumothorax, dislocated shoulder and fractured humerus. The climbers were unable to raise help with their radio and began a self-evacuation to the landing strip on the west fork of the Kahiltna Glacier. On April 28, they were able to contact their air taxi and were flown out to Talkeetna. *Falls with Injuries, Frostbite, Acute Mountain Sickness:* On May 14, four members of the Korean Blue Fire Expedition left their high camp at 18,200 feet at Denali Pass on the West Buttress and climbed to the summit. Due to fatigue, acute mountain sickness and poor weather, the climbers became separated on the descent. Go Il-Soon, Ann Jong-Ho and Lee Beom-Kyou bivouacked in the open. On the morning of May 15, frostbitten Ann fell 100 feet while descending to camp, sustaining minor head injury. Go had frostbitten hands. Meanwhile, Lee and Park Jun-Chan, who had been waiting at Denali Pass, fell 500 feet while attempting to descend to the 17,200-foot camp to obtain food and assistance. Park sustained fractured thoracic vertebrae and Lee a cervical strain. On May 16, mountaineering rangers and the NPS Lama helicopter evacuated Ann and Go from Denali Pass and Lee and Park from 17,200 feet. *High-Altitude Pulmonary Edema, High-Altitude Cerebral Edema, Frostbite:* On May 22, Korean Kin Hong-Bin, who was camped at Denali Pass became seriously ill with severe acute mountain sickness and high-altitude pulmonary edema. Kim was lowered to the 17,200-foot camp by other climbers. On May 23, he was lowered down the Rescue Gully to 14,200 feet by the para-rescue team from the 210th Air National Guard, assisted by rangers and other climbers at the 14,200-foot camp. On May 24, he was airlifted from 14,200 feet by an Air National Guard Pavehawk helicopter. He suffered severe frostbite to both hands and pneumonia complicated by high-altitude pulmonary edema. In a related accident on May 23, Kim Geo-Bong of the Korean Mokpo University Expedition fell seriously ill with high-altitude cerebral edema while camped at 17,200 feet on the West Buttress. He was lowered down the Rescue Gully to 14,200 feet by members of his own expedition. On May 25, his condition remained critical and a ground evacuation was determined not feasible. He was airlifted from 14,200 feet by the NPS Lama helicopter. *Crevasse Fall, Multiple Injuries:* On May 29, New Zealander Tara Wingfield of the Taking the Dog for a Walk Expedition was ascending from Windy Corner to the 14,200-foot camp. While crossing a heavily crevassed area near 13,400 feet, a large snowbridge collapsed. Wingfield fell about seven feet before her rope team arrested her fall. She was immediately hoisted from the crevasse. She sustained a dislocated patella, knee sprain and fractured ribs. With assistance, she continued to the 14,200-foot camp. On May 31, she was airlifted by the NPS Lama helicopter after it was determined that a safe ground evacuation by the remaining members of her expedition was not feasible. *Acute Mountain Sickness, Search, Self-Rescue:* On June 21, Japanese climbers Hiroshi Sakurai and Hiroshi

Urayama arrived at 15,500 feet on the Haston-Scott route on the south face of McKinley. They had ascended 3500 feet from the bottom of the face that day. Urayama was struck by acute mountain sickness and felt he should be rescued. That evening, the pair began calling "May Day" on their radio. The National Park Service responded with a search plane attempting to locate the "May Day" calls. Numerous contacts were made with climbers, including the Japanese, but due to a communication barrier, the two remained unidentified. "May Day" calls were again reported on the 22nd and the NPS Lama helicopter began to search. Again the two Japanese were not identified. Urayama decided that he wasn't going to be rescued and so the pair began ascending the route very rapidly, summitting the next morning. They then descended and reported to the NPS ranger camp at 14,200 feet that they were the ones calling "May Day." With this information, the search was called off. *Open Bivouacs, Frostbite:* Late on July 3, Polish climber Krzysztof Wiecha began climbing alone to the summit of McKinley from the 17,200-foot camp on the West Buttress route. As he approached the summit from the 19,500-foot area, the weather rapidly deteriorated with clouds, snow, high winds and zero visibility. He became disoriented. Early on July 4, he sought shelter in a small snow cave he dug at 20,000 feet. He carried no bivouac or survival gear. At seven A.M., he was reported as overdue to the NPS mountaineering rangers. The weather remained extremely poor on July 4 and 5 with heavy snowfall, strong winds and high avalanche danger prohibiting air and ground search. Meanwhile, Wiecha wandered around near the summit, seeking the descent route, taking shelter in several locations. He suffered severely from the cold, altitude, dehydration and exhaustion. By midday on July 6, it began to clear and an air search began. Miraculously, Wiecha was spotted crawling from a crevasse just below the summit. The NPS Lama helicopter was dispatched from Talkeetna and two rangers were flown to the "Football Field" at 19,500 feet. The rangers climbed to Wiecha, who was coherent but could barely move due to exhaustion and severely frostbitten feet. He was lowered 900 feet to the "Football Field", where the helicopter landed once again. Wiecha was flown off the mountain early on July 7. Both his frostbitten feet were amputated. There were a number of other incidents of altitude illness and frostbite. Many were treated at the National Park Service first-aid-and-rescue camp at 14,200 feet on the West Buttress.

Trends and Items of Special Concern: *Heavy Use:* Nearly record numbers of climbers attempted to climb Mount McKinley this year. They spent more than 17,000 user days on McKinley alone. Over 12,000 of these were on the West Buttress. The use on the West Buttress is even higher when considering that many other routes are accessed via the West Buttress. Also, many climbers acclimatize there too. *Rescues:* Ten of the 11 climbers (91%) that were rescued by helicopter this year were foreigners. 1.2% of climbers attempting McKinley this year required rescue. *Sanitation:* With the heavy use, it is more important than ever for mountaineers to dispose properly feces and urine. Many camps, especially at higher elevations, are littered with feces and frozen urine spots that are not covered by the annual accumulation of snow. Not only is this an

DENALI NATIONAL PARK AND PRESERVE
1991 MOUNTAINEERING SUMMARY

	Expeditions	Climbers	Successful Climbers
Mount McKinley			
West Buttress	145	475	275
West Buttress (guided)	24	205	137
W. Buttress/Muldrow Traverse	7	26	15
W. Buttress/Muldrow (guided)	3	23	20
Muldrow Glacier	2	4	0
Muldrow Glacier (guided)	2	22	10
Muldrow/W. Buttress Traverse	3	9	7
West Rib	15	58	33
West Rib (guided)	3	15	11
West Rib Cutoff	19	46	16
Cassin Ridge	18	37	24
Cassin Ridge (guided)	0	0	0
Haston-Scott	1	2	1
South Buttress	2	4	2
Reality Ridge	1	2	0
Northwest Face	1	3	2
Northwest Buttress	2	4	0
Wickersham Wall	0	0	0
	248	935	553
Mount Foraker			
Archangel Ridge	1	4	0
Infinite Spur	1	2	0
Northeast Ridge	3	8	0
Southeast Ridge	3	10	4
Southeast/Viper Ridge	1	2	0
Talkeetna Ridge	1	2	0
	10	28	4
Mount Hunter			
Kennedy-Lowe	1	2	0
North Buttress	1	3	0
Southeast Spur	1	2	0
Southwest Ridge	1	3	3
West Ridge	5	16	2
	9	24	5

	Expeditions	Climbers	Successful Climbers
Mount Huntington	6	18	2
Moose's Tooth (west summit)	9	26	9
Mount Silverthrone	1	6	6
Mount Dan Beard	1	7	0
Peak 11,300	2	5	3
Ruth Gorge Peaks	4	9	7
Mount Brooks	2	5	5
Mount Russell	0	0	0
Middle Triple Peak	1	2	2

NOTE: Since registration is required only for mountaineers attempting Mount McKinley and Mount Foraker, statistics for other mountains represent those climbers who voluntarily checked in with the mountaineering rangers. Other climbs, especially in the Ruth Glacier area, are likely to have occurred.

environmental degradation of the mountain, but there is risk of contamination of snow that might be melted and used for drinking water by future expeditions. We still suggest the use of plastic bags for latrines, which should be disposed of in deep crevasses. The Park Service maintains pit latrines dug deeply into the snowpack at the Kahiltna Glacier Base Camp, at 14,200 feet on the West Buttress and at the landing area in the Ruth Amphitheater. *Trash:* Many expeditions haul trash to Base Camp where it is flown off the mountain. Still others continue to dump trash in crevasses. Mountaineers of all nationalities must take the responsibility for, and the initiative in, preserving the quality of the world's mountain environments. A combination of education, leading by example and peer pressure are probably the most effective tools that can be brought to bear against less considerate mountaineers. Citations were issued for unauthorized guiding, littering and improper disposal of human-body waste. *Administrative Notes:* A portable radio repeater was again installed in the Ramparts west of the lower Kahiltna Glacier. This helps to improve communications between the Talkeetna Ranger Station and the mountaineering patrols. The newly constructed Park Service building in Talkeetna was occupied this year. It serves as seasonal quarters, year-round office for the South District Ranger and search-and-rescue coordination center. For more information or to request mountaineering information and/or registration forms, please contact the Mountaineering Rangers, Talkeetna Ranger Station, PO Box 588, Talkeetna, Alaska 99676. Telephone: 907-733-2231.

ROBERT SEIBERT, *South District Ranger,*
Denali National Park and Preserve

PLATE 32

Photo by Bradford Washburn

MOUNT McKINLEY rising above Thayer Basin. Solid line shows ascent. Dashed line indicates descent variant.

McKinley, Southeast Face from Thayer Basin. On May 28, Bob Gammelin and I flew to Kahiltna Base to attempt a new route on Denali, one rising out of Thayer Basin to join the southeast spur at P 18,900. It was our perhaps perverse intent to approach the Basin via the East Fork of the Kahiltna and the Japanese Ramp, which would require a descent of 1500 feet from the crest of the South Buttress—should we be fortunate enough to survive the objective hazards of the Ramp and reach the South Buttress at all! We spent four days hauling up the East Fork, establishing our final glacier camp on June 1 at 12,000 feet. The technical crux involved wild stemming between a sérac flake and the main crevasse wall early on in order to gain the Ramp as the lower section was badly broken. Our only camp on the Ramp was made on June 3 at 14,000 feet beneath a sheltering sérac, just left of the icefall which separates the Ramp from the Wyoming Spur. This icefall provided interesting moments, fortunately the only area active during our time on the Ramp! On June 8, we moved up over the South Buttress, picked up a food cache and staggered into Thayer Basin, where we were greeted by an unrelenting ground blizzard which continued for the next three days. On June 13, the weather let us move onto new ground. We climbed the right branch of the great couloir that splits the southeast face to its junction with the east ridge on 50° to 60° ice and snow, with a camp at 16,000 feet below the top of the couloir. Beautiful weather held and the following day we climbed to 17,800 feet on the ridge, finding moderate to easy climbing on snow and weaving a line through rock buttresses and outcrops with only intermittent rock or mixed moves necessary. At that point, the weather deteriorated and the next five days were spent tent-bound, watching food and fuel supplies evaporate mysteriously, as it didn't seem we were eating all that much! A second crux, this one psychological, was encountered when, on June 20, the weather broke and we were able to complete our climb of the ridge to P 18,900 and follow the Southeast Spur to the summit—an exhilarating finish up a sharp, exposed ridge with 8000 feet of the South Face falling below us! We retraced the route of ascent on our way down, with a variation involving a traverse south into the main branch of the great couloir just above the narrows at 16,000 feet, which allowed us to avoid down-climbing some rock encountered on the way up. We left Thayer Basin on the 22nd, beginning a 40-hour marathon, reaching Kahiltna Base on the evening of the 23rd, after climbing through the night on our descent of the Ramp. The route is moderate and enjoyable, yet committing and remote. Aside from the summit day and some specks on the Cassin, we saw no one for over three weeks . . . on Denali!

Lee L. James, *Hosemeisters International*

McKinley, Cassin Ridge Variant. Our Slovak expedition was composed of Emil Hasík, Josef Nežerka, Igor Valiga and me as leader. After landing on the Kahiltna Glacier on May 20, for acclimatization we climbed that same day to 3000 meters on Mount Crosson and reached the summit on the 21st. While Hasík and Valiga climbed the West Buttress, Nežerka and I left for the southwest

Photo by Bradford Washburn

PLATE 33

**Czechoslovak variant on
McKINLEY's Cassin Ridge.**

face on May 25 via the northeast fork of the Kahiltna Glacier. We headed up the southwest face to the left of the usual Cassin start and to the right of the Denali Diamond route. We started about 150 feet to the left of the Henrich-Volkman route. We bivouacked at 4200 and 4400 meters on May 27 and 28 and then were forced to the right to join the Cassin route at 4700 meters by very strong winds and heavy snowfall. We were on new ground for 1100 meters or 3600 feet. This was difficult mixed climbing (up to 5.9) with long sections of 60° ice. The lower face offered only hanging bivouacs or bivouacs on ice-chipped ledges. We found some old fixed ropes early on, probably from Japanese attempts in the 1970s. After our bivouac on the Cassin Ridge at 4700 meters, we again bivouacked on May 30 at 5600 meters. We climbed to the summit on May 31 and were back at the airstrip on the Kahiltna on June 2.

ZOLO DEMJÁN, *Spectrum Alpine Club, Bratislava, Czechoslovakia*

McKinley South Face, New Route. Josef Rakoncaj and I came to Alaska at the end of April. We flew to the Kahiltna Glacier. We climbed slowly as high as Denali Pass on the West Buttress. After acclimatizing to the altitude and cold, on May 17, Rakoncaj climbed the Messner Couloir in half a day. The next day, I climbed a new route between the Messner Couloir and the Orient Express. The maximum difficulty on rock was 5.8 and the ice was up to 70°. I descended to the 14,000-foot camp without going all the way to the summit. We two then climbed with skis over Denali Pass and continued in storm, cold and wind to the north on the Harper Glacier. We descended to the Muldrow Glacier and out to Wonder Lake. Rakoncaj flew home. I returned to Talkeetna, where I spent several days drinking beer in the Fairview Inn and loving Alaska. In early June, I flew again to the Kahiltna and then climbed the Cassin Ridge in five days. This was a great climb for me with very hard ice and a very heavy rucksack. As I bivouacked in the first rock band, at five A.M. I became aware of someone passing my tent. Was it a yeti? I looked outside and saw a solo climber with a small rucksack. "Hi. Good morning. If you like tea, we can do five-o'clock tea." We spent twenty minutes in my tent. "What are you doing here?" "Climbing the Cassin." "And you?" "The same." "And what is your name?" The man was Mugs Stump. And he took only a few hours to climb the Cassin!

MIROSLAV ŠMÍD, *ADR Rocks, Czechoslovakia*

Mount McKinley, Northwest Face of the West Buttress. A full article on this climb appears earlier in this *Journal*.

McKinley, Rapid Ascent. On June 4 late in the afternoon, Mugs Stump left the camp at 14,000 feet on the West Buttress of McKinley and crossed to the West Rib, which he descended to the northeast fork of the Kahiltna. He then climbed the Japanese Couloir and the whole Cassin Ridge to the summit in 15

PLATE 34

Photo by Bradford Washburn

**Šmid's new route between the
Messner Couloir on the left and the
Orient Express.**

hours and descended to the 14,000-foot camp, which he reached just 27½ hours after he had left it.

McKinley Climbed by a 12-Year-Old. Taras Genet, 12-year-old son of Kathy Sullivan and the late Ray Genet, climbed on July 21 to the summit of McKinley via the West Buttress. He is probably the youngest person to do so. The group of seven was guided by Chip Faurot and José Boza. His father died on the descent from Everest when Taras was 18 months old and was awaiting in Base Camp with his mother the arrival of Ray in vain.

Huntington Winter Attempt, West Face to the Harvard Route. Leo Americus, Dave McGivern, Charlie Sassara and I flew to the upper Tokositna Glacier on March 11. From an 8000-foot Base Camp, we moved through an icefall to a secondary camp on a bench below the notch where the Harvard route joins the west face at 9000 feet. On February 11, we fixed 750 feet of rope over nearly 2000 feet of terrain to the base of an ice couloir over mostly 35° to 45° ice and snow. Two days later, we jümared and climbed to that 1500-foot water-ice gully that joins the upper Harvard route above the "Nose Pitch." The first lead was the steepest with a 30-foot vertical section at the onset. The second was on 75° black ice. The third 300-foot pitch began with a 20-foot vertical apron and eased to 55° to 60° ice. The final two pitches varied from 45° to 55° ice, some covered with snow. On the traverse that leads to the upper snow face, night closed in and forced a bivouac on a tiny 15-foot ledge. The next day, we completed the traverse and climbed 600 feet of 40° to 60° blue ice to a rock outcrop, where we hacked a tiny ice ledge out of an ice bulge. A weather system moved through and created high winds at the exposed bivouac site. Short calm breaks were never long enough to complete the remaining 700 vertical feet to the summit. We had begun with only 2½ days of food. By rationing, we held out for three days of high winds on this tiny perch. On the fifth day, we packed our gear. During a slight break at midday, we went for broke on a summit bid in questionable weather. Sassara led 300 feet on 50° ice to the French ridge, followed by McGivern, but hurricane-strength winds on the ridge made them bail out. We began to rappel off, but darkness fell and we spent the night at the lower bivouac site. None of us could sleep that night. It was a relief to descend the ice couloir in daylight to the lower snowfields.

JOHN BAUMAN, *Unaffiliated*

Huntington, South Face. Jay Smith and Paul Teare climbed a difficult new route on the south face of Huntington to the right of the Harvard Route. This is described in a full article earlier in this *Journal*.

Huntington, West Face Attempt. In April and May, William Kito and I, both recipients of the American Alpine Club Climbing Fellowship grants, flew to the

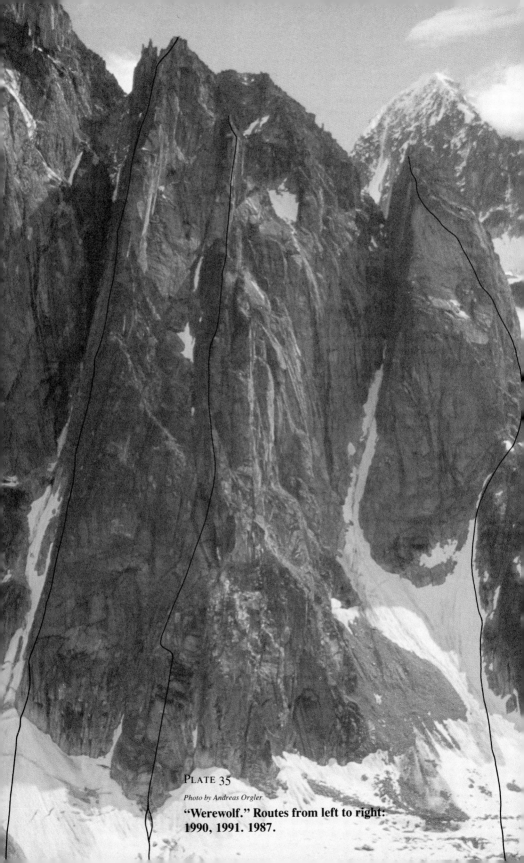

PLATE 35

Photo by Andreas Orgler

**"Werewolf." Routes from left to right:
1990, 1991. 1987.**

Tokositna Glacier below the west face of Huntington. Our objective was the unclimbed rock buttress immediately to the right of the Colton-Leech route. Of great help logistically and morally was the support of Rit Kellog. It took us 27 days to fix nine pitches (V, 5.9, A3) because of poor weather and snow-and-ice conditions on the face. We successfully surmounted the "bottleneck," a 150-foot section of overhanging wall at the apex of the rock climbing. We turned back at that point. Unconsolidated snow and ice covered rocks upwards from this point for 1000 feet to where our buttress intersected the Colton-Leech route.

CLAY WADMAN, *Unaffiliated*

Foraker and Barrille. A full article on remarkable new routes on the southeast ridge of Foraker and the east face of Barrille appear earlier in this *Journal*.

Mount Dickey South Face. A full article is found earlier in this *Journal*.

P 7500+ ("Werewolf"), Anenome Buttress, Ruth Gorge. On July 14, Klaus Geisswinkler and I were flown by Doug Geeting to the Ruth Gorge. On the 6th and 7th, we climbed on a rock face on the west side of the gorge but had to give up the attempt because of the outbreak of a storm. Bad weather continued until July 17. Nevertheless, we started on July 9 up the southwest buttress of "Werewolf." In ever-increasing rain, we climbed 12 pitches but had to wait for two hours on a big shoulder when it turned to snowfall. At about eight P.M., the precipitation stopped and we continued up the pillar, reaching its summit at midnight in damp cold. The 18-pitch route is mostly 5.8 to 5.10. After a two-hour rest we rappelled down the route and reached Base Camp at nine A.M. after I had fallen into a snow-covered glacial stream. Geeting was able to pick us up during a window in the clouds on July 16.

ANDREAS ORGLER, *Österreichischer Alpenverein*

P 6850. There are two Bugaboo-like rock peaks that rise between the lower Kahiltna and Lacuna Glaciers, which had never been attempted. Jim Okonek flew Clay Wadman and me to a glacier landing at 4000 feet. After setting up camp, we immediately set out for a long, steep snow couloir that splits into the northern and highest of the two peaks (62°38′N, 151°29′W). Our all-night climb took us to the top of the couloir, a few pitches being of steep ice. The crux of the ascent was a series of traversing leads on the northwest face on frozen, but sometimes breakable, snow. Fortunately we were able to protect with rock pitons some of the exposed pitches here and along the narrow, technical summit ridge. The descent took the same route.

FRED BECKEY

Whale's Back, Avalanche Peak and Citadel, Kichatna Spires. My husband Gino Buscaini, Helma Schimke and I were flown to the Shadows Glacier by Doug Geetings. We all climbed Whale's Back by the north ridge on May 22, Avalanche Peak by the east face and north ridge on May 24 and Citadel via the first gendarme on the north ridge, climbing from the north left of the icefall and descending to the Shelf Glacier and the couloir in the south face of Avalanche Peak and back to the Shadows Glacier on June 2.

SILVIA METZELTIN BUSCAINI, *Club Alpino Italiano*

Mount Thor, North Ridge, Chugach Range, Winter Ascent. Leo Americus and I spent four days skiing the 32 miles to the base of the north side of Mount Thor via the Nelchina and Sylvester Glaciers, starting on February 10. From there we made the first winter ascent of the north ridge, which rises 3750 feet from 8500 feet on the Sylvester Glacier. Thor (3734 meters, 12,251 feet) is the third highest peak of the Chugach Range. A storm moved in. A window in the multiple fronts opened on the sixth day and allowed us to climb. The first 1500 feet were a well defined ridge of blue ice and rotten snow, sometimes knife-edged, with a drop of 1000 feet or more on both sides and at a 35° to 50° angle. The ridge broadened as it met the north face, crossing a 250-yard area of crevasses. The upper 2250 feet were on good snow. We summited on February 16 after only six hours, having placed one ice screw on the lower section. We spent three days skiing 33 miles out the Powell Glacier to the south fork of the Matanuska River.

JOHN BAUMAN, *Unaffiliated*

Ptarmigan Peak, Western Chugach. In mid February, Tom Walters and I climbed the prominent north buttress of Ptarmigan Peak. The route ascends steep corners formed by massive blocks. With four 5th-class pitches on relatively sound rock, the climbing was steep and varied. (III, 5.8.)

CHARLES SASSARA

Mount Jarvis Ascent and Tragedy, Wrangell Mountains. Japanese climbers Hiroshi Oda and Ichiro Mitoda were flown to the Nebesna Glacier by bush pilot Ken Bunch on April 4. They started alpine-style up the southeast ridge of Mount Jarvis (4091 meters, 13,421 feet). (The first ascent was made on July 26, 1967 from the saddle between Mount Jarvis and Wrangell by Ed Lane, Barbara Lilley, Bill Morris and Dick Beach.) On April 6, Oda climbed to the summit, while Mitoda quit some 650 feet lower. The next day, they both returned to the summit and descended to the landing point, hoping to be picked up on the 10th. Bad weather intervened and it was not until April 16 that Bunch could return to pick them up. There was so much new snow that they failed to take off after a run of 1000 feet. They began to pack the runway with skis. Bunch emerged from the plane to help, took ten steps, collapsed and died immediately from a massive heart attack. When the skilled bush pilot with 45 years of experience did not return, other pilots set out to search for him. After they located the problem, eventually the Japanese were evacuated by Army helicopter. A full account appears in *Iwa To Yuki* N° 147, August 1991.

P 12,200, Wrangell-Saint Elias Mountains. On April 23, my wife Siri, Paul and Donna Claus and I made the first ascent of P 12,200, a border peak due west of Mount Logan. Landing at 8400 feet on an unnamed glacier west of our summit, we established Base Camp. The next day, we skied three miles up the glacier to 10,000 feet and camped below the route. The next morning, we ascended a 1000-foot high gully on the southern flank of the peak's western buttress. We then wandered up through snow patches and around rock outcrops at times on terrain up to 60°. A final pitch of shattered rock through a steep chimney brought us to a glaciated plateau a half mile west of the summit. After crossing the plateau, we turned our attention to the summit pyramid and the many crevasses that guarded the top. Two hours later, after snaking our way up the crevassed knoll, we looked at the last large crevasse, whose upper overhanging edge was six feet above us. Donna and Siri decided to wait it out while Paul and I finished the last section. With shoves from our wives, we climbed the overhang. An exposed, nearly vertical snow lead and another pitch brought us to the summit.

CHARLES SASSARA

Neacola. A complete article on the ascent of this remote peak appears earlier in this *Journal*.

P 7205, Philip Smith Mountains, Brooks Range. After a failed attempt on the south face of P 7240 above Echooka, our party passed to the Marsh Fork of the Canning River. The canyon here is reminiscent of the Alberta Rockies. We followed it west and then south to twin-glaciered P 7205 on the Continental Divide. From an unmapped lake, we ascended the east ridge, traversed the snow domes to the summit and descended by the glaciers.

DENNIS SCHMITT, *Unaffiliated*

Northernmost Peaks on the Continental Divide, Romanzof Mountains. I began this soujourn at Okpilak Lake with three Swiss climbers. After an ascent of Mount Michelson, we entered the Arey Creek drainage. Granite P 8405 stood directly north of our camp on the glacier. We climbed directly up the south ridge, finishing with a harrowing ice ridge to the summit. The ice wall of the north face feeds the Bravo Glacier basin. The following day, we waded through deep snow to the pass atop the icecap and camped below the north face of P 8715. We climbed again that night. Our route veered to the west of the icefall where it meets the triangular rock cliff of the upper northwest face. We placed two ice screws where the steep ice dropped over the face. After traversing the icecap, we descended into a stream canyon that took us to the Jago River. We turned south to Gothic Mountain (8620 feet). I had made the first ascent of this peak ten years before. New maps depicted an icefall along the summit ridge, which I had not encountered. We ascended the eastern canyon, entered the icefields and followed them to the south summit in good weather. From this summit, I witnessed the same gothic formations I had seen from the summit a decade earlier. The icefield on the new maps was misplaced. In correcting the old errors, these maps had created new ones. Further up the east fork of the Jago, we ascended to the icefields south of P 7800, the westernmost high Alaskan Arctic peak. Three of us reached the summit from the south. Heading west the next day, we crossed a 7100-foot pass just south of the Obolisk (8440 feet), which two of us climbed by the narrow southwest ridge. Descending into the Sheenjik drainage, we camped at the base of the glacier. That night I climbed the twin-horned P 7985, traversing the ice wall to the unnumbered peak to the west and descending to the point where the stream on the icecap splits north and south. This is the northernmost point on the Continental Divide.

DENNIS SCHMITT, *Unaffiliated*

Fairweather, Eliza and Other Ascents and Traverse from Mouth of Alsek River to Davidson Glacier and Chilkat Inlet. Our trip members were Betsy Fletcher, Craig Hollinger, Markus Kellerhals, Peter Stone and I as leader. After placing food caches by ski plane with Mike Ivers of Gulf Air, on May 7 we headed from its mouth up the Alsek and then up the Grand Plateau Glacier. Six-and-a-half days later we stood on the summit of Mount Fairweather, having climbed the west ridge from the plateau to the north. After feasting, we spent five days climbing some of the technically more difficult minor peaks near the plateau. These included P 11,105 (3354 meters) 3¾ miles northwest of Fairweather by its south ridge and the 3280-meter (10,761-foot) bump 2 kilometers east of Mount Root from the south. (Peaks in Alaska are given in feet and those in Canada in meters.) We also made a tiring ascent to the Fairweather-Quincy Adams col. After completing the first two weeks, we headed on the second leg of the trip with seven days of food. From lower on the Grand Plateau Glacier we crossed on skis a mile north of Mount Lodge and skied along the Grand Pacific Glacier to our next food cache near its junction with the Malbern Glacier. With three days to spare, we moved into the Mount Eliza area. We unsuccessfully attempted Eliza from the south but did climb P 2360 (7743 feet). The next day, two of us climbed to the summit of Eliza (2960 meters, 9711 feet) via the north ridge, a thrilling knife-edged, snow-and-ice route. We also climbed two minor bumps 1½ and 3 kilometers north and northeast of Eliza (2720 and 2632 meters, 8924 and 8635 feet). On skiing back down to the Grand Pacific Glacier, we took a two-hour side-trip to climb the higher of "The Rabbit Ears," (1680 meters,

5512 feet), located 7½ kilometers northeast of Eliza. After picking up our next load of food, we started up the Tenas Tikke Glacier. The weather turned poor. We spent five days, from May 27 to 31, either in the tents and at other times crawling along with the aid of map, compass and altimeter. We crossed the Carroll Glacier to go along the Tsirku Glacier, entering Alaska again just south of Mount Harris. We arrived at our final food cache in the upper cirque of the Riggs Glacier a day behind schedule. After descending the glacier 5½ kilometers the following day, we were held up by Peter Stone's snow-blindness for 2½ days at 3500 feet on the Riggs. In good weather for the first half of a day, we climbed P 5280 (1609 meters) on the western flank of the Riggs. With the recovery of Peter's eyes, we continued on in "in-and-out" weather. We ascended a glacier to a pass north of Sitth-gha-ee Peak and descended south to the Casemate Glacier. We ascended it over the divide to the Davidson Glacier. The Davidson was formidable, spectacular and time-consuming but possible on its southern ice and moraine. On the shores of Chilkat Inlet, we attracted a local fishing boat with an explosive white-gas fire. Haines Airways then was alerted and picked us up and dropped us off in Haines on the morning of June 9.

DAVID E. WILLIAMS, *Varsity Outdoor Club of the University of British Columbia*

St. Elias, Fairweather and Peaks in the St. Elias National Park and Glacier Bay National Park. Many expeditions made their access to the mountains which lie within these parks or near them through Yakutat. Of eight expeditions, only three were truly successful. The weather was the predominate cause of the low success rate. Yakutat received over 240 inches of precipitation in 1991 in both rain and snow. Americans Rick Holmes and Bob Branscomb attempted the south ridge of St. Elias but did not have enough time to complete the climb. Four attempts were made on Fairweather. Canadians Conrad Baumgartner, Alan Massin and Steve Bertollo made a successful five-day round-trip from the Grand Plateau Glacier up the west ridge. The splendid Canadian ascent of Fairweather and the crossing to Chilkat Inlet led by David Williams is described in another report in this *Journal*. Americans Joe Carriveal and Bill Mickel were turned back by the weather on the Carpé Ridge. Americans Tom Nickerson, Dave Baratt, Steve Wheeler and Mexican Vince Radice could not complete the climb on the west ridge, also because of the weather. Americans Patrick Simmons and Phil Kaufman were turned back on the south ridge of Mount Orville by rotten snow and technical difficulties. Silas Wild describes his and Sam Grubenhof's expedition to the same region in a separate note. A successful expedition to Mount Logan in Yukon Territory was made from Yakutat. Englishmen Dean James, Mid Glamorgan, Tim Stimson, Scot Alex McNab and American Rick Wentz took 19 days to make the climb and commented that it was easier access to Logan logistically through Yakutat than through Canada. Climbers may contact the National Park Service Yakutat District Ranger Station for information on mountains and weather. The Ranger Station is open year-round and serves the Yakutat

District for both Wrangell-St. Elias National Park and Preserve and Glacier Bay National Park and Preserve. Climbers are encouraged to submit a voluntary registration form with the Ranger Station for climbs. For forms or information, please contact National Park Service, Yakutat District Ranger Station, PO Box 137, Yakutat, Alaska 99689. Tel.: 907-784-3295.

RICK MOSSMAN, *Yakutat District Ranger*

Mount Orville Attempt and Ascents of P 8900 and P 7209. On June 14, Sam Grubenhof and I were flown by Mike Ivers from Yakutat to 4000 feet on the North Crillon Glacier. We did a double carry the next day and set up Base Camp at 5300 feet. On the 16th, we set off at four A.M. with bivouac sacks and two days of food. We cramponed up a wide gully on the south slopes of Mount Orville (3199 meters, 10,495 feet), using pickets for running belays and reached a 7000-foot gap on the southeast ridge at 6:30 A.M. Then we climbed mixed snow and fourth-class rock to a flat area at 8000 feet where we could finally see the next 2000 feet of the climb. We belayed along the ridge on rotten snow and loose rock to 8400 feet where, at three P.M., we decided to abort the climb since the route ahead looked steeper and just as rotten. The following day, we rappelled and climbed down to Base Camp. On June 19, we climbed to a ridge just east of camp and purposely set off many slush avalanches to clean the route toward the gap between Orville and P 8900 (2713 meters). This is incorrectly named Mount Wilbur on the Mount Fairweather C-4 quadrangle. It lies on the ridge between its foresummits: P 8826 and P 8632. Trying to climb in the safest snow conditions, we set out for P 8900 at nine P.M. on June 20. We reached the summit of this spectacular viewpoint at 7:30 A.M. after a challenging glacier climb, weaving our way through numerous Alaska-sized crevasses. On the 23rd, we moved our camp back to the landing site and then walked under the northwest face of Crillon through the gap where Loren Adkin's party began their west ridge climb in 1972 and on to P 7209 (2198 meters), which afforded a marvelous panorama. We called our pilot to change return plans and retraced our steps to camp. The next morning Mike picked us up and returned us to Yakutat.

SILAS WILD, *Boeing Alpine Club*

Mount Abbe, Main Peak. A full article on the first ascent of the main peak of Mount Abbe and its approach by kayak appears earlier in this *Journal.*

Devil's Thumb, New Routes. There is a full article on new, difficult routes on the Devil's Thumb earlier in this *Journal.*

Devil's Thumb, West Buttress, 1990. In pounding rain in May, 1990, Jim Haberl, Michael Down and I helicoptered from Petersburg to set up Base Camp at the fork of the Witch's Cauldron just north of the Devil's Thumb. When theweather cleared, we learned two things. First of all, there is no north face, per se, but rather a northeast face (solo attempt by Krakauer in 1977), a north buttress (climbed by Stutzman and Plumb that same year, 60 pitches, 5.9) and a huge northwest face (attempted by Bearzi and Klose in 1982). Second, we learned we didn't want to climb there. We shifted our focus to the unclimbed west buttress, which Bearzi and Klose had attempted in 1980. We moved camp up the south arm of the Witch's Cauldron and ascended the icefall and glaciers under the Fox Head (the double summit immediately west of the Cat's Ears). In deteriorating weather, we set up a gear cache at the bottom of the 55° ice couloir leading to the Cat's Ears-Devil's Thumb col. When the weather cleared, we moved to camp at the cache and climbed the couloir and the first two rock pitches (5.6), but severe weather forced us to fix ropes and descend. Our third attempt took us six pitches up steep corners and huge flakes (5.9, A2) to below the prominent roof which splits the route at half height. Again, the weather pushed us down. An early start on June 7, 1990 put us at our previous high point just as clouds began to move in. A few dicey A2 moves surmounted the roof and delicate slab-and-corner climbing led to a good ledge. The next two pitches followed steep dihedrals visible from the glacier. The climbing was on wild flakes and steep corners (5.10). The weather turned ugly: 10-meter visibility, strong winds and snow, and rime on the rock and ropes. At the top of the buttress, some 20 meters from the true summit, the difficulties lessened to fourth-class. We turned back there in truly miserable conditions. A lengthy descent followed in blowing snow, darkness and rime. We had prepared the rappel stations on the way up but were unable to find them under the ice on the way down. In the interests of climbing light, we had not carried boots and had only one headlamp between us. There were several hanging stances, cold and slippery feet and much fumbling about. We continued rappelling down the couloir, finally arriving back at our high camp at 7:30 A.M., after a 27-hour round-trip. We walked out to Thomas Bay via the Baird Glacier in four days.

ALASTAIR FOREMAN, *Alpine Club of Canada*

Washington—Cascade Mountains

Liberty Bell and South Early Winter Spire. On August 16 and 17, Keith Hertel and I completed the first free ascent of the Independence Route. During the summer of 1990, with Bruce Anderson we had climbed the first six pitches, which were enjoyable climbing up to 5.11c. Unfortunately the next two pitches, originally A4 and A2, have several sections of decomposing granite cracks and seams, which required some yo-yoing but were done at 5.12a (V, 5.12a). Over Labor Day, Brooke Sandahl, Kurt Schmier and Adam Grosowski freed Liberty Crack with the crux at the Lithuanian Lip (V, 5.13a). Passenger route on South Early Winter Spire follows a line directly up the center of the southeast face. It was completed in August by Brian Burdo, Pete Doorish and Greg White. It features eight pitches, all but one of which are 5.10d or harder (V, 5.12a).

STEVEN RISSE

The Tooth, Snoqualmie Pass. Cindy Long and I established a direct route up the east face of the Tooth on August 3. We started up the steep but mostly easy 5th-class corners past a tree. We then moved left onto a high-angle slab and up an exposed nearly vertical dihedral (the crux) to an easy off-width crack. We angled left and up several more pitches to join the east-face slab route.

TIM OLSON

Ingalls Peak, North Peak, Northwest Ridge. On October 6, Dred Dunham and I completed this short but interesting route. We gained the ridge from a polished ramp on the west about 150 meters from the start of the ridge proper, which was too rotten to climb direct. (II, 5.7.)

STEVEN RISSE

Oregon

Mount Hood, Illumination Rock. In early August, Jim Petroske and I started up what we thought was the South Chamber Route. We ascended steep snow and ice to the base of the wall at the upper end of the chamber and directly below the South Pinnacle Notch. From a large, flat ledge at the north corner of the wall's base we climbed two pitches to gain the notch. The first (5.7) was a crack and mantle out of an overhanging slot choked with loose rocks and grit. The second was easy but delicate climbing over big ledges of large, loose blocks. From the notch we climbed steep, crumbling rock directly toward the summit ridge's crest, keeping on the east side of a small arête. On the crest we joined the standard route to the top.

BILLY PETROSKE

Razorblade Pinnacle, Mount Hood. On September 29, Cindy Long and I climbed the beautiful west arête of this hidden classic in the Sandy River Basin on Mount Hood. After a 2½-hour approach, we began up a grungy but easy first pitch that was followed by an exhilarating, steep climb up the right corner of a box-shaped arête (II, 5.10b). We call it "Gillette Arête." Wayne Wallace and I returned on October 20 and established another new route near the overhanging northwest ridge of the pinnacle. We climbed the first pitch of Gillette Arête, then down-climbed and traversed left to a notch. We nailed up slanting, thin cracks to the summit (III, 5.4, A3).

TIM OLSON

California—Sierra Nevada

Mount Whitney, East Face. On June 16, David Wilson and I ascended a new all-free route, *Left Wing Extremist* (V, 5.11a, 16 pitches) on this 2000-foot granite wall to the left of the old Direct East-Face route. We ascended a pedestal for two pitches, then veered slightly right up vertical and overhanging cracks for four continuous pitches of 5.10 and 5.11 into a huge open book joined by an overhanging seam without a continuous crack. On the right wall is a full-pitch, five-to-seven-inch, off-width crack with parallel sides and rounded edges. Lack of protection stopped a 1990 attempt here with Kike Arnal of Venezuela. This time we brought #5 and #6 Friends plus a Big Bro for what turned out to be a 5.10d groaner at nearly 14,000 feet. Above, the difficulties eased into superb 5.8 and 5.9 plates and knobs on a rib that stayed left of the upper part of the standard east-face route. The route took a full day and is similar in length, rock and steepness to Keeler Needle, but with more continuous difficulty and fewer cracks.

GALEN A. ROWELL

Keeler Needle, East Face, The Crimson Wall. During the first week of August, Mike Carville, Kevin Brown and I added a new long, free route to Keeler Needle. Possibly the hardest free wall above 10,000 feet in California, the route strikes straight up the center of the east face of Keeler Needle, following an obvious line between the Harding route on the left and the Lowe route on the right. We named it the *Crimson Wall* (V, 5.12−) due to the incredible pre-dawn alpine glow that colored the face each morning. We ascended ten full pitches before connecting with the Harding route for the final four pitches. We originally intended to finish straight up the virgin headwall but, alas, cracks that appeared finger-width through binoculars turned out to be incipient when we arrived. Short on bolts that would have been necessary to protect the headwall pitches, we vowed to return to complete the direct route. (In fact, as you read this, it is likely that the headwall is virgin no more—we are returning in May, 1992.) The Crimson Wall is characterized by its diversity of pitches; corner systems, blank faces, cracks and dikes lead the eye upward from the base. Three pitches of superb climbing form the soul of the route. The 7th, 8th and 9th link an arching corner, a huge flake and a sustained and steep layback corner that go 5.11, 5.10 and 5.12 respectively. The rock is solid and a full rack is called for. A total of 20 bolts was needed to protect the first ten pitches. Pitch 1 begins at the very center of the base of the wall and ascends to a belay just under a three-foot roof. The line is straightforward from there.

KEVIN STEELE

Day Needle. On June 16, Cameron Burns and I climbed an all-free variation of the Beckey-Reese route on Day Needle. (IV, 5.10b). The crux came in the second to last pitch, which followed left-angling cracks up steep rock that offered knobby face-climbing. It bypassed the bottom of an enormous off-width that slants up and right in the center of the face. The off-width is clearly visible from the base of the needle. Although we climbed the route in 16 pitches, it could have been accomplished in less.

STEVE PORCELLA

PLATE 36

Photo by Kevin Steele

On the Crimson Wall of KEELER NEEDLE.

Mount Russell, West Face. Steve Untch and I did a new route on the west face of Mount Russell (III, 5.10d). We started about 20 feet right of the Rowell-Jones route and kept straight up for nine pitches. The short fourth pitch was 5.10a and the fifth was 5.10d.

PATRICK BRENNAN

P 13,680+, Mount Sill, Mount Mendel and Other climbs, 1990. In June, 1990, Ken Kenega and I climbed a dihedral on P 13,680+ for seven pitches on the right of the Rowell route (III, 5.10a). In July, Kevin Malone and I did a direct finish of Mount Sill's east face. Where the Roper guide says that at one point there are two choices, we went in between. Three of the last five pitches were 5.9. In September, Kenega and I did a route on the north face of Mount Mendel on the rock rib right of the Mendel Couloir (III, 5.8). It was very loose and we wandered a lot.

PATRICK BRENNAN

Sierra Nevada Ascents. By the time you read this, a new *Sierra Nevada Climber's Guide* will have appeared, authored by R.J. Secor and published by The Mountaineers. The following is a list of previously unreported Sierra Nevada routes that arrived too late for publication and will *not* be given in the new guide. These reports were submitted by Claude Fiddler, Bart O'Brien and Sam Roberts. *Wheel Mountain, Southeast Arête:* This is a pinnacled ridge. FA (first ascent) by Sam Roberts, Brian West, August 1977 (II, 5.4). *Stonehouse Buttress, "Rots of Rock:"* This route begins right of Milky Way and passes through an area of very loose rock. FA by Sam Roberts, Mark Bowling, April 1987 (IV, 5.9, A2). *The Miter, North Ridge:* FA by Claude Fiddler, Vern Clevenger, September 1979 (Class 5). *Mount Muir, East Buttress Direct:* By staying on the prow of this buttress, a fine route can be completed. FA by Claude and Nancy Fiddler, 1980 (III, 5.9). *Mount Hale, West Face:* Follow a gully and face ending a few feet from the summit. FA by Claude Fiddler, Bob McGayren, Danny Whitmore, September 1991 (II, 5.8). *Mount Barnard, North Face:* Follow a rib directly to the summit. FA by Claude and Nancy Fiddler, July 1986 (III, 5.8). *Mount Williamson, "The Long Twisting Rib:"* As seen from Highway 395, this climb from Williamson Creek leads to Williamson's satellite summits. FA by Claude Fiddler, Jim Keating (III, Class 5). *Vandever Mountain, North Face:* FA by Claude and Nancy Fiddler, August 1985 (II, 5.6). *Needham Mountain, North Face:* FA by Claude and Nancy Fiddler, August 1985 (III, 5.6). *P 11,861, "The Wall above Big Five:"* This peak is 1.5 miles northeast of Needham Mountain. Climb a crack system up the center of the face for 17 pitches. A committing route. FA by Claude and Nancy Fiddler (V, 5.11). *"Two Fingers Peak," Northeast Ridge:* This is listed as being 1.3 miles northeast of Needham Mountain in the Roper guide. The route is a traverse from P 11,861. FA by Claude and Nancy Fiddler (Class 3). *P 11,772, Northwest Ridge:* Roper lists this as 1.2 miles north-northwest of Needham Mountain. From Cyclamen Pass, follow the ridge to the summit. A rope was thrown over the true summit and handwalked to the top by Claude Fiddler, who left a small stopper for a rappel. FA by Fiddler, August 1985 (Class 5, A0). *Lippincott Mountain, North Face:* Follow a crack system in the center of the face. Excellent climbing on superb rock. FA by Claude and Nancy Fiddler, August 1985 (III, 5.10). *Mount Chamberlain, Northeast Face:* This route is about 200 meters left of the West Pillar Route (Rowell-Farrell). Follow the crack systems leading directly to the summit. Fiddler says this is the finest wall he has climbed in the High Sierra. FA by Claude Fiddler, Bob Harrington, 1980 (V, 5.10, A2). *P 13,920+, East Ridge Direct:* This peak is 0.6 miles west of Mount Russell. This route follows the ridge from Russell. Roper describes this as being Class 3, but that means dropping well off the ridge when difficulties are encountered. By staying directly on the ridge, an airy traverse can be had. FA by Claude Fiddler, Vern Clevenger, September 1979 (II, 5.6). *"Mount Carl Heller," West Rib Center:* This is a proposed name for P 13,211, southeast of Vacation Pass in the Roper guide. It has also been called "Vacation Peak." Climb the southernmost arête on the west face, which leads directly to the summit. FA by Claude Fiddler, Vern Clevenger (II, 5.6). *"Mount Carl Heller," West Rib North:* Follow the prominent rib on the north side of the west face. Both this and the previous route are excellent climbs. FA by Claude Fiddler, Vern Clevenger, Bob Harrington, 1984 (II, 5.9). *Eagle Scout Peak, North Face:* Many possible routes. FA by Claude Fiddler, Vern Clevenger, August 1985 (II, 5.6). *Koontz Pinnacle, East Face:* Not recommended: loose rock. FA by Claude and Nancy Fiddler (IV, 5.9). *Second Kaweah, East Spur:* A loose, undesirable climb. FA by Claude and Nancy Fiddler, August 1985 (IV, 5.9). *P 13,520+, Northeast Ridge:* [Probably the flat-summited peak 0.5 miles southeast of Milestone Mountain — *Editor.*] FA by Claude and Nancy Fiddler, Dieter King (Class 3 or 4). *Ericsson Crags, Traverse from 1A to 3.* Crag 1A shares a notch with Mount Ericsson. The western gully to this notch is a good route. About 100 meters below the notch, head up and left to the summit of 1A (Class 4). Descend and head northeast to the broad shoulder between 1 and 1A. Follow the south ridge of 1 to its summit (5.8). A Class 3 ridge goes out to 1W (no record of prior ascent). Crags 2 and 3 can be climbed from the notch between them, which can be approached from either the east or west. The north ridge of Crag 2 is Class 3 or 4. The south ridge of Crag 3 is Class 5. The traverse is on great rock in a remote setting and is highly recommended. The entire traverse was first climbed by Claude Fiddler and Jim Keating in July 1991. *Center Peak, Northwest Arête:* Follow the prominent arête which drops into Bubbs Creek. FA by Vern Clevenger, Claude Fiddler, 1983 (III, 5.7). *Mount Goode, North Buttress Left:* This is left of the north buttress route described in the Roper guide. FA by Claude Fiddler, Vern Clevenger, 1979 (IV, 5.10). *Mount Gilbert, West Face:* FA by Vern Clevenger, Claude Fiddler, 1985 (II, 5.7). *Mount Haeckel, East Arête:* FA by Claude Fiddler, Leon Borowsky (III, 5.8). *Wheeler Peak, North Arête:* Climb from the junction of the north and northwest faces. An excellent mountaineering route. FA by Claude

East face of KEELER NEEDLE at Sunrise. Route took a straight line up the middle of the face.

Fiddler, Jim Keating, 1991 (Class 4-5). *Peak near Mount Ritter, Southwest Ridge:* Follow the long ridge from the San Joaquin River to the summit. The first-ascent party continued over the Ritter Pinnacles to the summit of Mount Ritter, making for a long, classic climb. FA by Vern Clevenger, Claude Fiddler, 1984 (IV, 5.9). *Minaret Traverse:* This is a multi-day classic. FA by Claude Fiddler, Vern Clevenger, 1980 (VI, 5.9). *Mount Lewis, East Face:* Loose and not recommended. FA by Claude Fiddler, Jim Keating, 1980 (IV, 5.10). *Kolp Crest Traverse:* A long traverse beginning at the Kuna Crest and ending at P 11,601. FA by Claude Fiddler, Rick Cashner, 1986 (V, 5.7). *Matthes Crest, Main Summit:* FA by Claude Fiddler, Dieter King, 1981 (III, 5.9). *Matthes Crest, North Summit, West Face:* FA (?) by Alan Bartlett, Bob Bartlett, October, 1974 (II, 5.6). *Cleaver Traverse:* FA by Vern Clevenger, Claude Fiddler, 1984 (Class 5). *Sawtooth Ridge Traverse via the Cleaver:* FA by Claude Fiddler, Vern Clevenger, 1984 (VI, 5.9). *Finger Peaks Traverse:* FA by Claude Fiddler, 1989 (II, Class 4).

BART O'BRIEN *and* ALAN BARTLETT

Half Dome, Tis-Sa-Ack Climbed by a Paraplegic. Mike Corbet and paraplegic climber Mark Wellman, who serves as a Yosemite Park Ranger, climbed the Tis-Sa-Ack route on Half Dome, reaching the top on September 16 after 13 days on the wall. They suffered from bad weather and lack of food. Wellman had been injured in a climbing accident in 1982 but refuses to consider himself disabled.

Mount Hooker Correction. On page 173 of *AAJ 1991*, a report of the ascent of the north face of Mount Hooker was incorrectly said to have been written by Annie Waterhouse. The correct name is Annie *Whitehouse*. This account states correctly that they spent three days route-finding, leading and fixing the first five pitches and another 3½ days on the actual climb. This is very much less time than the 21 days stated on page 132 in the full article on another ascent of the north face.

Utah

San Rafael Swell, 1990. On April 25, 1990, I climbed *Lightbulb,* a bizarre 170-foot tower named for its overhanging bulbous shape. Located near the San Rafael River Campground, it is clearly visible from the road and requires a 30-minute approach. The first pitch, which goes free, starts on the far right or northern edge. Fingers to hands to fists, it wraps around left to a good ledge. The final short pitch ascends bolts up the inverted bulb. (II, 5.10, A1.) On October 29, 1990, Allan Murphy and I climbed *The Daughter* (III, 5.10, A1) in the Southern Swell, south of I-70. It is the middle tower of the five-tower formation called Family Butte. Mike Friederichs and Gene Rousch made the first free ascent during the second climb of the tower, rating it 5.11b. Friederichs and I added a second route (III, 5.10+, A2) on the same tower on November 3, 1990.

Both routes ascend the south side on excellent Wingate sandstone. On *P 7601*, north of and visible from Family Butte, Friederichs and I then climbed the west face (III, 5.10d, A2). Mike led an impressive 165-foot, left-facing dihedral hand-to-finger crack in the first steep pitch. On the same tower but on the northeast corner, Seth "ST" Shaw and I added another route (III, 5.9, A2) on November 19, 1990. These two climbs are actually on separate towers as a 20-yard cleft divides them.

JAMES GARRETT

Angel's Landing, Zion National Park. Two new routes were put up on the north face of Angel's Landing. The *Swiss-American Route*, done in October by Xaver Bongard and me, climbs the major crack line to the left of the Lowe route and ascends directly to the summit. We drilled no holes on pitches (14 holes for belays only). This is a very clean route with several very serious leads. (VI, 5.10, A4.) Barry Ward and I climbed *Days of No Future* on the far right side of the north face, ascending an overhanging, loose and soft natural crack system. We used no bolts on pitches (10 holes for belays only; VI, 5.9, A3+.) Elsewere in Zion, Conrad Anker and I climbed a new pitch at the base of the Watchman (5.9+) and did the first link-up of two Zion walls in a day: *Touchstone Wall* and the *Northeast Buttress* of Angel's Landing.

JOHN MIDDENDORF

Climbs on the Colorado Plateau in Arizona and Utah. In early 1991, Bill Hatcher, Barry Ward and I climbed *The Teapot* (III, 5.8), an interesting 350-foot formation near Jacob's Ladder on the Navajo Reservation. In June, I made the first solo ascent of *Standing Rock* by the original Kor route in eight hours' climbing time. In October Karen Lysett and I found a short spire to ascend, *Mr. Potato Head* (I, 5.9), located on a dirt road 6.6 miles southwest of Natural Bridges National Monument on Route 276. Also in October, Xaver Bongard, Melissa Wruck and I climbed *The Sitting Hen* (II, 5.8) in the Valley of the Gods. In November, Jimmy Dunn, Betsy McKirkick and I made the first ascent of *The Bear* (IV, 5.10, A2) in Monument Valley. This spectacular route on the 650-foot tower climbs through a window near the top of the formation, 70 feet high and 50 feet wide, to the other side of the formation and then on to the summit. There are pitches both of loose and solid free-climbing and pitches of moderate aid on relatively good rock. The tower had previously been attempted by at least three other parties.

JOHN MIDDENDORF

Canyonlands National Park. The Monument Basin Towers are located off the White Rim of the park. A number of climbs were made there. *Staggering Rock* (IV, 5.9, A3, 3 pitches) by Strappo and Crusher; *The Meemohive* (IV,

5.9+, A2, 4 pitches) by Crusher solo; Shark's Fin, west ridge, *Fetish Arête* (IV, 5.10, A2, 4 pitches) by Rob Slater, Jim Bodenhamer, Tom Cotter. This was the third ascent of the tower and the second route. On Enigmatic Syringe, *Altered Sanity* (III, A3, 2 pitches) by Strappo solo. In the region of Moses in Taylor Canyon, the west ridge of Aphrodite, *Swedish-American Route* (III, 5.9, A2, 6 pitches) was climbed by Anders Bergwall, Anders Swensson and Ed Webster. Jim Beyer, solo, climbed a line on Moses between the Primrose Dihedrals and Desert Prophet. This IV, 5.9, A3 ascent used no bolts and was the fifth route to the summit of the tower. Later in the year, Webster soloed Beyer's climb (adding bolts at belay stations), making the second solo and the second ascent of the difficult route. On the approach to Taylor Canyon, Bret Ruckman and Marco Cornacchino freed *A Circle of Quiet* at 5.11d, a route they had pioneered in 1988. In the Needles area, Angel Arch received its first ascent by Steve Anderton, Mike Colacino, Bill Duncan and Paul Midkiff (III, 5.10+, A2). It is a climb frowned upon by the Park Service and if done would call for a stiff fine. The ascent is documented here for historic record, but repeat ascents are discouraged.

ERIC BJØRNSTAD

Moab Area. On the Merrimac Butte, 200 feet left of its prow, Stuart and Bret Ruckman established *The Albatross* (I, 5.11c). There have been at least six new lines climbed on the butte that are still to be documented. Jim Dunn and Betsy McKittrick climbed a tower up Mill Creek about a half mile from the trailhead. They rate *Little Big Man* at I, 5.8. Along Kane Creek Boulevard, the same pair climbed *Pit and Bear* (5.10+). It is located 50 feet right of the first "Chicken Cave" reached from Moab while driving along the paved portion of the road. Also in the Kane Creek region, Dunn, Kyle Copeland and Eric Johnson made the first ascent of *The Predator*, naming their route "Rain of Terror" (II, 5.11−). Dunn and McKittrick teamed with Chad Wiggle for an ascent of a spectacular hoodoo *Cobra* I, (5.10+) located between Ancient Art and the Echo Pinnacle/Cottontail landforms of the Fisher Towers. Dunn and Copeland freed the Corkscrew summit route on Ancient Arts (III, 5.10). Also in the Fisher Towers, H.T. Carter and Bruce Hamilton climbed *Fine Endeavor* above Lizard Rock (II, 5.10). Directly above the Mystery Towers of the Fisher Towers area at the "Top of the World," Strappo and Crusher climbed *Cooler than Jesus* (2 pitches at 5.10−). Just beyond the Rhino Horn, up the Sand Flats Road, the hoodoo *Elvis' Hammer* was climbed by Glenn Dunmire and Stew Sayah, who named their north-side route *Harmones in Waiting*. The south side was soloed by Dunmire, who named it *Black Elvis* (5.10). In Arches National Park, Dunn and Bob Palais pioneered a third line up the popular Owl Rock, *Rasta Magnola* (5.9, A2). *Jr. Buttress* on the Convent was climbed by Jim Bodenhamer, Rob Slater, Bruce Hunter and Tom Cotter (IV, 5.10). In the Corona Arch area up the Potash Road, Laytor Kor and Copeland did a three-pitch, 5.10 fin. The first free ascent of Big Indian Rock, *It's a Gas*, was made by Jim Howe and Keith Maas. The freed ascent had a slight variation at the bolt ladder (5.11). The first free ascent of Texas Tower (IV, 5.11c, 8 pitches) was done by Derek Horsey and party. The second free ascent was accomplished by Bret Ruckman and Tim Coats. The remote spire is south of Canyonlands National Park near Arch Canyon and Natural Bridges National Monument. Closer to Moab, in Bluff, Utah, six short but exacting routes were climbed near the Navajo Twins landform by Mike Friedrichs, Jay Anderson, Manuel Rangel and Jean Rousch. They were all of 5.10 to 5.11 difficulty.

ERIC BJØRNSTAD

New Mexico

Sandstone Towers near Ghost Ranch, Abiquiu. There are numerous sandstone towers near my home in northern New Mexico and until February they were all unclimbed. When I set out to ascend them, little did I know that I'd be pushing the limits of "soft rock." Mount Ethan Putterman and Ghost Tower, above Ghost Ranch, were ground-breaking because of the consistency of the rock. On lead I used more three-foot gardening stakes than anything else. This rock makes the Arches and the Fisher Towers in Utah look like concrete! *Mount Ethan Putterman*, which Mike Baker and I climbed over four days (March 13, 17, 18 and 28), offers some of the softest sandstone in the Southwest. The upper half of this tower is a bizarre conglomerate of loose, brittle calcite, black shale and gypsum. Three bolts were used for a rappel anchor, three for a belay station and five for a bolt ladder. (III, 5.9 R, A4+, 2 pitches.) *Ghost Tower* appeared in the March, 1991 issue of *New Mexico Magazine* and on the cover of the book, *Ansel Adams in the Southwest.* It has the same soft rock. The capping layer is part limestone, part sandstone, part mud. Mike Baker and I made its first ascent on February 14. It overhangs on all sides. The crux was an overhanging off-width crack on the first pitch, belayed in the eye that pierces the entire tower. This pitch was very soft and, in retrospect, crazy. The second pitch moves through the west face and up the north side of the west face. We placed several knifeblades and small angles there. (III, 5.10 X, 2 pitches.) *Animas Spire* is located just 50 feet downhill from Ghost Tower. Baker and I climbed it on February 15. Baker led the single pitch by first threading the lead rope through the middle of the spire, tying it off and then jümaring the fixed "sling" around to a stance on the northern side of the tower. An awkward off-width followed. Descent was made by using simul-rappel techniques. (I, 5.7+, A3.) *Crackerjack Tower* is a tiny tower located up a canyon directly north of a rest area on NM Route 84, a few miles south of Ghost Ranch. Baker and I made its first ascent on February 25. He led, placing several pitons and drilled angles. (I, 5.9, A2.) *Coyote Pinnacle* was climbed in June, 1990 by Mike Baker and Leslie Henderson. It lies in a canyon west of Crackerjack Tower and is almost invisible to passers-by as it blends into the cliffs beyond. (I, 5.9, A2.)

CAMERON M. BURNS

Kokopelli Spire. This intriguing spire, located across the river from Farmington, had seen several attempts before Mike Baker and I made the first ascent on February 3. Seven drilled angles were used as a bolt ladder and several pitons, ranging from bongs to baby angles, were placed. The rock was quite loose. (II, 5.9 R+, A2+, 1 pitch.)

CAMERON M. BURNS

Zuni Needle, Gallup Area. Mike Baker and I made the first ascent of this beautiful 250-foot tower on April 7 and 8. Mike led a long pitch with a short section of 5.10. A second short lead (5.8) put us on a ledge two-thirds of the way up the tower. We rappelled off double ropes. The following day, after jümaring to the high point, I led a beautiful, overhanging A2 seam that quickly turned into 5.6 face-climbing. The descent required two double-rope rappels. We placed five drilled angles for rappel anchors and three knifeblades. (III, 5.10, A2, 3 pitches.)

CAMERON M. BURNS

Animas Spire (I, 5.7+, A3) is located just 50 feet downhill from Ghost Tower. Mike Baker and I climbed it on February 15. Baker led the single pitch by first threading the lead rope through the middle of the spire, tying it off and then jümaring the fixed "sling" around to a stance on the northern side of the tower. An awkward off-width followed. Descent was made using simul-rappel techniques. *Crackerjack Tower* (I, 5.9, A2) is a tiny tower located up a canyon directly north of a rest area on NM Route 84, a few miles south of Ghost Ranch. Baker and I made its first ascent on February 25. He led, placing several pitons and drilled angles. *Coyote Pinnacle* (I, 5.9, A2) was climbed in June 1990 by Mike Baker and Leslie Henderson. It lies in a canyon west of Crackerjack Tower and is almost invisible to passers-by as it blends into the cliffs beyond.

CAMERON M. BURNS

Ford Butte. Ford Butte is mentioned in Herbert Ungnade's *Mountains of New Mexico*, but precious little history of climbing on it is recorded. This volcanic plug has three separate and distinct summits, the highest being either the north or south summit. On April 6, Mike Baker and I made the first ascent of the south summit (II, 5.9, R). We then climbed the regular route to the north summit (5.7). The lower west summit remains unclimbed.

CAMERON M. BURNS

New Mexico

Angel Peak Correction. In *AAJ 1991*, page 169, Angel Peak was incorrectly placed. It rises in northeastern New Mexico.

PLATE 37

Photo by Michael Baker

**Cameron Burns rappelling off
Kokopelli Spire after the first ascent.**

Idaho

Chimney Rock, Selkirk Crest. On August 19, Ann Robertson and I made the first ascent of a new three-pitch route on the north side of Chimney Rock. The first lead was a superb 5.10c crack system that split the middle of an obvious prow just a few feet left of Greymatter. The crux was a 4-inch roof near the top of the lead just three feet from the Greymatter dihedral. The second pitch was of continuous A2 up a very thin seam that burst into an off-width after 40 feet. Because Ann did not want to jümar the second lead, I fixed a bomber second-pitch anchor, then clipped my 180-foot rope through it and ran out the third 100-foot lead to the top. On the third pitch, I turned progressively easier roofs (5.9+, 5.9, 5.8). When I tried to pull up the rope to rappel, Ann accidentally left a knot on her end, making the rope jam through my second-pitch belay. Since the rope had logged over 100 leader falls, I left it, as well as my second rope as Ann and I rappelled off. Ann was hypothermic by the time I reached her and when we reached the ground, she vomited repeatedly. We left the retired ropes hanging and hiked out to the car. Karl Birkinkamp cleaned my mess for me. I am very grateful to him. I did not want to trash out a climbing area where I was just a visitor, but I just had to get my partner off.

CAMERON M. BURNS

Wyoming—Wind River Range

Square Top Mountain 1990. Doug Colwell and I climbed an excellent new 17-pitch route (V, 5.10d) on the east face of Square Top Mountain in September, 1990. We began by scrambling up a series of obvious ramps to an intersection with the main crack system that splits the lower quarter of the east face. We then climbed three 5.5 to 5.8 pitches up the crack system to a grassy ridge. We traversed the ledge 300 feet left to the base of the lower right-facing dihedral marked by a fixed pin. Beginning at the dihedral, we followed the corner system by climbing a 5.10 face pitch with sketchy protection and two more 5.10 crack pitches that led to a large ramp. We traversed the ramp left for 165 feet to a semi-comfortable bivouac. The next morning, we climbed a 5.8 pitch a short distance up the face and left to a small ramp. We continued up another 5.8 pitch that followed the ramp left to a small steep seam. We then climbed the 5.10d crux pitch, placing limited but good protection. We next moved right and ascended a 5.7 slab to a prominent ledge, followed a 5.6 ramp to a second corner on the southwest and climbed straight up the corner system through a 5.9 chimney. We continued up a 5.7 crack to a belay at the right of the big roof, stepped left on small 5.10 holds that led to easier climbing and a big ledge and finally finished with a short 5.2 pitch to the expansive moonscape that forms the summit of Square Top.

DOUGLAS ABROMEIT

"Cloudburst Buttress," near Temple Lake. While in the Temple Peak area during the first week of September, Reid Dowdle, Jeff Niwa and I made the first ascent of a very attractive buttress on the west valley wall immediately north of Temple Lake. The rock was excellent (not a loose stone) and the climbing superb on massive granodiorate—with just enough cracks and holds to make the route possible. There were five pitches, 5.8 to 5.10c, and two scrambling pitches at the finish to the divide overlooking Big Sandy Opening.

FRED BECKEY

Little El Capitan, Southern Wind River Range. In August, Jeff Alzner and I hiked 16 miles to climb a half dome marked on the map as Little El Capitan. The first day, we free-climbed two 5.10 pitches, fixed two ropes and rappelled off. The next day, we free-climbed toward the top. The crack ran out one pitch from the top and, lacking a bolt kit, we rappelled off. After another bivouac at the base, we chose another line, left of the first attempt. We ascended 350 feet of strenuous climbing, fixed our ropes and bivouacked again at the tarn. On the fifth day, we free-climbed 5.10 until we were benighted at 13,000 feet. We wedged ourselves into coffin-shaped cracks. In the morning, Jeff bolted the 95° off-width crack above and then free-climbed the triple visor to the summit. (V, 5.10, A2.)

ROBERT MCGOWN

Colorado

Climbs in Colorado National Monument. Mike Colocino and Calvin Herbert climbed *Tunnel Vision* (III, 5.10+, A1, 4 pitches). The route ascends the second crack system right of the tunnel located right of Ribbed Buttress. Fred Knapp, Sharon Sadleir, Jules Raymond and Richard Starness climbed *Queen and Her Jewels* on Remnants Tower (II, 5.9). The route follows the crack system just inside the right profile of the topo in *Desert Rock* on page 51.

ERIC BJØRNSTAD

CANADA

Yukon Territory

Mounts Logan, Queen Mary, McArthur and Hubbard, Icefield Ranges, Kluane National Park Reserve. During the 1991 climbing season, there were 16 groups that climbed or skied in the park. A total of 83 people spent 1497 person-days in the mountains. A large number of these climbed or attempted Mount Logan via the King Trench route. They were Canadians Al Dennis, Jack Bennetto, Tony Moore, Linda Zurkirchen, Garry Nixon and Rob Whelan; Swiss

Rudolf Homberger, Hansvelt Brunner, Doug and Renoud Rossillon; Germans Walter Goetz, Reto Ruesch, Thomas Speck, Uwe Nootbaar, Matthias Berndt and Hermann Konrad; Canadians Martyn Williams, François Tremblay, Jacques Grenier, John Bond, Patrick McCool, Clifford and Ruth Holtz, Pat and Baiba Morrow; British Dean James, Tom Stimson, Rick Wentz and Alex McNab. Americans led by Mike Marolt and Canadians led by Don McLeod were unsuccessful on the same route. Canadians Hugh and Dan Culver, Brian Finnie and Alan Fletcher and French Ken Delbos-Corfeld, Michel Alexandre, Pierre Bay, Fernando Pintado, Daniel Vargas, Daniel Dupuis, Jean-Louis Bonnentien and Xavier Taupin climbed Logan by the east ridge. Canadians Chic Scott, Don Vockeroth, Don Forest, Brad Robinson, Terry Duncan, Neil Jolly, William Louie, Tom Swaddle, Bill Hawryschuk and Robert Bellis reached Logan's west summit. Canadians Jeff Marshall, Dave Chase, Jeffrey Everett and Glen Reisenhofer climbed the Schoening ridge to King Col but were weathered off King Peak. Canadians Andrew Lawrence, Rosemary Buck, Debbie Maclean and Wade Angevin skied around Mounts King George and Queen Mary and climbed the latter. Canadians Michael Down, Jim Haberl and Don Serl climbed Mount McArthur by the west ridge. Canadians Al Bjorn, Ron Breneman, Bruce Sundbo and Rick Mossman were unable to climb Hubbard because of bad weather.

LLOYD FREESE, *Kluane National Park Reserve*

Mount Upton and Other Peaks. In 1968, Philip P. Upton made the first landing at the Arctic Institute of North America's Mount Logan High Camp at 5300 meters. There followed 500 more plane trips without incident to that most inhospitable site. The mountain named in his honor was ascended for the first time 23 years after that first landing. Mount Upton is located at the heart of a triangular massif bounded by the Logan, Hubbard and Walsh Glaciers. The 3520-meter (11,550-foot) summit is 22 kilometers north of McArthur Peak. Barry Blanchard and Troy Kirwin, co-leaders, Ron Van Leeuwen, Dale Cote and I flew from Kluane Lake to 2560 meters in a sheltered basin at the southerly foot of Mount Upton. The first of eight days on the glacier, when light snow fell, was the only bad weather experienced. A two-kilometer traverse of part of the easterly arm enclosing the cirque was made on June 11. We encountered thigh-deep snow, steep ice and rocky pinnacles. From the first summit climbed (3068 meters) we had a spectacular view of Mounts Queen Mary and King George across the crumpled expanse of the Hubbard Glacier. We reached another summit (2840 meters) that day and descended from the 2600-meter col. The ascent of Mount Upton began at 4:30 A.M. on June 13. By nine o'clock we had reached the crest and continued to the windswept summit of Mount Upton. A small Canadian flag was placed in honor of a great aviator. After a day of reflection, we completed the six-kilometer trek of the eastern ridge, reaching summits of 2760, 2840 and 2680 meters.

DOUGLAS SMITH, *Alpine Club of Canada*

Coast Range

Mount Crawford, Chatsquot-Smaby Icefields, North Central Coast Range, British Columbia. Pete Parrotta and I were helicoptered to the remote Chatsquot-Smaby Icefields and established Base Camp 110 kilometers north-northwest of Bella Coola beside the beautiful snow dome, Mount Crawford (1951 meters, 6400 feet). We were on the gigantic, unlogged Kitlope-Gamsby watershed. We climbed and skied in the region from May 11 to 23. We made four first ascents, the first of which was Mount Crawford. Our most productive day was a grueling fourteen hours of climbing and skiing to climb three unnamed mountains. The highest was a peak of 7260 feet, four miles northeast of Crawford. The other two of 6255 and 6310 feet were about a mile farther south; all were measured by my altimeter. Although the mountains only range from 6500 to 7500 feet, the low glaciation and treeline offer ascents up to 4000 feet above the trees and opportunities for intermediate to extreme ski-mountaineering.

PETER WALLBRIDGE, *British Columbia Mountaineering Club*

Interior Ranges of British Columbia

South Howser Spire, Northeast Buttress, Bugaboos. In the summer of 1990, Jon Turk and I climbed an excellent route on the left side of the east face of South Howser Spire. On the approach, we could see other inviting lines. In August of 1991, we returned to one of these and found it at least as good as the 1990 route. We ascended the edge between the east and north faces and finished on the north face. Two pitches of ice and seven of rock led directly to the summit. We climbed two intricate pitches of ice to a small cave at the bottom of the Ice Hose route. The Ice Hose had degenerated into a dirty, loose gully mostly devoid of ice. We stemmed out of the cave to gain the wall above and moved right for an easy pitch to a crack leading through a roof at 5.9. The crack led upward for two pitches to a rubble-strewn ledge on the northeast edge of the spire. We scrambled westward across the ledge for 75 feet to two soaring dihedrals, the second of which rose from the end of the ledge. Each of the left-facing corners was split by many cracks. We chose the first and followed it for two pitches of 5.10 to a tiny but level stance. From there a short, unprotectable pitch of 5.9 led to easier ground and the summit. We rappelled the Beckey-Chouinard gully directly back to our ice gear in the cave. The upper part of our route may or may not coincide with the north-face route done at 5.6, A2 as a part of the 1965 Chouinard-Lang-Rayson-Tompkins traverse of all three Howser Spires. In any case, it goes free on some of the best rock in the Bugaboos. (9 pitches, IV, 5.10.)

GRAY THOMPSON

Mount Harmon, Olive Ridge Spires and Black Fang, Scottish Peaks. The Scottish Peaks rise from the Catamount Glacier about 15 miles south of the Bugaboos. Although smaller and lower than the Bugaboos, their rock is of the same excellent quality. We spent a week in August among the spires of this lovely range. Chris Seashore, Jon Turk and I climbed the southwest buttress of Mount Harmon, the highest of the range. We chose the only buttress of the three that leads directly to the summit. The route began in a steep crack system on the southeast side of the buttress. The cracks led to the backbone of the ridge in a single long pitch. Five more fine, moderate pitches led to the summit. (III, 5.9.) A ridge of sharp spires rises directly behind the new Olive Hut on the east side of the Catamount Glacier. Hank Abrons, Eloise Thompson and I climbed two 5.8 pitches on the east face of the first sharp, distinctly separate spire, a half mile from the hut. We found no signs of previous visitors to the summit. (II, 5.8.) Later the same day, Abrons and I did an excellent three-pitch 5.10 route on the west side of the second spire. (II, 5.10.) Turk, Abrons, Lili Thompson and I next climbed a mixed route on the north face of Black Fang on the southeast side of Catamount Glacier. We followed steep snow to rock gullies and deviated onto the east side of the peak for the final 100 feet. (III, 5.8.)

GRAY THOMPSON

Middle Scottish Peak, East Face. From the setting, rock and quality, this 5.6 climb deserves mention. From the North Star Glacier, the east face rises as a smooth slab. We climbed a pitch up the right side of the face to a prominent ledge, moved 100 feet to the left to an obvious crack and climbed to the summit. These top three pitches were unusual in that every move was 5.6, nothing harder, nothing easier. Protection was poor where the crack sealed off into a seam, but it would be hard to find a better climb at that grade. (II, 5.6.)

JON TURK, *Unaffiliated*

Canadian Rockies

Mount Alberta's North Face and Northeast Ridge. Mark Wilford's remarkable solo climb of this route is described in a complete article earlier in this *Journal*.

Mount Alberta, Northeast Ridge. During the first week of August, Jack Lewis and I climbed the northeast ridge of Mount Alberta. We bivouacked the first night at the base of the upper black band, the second on an airy site on the knife-edged cornice just below the summit and descended the Japanese route on the third day. The rock was loose. We climbed two pitches of 5.10 with a lot of moderate 5th class and mixed. The snow at the top proved to be the scariest part of the route, although both ropes got chopped on the Japanese descent.

THOMAS KIMBRELL, *Winthrop Mountain Sports*

Edith Cavell, North Face Solo. Robert Cordery-Cotter soloed a route on the north face of Edith Cavell at the end of September previously climbed by Colin

Grissom and Neil Sanford in 1987. He climbed ice runnels and steep mixed terrain from the Angel Glacier to the right of the route done in 1961 by Yvon Chouinard, Dan Doody and Fred Beckey.

Mount Bryce, Winter Ascent. The east ridge of Mount Bryce was climbed in January by Joe Mckay and Greg Colorach for the first winter ascent of the peak. The pair bypassed the central peak to reach the summit. This had been the elusive goal of many a serious party over the past few years.

BRAD WROBLESKI, *Canada*

Correction, Mount Dawson. In *AAJ 1991,* pages 185-6, the description of a 1988 ascent of "the ice couloir that is the most prominent feature of the north face of Mount Dawson" seems to imply that it was a new route. The couloir, termed the Comstock Couloir in the AAC's forthcoming *Columbia Mountains of Canada: Central,* was in fact first ascended by Benjamin Sayre Comstock, guided by Edward Feuz, Sr. and Friedrich Michel, on July 16, 1901. The 1901 party went on from the 3265-meter Dawson Col to make the first ascent of Feuz Peak, the slightly lower central summit of the Dawson massif. They required seven hours from the bivouac, which was on the Dawson Glacier side of the peak and lower than the 1988 party's. Comstock and the guides climbed first by rock on the left margin of the couloir and then in the couloir itself. Climbing earlier in the season and prior to the great glacial recession of the 1920s and 1930s, they certainly encountered more snow and less ice than the 1988 party.

JOHN KEVIN FOX

Labrador

Mealy Range Ski Traverse, Southern Labrador. Dartmouth student Dean Engle (recipient of an American Alpine Club Climbing Fellowship grant) organized our team of Dave McIndoe, Joe Catarini and me to conduct the first-known ski traverse of the Mealy Range, low peaks running along the lower edge of Lake Melville. We remained faithful to the traditional winter-camping methods of the Labrador fur-trapper. We flew to Goose Bay and were grounded for several days. Our Labrador Air single-otter plane got off on March 14 and set us down on a lake in the eastern-central Mealies. We headed southwest for eight days within lake and river valleys. Six feet of snow covered the ledgy, sparsely vegetated landscape. Excellent weather (sunny; no wind; $-30°$ F at night and $30°$ F in the daytime) permitted speedy travel. Minor difficulties were encountered while navigating our sledges through the steep, winding river gorge down to the edge of Lake Melville. The final four days along the lake's edge were monotonous. We reached Goose Bay on March 25 after covering 90 miles in twelve days.

GREGORY KNOETTNER, *Yale Mountaineering Club*

Canadian Arctic

Tirokwa, Bilbo, Asgard, Auyuittuq National Park, Baffin Island. From June 20 to July 29, Nicholas D. Wood, Jonathan Ison, Ian Marriot, Sean Walsh and I took part in the Leeds Baffin Island Expedition. We centered around Summit Lake. To reach there, we took skidoos up the frozen Pangnirtung Fiord. This was followed by numerous load carries. On June 28 Ison, Wood and Marriot pioneered a route on the west face of Mount Tirokwa, up a 3500-foot-high obvious corner gully. The bottom two-thirds was on good 5.6 to 5.7 rock. Then loose, broken ground gave way to a snow-filled gully that led to the top. On July 3, Wood, Ison and I made the first ascent of the central buttress on the south face of Mount Bilbo, some 25 pitches of 5.6 and 5.7. The top three pitches were very icy. On July 7, Wood, Marriot and Ison climbed the Swiss route on Asgard (5.4 to 5.5). We also attempted the north face of Breidablik, the southeast ridge of Adluk and a route on Loki but were turned back by a combination of bad weather and ill health.

NICHOLAS J. PHILLIPS, *Leeds University Mountaineering Club, England*

Breidablik, Asgard and Other Peaks, Cumberland Peninsula, Baffin Island. Our German Alpine Club (DAV) Training Expedition was active on Baffin Island from June 30 to August 18. We established our Base Camp on the southeast bank of the Weasel River at the foot of the west side of Mount Thor. We believe that all climbs we completed were new routes. Fritz Mussner, Wolfgang Wahl, Thomas Holzmann and Johannes Göppl climbed the 500-meter high north buttress of Breidablik with a bivouac on the route. On July 19, Robert Tanner and Jörn Eysell climbed a 450-meter-high route on the south face of the south tower of Asgard. On July 20 and 21, Franz Perchtold, Andy Fuchs, Wahl and I made a partially new route on the 1000-meter-high east face of the north tower of Asgard. We followed the Scott route for eight pitches and then deviated to the left up a crack system that led directly to the summit. On July 27, Eysell, Holzmann and Göppl climbed the 450-meter-high south face of an unnamed peak, which we called "Mount Annie." To get to this peak we hiked up the Fork Beard Glacier and turned to the left up the second valley. At the head of the valley, one can see the rock face and a beautifully curved snow ridge on the left. Our last new climb was on the second peak to the right of the Fork Beard Glacier behind Mount Thor; we called it the "Chinese Tower." This 50° to 60° ice climb was first done by Perchtold and Günter Bahr and repeated later by Mussner, Wahl, Holzmann and Göppl. We also made two unsuccessful attempts. Perchtold, Bahr, Fuchs and I attempted to repeat the 1986 Refern route on the 1500-meter-high granite face of Mount Thor but gave up after 400 meters because of objective danger. Perchtold, Bahr and I tried to climb the direct north buttress of Mount Tyr but quit after climbing 250 meters because compact slabs prevented access to a crack system unless we drilled many bolts.

CHRISTOPH KRAH, *Deutscher Alpenverein*

PLATE 38

Photo by Christoph Krah

South and North Towers of MOUNT ASGARD.

GREENLAND

Cathedral Peak Attempt, Lemon Bjerge, East Greenland. Our expedition was organized to send a small, unsupported party of mountaineers into the interior of Greenland to scale unclimbed Cathedral Peak. We wanted to be self-sufficient and therefore planned to sail to the nearest fjord, land the climbers, find a safe anchorage whilst the climbing party was away and survey the anchorage before all sailing home. The team had co-leaders: Robin Knox-Johnson for sailing and me for mountaineering. It also included Jim Lowther, Perry Crickmere, James Burdett, Jan Pester and Allen Jewhurst. We sailed from Whitehaven, Cumbria on July 20 in the 32-foot ketch *Suhaili,* having on board climbing-and-sledging equipment, food and supplies. Only fuel and fresh provisions were loaded in Reykjavik, where we obtained information on the latest pack-ice situation. The ice normally clears during August, but in 1991 it moved away a month earlier, providing a clear path to the southeast coast of Greenland. On August 3, Greenland was clearly in sight and more than a dozen icebergs were visible to the north. A mass of bergs between us and the mountains ashore then indicated the presence of Kangerdlugssuaq Fjord. Despite the ice, we managed to find the previously selected anchorage, which lay in shelter behind Mellamo Island at the entrance of the Uttental Sund. With a secure base established, *Suhaili* got underway again and proceeded up Kangerdlugssuaq Fjord. At the entrance to Watkins Fjord, the ice became much more dense. Our destination was the foot of the Sidegletscher, which empties into the fjord. Despite having to work our way through the pack-ice, we made the 14 miles from the anchorage to the foot of the glacier in seven hours. August 4 was spent by the shore party getting the loads organized and making a carry up the side of the moraine of the Sidegletscher to where the glacier flattened and it would be possible to start hauling the pulks. The following day, the team made two more heavy carries and established camp at 210 meters, about two miles from the sea. After an 11:30 P.M. start on August 6, we ascended first ice and then glacier snow where we could ski to a col at 1000 meters. After a day's rest, we made a pleasant, easy ski down to and up the Federiksborg Gletscher. Despite awkward stream crossings and many crevasses, we camped on the night of August 8 at the foot of the glacier leading up towards the southern aspect of the Lemon Bjerge. We were probably the third expedition to ascend the Federiksborg Gletscher after Wager in 1936 and Stan Woolley in 1972. On the morning of August 9, Lowther and I reconnoitered the southern approach and, after consulting the map, decided that the mountain we had perceived to be the Cathedral was in fact P 2600 and that the real Cathedral was a massive rock peak at the head of the left fork of the glacier shown on the map as Domkirkebjerget (2660 meters, 8727 feet). We established camp on August 10 below what we believed was the Cathedral in a magnificent granite cirque. At 5:30 A.M. on the 11th, Lowther, Knox-Johnson and I set out up a 500-meter ice gully leading to a col at the base of the south ridge. Reaching its top at 8:30 A.M., we continued up the ridge over broken rocks interwoven with steep little walls. At four P.M., we reached the base of a pinnacle that barred the ridge. We climbed a couple of difficult pitches and reached the top of the pinnacle at 2450 meters, still 400 meters from the summit. It was now six P.M. and so we decided to retreat. There was only enough time left for a final attempt by Lowther and me while Knox-Johnson and the two-man film team started back for the coast. We made a reconnaissance on August 13 and found what was marked on the map as a high linking wall between the two mountains was, in fact, a comparatively low col leading to a narrow glacier that dropped to the Courtauld Gletscher. The approach to the other peak looked steep and difficult and so we decided to retrace the previous route. Starting at 4:30 A.M. on August 15, we took only three hours to reach the shoulder below the pinnacle that had been our high point. We abseiled from there down steep ice into the gully that led up to a col behind the pinnacle. In four hours, we climbed difficult ice back to the same altitude as at the beginning of the abseil. From the col the ground was more broken but also steeper. It was six P.M. when we reached what had appeared to be the top, only to find ourselves at the end of a pinnacled summit ridge with the highest pinnacle some 20 meters higher and six pinnacles away. The altimeter read 2590 meters. The mountain we had first considered to be the Cathedral seemed slightly higher than the peak we were standing on. The descent had long, tricky abseils and was tiring, ending at 7:30 the next morning. It took us two days to get back to the coast to be picked up. The sail home was eventful. We eventually ended the voyage in the Thames on September 12. The total distance sailed was 3092 nautical miles.

CHRISTIAN BONINGTON

Mont Forel, East Greenland, 1990. A Norwegian expedition was led by Allan Sande and the other members were Otto A. Bårholm, Erik Brendehaug, Steiner Bekkevolt, Anders Naess, Johan H. Lundo and Thorstein Lunde. They made the first Norwegian ascent of Mont Forel by the classic Swiss route. To get from Tasilik Fjord over the Glacier de France to the top took them ten days. They tried to make the ascent on skis, which no one has yet done. Hard ice and steepness forced them to give this up. On July 30, all seven reached the summit as the tenth expedition ever to do so. On the way back to Tasermiut Fjord, they tried to climb Lauper Bjerg but were defeated by bad weather. They did, however, climb Conniat Bjerg. The expedition lasted from July 15 to August 10.

DOLFI ROTOVNIK, *Danish Mountain Club*

Rødebjerg, East Greenland. An expedition was in the Angmagssalik area from July 2 to August 1. The leader was Scot Jackie Gorden, accompanied by Scot Wendy Gudmundsson and Englishmen Graham Butler and Nigel Dyson. They flew by helicopter to the Håbets Gletscher and spent two weeks there. They made the first British ascent of Rødebjerg (2140 meters, 7021 feet) and made five other first ascents. The conditions were perfect and there were no problems with glaciers, crevasses, etc. They returned on skis via Slangens Pass to

Sermiliqaq Fjord by the Karale Gletscher and from there by boat to Kap Dan (Kulusuk).

DOLFI ROTOVNIK, *Danish Mountain Club*

Sangmissoq. Our French expedition climbed Sangmissoq (2060 meters, 6759 feet) on the south shore of Evinghedsfjord. The first ascent had been made by the Gréloz Franco-Swiss party in 1958. There was a crumbling cairn on the summit. The only other signs of humans were some old boxes at our Camp III.

PIERRE CHANEL, *Club Alpin Français*

SOUTH AMERICA

Peru—Cordillera Blanca

Huascarán Sur, North Face. In 1990 after my solo ascent of the Richey-Brewer route on Chacraraju, I tried to climb an obvious line on the north face of Huascarán Sur, but was driven back by dangerous falling ice and rockfall. In 1991, it was colder and so I tried again, although the conditions were really not good. On July 13, I crossed the dangerous glacier below the face and ascended 300 meters. I ascended the couloir to the left of the 1984 French Benoît-Grison route. On the 14th, I joined the French route at 6100 meters. In changeable weather, I descended the French route. I rate my route as V, 60° to 65°.

PAVLE KOZJEK, *Planinska zveza Slovenije*

Huandoy Este, 1988. In May, 1988, Adrian Baker and I climbed a new route on the southeast face of Huandoy Este. This direct, 900-meter-high line to the summit had some truly frightening snow formations. We abseiled down the north face.

GRAHAM E. LITTLE, *Scottish Mountaineering Club*

Pukarashta Group and Pukahirca Sur and Tragedy. Above an Alpamayo Base Camp in the Arhueikocha Quebrada is the long Pukahirka-Pukarashta ridge, which had remained untouched from the south until a British team climbed five lines on it in June. Australians Neil Kemp and Duncan Thomas and I, a Scot, climbed an easy gully between Pukarashta Central and Pukarashta Oeste on June 15 to link with the west-ridge route climbed by Kekus and Howard in 1980 and continued to the summit of Pucarashta Oeste (c. 5450 meters, 17,881 feet). The next day, Phil Moorey, Mick Davie and Steve Di Ponio reached the summit of Pukarashta Central (5500 meters, 18,045 feet) after climbing the south face. The team then divided into three pairs with Simon Lee joining Kemp to climb a Scottish-style gully on the southwest face of Pukarashta

PLATE 39

Photo by H. Adams Carter

HUASCARÁN's West Face. Kozjek's route on left; French 1984 route on right.

Oeste on June 19. Thomas and I trudged further along the glacier to the obvious couloir on the southwest face of Pukahirca Sur. We reached the top (6039 meters, 19,814 feet) early on the morning of July 20 while Moorey and Davie were climbing the difficult south face of Pukarashta Este (5500 meters, 18,045 feet). Upon reaching the summit, Moorey fell in an abseiling accident, leaving Davie to solo down the route and seek help. Moorey subsequently died on June 21 whilst being evacuated.

DAVID SHARMAN, *Scotland*

Kurikashajana. On July 14, Briton Mick Davie soloed the southeast face of Kurikashajana (5510 meters, 18,078 feet) from the Quebrada Santa Cruz. He followed the obvious left-to-right traverse of the southeast face.

DAVID SHARMAN, *Scotland*

Abasraju Attempt, Paqtsaraju, San Juan, Shaqsha. I climbed the south side of Abasraju, thinking I was on a different mountain. Becoming confused in clouds, I did not go to the summit. Teamed up with Austrian Gerhard Feichten-schlager, I did the whole southwest ridge of Paqtsaraju (5741 meters, 18,835 feet), including two lesser summits on the way. On August 4, Duncan Thomas and I climbed San Juan (5843 meters, 19,170 feet) by a new route, the east arête. I finally soloed on August 14 a possibly new route on the west-northwest ridge of Shaqsha (5703 meters, 18,711 feet).

DAVID SHARMAN, *Scotland*

Cayesh, Cordillera Blanca. The west face of Cayesh has lost a great deal of snow and ice in the past few years. In 1988, Germans Jörg Steinsberger and Malte Roeper climbed a new direct route on the west face of Cayesh. (See *AAJ, 1989,* page 168.) On August 4 and 5, British climbers Manuel Anson and Paul Harrington repeated the route. They climbed rightward-slanting ramps for five pitches and then climbed eight pitches straight up to reach the south ridge just below the summit. Despite the lack of snow making the climbing on the face easier, they decided not to climb the last 15 meters of unstable mushrooms.

Bolivia

Casiri, Cordillera Real, 1990. After being attacked twice by locals on the three-day hike from Achacachi to the southern base of Casiri, Jim Petroske and I camped below the icefall that tumbles down the southeast section of the glaciers that cover Casiri's southern slopes. On August 13, 1990, we meandered for 500 meters through the icefall to the upper glacial bowl. We continued west up the bowl and up a 60° ice slope to the saddle beneath the striking granite finger a half-kilometer southwest of Casiri's main summit. After traversing toward a false summit, we retreated to find our camp frozen into a glacial pond that had formed during the day. On August 15, we retraced our steps to our previous high point and climbed the southwest ridge on mixed rock and ice over the false summit and along the corniced crest to the summit of Casiri (5857 meters, 19,216 feet). The round-trip took fifteen hours.

BILLY PETROSKE

Illampu West Face, Three Routes and Other Climbs. On June 25, Miha Vreča and Marko Vrevc climbed a new route on the west face of Illampu Norte (6342 meters, 20,798 feet). This is Number 1 on the accompanying drawing. They rated it UIAA VI−, 85°, A0. The 900-meter-high climb took twelve hours to complete. On June 28, Matjaž Jamnik and Miha Kajzelj climbed a new route on the right side of the west face of Illampu Sur (6368 meters, 20,891 feet). They first tried unsuccessfully on June 24. They rated the climb UIAA VI+, 75°. The 850-meter-high climb took them 20 hours. This is shown in the drawing as Number 2. From April 25 to 27, Dušan Debelak and Tomaž Žerovnik climbed a new route on the same face, shown as Number 3. The 1000-meter-high climb took them 30 hours of climbing over the three days. They rated the climb as UIAA VII−, 90°, A3. Bolivian climbers estimated the route as the most difficult in this part of the Andes. Other Slovene climbers made ascents, which were probably not new. Three women, Tatjana Cerar, Simona Košir and Nataša Pristov, climbed Mururata on June 20 and Huayna Potosí on July 5. Matjaž Jamnik and Marko Vrenc climbed a route in the center of the west face of Huayna Potosí, which probably followed one of the previously ascended routes.

FRANCI SAVENC, *Planinska zveza Slovenije, Yugoslavia*

Huayna Potosí, East Face, 1990. Juan Carlos Vázquez, Enrique Rey. Julián Hevia and I made a new route on the east face of Huayna Potosí on July 19, 1990. Our route ascended between the normal route and that of the French. It had a rise of 300 meters and ice up to 75°. We started up the right side of the east face and ascended a ramp of hard snow. We then traversed left under a series of séracs before ascending to the right onto the northeast ridge, which we followed to the summit.

ELISA GONZÁLEZ, *Spain*

Huayna Potosí, West Face, 1990. Argentines Horacio and Carolina Godó, Marcelo Pagani and Spaniard Alvaro Enríquez climbed a new route on the right side of the west face of Huayna Potosí, which rose 1000 meters with a maximum angle of 80°. Both of these routes are illustrated on page 23 of *Desnivel* N° 60.

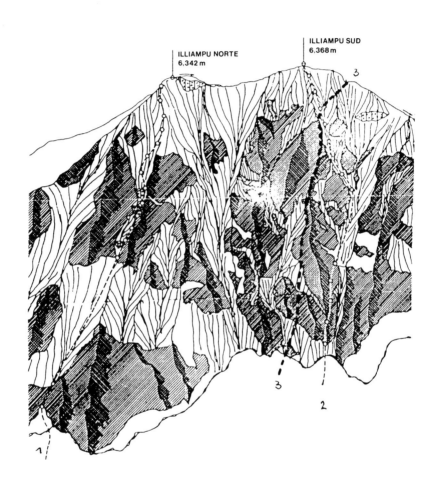

ILLIAMPU NORTE
6,342 m

ILLIAMPU SUD
6,368 m

Huayna Potosí Corrections. On page 192 of *AAJ, 1991*, there were reports of several "first ascents" of routes that had already been climbed previously. The west rib of Huayna Potosí reported by Matt and Julie Culberson sounds like the west ridge first climbed in 1969 by John Hudson and Roman Laba (and incorrectly identified in the *AAJ, 1970*.) It had previously been attempted by George Urioste, Gustavo Iturraldi and me when we were forced down by Urioste's altitude problems and by Roger Whewell and friends when a crampon fell off. This route was subsequently done twice more, making the Culbersons' ascent the fourth. The "Lyon" route on the west face proper was actually first done by Dobbs Hartshorne and companion in 1970. French climbers repeated the route, believing it to be a first. Finally, the Ala Norte west ridge was also not a new route, having been done some 20 years ago by Roger and Elspeth Whewell.

STANLEY S. SHEPARD

Cordilleras Real and Quimsa Cruz, 1990. Neil Howell and I arrived at Mina La Argentina on the eastern side of the Cordillera Quimsa Cruz in the third week of June, 1990. Despite bad weather and intense cold, we managed to make the first ascent of the south face of Nevado Nina Collo (5280 meters, 17,323 feet). We then crossed the Paso San Enrique to the Chatamarca Lake basin. We climbed Cerro Chamac Collo (c. 5350 meters, 17,553 feet) by its northeast face and descended the west gully. This rock peak lies in the southwest corner of the basin. Marching along the west shore of the lake, we saw a magnificent rock climb with a chess knight-piece summit. The protruding pinnacle belongs to the east side of the Cerro Chamacani, which is a long ridge with many spikes. We climbed it by a crack straight up the east side. After reaching the Viloco and Araca valleys, we ascended between July 10 and 15, 1990 the following: *First Wall* (4700 meters, 15,420 feet) (See map on page 167 of *AAJ 1988*), fourth ascent; "The Lookout," a small pinnacle left of the Big Wall, and "La Astilla," a granite finger, both first ascents; a peak west of Lake Chilihuani Khota and "Ridge Peak," west of the former, the last two second ascents and probably new routes. Later, after several attempts, we managed to climb free the right of the central side of the north face of the *Big Wall* (4890 meters, 16,044 feet). We then went to the Cordillera Real. After an ascent of Huayna Potosí, Howell left for England. I then teamed up with Argentines Federico Chippitelli and Antonio Rodríguez. We made a new route on the south face of *Tiquimani* (5519 meters, 18,108 feet), where we climbed a steep gully and ridge to the summit. It involved four days and three bivouacs, a challenging and cold route. We got to the summit on August 11, 1990.

ANGUS ANDREW, *Castlefields, Shrewsbury, England*

Cordilleras Quimsa Cruz and Santa Vera Cruz. During a six-week stay in the area of La Paz, I made three solo trips into these seldom visited ranges. From the Mina Bajaderías, above Pongo, I reached the Coricampana Glacier and the northeast side of the Huayna Cunocollo massif, camping at 5100 meters. On May 22, I climbed the northeast side of Nevado San Luis (5620 meters, 18,439 feet). The summit ridge is long and narrow, all ice and corniced. Its main point was reached from the northwest by the 1982 Regensburg expedition when descending from Huayna Cunocollo. I climbed a new route. On May 25, I placed another camp at the head of the San José valley and on the following day climbed the north ridge of Nevado San Juan or Altarani (5540 meters, 18,176 feet). The peak was first climbed from the west in September of 1938 by Germans Josef Prem and Wilfried Kühm. In my second campaign, I first attempted Cerro Chatamarca (5180 meters, 16,995 feet) and then made another second ascent, that of Cerro Chamac Collo (c. 5350 meters, 17,553 feet), climbed from the northeast in 1990 by two Britons (see above); I ascended instead the steep western gully. In my last campaign, I reached the Monte Blanco mine, crossed the Huallatani Pass (5100 meters) and dropped west into the Chocñacota mine basin. On July 5, from a 5000-meter camp, I traversed the west arm of the flat Chocñacota Glacier and climbed the easy but unstable northeast side of Cerro Santa Rosa (5520 meters, 18,111 feet), located north of the mine, a first ascent. I then returned to the Huañayacota hamlet and transferred activities to the Cordillera Santa Vera Cruz, which is a cluster of some ten peaks from 15,000 to 18,000 feet, south of the Quimsa Cruz. From a camp on the Huariananta lake, I attempted 5100-meter Cerro Chupica, whose sharp summit pinnacle I could not climb. Judging from photographs dating back to 1903, I feel that the Cordillera Vera Cruz has lost more ice and snow than any other Bolivian range.

EVELIO ECHEVARRÍA

Araca Group, Northern Quimsa Cruz. From June 16 to 27, our party of six climbed in the Araca group, a forest of granite towers of exceptional beauty that I had first visited in 1967. Gregory Johnson, Virginia Louise Porter and Scott Titteringham flew down from the United States and joined Juan Pablo Ando, Douglas Daken Cook and me, residents of Bolivia. In various combinations, we did a half dozen climbs, generally short and hard. The most spectacular was the Cristal, a needle hardly 40 meters high and perhaps six wide. On aid, Titteringham and Johnson placed six solid bolts on the first short pitch. Then Ginger Porter, our best rock climber, finished it, accumulating air time trying to redpoint it. She expects it all to go at 5.11; I think it may prove harder. The climb was repeated by Swiss later in the year. (See below.) Before we turned to the Cristal, Cook and Ando climbed the west ridge of a big rock peak while Porter and Johnson did its north face via a chimney system which ended in a difficult slot as night fell and a windstorm flattened our Base Camp. The "big rock peak" is the southernmost of the granite summits forming the cirque enclosing the usual Base Camp. Then come the Block Tower, Handsome Splinter and Cristal (in that order, south to north.) While our friends rested the following day, Titteringham led me up another small classic on one of the unnamed rock towers cluttering the ridgelines. Cook, Ando, Porter and I then turned our attention to Handsome Splinter, left of the Cristal. Overcome with nostalgia for the old days, I hammered and friended an A2 start directly out of the Cristal-Handsome Splinter notch, while Cook and Ando found the modern alternative, a bomb-bay layback around the corner. Porter and Ando finished the climb the next day. Cook and Ando later did a third pinnacle, the second to the right from the Cristal. One expects the Cristal and its neighbors, as well as the fine routes done by the few earlier parties in the region, to become popular. They are short, hard, spectacular climbs, easy of access once you set up Base Camp. We do not recommend June for the days are cold and short. Try August or September. Later Cook and I did yet another route—my 14th—on Charquini. A huge amount of snow and ice has disappeared since my last visit to this group eleven years ago. The Bolivian glaciers are just withering away.

STANLEY S. SHEPARD

Cerro Taruj Umaña, East Face and Other Climbs, Araca Group, Cordillera Quimsa Cruz. Our Swiss expedition was composed of Hanspeter Bricher, Gian-Andri Tannò and me. We placed Base Camp in the eastern fork of the Taruj Umaña valley at the same spot as the German Bayreuth party of 1987. We did the following climbs in the Araca group: *Cristal* (4850 meters, 15,912 feet) by the bolted route of the Bolivian-American party (see above). Because of high winds, we did not try to free-climb it. It was impressive and quite hard to protect in the upper part. (5.10a, A1); *Cerro Taruj Umaña* (4852 meters, 15,918 feet), first ascent of the red east face. We called the route "Buscando el sol" (Seeking the Sun). Although this interesting five-pitch route follows the central crack system, it offers mainly face climbing. The cracks are used for protection. (5.10a); *P 4900* (16,076 feet) in the northern fork of the Taruj Umaña valley, easy, good views, a first ascent; *Calsonani Sur* (5050 meters, 16,568 feet), east ridge, second ascent; *Cuernos del Diablo* (5271 meters, 17,293 feet), a repetition of the route "La Clásica," very beautiful, 5 pitches, apparently a third ascent (5.8). The climbing, all in July, was generally good but it was quite cold and windy. The Base Camp site needs a lot of cleaning! We also ascended Nevado Ancohuma (6430 meters, 21,096 feet) in the Cordillera Real from the Sorata valley and Cerro Parinacota (6330 meters, 20,768 feet) from Chungará, Chile.

CHRISTIAN PLÜSS, *Schweizer Alpen Club*

P c.5030, Near Torrini, Quimsa Cruz, 1990. From Viloco, Jim Petroske and I followed the road to Araca for 10 kilometers and switched to a mule path where the road begins to descend to Araca. We continued along the mule path up a side valley to an abandoned mine and then on a faint path to Lago Warus Kolas. On

July 28, 1990, we ascended the valley to the northeast for two kilometers to a col, and after dropping down the other side, climbed the northeast face for five pitches to the top of a boxlike tower (c.5030 meters, 16,503 feet). This monolith is the second summit from Cerro Torrini along the ridge running northwest of Torrini.

BILLY PETROSKE

Chile—Northern Andes

Aguas Calientes, Second Ascent. Brian Baker and I formed the 1991 British Andean Volcanoes Expedition, which lasted from July 28 to September 7. We climbed Licancabur (5916 meters, 19,411 feet) on August 5, Aguas Calientes (5924 meters, 19,435 feet) on August 15 (The local name is Volcán Simbad.), Pili or Acaramachi (6046 meters, 19,837 feet) on August 17 and Láscar (5641 meters, 18,507 feet) on August 20. All had been ascended several times before, but Aguas Calientes had had only one ascent, by two Chileans in October, 1971. At the end of the month, we ascended the Ojos del Salado.

GRAHAM E. LITTLE, *Alpine Club*

Argentina—Northern Andes

Nevado de Pissis and Other Ascents, 1990. Italians led by Luciano Gadenz was active in early 1990 in the high, barren area south of the Ojos del Salado. The other members were Giacomo and Renzo Corona, Giampaolo Depaoli, Silvio and Tullio Simoni and Giuliano Zugliani. On January 11, 1990, they drove from Chilecito, in the province of La Rioja, to Laguna Brava. On January 17, they finally camped within the *caldera* or depression that lies south and east of the Pissis-Veladero system. They then placed several high camps and on the 21st climbed the south side of Nevado de Pissis (6780 meters, 22,244 feet on older maps and 6882 meters, 22,579 feet according to a new Argentine survey.) It seems to be a new route. Getting to the summit were Gadenz, R. Corona, S. Simoni and Zugliani. That same day, Depaoli soloed a P5600 (18,373 feet), near their Camp I, a first ascent. On the 23rd, G. Caroni and T. Simoni ascended Cerro Veladero (6430 meters, 21,096 feet).

MARCELO SCANU, *Grupo Andino Huamán, Buenos Aires, Argentina*

Argentina—Central Andes

Cerro Natividad and Other Ascents, 1990-1. On March 19, 1990, four Argentine climbers led by Antonio Beorchia made the second ascent of the highest point of the Cordón de Manrique (5026 meters, 16,490 feet). On the summit, Boerchia found pieces of old lumber, possibly of Inca origin. The peak had been climbed only once in modern times, 31 years ago. On December 28, 1990, M. Manzi and H. Campodónico made the second ascent of Cerro Negro Aspero (5500 meters, 18,045 feet), this time by the southeast ridge, a new route.

They went on climbing along the ridge that connected their peak to Cerro Natividad and completed the first ascent of the latter (also 5500 meters). They then descended to the high plateau between the two former peaks and the long Olivares chain. On the 29th, they made the first ascent of a peak in that chain that they named Cerro Olivares Norte (c. 6000 meters, 19,685 feet). It is seven kilometers west of Cerro Negro Aspero and wholly within Argentine territory. Another group, F. Pascual, R. Pereira and I, reconnoitered the Quebrada de las Trancas and attempted Nevado de Pismanta (5400 meters) but a storm forced us down. On January 16, 1991, we explored the Quebrada de San Lorenzo and placed a camp at 4300 meters. That same day, my two companions made the first ascent of Cerro Bifurcación (5223 meters, 17,135 feet). I repeated the ascent the next day. Finally, on January 20, again alone, I made the first ascent of the very fine rock pyramid of Cerro de la Fortuna (4376 meters, 14,358 feet), which I climbed by the north side.

MARCELO SCANU, *Grupo Andino Huamán, Buenos Aires*

Aconcagua South Face. On January 3, I managed to climb the south face of Aconcagua on the direct (Messner) route, solo, in 15½ hours. It took another 5½ hours to descend the normal route. I was the only climber to do the direct route in the past two years. Three other parties were successful in December, 1990 and January, 1991 on the original French route: Japanese in four days, Koreans in five days and a solo Chilean in four days.

THOMAS BUBENDORFER, *Deutscher Alpenverein*

Aconcagua, Ascent by the Youngest Female. Nerea Ariz, daughter of the well known Spanish climber, Gregorio Ariz Martínez, climbed to the summit of Aconcagua by the normal route on January 3. At the age of fourteen years and eleven months, she is the youngest female to have climbed to the highest point in the Americas. She matched the record set by American Richard Garret who ascended Aconcagua in the summer of 1984 when he was also fourteen years old.

Cerro Agua Negra, 1990. A very fine route, the southeast ridge of Cerro Agua Negra (5484 meters, 17,991 feet), near the international pass of the same name, had been attempted four times in the 1960s. Climbing alone, Roberto Pereira of San Juan managed to overcome all obstacles and reached the summit in the late afternoon of November 2, 1990.

MARCELO SCANU, *Grupo Andino Huamán, Buenos Aires, Argentina*

Cerro Imán from the Southeast. Miguel Beorchia and local hillman Roberto Vega approached by the Arroyo Caserones and on May 17 made the first ascent of the southeast face of Cerro Imán (5467 meters, 17,938 feet). The mountain

PLATE 40

Photo by Thomas Bubendorf

**Steep ice on the direct (Messner)
route on ACONCAGUA's South Face.**

had been previously climbed by a different route by pre-Columbian Indians and in 1969 by an Italo-Argentine party.

MARCELO SCANU, *Grupo Andino Huamán, Buenos Aires*

Argentine and Chilean Patagonia

Campanile Esloveno, Above Bariloche, Northern Patagonia, 1992. February 13, 1992 was the 40th Anniversary of the first ascent of the Campanile Esloveno, which caused quite a stir when it was first done. In celebration of the event, Dinko Bertoncelj climbed "his" tower along with his sons, Bogdan and Andrej. Simultaneously, the two best Bariloche climbers, Sebastián de la Cruz and Rolo Garibotti, made a new route on that bold pinnacle.

VOJSLAV ARKO, *Club Andino Bariloche*

P 3385 and P 2517 near San Lorenzo, 1989. S. Scarvarda and I made the first ascent of P 3385 (11,115 feet) by its west face on November 27, 1989. We climbed it in 13 hours from Camp II on the Paso de la Cornisa. The peak lies three kilometers southwest of San Lorenzo. That same day G. Borsani and M. Bascialla climbed P 2517 (8208 feet) by the south face and west ridge. This peak lies due west of the Paso de la Cornisa and six kilometers northwest of San Lorenzo.

CORRADINO RABBI, *Club Alpino Italiano*

New Altitudes in the Chaltén (Fitz Roy) Area. Until now, heights in use have come from the basic survey made by Professor Luis Lliboutry, a member of the French expedition that in 1952 made the first ascent of Chaltén (Fitz Roy). His task was meritorious and accurate in most cases, despite the short time he had and difficulties imposed by the logistics of the era. Both the names Chaltén and Fitz Roy have now been officially accepted. The first was the original one, meaning "Volcano" in Tehuelche, a name given by the ancients because this remarkable rock peak is almost always crowned by a cloud cap and it was thought then that it was smoke from a possible crater. The peak was renamed Fitz Roy, after the commander of the ship *Beagle* by the Argentine explorer Mariano Moreno. [Vice-Admiral Robert Fitzroy's name is spelled on Argentine maps as noted above. —*Editor*] A survey by the Argentine Instituto Geográfico Militar was made a few years ago but the results were not released because of a border controversy with Chile. These new heights are now official and appear on the new maps. On Hoja (sheet) *Monte Fitz Roy* 4972-19, 1:100,000 are: Chaltén (Fitz Roy) 3405m (11,160'), Gorra Blanca 2907m (9539'), Marconi 2210m (7251'), Rincón 2465m (8028'), Pollone 2579m (8462'), Domo Blanco 2507m (8225'), Pier Giorgio 2719m (9821'), Poincenot 3002m (9849'), Cerro Torre

3102m (10,177'), Cerro Eléctrico 2257m (7405'). On Hoja *Viedma* 4972-25 and 4972-30 are Cerro Solo 2121m (6959') and Cerro Grande 2751m (9025').

MARCELO SCANU, *Grupo Andino Huamán, Buenos Aires, Argentina*

Austral Summer Season in the Fitz Roy Area, 1991-2. News is beginning to reach us now on February 14 about the climbing season during the end of 1991 and the beginning of 1992. Aguja Poincenot was climbed by Argentines Máximo Schneider and Oscar Pandolfi on January 28, 1992, by Argentines Teo Plaza and Ramiro Calvo and by two Brazilians. All climbed the Whillans route. Later, Plaza climbed Fitz Roy by the Argentine route with a Spaniard. The Aguja Guillaumet was climbed by Horacio Bresba solo. The same peak was also climbed by two women from Buenos Aires. Casimiro Ferrari and two other Italians climbed the highest (north) summit of Bifida, thinking they had made a first ascent. They later learned that Swiss Peter Lüthi and Argentine Horacio Bresba had made the first ascent in 1989. There is a rumor that Italian Ermano Salvaterra climbed Poincenot by the west face, but we have no details as yet. Aside from Andy DeKlerk's and Julie Brugger's ascent of Cerro Torre, a group of Mexicans made the ascent in five days.

VOJSLAV ARKO, *Club Andino Bariloche*

Cerro Torre, El Mocho, Torre Innominata. Cerro Torre repulsed all attempts until January 28 when numerous parties reached the summit via the Maestri compressor route. This included Andy DeKlerk and Julie Brugger of Seattle. Previously, they had repeated the Piola-Anker route on the east buttress of El Mocho. After the Cerro Torre ascent, they went on to repeat the Piola-Anker route on the north spur of the Torre Innominata.

TODD SWAIN, *Unaffiliated*

El Mocho, Aguja Poincenot and Cerro Torre, 1991-2. Steve Gerberding and I arrived at Campo Bridwell in the Torre valley on November 22, 1991. That same day, we made two carries, set up camp and finally got to sleep at three A.M. the following morning. At eight A.M., the sun spurred us into action. We immediately headed up the glacier and made a cache under El Mocho. The next day was also fine and we carried more gear and bivouacked on the shoulder of El Mocho. The following day was also beautiful and we made our first foray to Cerro Torre's south face. After studying the face through binoculars from various angles, we found our hopes of climbing a new route on this 6000-foot-high face dashed. We continued to the base of the face to confirm the desperate nature of the cracks. The amount of drilling required immediately made our decision easy to abandon the attempt before we wasted our entire stay. Since we were already in the area with equipment in hand, we set our sights on the beautiful unclimbed south face of El Mocho, the Half Dome look-alike next to

PLATE 41

Photo by Michael Horan

From left to right: Cerro Adela, Cerro Torre, Torre Egger, Cerro Stanhardt, Perfil del Indio, Bifida, Cuatro Dedos, Domo Blanco. Flat-topped El Mocho stands before Cerro Torre group.

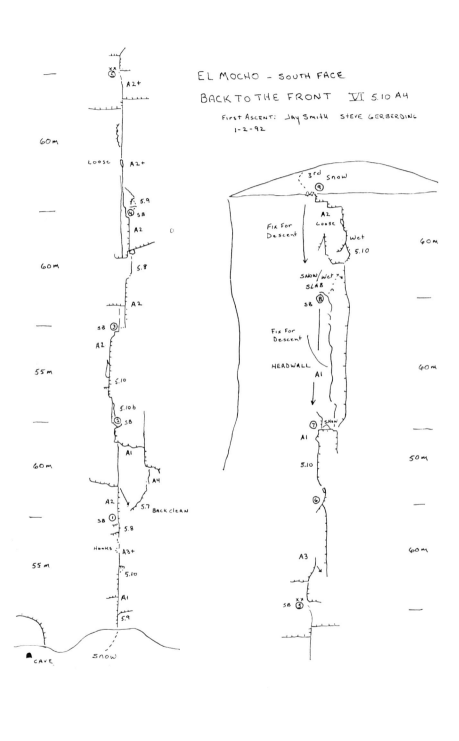

EL MOCHO - SOUTH FACE

BACK TO THE FRONT   VI 5.10 A4

First Ascent: Jay Smith Steve Gerberding
1-2-92

Agujas Poincenot SW Face (1200m)

Judgement Day VI 5.11 A1

First Ascent - 1-28-92   Jay Smith & Steve Gerberding

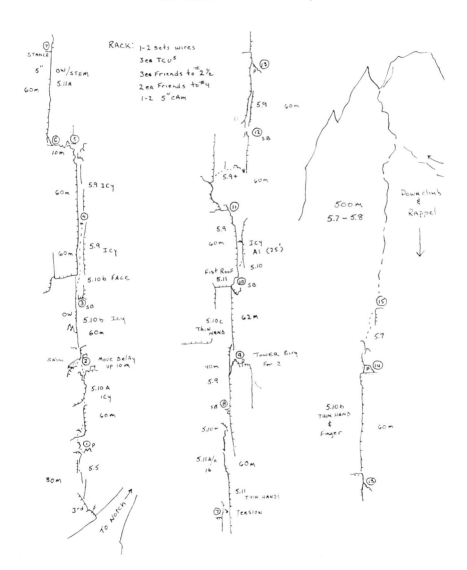

PLATE 42

Photo by Jay Smith

On the 1800-foot-high face of El Mocho.

COLOR PLATE 11

Photo by Jay Smith

AGUJA POINCENOT. Southwest
Face on right. Route ascends obvious
system in center of face. Tower
Bivouac is in center of wall.

Cerro Torre. We figured we could make the climb in two days and then move on to the larger peaks. We dug a snow cave at its base and cached our gear as we greeted our first storm. Several weeks later, after two partial days of fixing rope, we were well established. The climbing had been difficult: A3 and A4 in bottoming cracks requiring hooks, birdbeaks, questionable nuts and dicy free climbing off poor protection while the face ran with water and a continuous bombardment of ice and snow added to the excitement. After 1½ months, on January 2, 1992, we finally summited. We had left Base Camp at three A.M. and arrived at our cave at ten o'clock. After digging it out from eight feet of snow, it was noon. However, we decided to go for it or perhaps wait weeks for another chance. Under threatening, though calm, skies, we arrived on the summit at 1:30 A.M. in total darkness. The 1800-foot-high route was completed in nine stretched 60-meter pitches, with all fixed ropes left in place on the final headwall to facilitate the descent down this very overhanging section. By eight A.M., we were back on the glacier with the route totally cleaned of all but rappel anchors. The following two days, we ferried loads across the valley to the foot of the southwest face of Aguja Poincenot. This 1200-meter-high face had been climbed by Argentines to three-quarters height several years before. In 1968, Argentines José Luis Fonrouge and Alberto Rosasco climbed a route on the far left side. We chose a difficult, direct route up the center. On January 14, we departed Base Camp at four A.M. in promising weather. By the day's end, we had made a carry to the start of the route, fixed three ropes and descended to an exposed bivouac at the foot of the initial slabs. Dawn was ominous. Storms seemed imminent. We returned to Base Camp late in the evening. Then it cleared. We again raced up to the face only to be greeted once more by blustery squalls, but this time we swore to remain at the foot. Extreme cold and wind grounded us all the next day. By the next morning, we scrambled for shelter under a large boulder in 100-mph winds where we were pinned down for two days, unable to cook or get out of our bivouac sacks for fear of being blown away. During a lull on the third day, we made our escape. On January 24, we again made our alpine-style attempt on Poincenot and climbed to half height by ten P.M. to the only bivouac ledge on the face. The climbing had been fantastic, all free except for one short tension traverse to change crack systems on the vertical headwall of the central band of the wall. In gusty wind, Steve and I fashioned tiny wind breaks on our two independent 2x4-foot ledges. By morning, we were in a full Patagonian tempest and I was unable to communicate with Steve, 15 feet away, for more than 18 hours. We endured a second day in our exposed perch before the wind died enough for us to get out of our bivouac sacks for a brew of warm cocoa and a discussion. We had precious little food, fuel and water. The next day was either up or down. By six P.M., the weather was much better and so we ate our last micro portions of food and I cast off for the summit. At the end of the 200-foot pitch, the winds were back and so I rappelled back to the bivouac with the rope rigged for retrieval. The skies cleared. The oncoming next front out on the icecap to the west stood still and the evening sky glowed pink with promise. Climbing by eight A.M. in calm, cold, clear conditions, we

PLATE 43

Photo by Gino Buscaini

EL MOCHO. The face climbed is in profile on the left. The snowy summit of Cerro Torre towers above the clouds.

ascended 800 feet of 5.10 to 5.11 with only 35 feet of aid through an icy section. From there on, we climbed roped but not belaying up the remaining 1600 feet to arrive on the summit at four P.M. We were back down twelve hours later. With only two weeks remaining, we focused on the Maestri Route on Cerro Torre. Six teams had been attempting the route over the last two months. Only Mexicans Carlos Carsolio and Andreas Delgado had been successful and they had spent two nights out without stove or bivouac gear through life-threatening storms. On February 17, we climbed the initial ice pitches to the snow cave on the shoulder, some 3000 feet below the summit. A day and a half of storms followed, leaving the wall covered with fresh snow, but by afternoon the weather was perfect and the walls were rapidly drying. At four A.M. on February 20, we set off for the summit and were on top by ten P.M. We were followed by an Argentine, a Brazilian and a Spaniard who joined us at 11:30. Twelve hours later, we were all safely back at the snow cave as the first clouds began to enshroud the Torre once more.

JAY SMITH

Cerro Adela Central, Southeast Face, Winter Ascent. Because of the war in Slovenia, my climbing partner was unable to leave our country to join me. I therefore modified my plans and headed for Cerro Adela instead. I believe I was the only climber in the region. Actually in mid-winter I found the weather stabler and less windy. The glacier approach was very dangerous when done solo. On July 5, I took seven hours to climb the 1200 meters of ice and mixed terrain. There were two pitches of 70° to 80° ice but the big problems were cornices. I descended the ridge to Adela Sur and then took the delicate ridge to the pass between Adela Sur and Cerro Ñato and down the steep side of Adela Sur. Two other different routes had been done on the face previously. Giancarlo Grassi and M. Rossi in 1986 climbed a route well to the left of mine to the summit of Adela Sur. In 1987, Sebastián de la Cruz climbed solo a route which I crossed twice, having started to the right of his route and also finishing to the right of his.

PETER PODGORNIK, *Planinska zveza Slovenije*

Aguja Guillaumet West Face, Solo, 1990. With my wife Rosanna, I arrived on November 24, 1990 at Base Camp at Piedra del Fraile. I wanted to climb the west face of Agjua Guillaumet over a new route for the first 600 meters where I planned to join the Argentine route. On December 7, 1990, Rosanna accompanied me to the foot of the face. I planned to climb fast against a possible worsening of the weather and so climbed primarily not self-belayed. I did have five pitons, some Friends, a 90-meter rope for rappelling, crampons and ice axe, for despite the smooth rock, the final part might have ice. I took no bivouac gear, counting on climbing through the night, which at that latitude is very short. At five P.M., after seven hours of climbing, I had ascended the 1100 vertical meters, 600 meters of which were new with an UIAA difficulty of VI+, A2. I descended with 20 rappels in deteriorating weather.

MAURIZIO GIORDANI, *Club Alpino Italiano*

Aguja Saint Exupéry, South Buttress, Fitz Roy Region. After the climbs in the Paine Towers, on December 6 Argentine Sebastián de la Cruz and I camped on the glacier right below the Aguja Saint Exupéry. We intended to climb the Metzeltin-Buscaini route on the north buttress but there was so much snow that we turned our attention to the south buttress. Finally, on December 10, the weather improved and we first climbed an easy 200-meter-high couloir. Then the rock began. The route ascends some perfect, vertical dihedrals, in which we found some pitons and bolts. At nine P.M., we reached the summit, having climbed 15 pitches. We descended the same way. The climb took us a total of 24 hours round-trip. The major difficulties were caused by the great accumulation of snow. The route was first climbed in 1987 by Austrians Hans Bärnthaler and Ewald Lidl.

JON LAZKANO, *Guipuzcoa, Spain*

P c.1400. In late November, Steve Hayward, Chilean José Muriez and I completed a new trekking route, leaving the Río Ascencio via a steep glaciated pass northwest of the Japanese Camp. We climbed steep, unstable avalanche debris on the right side of the heavily corniced pass. We made what was probably the first ascent of P c.1400 (c. 4593 feet), a small peak to the right of the pass, before continuing down to join the regular trekking circuit around the Torres near Lago Dickson.

ERIC BRAND

Torre Central de Paine, East Face, "Riders on the Storm" Route 1990-1991. We climbed a new route on the central part of the east face of the Central Paine Tower. The wall is about 1300 meters high with excellent quality, vertical, compact granite. There were 36 pitches with difficulty up to 5.12d, five pitches of aid (A3 and one pendulum traverse). The route was done by five Germans: Norbert Bätz, Peter Dittrich, Bernd Arnold, Wolfgang Güllich and me. We arrived at Base Camp on December 5, 1990 at 600 meters on the east side of the Paine Towers. After a short reconnaissance of the north buttress, which we rejected because of rotten rock, we turned to the center of the east face. We placed a kind of Advance Base ¾ of an hour below the face. After a typically severe windstorm ripped our tents apart there, we gave the name of "Riders of the Storm" to the route after the popular song. On December 14, Güllich and Bätz climbed the first 150 meters on marvelous granite. Iced cracks and terrible weather slowed progress. Finally, the route was established to a bivouac site at the top of the buttress. On December 28 and 29, 1990, Güllich, Dittrich and Bätz climbed the three pitches above the top of the buttress and into the crack system that led up the final wall to the summit. The next day, Arnold and I took over and pushed the route higher, including a poorly protected pendulum traverse. More bad weather ensued. Finally, the other trio made a spectacular, 25-meter, horizontal traverse beneath a giant roof with a 1000-meter drop below them. This took 5½ hours. They returned to Base after a 20-hour day. Bivouacs on the wall were unpleasant, but on January 23, Arnold and I climbed the fixed lines for two hours and continued up difficult terrain until the angle eased somewhat. More ice now clung to the rock. I led on the rock while Arnold went ahead on the ice sections with crampons and ice tools. Luckily, we were mostly in the lea from the wind. A difficult ice hose was overcome before we two reached the summit at ten P.M. We were back at the bivouac at midnight. At that time, Bätz had to leave because of a badly infected foot and professional obligations. We then had three totally unexpected days of lovely weather. On January 27, Güllich and Dittrich also stood on top. They bivouacked on the buttress top on the descent. The next day they then ascended again to climb free some of the pitches where we had been forced to use aid. Arnold and I climbed free a new route to the right of the original route on the buttress, where ice had forced us to use some aid. We met the other pair on the top of the buttress. They were delighted to have done, among other things, a 25-meter crack and the roof free.

KURT ALBERT, *Deutscher Alpenverein*

Paine Towers, Torre Norte and New Route on the Torre Central, West Face, 1990-1. Our expedition of Spanish Basques was active in the Paine Towers in late 1990 and early 1991. On December 8, 1990, Guillermo Bañales and I ascended the Italian route on the Torre Norte in 14 hours from camp. We first had to climb a 1000-meter snow-and-ice couloir. The actual climb had two or three pitches of mixed climbing but the other ten pitches were of moderately difficult rock. Our main objective, however, was a new and extremely difficult route on the west face of the Torre Central, to the left of the Wild, Wild West Route (see *AAJ, 1991*, pages 74-85). This had been unsuccessfully tried previously by Japanese and Italians. We worked on the route for some 45 days, mostly in poor weather. Bañales and I prepared 14 pitches before he had to leave to go back to Spain. I continued with Kike de Pablos. The first nine pitches were mostly free-climbing on somewhat rotten rock. In the middle part, the rock was fine but the climbing was direct-aid. After having fixed 700 meters, on January 27 Kike and I free-climbed the last 200 meters to the summit on somewhat decomposed rock in perfect weather. We descended the same route. We called the route "Kanterarik ez."

JON LAZKANO, *Guipuzcoa, Spain*

Paine Towers, Torre Sur and New Route on the Torre Central, South Face. On October 26, José Carlos Tamayo and I moved into the Italian Base Camp at 600

PLATE 44

Photo by Olaf Sööt

**Torre Central del Paine on left.
Spanish-American-Argentine route on
South Face on left; German route on
East Face on right.**

meters. Our first objective was to climb the Torre Sur by the north ridge, the first-ascent route. In the next three days we carried supplies to the base and fixed rope on the first 300 meters. On November 1, we jümared the ropes and climbed the remaining 700 meters to the summit, arriving in bad weather (V+ or VI, 21 pitches). We descended in 22 rappels. The rock for the first 300 meters was rotten but was excellent above. We then joined forces with two Californians, Eric Brand and Steve Hayward, to attempt a new route, the south face of the Torre Central. We made a camp at the base of the face and began fixing rope. After three days, we were joined by Argentine Sebastián de la Cruz. The route started in an eight-pitch corner system on the grey rock. The climbing here averaged V+ (5.9) with sections of VI (5.10 b/c) and A2. The free climbing on this initial section was often loose and difficult to protect. At the beginning of the red rock the route ascended a continuously overhanging, 50-meter, thin crack (A3). We continued up steep consistently difficult climbing (V+) for ten more pitches before the angle backed off. After 20 days, the route was ready for the summit attack. On November 24, all five of us jümared 850 meters and climbed 200 meters to reach the summit. We descended the same route and removed all fixed rope. The first part is on mediocre rock, but the upper rock is excellent. The upper part ascends marvelous walls and overhangs. We called the route "The Whale of the Winds."

JON LAZKANO, *Guipuzcoa, Spain*

Peaks in the Valle del Francés, Paine Group. Santiago youths led by Rodrigo Mujica climbed in the valley of El Francés, whose sources are some five kilometers west of the Paine Towers. During January and part of February, they made the following climbs: *Aleta de Tiburón* (1850 meters, 6070 feet) by Esteban Chacón, C. Porcila, Andrés Zegers; *Trono Blanco* (or Mellizo Este; c. 2400 meters, 7874 feet), third ascent, by Juan Montes, Mujica, Mauricio Rojas on January 24; *Cuerno Principal or Central del Paine* (2110 meters, 6923 feet) by Zegers, Mujica on February 4; *Gemelo* (or *Mellizo*) *Oeste* (c. 2400 meters, 7874 feet), second ascent via a new route on the south by way of 5.9 cracks and a 200-meter ice couloir by Boitano, Chacón on February 4; *Fortaleza* (2755 meters, 9037 feet) by two different routes. One was a center line between the first-ascent (southwest) and the southeast routes by Rojas and M. Bovey. Boitano and Montes made the second alpine-style ascent of the 1968 Ian Clough route on the Fortress. To their surprise, after the first snow-and-ice couloir, they found they could not continue up the dihedral. They had to make a variant of six pitches to the left, 300-meters-high, 5.9, A3. The ice on the original route had become impracticable because of the warm weather. They followed an English team that had made the first alpine-style ascent a week earlier on the ice. [The names Mellizo and Gemelo are apparently used, both meaning twin. — *Editor.*]

EVELIO ECHEVARRÍA

South Face of Central Tower of Paine
"The Whale of the Winds"

VI - 6a/b - A3+ 1000 m

PLATE 45

Photo by Gino Buscaini

**FORTALEZA from the northeast.
The route follows the right skyline.**

Peineta, 1990. On page 201 of *AAJ, 1991*, a report appears of the ascent of a peak in the Paine group, the location of which was not known to us. The mountain lies a kilometer to the northeast of the Torre Norte del Paine and is connected to it by a ridge. The peak is given on the map on page 250 in Gino Buscaini's and Silvia Metzeltin's *Patagonia* as Nido Negro de Cóndores. The French called it Paineta, which probably should have been Peineta, which means "comb" in Spanish. Argentine authority, Marcelo Scanu, confirms the name as being Peineta. The confusion with this name will certainly be even greater since there already is a Peineta on the eastern edge of the Southern Patagonian Icecap some 15 kilometers north of Cerro Mayo and 7 kilometers south of Cerro Heim.

Cerro Barros Arana, 1990. In December, 1990, Doug Tompkins and my wife Barbara flew two Cessna T206s to Patagonia. Doug and I reconnoitered unclimbed peaks from the air. We originally thought of trying Cerro Castillo, but when we flew close to the summit, we saw rock of poor quality and a cairn on top. Farther north we saw tempting summits and chose Cerro Barros Arana in the Río Milta valley. With Cado and Josh Avenali, we drove down the Carretera Austral, a road opened in 1988, until we could see the peak from the road, 13 kilometers north of La Junta. Although we were at sea-level, timberline on our mountain appeared to be a two-or-three-hour walk away, had there been a good trail. An estancia owner said, that, to the best of his knowledge, no one had ever been to the base of the ice-draped peak, We smiled when he said he doubted we would make it to timberline. The approach took 2½ days as we thrashed our way through primeval rain forest filled with chasms, waterfalls, bamboo and leeches. Whenever we encountered bamboo, we knew that within 100 yards we would be crawling on our bellies with 60-pound packs through a forest that seemed impenetrable. In a fit of ecological passion, we had left machetes behind. The weather stayed poor. After waiting out two days of storm, our party of four headed up snow slopes that led to a glacier on the north side. In a whiteout we climbed a steep couloir with crampons and exited onto 5.5 rock that brought us to an easier ramp above. Higher on the ramp, we began to find ice over the rock. Then we came to a notch below a 200-foot headwall of verglas and 5.8 rock that Doug led in crampons with zest. Josh and Cado decided not to climb the ice. As Doug and I climbed higher, the mist parted. The corniced ridge leveled out and in a few hundred feet we were on the 7560-foot summit. At the top, we wondered about a 360° sun halo before we hurried down to meet our friends in the notch below the technical difficulties.

GALEN A. ROWELL

Sea Kayaking and Climbing in Chilean Patagonia. Rick Ridgeway describes this in a full article earlier in this *Journal*.

COLOR PLATE 12

Photo by Olaf Sööt

Paine Towers seen from the east. In the background rises Paine Grande.

Tierra del Fuego

Monte Cloven, Hoste Island, 1989-90. A four-man American-Canadian expedition, T.J. Thomas, Doug Krause, Steve Gayner and I, made the first exploration and ascents on the uninhabited and unexplored Hoste Island. The trip took place in December, 1989 and January, 1990. Base Camp was at sea level on Fromunda Bay at the tongue of the main glacier. We persevered despite violent winds, poor snow conditions and endless rainfall. Our first climb was of P 1120 (3675 feet) where we followed the southwest ridge to the summit. The second climb was of Monte Cloven (1340 meters, 4397 feet), the highest on the island. We had ascended an icefall and then a steep couloir to camp on a rocky ridge. Three days later, on December 28, 1989, we had one of the few clear days in the region. After crossing the plateau, we climbed the west ridge to the summit. From the summit we could see Cape Horn. Due to poor weather and conditions, we were limited to non-technical ascents. There are great possibilities for technical ascents on fantastic granite spires. The only problem is the weather, which is so bad that it makes Patagonia look like Hawaii.

BRAD WROBLESKI, *Canada*

Monte Bove, Cordillera Darwin, 1990. I directed an expedition for Spanish Television called "Al filo de lo imposible." On December 12, 1990, we climbed Monte Bove (2300 meters, 7546 feet) by its east face. This peak had been climbed only once before, by Eric Shipton, John Earle, Peter Bruchhausen and Claudio Cortés on February 25, 1964, who ascended the south face and the west ridge.

SEBASTIÁN ALVARO, *Televisión Española*

ANTARCTICA

Traverse of Antarctica via the South Pole, 1990-1. Four Norwegians, Ralph Hoibakk, leader, Herman Mehrem, Simen Mordre and Sjur Mordre, traversed the Antarctic Continent, setting out from the Ronne Ice Shelf in October, 1990, with dogs but without any motorized assistance. On the way to the South Pole, which they reached on December 14, 1990, they did have several supply depots. They continued on to McMurdo without depots. The 3000-kilometer traverse was accomplished in 120 days.

South Georgia. We left Cape Town in December, 1990 in the 19-meter yacht *Diel*, which was specially fitted with a lifting keel and other equipment for polar travel. We were four climbers: Paul Fatti, Doug Jamieson, Hilton Davis and I as leader; three sailors: Berhard Diebold, Nigel Jarman and Tako Palthe; and a movie maker: Fanie van der Merwe. After 31 days of sailing, we reached South Georgia and spent a month climbing. We made the first ascents of Mount

Norman (4016 feet) and an adjacent peak, Mount Senderens (4315 feet). The expedition was to commemorate the centenary in 1991 of the Mountain Club of South Africa. We also made the first South African ascent of Admiralty Peak (3100 feet) and several other minor peaks. Jamieson and I explored the Kohl-Larsen Plateau on skis, reaching this from a camp on the edge of the Konig Glacier. We made a determined attempt on Mount Paget by a new route on the east face but were driven back by high winds, bad snow conditions and unpredictable weather. The return voyage back to Cape Town was completed in 16 days. The total distance sailed—Cape Town-South Georgia-Cape Town—was 15,000 kilometers.

JOHN R. MOSS, *Mountain Club of South Africa*

EUROPE

Eiger. A full article on the remarkable solo climb of the north face of the Eiger in winter by Jeff Lowe appears earlier in this *Journal*. It should be noted that Lowe's good friend, Catherine Destivelle, made the first female solo winter ascent in the late winter of 1992.

Stortind Southwest Ridge, Norway. There is a complete article on this climb in Norway earlier in this *Journal*.

OCEANIA

Sabah, Borneo, Malaysia

Mount Kinabalu. On July 24, my daughter Helene, Dr. Karl Lengauer and his wife Bertl Lengauer and I climbed through the gorgeous jungle with rare and beautiful flora to the Laban Rata Hut. On July 25, we climbed in three hours to the highest point of Mount Kinabalu (4101 meters, 13,455 feet) on the normal ascent route, which is secured in part by fixed ropes. We were very impressed with the beauty of the mountainous region and by the excellent organization and comfortable facilities in the Kinabalu National Park. This was obviously no new ascent. The first recorded climb was made in 1851 by Sir Hugh Low. However, we were particularly impressed by the north faces of the Kinabalu Massif, which rise precipitously for over 1000 meters. This is an untouched paradise for the extreme rock climber in a setting of incredible natural beauty.

MARCUS SCHMUCK, *Österreichischer Alpenverein*

ASIA

India—Arunachal Pradesh

Gorichen, Pachakshiri Range. A 12-man team from the Assam Regiment was led by Captains R.K. Bhardwaj and G.V.S. Prasad. Base Camp was set up at Merathang beyond Ghokarsomon on September 25. They established two high camps. On October 5, Captain Bhardwaj, Sepoys Salow Mao and Darwan Singh and Naiks Jogendra Singh and B.B. Thapa reached the summit (6328 meters, 20,762 feet) via the northwest face. The first ascent was made by an Indian Army expedition in 1966.

KAMAL K. GUHA, *Editor, Himavanta, India*

Bhutan

Basingthang Peaks. During October, Peter Mould led a combined climbing-trekking expedition to northwest Bhutan which had permission to tackle unclimbed "trekking peaks" up to 5700 meters from a Base Camp at 4200 meters on Basingthang yak pasture, 12 miles southeast of Chomolhari. The climbers were John Blacker, John Innerdale and son Jonathan, Eric Langmuir, Jerry Lovatt, Peter Mould, Dr. John Nixon, Stephen Town and I. On October 12, Mould, Blacker, Lovatt, Nixon and I climbed P 5640 (18,504 feet) in the Ngum Tang Gang group from a camp at 4800 meters near the top of the Riburi Ridge. The peak lies 2½ miles west-northwest of Base Camp. A satisfying steep ridge of snow and ice led to an airy summit. There are two more unclimbed peaks in this group. On October 15, Nixon climbed P 5487 (18,002 feet) solo after his companion retired unwell. The north summit of this easy saddle-shaped peak was visible from Base with two small rocky summits of 5487 and 5450 meters at either end. We propose the name Ganae Gang, which means "Saddle Peak" in Bhutanese. On October 16, the Innerdales, Town and I climbed both summits in a 10½-hour round-trip from Base. On October 15, Wohney Gang (5589 meters, 18,337 feet) was climbed by Langmuir, Lovatt and Mould in a 12-hour round-trip from a camp 100 meters below the 4969-meter Wohney La to the north of the peak. It lies 3½ miles south-southwest of Base. This was the best climb. It went up a steep snow rib on the flank of the northwest ridge and led unexpectedly without further great difficulty to the summit. There are other fine peaks, but the rock is poor and so it is better to concentrate on snow-and-ice climbs.

GEORGE BAND, *Alpine Club*

Chatarake and Kang Bum. Bas Gresnigt and I made a climbing expedition to western Bhutan. Our first objective was a mountain that the Swiss trekking map of Bhutan calls Chatarake and is given as 6500 meters high. This is also called Djodrake by locals. From Paro we trekked via Drukgyal Dzong into a region probably not previously visited by Westerners. On October 27, we reached the foot of the northeast buttress on a 4800-meter pass. We climbed the next day to

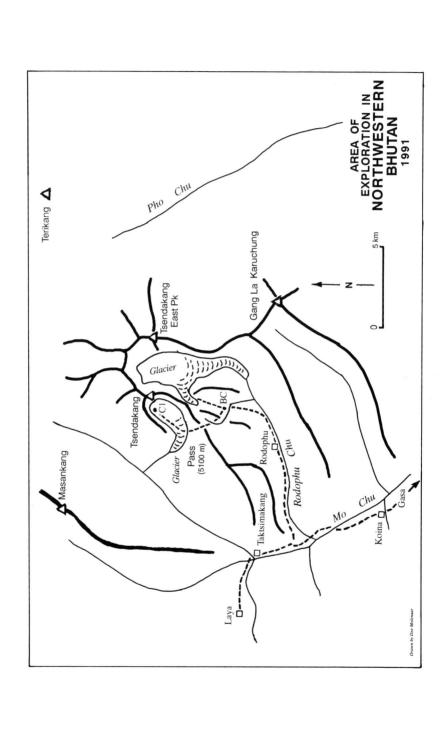

Terikang △

Pho Chu

Tsendakang
East Pk

Gang La Karuchung

Glacier

Tsendakang

BC

C1

Masankang

Glacier

Rodophu

Rodophu Chu

Pass
(5100 m)

Tsendakang

Taktsimakang

Mo Chu

Koina

Gasa

Laya

N

0   5 km

AREA OF
EXPLORATION IN
NORTHWESTERN
BHUTAN
1991

Drawn by Dee Molenaar

the summit, which we reached at 1:10 P.M. The height was a little disappointing, in reality "only" 5570 meters (18,275 feet). From there we traveled to the region just previously visited by the British party, the Basingthang peaks. The British had suggested that there was a hidden "Andean-type" mountain which was probably the highest in the Wohney-Gang group. After heading up several wrong valleys, we finally found our "Andean" mountain. On November 5, we reached a crevassed glacier and got to the summit of the peak (5780 meters, 18,964 feet). However, it was not the highest of the group. This proved to be a sharp rock needle, further south. After traversing a narrow ice ridge, Gresnigt climbed to its summit, while I belayed. From there, we headed for Kang Bum, given on maps as 6494 meters. However, the mountain looks lower although certainly more than 6000 meters. We crossed into and ascended the Thimpu valley. Our horse driver, who had accompanied the Japanese first-ascent party, explained the route. On November 9, we were camped on Kang Bum's southern glacier. In order to reach the upper glacier, we had to climb threatened slopes and both steep rock and ice. On November 11, we left our Camp II before sunrise. After a steep section to a foresummit, we climbed on over several false summits to the summit at nine A.M. where we had a magnificent view all the way from Everest and Kangchenjunga to the 7000-meter peaks of the Lunana district to the east. We were back in Thimpu, the Bhutanese capital, on November 14.

RONALD NAAR, *Koninklijke Nederlandse Alpen Veriniging*

Tsendakang. Our members were Hiroshi Kodama, Kosuke Honma, Ryoji Takahashi, Takeharu Shumiya and I as leader. After an approach from Thimpu, which began on October 12, we arrived at Base Camp at 4700 meters on October 20 on the south side of Tsendakang. We fixed rope up to 5300 meters in the icefall for two days, but were stopped by crevasses. We changed to the west side and made Advance Base under the southwest face of Tsendakang at 5350 meters on October 28. To get there took five hours, which included crossing a 5100-meter pass. From Advance Base, we climbed a couloir threatened by rockfall to reach the west ridge. We continued up the snow ridge, fixing 750 meters of rope to the base of a steep rotten-rock step. After leaving supplies, we returned to Advance Base. At 8:30 A.M. on November 6, Kodama, Honma and I started from Advance Base, climbed to the top of the fixed ropes and another 150 meters of rock. We continued up the steep ridge on unstable snow. As night fell, there was no place to camp. We bivouacked at 9:30 P.M. on the snow face at 5950 meters. The next day, we continued along the ridge until we found a flat spot for Camp II. At 6:40 A.M. on November 8, we headed for the summit. There was first a 180-meter-high icefall. We kept on along the slope to the summit wall. In three pitches we got to a shoulder below the top and climbed three more pitches to the summit, which we reached at one P.M. My altimeter indicated 6310 meters (20,702 feet), although the official altitude was given as 7200 meters. It is certainly much lower than 7000 meters.

FUMITAKA SAKURAI, *Chiba University Alpine Club, Japan*

India—Sikkim

Kangchenjunga from the East, Ascent and Tragedy. Our expedition was jointly sponsored by the Himalayan Association of Japan and the Indo-Tibetan Border Police under the auspices of the Indian Mountaineering Foundation. Hukam Singh was the overall leader and I was co-leader. The rest of the team was composed of Japanese Hideji Nazuka, Hideki Yoshida, Hirotaka Imamura, Osamu Tanabe, Shinsuke Ezuka, Mitsuyoshi Sato, Nobuhiro Shingo, Ryuzo Oda, Fumiaki Goto, Ryushi Hoshino, Tsuyoshi Akiyama, Ms. Miharu Kitagawa and Ms. Tamaki Kaizuka and Indians S.D. Sharma, Kanhaiya Lal, T. Smanla, Ms. Santosh Yadev, Chholden Sherpa, Ms. Pema Sherpa, Khem Raj, Pasang Sherpa, Sunder Singh Martolia, Govind Singh, Jor Singh, Sharki Bhutia, Phurba Lepcha, Lopsang Tshering and Ms. Suman Kutiyal. On March 14, we left Gangtok in four minibuses and seven autotracks with members and high-altitude porters. We drove 120 kilometers to Lachen and the next day to Tanggu along the Tista River. There are two routes to approach Base Camp on Green Lake on the Zemu Glacier. One is up the Zemu Chu (river) from Lachen and the other is a roundabout way in the northern area from Tanggu with three high passes: Lungnak La (5035 meters), Theu La (5212 meters) and Tangchung La (5150 meters). We took the latter despite snow conditions on the high passes for yaks in the middle of March. It took 44 days to transport all loads from the roadhead to Base Camp at Green Lake at 4935 meters. Without snow on the passes we would have reached Base Camp from the roadhead in four days! The advance party arrived at Base Camp on March 31 and the last group on April 26. A site for Advance Base was selected on April 1 and carrying supplies there began on April 10. It lay up the Zemu Glacier where the Twins Glacier joins the Zemu at 5200 meters. The first obstacle on the way to Camp I was an icefall an hour from Advance Base. The icefall was dangerous due to ice avalanches and rockfall. On April 16 we fixed 13 pitches of rope across crevasses and ice walls and the next day nine more to reach an ice plateau on the upper Zemu Glacier, where we established Camp I. On April 19, after both leaders and some members had reached the camp, we had a good view of the east face of Kangchenjunga. It was very steep with mixed rock and ice, constantly threatened by big avalanches. We judged that there was no feasible route up from the top of the upper Zemu Glacier. That same day, a huge part of the icefall just below the snow plateau broke up and our route was cut to pieces. We changed to attempt a repeat of the northeast spur route. A new Camp I was set up on the south face of the northeast spur at 5700 meters on April 20. We had to gain 300 meters up the steep ice-fluted, avalanche-swept face. On April 21, we fixed 20 pitches of rope across ice gullies and broken rock to 6150 meters. The next day, we climbed two more pitches up an ice wall to the crest of the northeast spur. From there, towers piled on towers, cliff on cliff, and columns tapered like spires and shining curtains of icicles hung down from the cornices. We found old fixed rope on the ridge from the 1977 and 1987 Indian expeditions. We fixed 34 pitches of rope from Camp I to Camp II, which was placed at 6300 meters on

April 27. From there, the spur continued to have monstrous mushrooms, cornices, crevasses and cliffs. Route fixing went arduously on. Camp III was placed at 6800 meters on May 4. At that point, the spur became a wide snow ridge with no technical difficulty. On May 6, we reached a huge ice cliff at 7250 meters, having strung 14 pitches of rope for two days. On May 9, we established Camp IV at 7450 meters. The route above the camp was a very steep arête which culminated in the highest point on the northeast spur. After four days' work, on May 14 four Indian climbers placed Camp V at 7850 meters. On May 15, Pasang Sherpa, Khem Raj, Sharki Bhutia and Lopsang Tshering reconnoitered to find a final camp. They reached the site of the 1977 and 1987 expeditions at 8000 meters. The way to the summit seemed clear. The same morning, Sato and I started a laborious carry to Camp V, where at noon we met the Indian climbers. On May 16, the four Indians started from Camp V at four A.M. They reached the old camp-site, deposited their loads and continued toward the summit, on their own, each with one oxygen cylinder. When Pasang Sherpa was about 100 meters below the summit, he radioed to Hukam Singh that he could not see his partners below him. Hukam Singh asked him to return immediately. As he turned to descend, he slipped and fell to his death thousands of feet down the north side. Hukam Singh heard his sharp cry. We went into mourning for Pasang Sherpa at each camp. We then entered the final stage of our expedition with heavy hearts. On May 23, seven Japanese reached 7950 meters, where they established Camp VI. Two climbers fixed seven pitches above the camp while the support party returned, leaving Nazuka, Imamura and Oda at Camp VI. Because there were only two oxygen regulators, Nazuka had to make his attack without oxygen. On May 24, they started at four A.M. in biting cold. Imamura's oxygen mask gave trouble and he too climbed without oxygen. They slogged on in deep snow and high winds. At 10:57 A.M. Nazuka reached the west col between the main peak and Yalung Kang. Traversing the summit ridge on the Yalung Glacier side, he partly escaped the fierce wind. At 11:50 A.M., he stood beside the summit. He left the last two meters untrodden, remembering the promise the team had given the people of Sikkim. He returned to the west col at one P.M., where he met Oda. Imamura was not yet there. Nazuka was safely back in Camp VI at three P.M. Imamura and Oda finally stood on the summit at 3:23 P.M. and returned to Camp VI in darkness at 10:30 P.M. Early the next morning S.D. Sharma, Kanhaiya Lal and T. Smanla left Camp VI for the summit. They reached the top at 2:30 P.M. and were back in Camp VI at 7:48 P.M. Time and weather prevented further summit attempts.

YOSHIO OGATA, *Himalayan Association of Japan*

Gurudongmar, Dongkya Range. Four members of an expedition led by G.C. Bhutia from the Sonam Gyatso Mountaineering Institute climbed Gurudongmar (6715 meters, 22,030 feet), which lies in northern Sikkim. The first ascent was made in 1936 by Eric Shipton and E.G.H. Kempson.

KAMAL K. GUHA, *Editor, Himavanta, India*

Kokthang. A 12-member team from Calcutta climbed Kokthang (6147 meters, 20,167 feet) via the northeast face from Camp II at 5425 meters. On May 12, Dipak Kumar Bose, Parijat Chowdhury and Sherpas Kami, Lhakpa Tsering and Tharchen Tsering reached the summit. The leader was Amulya Sen.

KAMAL K. GUHA, *Editor, Himavanta, India*

Nepal

Nepalese Peak Fees. Climbers are concerned with a sizeable increase in the fees that the Nepalese government charges for permission to climb its peaks. On September 20, the Ministry of Tourism announced that fees were being raised for the start of the spring 1992 season "in consideration of environmental conservation." A ministry official said that this means the government wants fewer climbers and their rubbish on Everest and the other popular 8000-meter peaks. He cited the view of Sir Edmund Hillary that Everest should be closed to all mountaineers for several years to give the mountain time to cleanse itself. The Nepalese authorities said they did not want to take such drastic action, but they would like to encourage climbers to go to peaks below 8000 meters, for which the fee increase is less extreme. He also pointed out that Nepal had devalued its currency by about 20% in July and the new rates were partly designed to make up for this. (The old rates had been fixed in Nepalese rupees.) A member of a Spanish team returning from Pumori and Lhotse observed that the new fee of $8000 for Lhotse alone is equal to half of their total budget for this autumn's climb. The leader of the Russian Cho Oyu east-ridge team said that he had previously applied for a permit for Dhaulagiri in the spring of 1993. This permit would now cost $8000 for a team up to nine members with an added charge of $800 per additional member and "I am afraid this is too much money. I will not be able to come." (The old fee was less than $2000 with no fixed limit on a team's size.) When Sergio Martini came back from his attempt on Kangchenjunga, he went to the Tourism Ministry to ask permission to return for a try next year. When he learned that he would have to pay four times as much as he had this autumn, he did not put in the application. Whether the drastic increase in fees for 8000ers will actually decrease the number of climbers is open to question. The obvious way to achieve this goal is to stop giving so many permits. Obviously, it is likely that there will be a drop in the number of self-financed teams, but there could be an increase in the commercial expeditions, which are organized for profit by adventure-travel agencies, mountaineering clubs and climbing schools. The commercial expeditions are joined by people who are strangers and so have never climbed together before and sometimes do not even speak the same language. They are led by professional guides who are hired to take them climbing by standard routes. By contrast, the self-financed teams tend to be small groups of friends—or a single individual like Svetičič—who try difficult and unclimbed routes, often on little-known peaks that do not attract commercial organizers. A third source of financing is finding sponsors. Potential sponsors are often not interested in unknown peaks, especially small ones. There can be a drawback to sponsorships. A French team received help from a television organization which reasonably required photographic coverage. Two members on a summit try did not arrive on top, having spent so much time photographing that when the wind rose, they had to turn back to be in camp before nightfall. None of the other members ever got so high again. The results of the higher fees could be 1) The Ministry's desired result, namely climbers turning to Nepal's lower, less costly peaks and to more difficult routes on them. Instead of having to find $8000 or $10,000, they would need only $1,000 to $3,000 depending on the mountain's altitude. (The old rate for "lesser" peaks ranged from $500 to $1400.); 2) Mountaineers say they will go where the cost is lower. An American who was on Lhotse this autumn with just one teammate said, "For a small two-man climb, I'll look instead at Pakistan." Of course Pakistan may follow Nepal's example and raise its fees; 3) There could be a rise in the number of people who climb in Nepal without getting permission. When discovered, they are subject to fines and banishment from entering and/or climbing in Nepal for some years, as happened to Martínez this autumn, but often the Nepalese authorities do not know of such cases. Only time will tell what the effects of the increase in fees will be.

ELIZABETH HAWLEY

Kangchenjunga. The Slovene expedition, which made a remarkable new route on the southwest ridge of Kangchenjunga South, ascended others of Kangchenjunga's summits, made a new route on Talung and attempted the difficult east face of Kumbhakarna East, is described in a complete article earlier in this *Journal.*

Kangchenjunga Attempt. A Spanish expedition led by Mari Abrego attempted to climb the north face of Kangchenjunga. They reached a highpoint of 8400 meters on September 23.

ELIZABETH HAWLEY

Kangchenjunga Attempt. The highly experienced Italian climber, Sergio Martini, managed to reach 8200 meters on the southwest face of Kangchenjunga on October 11. He and two Nepalese helpers became too exhausted to continue after a month's effort.

ELIZABETH HAWLEY

Yalung Kang, Southwest Face Attempt. Our international expedition was composed of Czechoslovaks Leopold Sulovský, Miss Zdeňka Pleskotová and me as leader and Italians Marco Berti, Gianluigi Visentin and Miss Dr. Monica Zambon. We had no high-altitude porters and used no supplementary oxygen.

PLATE 46

Photo by Jiří Novák

**Southeast Face of YALUNG KANG
from Camp I.**

We left Kathmandu on September 2 and got to Base Camp at 5300 meters on the 16th. We established Camps I, II and III at 6100, 6700 and 7400 meters on September 23, 27 and 29. After a rest, Sulovský and Visentin got to Camp III on October 8. The next day Sulovský alone climbed a steep couloir and pitched Camp IV at 7950 meters. During the night, the tent was destroyed by a strong wind. On October 10, he climbed to 8200 meters, which he reached at eleven A.M. He decided not to climb further. Climbing slowly because of the conditions, he figured that he could not climb to the summit and descend to Camp III past wrecked Camp IV and survive without bivouac gear. He was back in Base Camp on the 11th.

JIŘÍ NOVÁK, *Czechoslovakia*

Makalu Attempt. Todd Burleson was accompanied on the northwest ridge of Makalu by Lhakpa Rita and Gopal Tamang. They established Base Camp, Camps I and II at April 1, 4 and 5 at 5300, 6000 and 6900 meters. The plan was to climb the rest of the mountain alpine-style. Three summit attempts were made from Camp II in the next 20 days, all aborted because of high winds. On April 26, Camp III was placed at 7600 meters. After waiting out a day in strong wind on April 27, on the 28th the three left for a final summit attempt at six A.M. At 10:30 A.M., they reached a high point of 8200 meters when violent winds returned and ended the climb.

WILLI PRITTIE, *Alpine Ascents International*

Makalu Attempt and Kangchungtse Ascent. Our expedition was made up of Maurice and Marc van der Berge, Wim Willekens, Michel Schuitemaker, Dr. Frank Hoppenbrouwer and me as leader. We hoped to climb the northwest ridge of Makalu by the standard route. We got to Base Camp at 5350 meters on April 5 and established Camps I and II at 6000 and 6700 meters on April 7 and 10. More serious climbing started there as we ascended the Makalu couloir; we fixed rope on 90% of this part and so did not make a supply dump at Camp III until April 18. We occupied Camp III at 7400 meters on April 27. Because it was obvious due to snow conditions that Makalu would be a dangerous objective, we decided to climb Kangchungtse. On April 29, Willekens and I set out late, at 10:15 A.M., because of bad weather and a faulty stove, and reached the summit (7678 meters, 25,190 feet) at one P.M. By May 1, all members were safely back at Base Camp.

RENÉ DE BOS, KONINKLIJKE NEDERLANDSE ALPEN VERENIGING

Makalu, West Face Attempt. Makalu has never been successfully scaled by the vast central portion of its west face. A team of Italians attempted a line halfway between the one followed in the autumn of 1981 to 7900 meters by Poles Jerzy Kukuczka and Wojciech Kurtyka and Briton Alex MacIntyre and another which Kukuczka soloed after his two teammates had left the mountain. The Italians were Casimiro Ferrari, leader, Lorenzo Mazzoleni, Dario Spreafico, Marco Negri, Salvatore Panzeri, Mario Panzeri and Umberto Valentinotti. On May 7, Salvatore Panzeri and Spreafico managed to reach a high point of 7300 meters at the top of a small ridge and at the bottom of a very steep section. A fierce wind was blowing a lot of snow onto their route and their feet were beginning to freeze in the extreme cold. They retreated and the climb was over.

ELIZABETH HAWLEY

Makalu, Post-Monsoon. There were two successful Spanish expeditions on the Kukuczka ridge of Makalu in the post-monsoon season. An expedition led by Jordi Bosch placed Josep Permane on the summit on September 24 and Xavier Robiro and Carles Figueras on September 30. This group made two unauthorized ascents of Kangchungtse by its south ridge: Ramón Estiu on September 15 and Joan Cardona on September 30. (There has been an increase of illegal ascents of late. A Spaniard, Antonio Martínez, not a member of either of these expeditions, was stopped before he had climbed very high on Dhaulagiri by a government-appointed liaison officer with an authorized expedition. He was taken to Kathmandu, where he was fined about $1750.) The second Spanish expedition was led by Alberto Iñurrategi. On September 30, Alberto and Félix Iñurrategi and Felipe Uriarte reached the summit of Makalu.

ELIZABETH HAWLEY

Makalu, West Face Attempt and Rapid West Buttress Ascent. The west face of Makalu was first attempted in 1977 and first climbed solo by Jerzy Kukuczka in October 1981. The route followed the left edge of the face and finished via the northwest ridge. In October 1982, a new route was opened up the center of the face by a Polish team, and Andrzej Czok reached the top from the northwest side. In September 1984, Swiss Romolo Nottaris achieved an ascent along a route slightly to the right of the 1981 route. It was his second attempt from this side, having been accompanied by Swiss Jean Troillet on his first attempt in 1982. Troillet returned in 1988 with Swiss Erhard Loretan, but their plans for a completely new route up the west face were frustrated when Troillet fell ill at Base Camp. Three years were to elapse before this pair was able to put their plan into action. The Loretan-Troillet route follows the untried right section of the west face, starting with steep snow and ice and continuing above 7000 meters with difficult, in some places overhanging, rock directly to the steep summit headwall. The lower part is avalanche-prone, but the main difficulties are in the upper section. They set up Base Camp at 5300 meters at the foot of the west face on August 28. They were committed to alpine-style. During the next four weeks, between intervals of bad weather, they established a bivouac tent at 6500 meters and climbed in the upper rock section to 7800 meters. On September 19, they discovered that their bivouac tent had been wiped out by an avalanche with the loss of nearly all their equipment. At Base Camp, they were able to purchase essential items from a Japanese expedition. On September 26, they climbed to 7800 meters, but had to return when Troillet broke a crampon. With time running out, they fixed a rendez-vous at around 7900 meters near the top of the west pillar with Spaniards who had spent 50 days setting up camps along the ridge. Fully acclimatized by now, Loretan and Troillet left Base Camp at one A.M. on October 1, carrying light rucksacks with a minimum of food and equipment and a 50-meter rope. The weather was perfect. Starting up the lower part of the west face, they traversed out onto the west pillar and continued up it, reaching 7400 meters by ten A.M. After a rest, they left at five P.M. and reached the top Spanish Camp at 8000 meters, from which they set out at midnight, joined by two Spaniards Carles Vallès and Manu Badiola. At 8200 meters, beyond where the west pillar merges into the southwest face, they encountered a difficult rock section. By now they had moved well ahead of the Spanish pair and reached the summit at ten A.M. on October 2. They spent two hours on top until the arrival of the Spaniards. Returning the way they had come, Loretan and Troillet completed the descent to Base Camp in the amazing time of nine hours. This was the fifth ascent of the difficult west pillar and establishes a record as the fastest ascent of the mountain. It was Loretan's twelfth 8000er and Troillet's sixth. As noted below, the two Spaniards who made the sixth ascent of the west pillar met disaster on the descent when Badiola tragically fell to his death on the difficult rock section at about 8300 meters. (This information was kindly given by Erhard Loretan.)

TREVOR BRAHAM, *Alpine Club*

Makalu, Ascent of the West Pillar and Tragedy. A Spanish expedition led by Carles Vallès was further composed of Manu Badiola, Joan Jover, Gerardo Blásquez and Dr. Rafael Martínez. During a period of 50 days, the group worked its way up the very difficult west pillar. They established Camp III at 7350 meters and fixed rope up to 7700 meters, where Vallès and Badiola bivouacked on September 30. On October 1, they again bivouacked at 8000 meters. They had agreed to join forces with the Swiss pair, Loretan and Troillet. After the arrival of the latter at one A.M. on the 2nd, all four set forth. Around 8200 meters, they encountered a difficult rock section. The Swiss pair moved ahead of the Spaniards. Some time after the Swiss, the Spaniards completed the sixth ascent of the route; for Vallès, this was his fifth 8000er. On the descent on the difficult rock section at about 8300 meters, Badiola tragically fell to his death.

TREVOR BRAHAM, *Alpine Club*

Makalu, Ascent and Tragedy. Miss Taeko Nagao, Yuji Futamata, Yuko Okada, Takumi Ishizaka, Ayumi Nozawai and I were on Makalu's normal northwest route. We placed Camp III on the Makalu Col at 7400 meters on September 26 and Camp IV at 7800 meters on the 29th. On October 5, Futamata,

Photo by Carles Vallès

PLATE 47

Steep ice on the West Buttress of Makalu.

Okada, Ang Dorje Sherpa and I climbed to the summit. On October 7, Miss Nagao, Ishizaka, Nozawai and Furgerjen Sherpa headed towards the summit, but at 8100 meters Nozawai was forced to quit; he and the Sherpa descended. Miss Nagao and Ishizaka continued and reached the summit around four P.M. They descended to bivouac at 8200 meters. The next day, exhausted Ishizaka could not descend below 8000 meters. There, Miss Nagao dug a snow cave. She urged Ishizaka to enter; he responded but did not come in. She found him dead on the fixed rope in the morning. Though badly frostbitten, on October 9 she descended to 7600 meters where she was met by Futamata and me; she continued with us to Base Camp, which we reached on the 10th. She was helicoptered to Kathmandu for medical treatment.

HIROTAKA IMAMURA, *Bernina Alpine Club, Japan*

Baruntse. Our expedition was a commercial one. The members had a wide variety of experience in the mountains. The climbing team of nine was accompanied to Base Camp by ten trekkers. We flew to Lukla on April 19 and headed up the Hinku valley. After a night on the Mera La at 5400 meters, ten people on April 28 climbed Mera Peak (6654 meters, 21,830 feet), the high point for the trekkers and good acclimatization for the climbers. We arrived at Base Camp on May 1 by following the Honku valley. On May 4, the trekkers crossed the Amphu Labsta Pass (5780 meters) and dropped into the Imja valley. Craig Seasholes and I helped them and their porters over this technical pass. Some of them had never rappelled before! Meanwhile, the climbing team ferried gear to the base of the west col and fixed ropes up steep ice (40° to 50° with a stretch of 70°) to establish Camp I on the col at 6100 meters. On a commercial expedition, the issues of climbing teams and climbing styles can be rather complex. This was not a *guided* climb. People paid to be part of the expedition, not to be guided. I chose to take the strongest client, David Mondeau, and we put in the route to the summit. The rest then had steps kicked and ropes fixed for their attempt. We two bivouacked at the foot of the fixed ropes and on May 6 climbed to the col, picked up supplies and established Camp II at 6500 meters. On May 7, we left Camp II at 2:30 A.M. and were on the summit (7129 meters, 23,737 feet) at eleven A.M. The climbing above Camp II on the southeast ridge was straightforward, most done on the west side of the cornice, all snow and ice and no rock. There were stretches of 70° and great exposure. We fixed some 500 feet of rope for the subsequent climbers. A second team of Wesley Krause, Craig Seasholes and Dale Kruse followed. They spent a night at Camp I, two at Camp II and on May 9 climbed to the top. On May 10, they cleaned all the ropes and camps from the mountain and returned to Base Camp.

SCOTT FISCHER

Baruntse, Post-Monsoon Southeast Ridge Attempts. Two expeditions unsuccessfully attempted to climb the southeast ridge of Baruntse. Three Frenchmen and two Belgians led by Jean René Minelli got to 6135 meters on November 4, and three Swiss and a German led by Fridolin Hauser reached 6740 meters on November 13.

ELIZABETH HAWLEY

Chamlang. Our team consisted of Andrew Knight and me as joint leaders, Neil Howells, Angus Andrew, Annette Carmichael, David Gwynne-Jones, Peter Pollard, Dr. Carolyn Knight, and scientists David Collier and Richard Hancock. We set up Base Camp on October 2 by the Hongu Khola at 4700 meters. The route was a variation on the original 1962 Japanese ascent; the Japanese started further north, avoiding what was the crux of the climb for us: two rock towers at the start of the ridge. Advance Base was established on the 8th at 5170 meters on the moraine of a glacier flowing from the south end of the south ridge. Camp I was placed at the top of the glacier at 5740 meters on October 9. Six days were spent climbing the two rock towers and rope was fixed. Camp II was made on the 15th at 6280 meters on the crest of the south ridge. From there, we climbed alpine-style. Howells, Andrew, Ngatemba Sherpa and I bivouacked at 6840 meters and reached the summit (7319 meters, 24,012 feet) on October 20. Above Camp II there was much unconsolidated snow on knife-edged ridges. A rock band at 6500 meters slowed progress.

ANDREW POLLARD, *Alpine Club*

Kusum Kanguru. On October 16, Japanese Koji Asano, Hiroyoshi Manome and Atsushi Sakudo completed the ascent of Kusum Kanguru (6367 meters, 20,889 feet) via the north ridge alpine-style. They made three bivouacs on the way to the top.

Kusum Kanguru from the Southwest. Brian Davidson, Dick Renshaw and I hoped to climb Kusum Kanguru (6369 meters, 20,896 feet) from the southwest. The approach from the Dudh Khosi was difficult and we may well be the first to reach the head of the Kusum Khola; it took three days to cover four horizontal miles through dense forest. Base Camp was just above the trees at 4000 meters and Advance Base at 4800 meters, just below the unclimbed southwest face. Our intended direct line up the face was regularly bombarded by rockfall and so we opted for a safer line further right. On the first attempt, we climbed this southwest buttress, 26 pitches of mixed climbing, to the crest of the unclimbed south ridge, where Davidson developed symptoms of altitude sickness. We sadly abseiled down the buttress but after two days of rest at Base Camp, Renshaw and I returned for a second attempt. This time we took a more direct line up the buttress and by the second afternoon had started to climb the magnificent rock pillar of the south ridge. On the fourth day, November 20, we climbed the final ridge of ice towers and reached the summit, completing a

Photo by *Stephen Venables*

PLATE 48

Snow bollard rappel on South Ridge of KUSUM KANGURU.

PLATE 49

Photo by Stephen Venables

**Renshaw nearing summit of KUSUM
KANGURU on the South Ridge.**

marvelous route, 1250 meters high, alpine grade TD sup. By the evening of the fifth day, we were back in Base Camp.

STEPHEN VENABLES, *Alpine Climbing Group*

Mera. A group of fourteen French youths between the ages of 13 and 17 made the ascent of the trekking peak Mera (6414 meters, 21,043 feet). On the descent they skied from 6300 to 5300 meters at the tongue of the glacier. They were from the Collège Saint Exupéry of Bourg Saint Maurice and led by Michel Folliet and Philippe Bonano.

Lhotse Attempt. A Spanish expedition led by Juan Fernando Azcona attempted to climb Lhotse via the west face. They reached 7650 meters on October 4 before having to retreat.

ELIZABETH HAWLEY

Lhotse Attempt. American Peter Athans and a companion reached 7600 meters on the west face of Lhotse on October 11 but could not continue higher.

ELIZABETH HAWLEY

Mount Everest, Illegal Attempt. Frenchman Marc Batard has become so enmeshed in controversy with the Nepalese authorities that there is doubt that he will ever return to Nepal to climb again. He gained fame in September, 1988 by achieving what is still the fastest ascent of Everest, 22 hours and 29 minutes, from Base Camp at 5350 meters to the summit at 8848 meters via the normal South Col route. This was not a solo climb, for there were a number of other climbers at various points, and indeed several of them went to the top before him on his own summit day. He went to Everest's summit a second time in October, 1990 in an unsuccessful attempt to become the first person to climb Everest and Lhotse in the same day. Unfortunately, Batard manages to quarrel with other climbers. In that expedition there was a dispute between him and a Nepalese woman, Mrs. Pasang Lhamu Sherpa, whose ambition was to become the first Nepalese woman, and the twelfth woman from any nation, to surmount Everest. In late September, she left the mountain in great anger, claiming that Batard had stopped her from going to the summit from their highest camp. He has stated— and so have climbers from another expedition who were also at the high camp—that she was not strong enough at that time to reach the top. However, according to Batard, he invited her to join him in a second attempt soon afterwards, but she refused to continue climbing. Her husband, the head of a trekking agency in Kathmandu, lodged with the Nepalese Ministry of Tourism a protest against a foreigner's forcibly preventing a Nepalese woman from climbing a Nepalese mountain. Stories went around Kathmandu that Batard had manhandled her, even beaten her—all charges he has consistently denied.

Batard came to Nepal again this spring to try once more to try for a double Everest-Lhotse success, to reach Everest's summit late on an afternoon, spend the night there, descend the next day to the South Col and climb Lhotse. In Kathmandu he understood from a Tourism Ministry official that permission was again promised, and he went to the mountain. He climbed to 8200 meters on May 1, but strong winds stopped him and he retreated for a rest at Base Camp. There, he learned that he had not in fact been granted a climbing permit, and therefore he abandoned his climb. It is not clear why he had not received permission. However, for having climbed without an official permit, Batard is liable to be banned from entering Nepal for five years or from mountaineering activities in the country for as much as ten years. Whether the authorities will actually take action against him is not yet known, but the matter has become irrelevant. On his return from Everest, he stated, "I have been very badly victimized in Nepal this time by those making charges and withholding my permit. So, with my heartfelt salutation to those brave and powerful people in Nepal, I have decided to cancel all my future climbing activities in Nepal." He had planned to return to Everest in the autumn, but to those who were scheduled to climb Everest with him later this year, he would offer to go with them to a high mountain of their choice in South America or Pakistan.

ELIZABETH HAWLEY

Everest Attempt. A six-man Australian expedition was led by Michael Groom. They first attempted to climb the west ridge of Everest from the Western Cwm, getting to 7400 meters on April 24. They then turned to the South Col route, where they reached a high point of 7900 meters on May 1.

ELIZABETH HAWLEY

Everest, Southwest Face Attempt. Our expedition was composed of Chung Woo-Sub, Nam Sun-Woo, Heo Jeong-Sik, Jung Gwang-Sig, Choi Tae-Sik, Cho Kwang-Je, Lee Sang-Lock, Park Young-Seok, Kim Jin-Sung, Koo Kyeong-Mo, Kim Seok-Jun and me as leader. We attempted Bonington's route on the southwest face. We established Base Camp, Camps I, II, III and IV at 5400, 6050, 6450, 6920 and 7600 meters on March 31, April 5, 7, 17 and 23. Camp IV had two box tents. On April 28, we fixed rope to 8300 meters where we hoped to pitch Camp V with one small bivouac tent. On May 1, Nam Sun-Woo, Kim Jin-Sung and sirdar Ang Tshering pushed up to the Camp V site, where they could see the south summit across the rock band and the refuse from previous expeditions around the site. There was not enough snow on which to pitch the tent. After the sirdar descended, the two Koreans bivouacked sitting up in the fortunately not too cold night. On May 2, Nam tried to climb the rock band, but after only 50 meters he found it impossible. Three centimeters (1¼ inches) of new snow made it impossible to ascend the rock and the snow was too thin for crampons. On May 3, I gave up the expedition because the snow would not easily have blown away or melted at that altitude. We had an accident. On April 14, Park slipped and fell 100 meters at 7000 meters. Fortunately, his injuries could be treated by American Dr. Michael Sinclair before he was carried to Base Camp in a stretcher we borrowed from his American team, for which we were very grateful.

LEE KANG-OH, *Seoul, South Korea*

Everest Attempt. Our members were German Michel Dacher, Frenchwoman Chantal Mauduit, Swiss Pierino Giuliani, Louis Deuber, Hans Kessler and I as leader. We joined a number of other expeditions at Base Camp on April 8. On April 11, we climbed the Khumbu Icefall to leave a depot at the site of Camp I at 6500 meters. On the 14th, we occupied Camp I but high winds and cold drove us back. On April 18, Kessler and I established Camp II at 7200 meters, while the others went to Camp I. We were aided by the ropes fixed by the Sherpa expedition on the steep, icy Lhotse Face. Again wind and cold drove us back to Base Camp. Again on April 24, Kessler and I spent the night at Camp II, but wind, cold and stomach troubles forced us back. On May 5, Kessler and I set out again and reached the South Col the next afternoon. Our companions climbed to Camp II. With extreme temperatures and wind, we saw that we had no chance and luckily were able to descend to Base Camp. We are convinced that the only way to climb Everest is by "fair means," namely without supplementary oxygen, which essentially degrades the peak to a 6000er. The 250 or 300 discarded oxygen bottles litter the South Col. After five more fruitless days at Base Camp, we wanted to climb back up the icefall to retrieve our gear, but conditions were too unfavorable. After our departure on May 15, the Sherpas with an American expedition evacuated our material.

NORBERT JOOS, *Schweizer Alpen Club*

Everest. Ours was the first Everest expedition to consist solely of climbers from the Northeast of North America. We were Mark Richey, climbing leader, Marc Chavin, Barry Rugo, Gary Scott, Dr. Michael Sinclair, Dr. Richard St. Onge, Québecois Yves La Forest and I as expedition leader. We arrived at Base Camp on March 20. During April and the early part of May, working with the All Sherpa Expedition, we established four camps on the mountain, the highest on the South Col. On May 2, Rugo, Richey, Chauvin and I arrived at the South Col for a summit bid. After two nights of waiting for the jet stream to move into northern China, we returned to Base Camp, thoroughly exhausted and beaten by high winds and bitter cold. After a much needed rest, Rugo, Richey, La Forest, Sinclair, Scott and I returned to Camp II for a final attempt. On May 13, Rugo, Richey, La Forest and I climbed to the South Col. Scott arrived there early on the morning of the 14th. We rested that day and Scott decided to return to Camp III. Just after midnight on May 15, we four left Camp IV for the summit. At 8:30 A.M., Richey and La Forest reached the summit, where they spent 45 minutes.

At 9:45 I got there, followed by Rugo. We spent an hour on the summit in excellent weather. Rugo ran out of oxygen during the descent and, after being caught in a storm, had to fight his way back to Camp IV. On the afternoon of the 15th, Dr. Sinclair arrived on the South Col to help us down. On May 16, we had all returned safely to Camp II. All camps were removed by May 20. We left no trash on the mountain or at Base Camp.

RICK WILCOX

Everest. There is a full article on the successful Sherpa Everest expedition in the pre-monsoon period earlier in this *Journal.*

Everest. Our expedition consisted of Robert Link and me as co-leaders, Steve Gall, Dave Carter, Darrin Goff, Hall and Amy Wendel, Dr. Kurt Pappenfus, five high-altitude Sherpas and three cooks. We established Base Camp on March 20. Once Sherpas had established the route through the Khumbu Icefall, we were able to place Camp I at 20,000 feet on April 1. All expeditions on the South Col route paid a fee to Sherpas to fix and maintain the icefall and Lhotse Face. Camps II and III were set up at 21,500 and 24,500 feet on April 7 and 17. High winds plagued us and made carries on the face difficult. The 1991 pre-monsoon weather was very unsettled and we never experienced the typical 7- to 14-day calm which usually occurs in May. Our first summit attempt began at Base Camp on May 6 but was cancelled on May 11 after two windy nights at Camp III. On May 13, we made our second attempt from Camp II. After a night at Camp III, Amy Wendel and Carter descended while Hall Wendell, Goff, Wongchu Sherpa and I climbed to occupy Camp IV on the South Col. At 2:30 A.M. on May 15, only Goff and I left the col for the summit in calm, clear weather, using oxygen. We followed in the Wilcox team's footsteps. After an hour, Goff turned back due to fatigue and cold feet. I continued up snow gullies to the south ridge where I abandoned my malfunctioning oxygen system. The snow conditions were horrible — inconsistent, loose, dry powder snow. The weather began to deteriorate. I met the Wilcox team on their descent just below the South Summit. I finally reached the summit at 2:30 P.M. in a howling blizzard. There I met Andy Politz, who had climbed via the north ridge. After five minutes I descended to the South Col, which I reached at 6:30. I was back in Base Camp on May 17 and we left the mountain on the 18th. This was my second ascent of Everest. On May 8, 1990, I climbed the north ridge without oxygen.

ED VIESTURS

Everest Attempt by a Nepalese Woman. A group of ten Nepalese, four Frenchmen and a Belgian was led by Mrs. Pasang Lhamu Sherpa, the first Nepalese woman to lead a mountaineering venture. (Many of her leadership duties were performed by her husband, who runs a trekking agency and has been an active mountaineer; he was one of the Sherpa climbers.) Last year, she was a member of an expedition led by Marc Batard, but at that time she failed to climb to the summit and claims that Batard had prevented her from trying it. Despite two summit bids, on both of which she used artificial oxygen, Mrs. Sherpa was unable to reach the summit. On her first attempt, she got to the south summit on September 30 in the company of several of her group. They decided the wind was too strong to continue. On the second attempt, she got only to the last camp on the South Col. Some of the foreigners in her party were not enthusiastic about their experience. One French member said that he had to sleep in the tent of another expedition at the last camp on the night of September 29. Mrs. Sherpa's husband explains that the Frenchman was supposed to be in the second summit party, not the first.

ELIZABETH HAWLEY

Fees Collected for Preparation of the Route through the Khumbu Icefall. Much of the work of making the route through the Khumbu Icefall was performed by the Sherpas employed by Mrs. Pasang Lhamu Sherpa and a Spanish expedition. For their work in the icefall and for the ladders and other equipment they supplied to do it, these Sherpas demanded from other expeditions to Everest and Lhotse some payment in cash or in kind, preferably $300 per foreign climber using the route. This was not the first time that those who had established the route had asked for contributions from others, and as long as permits are granted to a number of teams to climb this route at the same time, it is likely not to be the last. According to German Hans Eitel, four or five Sherpas were posted at the beginning of the route to stop those from using it if they had not paid. "This situation is not good for climbing," he commented angrily later; he said that he gave $1,700 and 1000 meters of climbing rope. He was not the only person to object. The Russians, who were on a very tight budget, refused to pay and made their own Icefall route, which was dangerously close to avalanche-prone slopes. According to a Sherpa involved in making the general route, the Russians went their own way several times and then switched to the normal, safer route, wrapping their faces so that no one could tell whether they were people who had paid or not.

ELIZABETH HAWLEY

Everest. Our expedition was composed of former Soviets Vladimir Balyberdin, leader, Anatoli Bukreev, Gennady Kopieka, Roman Giutashvili, Vladimir Gorbunov, Aleksei Klimin, Yelena Kunshova and Americans Kevin Cooney, Greg Smith and me. I belatedly joined the group in Base Camp on September 21 after negotiations in Kathmandu as a late addition. By September 23, we established a new Khumbu Icefall route because we were unwilling to pay $300 per person to the Nepalese-French expedition for use of fixed lines and ladders. The "Russian route" was wiped out by a massive avalanche from the Lho La at

6:15 A.M. on the 30th. Balyberdin and Bukreev attained the summit without supplementary oxygen on October 7, while Cooney turned back at the Hillary Step. Giutashvili, 54-years-old, and I summited with oxygen on October 10 at 5:20 P.M. On the descent, Giutashvili collapsed in blowing snow and darkness at 8:05 P.M. I dug a snow hole for him, left the remaining oxygen and stumbled to the South Col, where I had seen a light. After four hours and several forays, Kopieka and Klimin, who had been waiting out the storm, managed to locate Giutashvili and carry him back to the col uninjured. Upon return to Kathmandu, Giutashvili announced that he had had the use of only one lung since the age of 10. Bukreev and Balyberdin had as their goal the establishment of a new Everest record by ascending the 3500 vertical meters to the summit from Base Camp and returning in less than 24 hours. They wanted to break the French climber Marc Batard's record of 22 hours and 29 minutes. After their summit climb, Bukreev set out on October 12 at five P.M., climbed through the night and managed to reach 8300 meters at eight A.M. before terrible winds forced him to retreat. He was safely back in Base Camp 24 hours after he had left it. Balyberdin took 17 hours on October 17 to cover the same distance. When he left Base Camp alone at six A.M., he actually intended only to go part way up and bring down a tent and other gear, but when he saw how fine the weather was, he kept on going. He was climbing without crampons which he thought he would not need when he set out. When he reached 8300 meters at eleven P.M., he found it impossible to go higher on the very hard snow and in gusting winds without crampons. He stopped and spent the night in a thin sleeping bag and a thin down jacket. At daylight, he descended, safe and well—with no frostbite!

DANIEL MAZUR

Everest and Examples of Self-Sacrifice. A Spanish expedition led by Juan Carlos Gómez sucessfully completed the ascent of Everest on October 6 when José Antonio Garcés, Francisco José Pérez and Rafael Vidaurre reached the summit from the South Col. Gómez stated that he was clearly bemused by the French group led by Denis Pivot, which he described as not really a team but a collection of individuals, each doing his own thing. Although he did not explicitly say so, he clearly has a different philosophy and his party closely supported each other. An Australian climber commented with some amazement how one Spaniard, Lorenzo Ortas, carried two oxygen bottles to 8500 meters where he deposited them, not for his own use but for that of his teammates to enable them and not him to reach the summit. The leader Gómez did not quite reach the top because when he was on the Hillary Step, he met Vidaurre, who was beginning his descent but was now nearly blind because of sun and wind blowing into his eyes. Vidaurre was weeping in his distress and begged Gómez to help him down. Gómez did not tell him to wait for a bit while he went to the nearby summit but immediately abandoned his summit bid and helped his friend descend without any accident.

ELIZABETH HAWLEY

Everest Attempt. Briton Jonathan Pratt attempted Everest without teammates or Sherpas, but he could hardly have been said to have been climbing solo since eight other expeditions were on the same route. Indeed, he made use of other people's tents, ate their food and used their fixed ropes. He brought such meager resources with him that, according to a Sherpa, he tried to borrow the equivalent of $3.50 to buy food in the nearest village. He twice tried to reach the summit in the company of other climbers. His high point was gained on October 9 with another Briton.

ELIZABETH HAWLEY

Everest, South-Col Post-Monsoon Attempts. Aside from the attempts noted separately, there were a number of expeditions on the route via the South Col that did not succeed in reaching the main summit. A primarily French expedition led by Denis Pivot also had two Britons and a Brazilian. Frenchman Jean Michel Asselin did reach the south summit along with Mrs. Sherpa and her companions. An eight-man expedition of Spanish Basques was led by Josu Bereziatua. The leader, Benanxio Irureta and Gurutz Larrañaga reached the south summit on October 3, but could not continue on to the main summit. On October 3, eight Japanese under the leadership of Yasuo Iwazoe also reached the south summit. Australian Michael Groom's expedition got to 8200 meters on October 6. Groom took a 900-meter fall, luckily without fatal results. German Hans Eitel led three Germans, two Swiss and an Italian, who got to a high point of 7900 meters on October 16.

ELIZABETH HAWLEY

Everest, West Ridge and South Col Attempt. An international expedition led by Pole Aleksander Lwow was composed of two Poles, a German, an Australian and three Americans. They first attempted the west ridge, where on October 2 they got to 7600 meters. They then shifted their efforts to the South Col route, where they reached their high point of 6700 meters on October 15.

ELIZABETH HAWLEY

Everest, Korean Winter Attempts. Two Korean expeditions unsuccessfully attempted to climb Everest in the winter of 1991-2. Led by Kim Kwang-Jin, seventeen climbers tried to climb the south pillar, getting to 8700 meters on December 14. Four other climbers under the leadership of Kim Teuk-Hee attempted the South Col route and had to turn back at 8600 meters on December 20.

ELIZABETH HAWLEY

Everest, Southwest Face, Winter Attempt, 1991-2. Sixteen Japanese climbers with 25 Sherpas to help them were led by Kuniaki Yagihara. Their goal was to make the first winter ascent of the formidable southwest face, which had previously been ascended only three times but never in winter. They spent three long months on the mountain, but in the end the wind defeated them. When deputy leader Yoshio Ogata and Fumiaki Goto made the first attempt to set up Camp V at 8350 meters on December 21, the wind broke their tent poles, forcing them to descend without establishing the camp. They had managed to climb a small distance above the camp site which turned out to be the team's high point. Camp V was occupied on January 8, 15 and 29, 1992, but none of the climbers was able to venture higher. A total of seven tents, including two at Base Camp, were torn apart. They decided on February 9 to abandon their effort, which had started on November 16.

Elizabeth Hawley

Everest Photograph Corrections. The captions on the photographs appearing on pages 53 and 55 of *AAJ 1991* were not correct. Plate 14 was taken by Mike Browning. In the photo are Ang Jambu, Nima Tashi, Dana Coffield and Brent Manning. Plate 15 was taken by Dana Coffield.

Everest Correction. On page 227 of *AAJ 1991*, the names of Ang Phurba and Nima Dorje were unfortunately omitted from those of Jean-Noël Roche's party who reached the top.

Nuptse, Southwest Ridge Attempt. Swede Magnus Lekman and three Sherpas tried a new approach to an unclimbed ridge on Nuptse, a southwest ridge to a south rib. They gave up on October 24 after only a week when they found strong winds and route difficulties prevented progress above 6500 meters.

Elizabeth Hawley

P 5886. On April 29, Canadian Barry Blanchard and I ascended the unclimbed west face of P 5886 (19,312 feet), which lies on the southwest ridge of Nuptse, northeast of Kongma Tse. We placed Base Camp at 4940 meters just west of the Kongma La and Camp I at 5200 meters. The climbing on the face began with two 45° icefields separated by a short rock-and-ice step. We then encountered three ice ribs which offered ice climbing up to 80°. Next we climbed a snow ramp leading left and completed three pitches on loose rock and snow. To gain the glaciated summit ridge, we ascended the last 250 feet of 75° ice. We were greeted with big smiles and cups of tea by two of our Sherpas, Tenzing and Dawa, who had climbed the glaciated ridge. We hiked along the summit ridge for 200 yards and were within 75 feet of the summit when darkness fell. A large crevasse at the base of the pinnacle and a short ice pitch separated us from the summit. Since it would have been less than prudent to continue in the dark, we regretfully descended the glaciated north ridge and an endless boulder field. We took 28 hours round-trip from Camp I.

JAMES SCOTT

Pumori. A Spanish expedition led by Josu Feijoo climbed Pumori (7161 meters, 23,494 feet) by the southeast face to the east ridge. On April 25, Jesús María Díaz and Luis Angel Rojo completed the 61st ascent of the peak.

ELIZABETH HAWLEY

Pumori, Post-Monsoon Ascents, Tragedies and Attempt via the Southeast Face to the East Ridge. Jean-Noël Roche led six Frenchmen on the normal route on the southeast face to the east ridge of Pumori (7161 meters, 23,494 feet). On September 15, the leader Roche, Laurent Feruglio, Stéphane Laurenceau and Dawa Rinje Sherpa got to the top. The expedition was marred that same day by the deaths in an avalanche of French teenager Saidi Brahim and Gyalzen Sherpa as they were moving towards the summit. On September 18, Spaniards Juan Fernando Azcona, leader, Juan Carlos Arrieta, Juan Lasarte and Josu Ulazia completed the 63th ascent of the peak. Eight Germans, an Austrian and a Swiss were led by Michael Roepke. On October 6, the leader and Teja Finkbeiner reached the summit, followed on the 8th by Hans Brüggler, Josef Daxlberger, Rainer Faulstich and Fräulein Helga Hoess. On October 9, Michael Breuer teamed up with Icelander Ari Gunnarsson from Malcolm Duff's party to reach the top. Tragically Gunnarsson fell to his death on the descent. Britons Malcolm Duff, his wife Elizabeth and Mark Warham climbed the peak on October 7. German Bruno Walmann's Austro-German-Swiss party placed Austrian Wolfgang Köblinger on the summit on October 11. Six Venezuelans were led by Armando Michelangeli. On October 12, Marcos Antonio Tobia, Alfredo Autiero and Kazi Sherpa climbed to the top, followed the next day by Raúl Castillejo, Martín Echevarría and Nima Rita Sherpa. On October 16, Japanese leader Hiroshi Nakamura and Kami Tshering Sherpa climbed the mountain. French leader Pierre Taule, Serge Mauran, Chowang Nuru Sherpa and Pemba Gyalzen Sherpa on October 25 completed the list of successful climbers on Pumori for the year. Less fortunate were French led by Philippe Djoharikian, who reached 6950 meters on November 8.

ELIZABETH HAWLEY

Pumori Winter Attempt. Glenn Rowley led a group of 14 English climbers on the normal southeast face of Pumori. They were unsuccessful, reaching 6250 meters on December 2.

ELIZABETH HAWLEY

Lobuje East, West Buttress. A full article on this climb appears earlier in this *Journal.*

Lobuje East. A Japanese expedition from Touhoku University led by Kazu-masa Yamada climbed Lobuje East (6119 meters, 20,075 feet). On March 18, A. Koyama and M. Yamagata reached the summit.

Ama Dablam Attempt, 1990. I originally intended to try the Lugunak (southeast) Ridge, but since my companions had backed out in the United States, I switched to a solo effort on the standard southwest ridge. I was added to the permit of a South Tirolean team. After a bout with pneumonia, I went back to Base Camp after the departure of the South Tiroleans and started up alone on November 1, 1990. The route had been mostly fixed by two strong Italian and English teams, though by the time I arrived, quite a number of the ropes were cut or worn through. I tried to free everything but stayed clipped in as much as possible. I went for the summit from a second bivouac, but at the end of the Mushroom Ridge at 21,000 feet, the violent cough and high fever came back, this time with pulmonary edema. I descended to Camp II and stayed awake all night, drinking and taking Diamox and Decadron against cerebral impairment. I was very ill, and so at first light I started the tricky down-climbing, rappelling and traversing. I descended to Pangboche, where French friends gave me antibiotics.

RUSSELL GORDON

Ama Dablam, Southwest Ridge, Pre-Monsoon. The southwest ridge of Ama Dablam continues to be the objective of numerous expeditions. In the pre-monsoon season only one group made the climb successfully to the summit. On April 4, Michael Murphy of the Irish expedition led by Cornelius Moriarty reached the top. The following made attempts: Italians led by Angelo Giovanetti to 6400 meters on March 25; six Americans, three Mexicans and a Canadian led by Paul Thorndike to 6040 meters on March 29; Americans led by Evan Smith to 6400 meters on April 12; and Americans led by Thomas Bol to 6475 meters on April 13.

ELIZABETH HAWLEY

Ama Dablam. In March and April, Irish climbers comprising Cornelius Moriarty, Ciaran Corrigan, Pat Falvey, Tony Farrell, Mick Murphy and Mike O'Shea were on the southwest ridge of Ama Dablam. They had bad weather and several of the party were incapacitated by food poisoning. Mick Murphy reached the summit alone on April 4 after Corrigan had turned back with respiratory problems. This was the only pre-monsoon ascent of Ama Dablam.

JOSS LYNAM, *Federation of Mountaineering Clubs of Ireland*

Ama Dablam, Northeast Face and Southwest Ridge Attempts. Our team was made up of Swiss Marie Hiroz, French Laurence Gouault and Americans Steve

Shea and me. We arrived at the rarely visited Base Camp northeast of Ama Dablam in mid-April after an acclimatization trek to Everest Base Camp, where we viewed piles and piles of rubbish. After fixing several hundred feet of rope and observing the face for several days, because of objective danger from séracs overhanging the route we got permission to change our objective to the frequently climbed southwest ridge. On April 30, we four set out from our new 14,000-foot Base Camp for a rapid ascent of the southwest ridge. The next afternoon, after a long, hard day of climbing on the ridge in unusually dry and icy conditions, we turned back 600 feet from the summit in the face of an oncoming storm and darkness. The following day, May 2, we returned to Base Camp.

DAVID BREASHEARS

Ama Dablam, Post-Monsoon Southwest Ridge Ascents. Swiss Norbert Joos led an international group of six Swiss, a German and a Briton. They ascended the normal southwest ridge as follows: Swiss Diego Wellig, Hans Jörg Bumann and Martin Fischer on October 12; Briton Adrian Ball and Joos on October 13; German Wolfgang Vollbrecht and Swiss Urs Braschler on October 14 and Swiss Peter Marugg and Joos again on October 17. On October 25, French Michel Pelle, leader, Raymond Bousquet, Renaud Gardelle, Jean François Grand and Swiss Claude Stucki made it to the top. On November 3, French leader Gilles Buisson and Jean-François Males were joined by Roger Lecompte from Michel Richard's expedition and climbed to the summit. French Michel Richard led 9 French and a Swiss climber. On November 4, French Robert Collard, Swiss Pierre Alain Rickli and Ang Dawa Sherpa reached the summit, followed on November 9 by Mlle Véronique Parein, Dominique Gombert, leader Richard, Dawa Sherpa and again Ang Dawa Sherpa.

ELIZABETH HAWLEY

Ama Dablam Winter Ascents. There were two expeditions on the normal southwest ridge of Ama Dablam during the winter climbing season. Warwick Baird, one of two Australians, paired up with members of the South Koreans in a climb to the summit on December 15. The members of the Korean expedition that reached the top that day were Yoo Byoung-Cheul and Ang Dawa Sherpa. On December 19, Korean leader Park Kyung-Lee, Dawa Sherpa and again Ang Dawa Sherpa climbed to the summit.

ELIZABETH HAWLEY

Cho Oyu from the South, Pre-Monsoon. Cho Oyu (8201 meters, 26,906 feet) continues to be a popular objective, the west side often being reached from Nepal. Alain Hantz, leader of a group of six Frenchmen, climbed to the summit of Cho Oyu with Nepalese Man Bahadur Gurung and Iman Singh Gurung on

April 22. A Brazilian, Sergio Beck, got to the summit in an unathorized climb that same day. Four Americans, led by David Houchin, failed in their attempt, reaching 6100 meters on April 8.

ELIZABETH HAWLEY

Cho Oyu, East Ridge Ascent and Tragedy. A team of 14 Russians, a Ukrainian and a Bashkir was led by Sergei Yefimov. They succeeded in climbing Cho Oyu (8201 meters, 26,906 feet) by the formidable east ridge, which has a 70-meter-deep gap with 80° rock on its sides at a very high altitude. They overcame this great obstacle partly by making an extremely difficult traverse on a rock ledge on the Tibetan side. This ridge had previously been unsuccessfully attempted by Japanese, British, Polish, American and Japanese climbers. Their highest fixed camp was at 6950 meters. At eight A.M. on October 20, six members set out from a bivouac at 7900 meters on the western side of this obstacle. Climbing without artificial oxygen, Ivan Plotnikov, Eugeny Vinogradsky and Alexsander Yakovenko gained the summit three hours later. Two more, Valeri Pershin and Sergei Bogomolov reached the top nearly two hours after that. Yuri Grebeniuk turned back at 8000 meters because his fingers were beginning to freeze and as a surgeon he wanted to keep them from being damaged. Tragically, the next day during the party's descent from the bivouac, Grebeniuk was hit on the forehead by a falling stone while he was climbing out of the gap. Like the summiters, he was not wearing a helmet. He received a deep wound and lived only a minute longer. His body had to be left in a sleeping bag on a shelf in the gully.

ELIZABETH HAWLEY

Cho Oyu, West Side from the South, Ascents and Attempt, Post-Monsoon. On September 29, Russians Vyatcheslav Skripko, leader, Mikhail Mozhayev and Yevgeny Prilepa reached the summit of Cho Oyu, having climbed in one day from 7200 meters. On October 1, the two Bulgarian members of the same expedition, Borislav Dimitrov and Miss Iordanka Dimitrova also got to the top. Miss Dimitrova is the first Bulgarian woman to have climbed an 8000er. She has climbed all 7000ers in what was the USSR, becoming the first foreign female "Snow Leopard." A French expedition was also successful from Nepal on the western side of the peak: Max Imbert and Dawa Sherpa on October 4 and leader Michel Zalio and Kilu Temba Sherpa on October 5. These were the 95th to 98th ascents of the mountain. Three Austrians led by Rudi Mayr were unsuccessful, reaching 6500 meters on October 28 and November 4.

ELIZABETH HAWLEY

Numbur. Helmut Müller and I traveled to Jiri by bus and then made a seven-day approach via Junbesi, Basa Drangka, over a 4352-meter pass to the

PLATE 50

Photo by Mathias Rau

**Southwest Ridge and South Face of
NUMBUR.**

Dudhkunda Khola. We set up Base Camp on October 10 at 4600 meters at Yüligolcha, a little lake on the west side of the Dudh Kund Glacier. From Base Camp we climbed grass slopes and scree to a col to rejoin the glacier at 5200 meters. We followed the glacier to its western top and placed Camp I at 5450 meters on October 28. We ascended a snow-covered rock spur which climbed westward to join the southwest ridge, the normal route on the mountain, at 5800 meters. On November 6, we climbed this spur and placed Camp II at 6000 meters just below a steep step on the ridge. On November 7, Müller and I climbed a 45° ice slope to easier terrain and the summit (6957 meters, 22,824 feet).

MATHIAS RAU, *Deutscher Alpenverein*

Dorje Lhakpa Winter Ascent. A South Korean expedition succeeded in making the seventh ascent of Dorje Lhakpa (6966 meters, 22,854 feet) and did it in the winter. They climbed the west ridge. On December 16, leader Song Ki-Bo, Jung Woo-Chang and Ang Kami Sherpa reached the summit.

ELIZABETH HAWLEY

Langtang Lirung, Post-Monsoon Southeast Ridge Attempts. Two expeditions attempted Langtang Lirung (7225 meters, 23,705 feet) by the southeast ridge in the post-monsoon period. British led by James Grey got to 6100 meters on October 31. Japanese under the leadership of Mitsuo Nomura reached a high point of 7150 meters on November 3.

ELIZABETH HAWLEY

Manaslu Attempt. Five Swiss led by Franco Dellatorre tried to climb Manaslu by the northeast face. They reached a high point of 6415 meters on April 6.

ELIZABETH HAWLEY

Manaslu Attempt. Our expedition was made up of Frank Nugent, co-leader, Calvin Torrens, Martin Daly, Harry O'Brien, Donie O'Sullivan, Philip Holmes, Dermot Somers, Mike Barry, Robbie Fenlon, Garry Murray, John Murray, William Forde, Leslie Lawrence, Nick Stevenson and me as co-leader. We attempted the normal route, the northeast flank. We got to Base Camp at 3850 meters on March 25. We established Advance Base and Camps I and II at 4200, 5050 and 5600 meters on March 29, April 2 and 14. Heavy snowfalls delayed progress. We made three attempts to get to Camp III on April 22, 25 and 27, the last one reaching 6000 meters. On April 29, we returned to Base Camp and left the mountain on May 1. The weather was continually bad from April 4 until we left. Though the camps were in safe positions, the route was threatened by avalanches.

DAWSON STELFOX, *Irish Manaslu Expedition*

Manaslu Traverse. A strong Soviet expedition from the Ukraine with 20 members, 16 of them climbers, was led by Dr. Vladimir Shumikhin and Sergei Bershov. They had hoped to ascend the still unclimbed east face of Manaslu (8163 meters, 26,780 feet). In 1987 a Polish pair climbed to 6800 meters on it and in 1990 a Soviet party got to 7200 meters but was stopped when three of them fell to their deaths. This year's expedition established Base Camp at 4200 meters on March 21. "There was surprisingly much snow," says Bershov, "and it snowed day in, day out." Depite bad conditions, three camps were placed at 5200, 6200 and 7000 meters, the last on April 8. A group led by V. Khitrikov made three attempts to finish the route but was driven back by bad weather. A late April snowstorm damaged camps and covered much equipment. They decided to try the Polish route from the south, climbed in 1984 by Lwow and Wielicki. On May 1, Alexei Makarov, Viktor Pastukh and Igor Svergun started alpine-style toward the Pungen La (6700 meters), the south ridge and southeast face to the summit, which they reached on May 6. They descended the normal northeast route, which took two more bivouacs.

JÓZEF NYKA, *Editor, Taternik, Poland*

Manaslu Attempt and Tragedy. Our expedition attempted to climb Manaslu by the northeast face, the first-ascent route. We were Albert Brugger, Gregor Demetz, Karl Grossrubatscher, Friedl and Hans Mutschlechner, Stephan Plangger, Christian Rier, Erich Seeber, Werner Tinkhauser, Roland Losso, Dr. Pavel Dolecek and I as leader. We set up Base Camp and Camp I at 4000 and 5600 meters on April 18 and 21. At Camp I, we found a thin film of oil on the water we had melted from snow. This may well have been carried eastward from the burning oil fields of Kuwait. Bad weather prevented progress for the next two weeks. On May 7, Friedl Mutschlechner, Grossrubatscher and I climbed to Camp I. On May 8 and 9, we set up Camps II and III at 6250 and 7000 meters. After a stormy night, we three started for the summit. Mutschlechner turned back an hour later, fearing frostbite. Shortly after that Grossrubatscher also began the descent. I kept on to 7600 meters, where stormy weather made me retreat to Camp III, where I found only Mutschlechner. I learned that Grossrubatscher was dead. While photographing, he had lost a crampon and fallen a few meters, breaking his neck. After placing his body in a crevasse, Mutschlechner and I climbed down to Camp II and then began to ski down to Camp I. It began to snow. At 3:30 P.M., when still only a few meters from camp, Mutschlechner was struck by lightning and instantly killed. I spent a sad night in Camp I and skied down to Base Camp the next day. Grossrubatscher was one of Italy's best rock climbers. He had been on numerous expeditions and had climbed the Uli Biaho Tower and Cerro Torre. Mutschlechner was also one of the most successful alpinists, having climbed three 8000ers with Reinhold Messner.

HANS KAMMERLANDER, *South Tirol, Italy*

Manaslu, Post-Monsoon Northeast Face Ascent and Attempts. An international party of 15 Swiss, an Austrian, an Italian and an American was headed by Bruno Jelk. On October 25, Swiss Mauro Ferrari and Horst Brantschen reached the summit, having climbed the normal northeast-face route. Less successful were Italians led by Oreste Forno who got to 7100 meters on September 28 and again on October 8 and Catalan Spaniards under the leadership of Antoni Llasera who reached 7900 meters on October 6.

ELIZABETH HAWLEY

Manaslu, South Face Attempt. An American expedition led by Austin Weiss was composed of John Owen, Craig Dobkin, Clyde Soles, Jim Graham, Mark Kightlinger, Deborah Eads and Mark Selland. Their high point on the south face was 7800 meters, reached on October 22.

ELIZABETH HAWLEY

Cheo Himal. The previously untrodden summit of Cheo Himal (6820 meters, 22,375 feet), which is north-northwest of Manaslu, was reached on October 13 by Japanese Shigeki Imoto and Nepalese Tshering Sherpa, Ful Bahadur Rai and Dambar Bahadur Gurung, members of a joint Japanese and Nepalese Police Force expedition, led by Japanese Masanobu Okazaki and Nepalese Gupta Bahadur Rana. Their route above Advance Base began on the south face of Himlung Himal on the lower part of the route which the Japanese had used when they made the first ascent of Himlung Himal in 1983. Camps I and II were established at 4800 and 5580 meters on September 22 and 30 on that face, despite serious rockfall. They then traversed a snowfield to the east to place Camps III and IV at 5800 and 6400 meters on the southeast ridge of Cheo Himal. The summit was reached by four of the nine who set out on a long summit day.

ELIZABETH HAWLEY

Himlung Himal Winter Attempt. British climbers led by Richard Emerson attempted to climb Himlung Himal (7126 meters, 23,379 feet) by a western spur to gain the south ridge. They were able to get to 6050 meters on December 19.

ELIZABETH HAWLEY

Kang Guru. Our expedition was composed of Domenico Bidese, Imerio Dal Santo, Paolo Ghitti, Fiorenzo Pagiusco and me as leader. On October 4, we established Base Camp at Meta, a deserted village at 3600 meters at the foot of the mountain. We placed Camp I on the 7th at 4900 meters below a rock wall which seals off the valley. On October 12, we climbed the wall up a steep couloir to place Camp II at 5600 meters. Camp III was set up at 6100 meters at the foot of the northwest ridge on October 20. On October 21, Bidese, Ghitti, Pagiusco,

Ang Dawa Tamang, Lhakpa Tamang and I climbed a steep ice spur for 400 meters to join the sharp, corniced northwest ridge and reached the summit (6981 meters, 22,904 feet). This was the German first-ascent route.

GIANCARLO CONTALBRIGO, *Club Alpino Italiano*

Bhrikuti, First (?) and Second (?) Ascents. There had been some question as to whether Bhrikuti (6364 meters, 20,879 feet) in northern Mustang had been successfully climbed before a joint British-Nepalese expedition, led by Elaine Brook and Lhakpa Sherpa, set out for it this autumn. Japanese claimed the first success in 1982 by three separate summit parties, but the leader of an unsuccessful French team four years later said that he had seen their photos and was certain that they had not reached the highest summit. In any case, it was not the British members who went to the top via the southeast ridge on October 22 but three Sherpas, Lhakpa, Ang Zangbu and Ang Kitar. The Britons, who were feeling the effects of altitude remained in Base Camp except for the doctor, who went to Advance Base. On November 3, a French expedition led by Bertrand Doligez also followed the southeast ridge to the summit. Those who got to the top were Doligez, Jean-Pierre Bourgeois, Patrick Blanfune, Jean-Marc Pillot, Frédéric Simond and Sherpas Ang Tendi and Mingma Tenzing.

ELIZABETH HAWLEY

Bhrikuti Winter Attempt. Romolo Nottaris and three other Swiss attempted to make a winter ascent of Bhrikuti by the southwest ridge, but they were able to reach only 5500 meters on November 30.

ELIZABETH HAWLEY

Manang Mountaineering School. The 11th course began on August 13. This year there were three Nepalese instructors: Lhakpa Norbu Sherpa, Ang Tsering Sherpa and Musul Kazi Tamang. We Slovene instructors were Alenka Jamnik (f), Darja Jenko (f), Tomaz Azman, Bojan Pograjc and I. The course was attended by 26 Nepalis, two Chinese and one Syrian. The first part, given in six days in Kathmandu, included theory and rock-climbing practice. The practical course in Manang took 20 days. One day was spent practicing on the Gangapurna Glacier, three days were for the ascent of Naur Peak and four days for ascent of Chulu Far East.

MARCO ŠTREMFELJ, *Planinska zveza Slovenije*

Annapurna IV Attempt. Our members were John McMenamin, Heather McComb, Ruth Gemperlein, Jim Tweedie, Base Camp Manager Pat Ballard and I as leader. Bad weather and deep snow severely hampered our efforts. Upon arriving on March 30 at Yak Kharak in the Sabje Khola valley on the northwest side of Annapurna IV, we encountered deep snow that extended down to 3800 meters which prevented our mule caravan from carrying loads higher. From a low Base Camp there, with a small porter contingent we were forced to ferry loads for five days to Advance Base at 4650 meters. On April 4, this was occupied on the south side of a high rock ridge on the Sabje Glacier. Crows were a problem to food and everything had to be securely covered. The campsite had obviously been used by other expeditions judging from the debris in the area. From Advance Base, it was an hour's hike to the foot of the icefall leading to the dome on the northwest ridge. It took several days to fix the route to Camp I. We had to rebreak trail each morning in new or drifted snow. Two caches were set up along the way. Again crows were a problem. Camp I was set up on April 17 on a small ledge in the icefall. Above Camp I, the route became steeper and a long section of hard 50° ice had to be crossed. We got only to the site of Camp II because on the night of April 20 our tent at Camp I was destroyed by an avalanche. One member was in the tent at the time, but he was not injured. We then abandoned the expedition because of dangerous conditions and lack of time.

RICHARD SALISBURY

Annapurna IV Attempts. A student from Osaka, Japan, Koichi Sugiyama, with Kami Tshering Sherpa, climbed to 6480 meters via the northwest ridge. They gave up on September 7 due to adverse weather. A South Korean Buddhist monk, Rim Jong-Bum, with five Sherpas, also was unsuccessful, reaching 7000 meters on October 9 on the same route before strong winds forced a retreat. Serbs led by Milenko Savić got to 6500 meters also on the northeast ridge before having to abandon the attempt.

ELIZABETH HAWLEY

Annapurna III, Post-Monsoon Attempts. There were two unsuccessful expeditions to Annapurna III (7555 meters, 24,787 feet) after the monsoon. American William Bancroft and a companion got to 4730 meters on the southeast buttress in September 30. Japanese led by Morimasa Ohtani attempted to get to the south ridge from the south and reached 6800 meters on October 13.

ELIZABETH HAWLEY

Gangapurna Attempts. There were two unsuccessful expeditions to Gangapurna (7455 meters, 24,457 feet) in the post-monsoon period. Eight Spaniards were led by Francisco José Palacios. After getting to 5900 meters on the north face on October 17, they turned to the north spur in order to reach the north ridge, where they got as high as 6400 meters on October 24. Three Swiss led by Hans Rauner climbed the north spur to the north ridge but could not get above 7200 meters, which they reached on October 23.

ELIZABETH HAWLEY

Gangapurna Winter Attempt. Timothy Brill led a group of six Americans, who attempted to climb Gangapurna (7455 meters, 24,457 feet) via the south ridge from the south. They were able to get to only 5800 meters on December 8.

ELIZABETH HAWLEY

Tarke Kang (Glacier Dome) Attempt. Four English climbers led by Keith Foster attempted to climb Tarke Kang (7193 meters, 23,600 feet) by its south ridge. They got to a high point of 5800 meters on October 24.

ELIZABETH HAWLEY

Khangsar Kang (Roc Noir) Winter Attempt. Seven Koreans led by Lee Dong-Myung were unable to complete the ascent of Khangsar Kang (7485 meters, 24,557 feet), which they attempted by the south face. They got to 6600 meters on December 12.

ELIZABETH HAWLEY

Annapurna, Solo Autumn Ascent, 1990. I approached Annapurna in May of 1989 but did not make a real attempt to climb the mountain because of bad weather. In the autumn of 1990, I returned. I flew to Jomosom and continued on with seven porters to the Annapurna Base Camp at 5200 meters on the north side of the mountain, which I reached on October 5. Two Sherpas helped me to establish Camp I at 5600 meters. From there on, I climbed solo, moving up a few hundred meters during the comparative lulls early each morning. I was plagued by wind, stomach problems and high-altitude sickness, but persisted. Finally on October 25, 1990, I got to the summit, having taken four hours to complete the last 100 meters. It took me another five days to descend to Base Camp, where my Sherpas awaited me. [Gazzola did not get permission to climb the mountain and so this was an illegal ascent. There is also actually a considerable amount of doubt in Italy that Gazzola accomplished this ascent. —*Editor.*]

GIANCARLO GAZZOLA, *Club Alpino Italiano*

Annapurna, Pre-Monsoon Attempts. There were two unsuccessful expeditions that attempted the Dutch route on the north face of Annapurna. Austrian Arthur Haid led five Austrians and a German, who reached 5900 meters on April 21. Ralf Dujmovits guided a group of 14 Germans who got to 5750 meters on April 26.

ELIZABETH HAWLEY

Annapurna Tragedy. A 14-man South Korean team led by Ko Yong-Chul abandoned its attempt after two members and four Sherpa porters were killed by an avalanche on September 19. The Korean victims were Lee Sang-Gu and Lee Seok-Jee; the Sherpas were Dawa Sange, Norbu Jangbu, Lhakpa Tendi and Tenzing. Their Camp IV at 7500 meters was swept down the mountain. Two other Sherpas were carried down by the avalanche but managed to survive. One of them broke a leg and the other escaped with bruises. As they fell, Jin Ang-Sung was observing them with binoculars from Camp I at 5050 meters. Others in Camp III at 6900 meters knew nothing about it until a surviving Sherpa came down to report the accident. Yul Bae-Sung, who was at Camp III, rushed to the site but found only five bodies. The body of one Sherpa could not be traced. They were given a snow burial. The victims had hoped to make a summit bid the next day.

KAMAL K. GUHA, *Editor, Himavanta, India*

Annapurna Attempt. Our group of ten Americans, mostly professional mountain guides, attempted to climb the north face of Annapurna by the Dutch Rib. We arrived at Base Camp on August 28, finding a large Korean expedition already at Camp I. We caught up with the Koreans' Sherpas along the rib and shared the work of trail breaking and rope fixing with them up to 7300 meters. Large avalanches poured down the mountain throughout our climb, destroying Korean Camps I, II and III at various times. Bill Crouse and we two occupied our Camp IV at 7325 meters on September 18. The next was to be a rest day prior to a summit attempt on September 20. All the technical climbing was below and our camp was at the final sérac barrier. At midday, six Sherpas and two Koreans passed our camp. The Sherpas were worried because the Koreans were forcing them to camp at 7500 meters, where there was no avalanche protection. Two hours later, a large avalanche roared over Camp IV, partially burying our tents. It also carried four Sherpas and two Koreans down. Five of them flushed out at 6275-meter Camp III, all to die within 20 minutes of internal injuries. One Sherpa was never found. We descended, helping the two survivors down and burying the dead. Five days later, Paul Valiulis, Ron Johnson and we two reascended to Camp III to find more new, unstable snow and constant winds. We retreated.

JULIE AND MATT CULBERSON

Annapurna, Northwest Buttress Attempt. An expedition of six Austrians was led by Hubert Fritzenwallner. On October 13, they reached a high point of 6120 meters on the northwest buttress.

ELIZABETH HAWLEY

Annapurna North Face, Ascent and Attempts, Post-Monsoon. A Russian expedition was led by Alexander Glushkovski. They climbed the Dutch Rib on the north face. On October 24, Sergei Arsentiev and Nikolai Cherny reached the summit. Two other groups were unable to get to the top. Spaniards led by Albino Quinteiro reached 6300 meters on September 19. Japanese under the leadership of Masaru Otani got to 6450 meters on October 1.

ELIZABETH HAWLEY

Annapurna, West Face Solo Attempt. From October 28 to 31, I climbed a new route on the west face of Annapurna solo alpine-style but did not ascend to the summit. I got to Base Camp at 4300 meters on October 19 and bivouacked at the foot of the west face at 5150 meters on October 27. I followed the 1985 Messner route to 6000 meters and after that climbed a new route to the left of his. After a bivouac at 6200 meters on the upper plateau, I climbed 70° ice and experienced some rockfall. I bivouacked again at 6900 meters after reaching a snow ridge. On the 30th, I worked left onto a safer part of the face. I climbed to 7300 meters, where I had to halt for two hours because of the wind. I then continued up snow-covered rock to 7800 meters where I bivouacked in what was left of my tent. On October 31, I got to 7900 meters near to the normal route but was forced back by the wind to bivouac again at 7800 meters. On November 1, I traversed the north face and descended the normal route and bivouacked at the site of Camp I. I was back in Base Camp on November 2. This had been packed up by my Base-Camp staff, who thought I had not survived, but I managed to walk down to a village on two frost-bitten toes.

SLAVC SVETIčIč, *Planinska zveza Slovenije*

Annapurna, South Face Ascent and Tragedy. The 13th ill-fated climber in Nepal in the post-monsoon season was a Belgian, who died in the season's most dramatic death, having disappeared with no final trace. Gabriel Denamur was a member of one of two international expeditions led by Poles on the Bonington route on the south face of Annapurna. His team was led by Mieczysław Jarosz. Denamur and a Polish teammate, Kazimierz Stępień who climbed without Sherpas or artificial oxygen, planned to go to the summit together from the last camp, Camp III at 7300 meters and made an abortive attempt on October 19. The next morning, Denamur started up alone, and he was never seen again. Stępień began his own ascent at noon on the 20th and did not see Denamur at any time. He lost the trail, darkness fell and he bivouacked at 7700 meters in the hope of climbing the rest of the way on the 21st. However, he had to descend because he was beginning to suffer from high-altitude sickness. He was met that morning by the leader of the other expedition, Krzysztof Wielicki, who was on his way to the summit. Wielicki found a line of fresh footprints on the snow ahead of him leading all the way to the top—and down the other side, the north face. He saw no other trace of Denamur, nor did members of his team who followed him to the summit on October 22 and 23. Jarosz hoped that other climbers on the north face would help Denamur and did not send out a search team. His expedition's food supplies were running low and they mounted no further summit attempts. Some

PLATE 51

Photo by Andrej Štremfelj

ANNAPURNA's West Face. . . . . . =
**Swiss Attempt, Autumn 1984; ——— =
Svetičič, 1991; – – – – = Messner,
1985; –..–..– = French Attempt,
1986; —.–.— = French Attempt,
Spring 1984.**

of the members had already left Base Camp on the 20th. They hoped Denamur would make his way to Kathmandu. But he did not. A Russian expedition was still on the north face when Denamur disappeared on the 20th, and two of their number went to the summit on the 24th. They saw absolutely no signs that anyone had descended their route. He might have plunged into some area where the Russians did not go. This possibility is perhaps supported by some footprints raised above the surface of the snow by wind scouring the snow around them. These were found by Svetičič west of the normal north-face route during his traverse from the west face on November 2. Without bivouac gear, Denamur could not have long survived.

ELIZABETH HAWLEY

Annapurna, South Face. Our international party was composed of Poles Mrs. Jolanta Patynoska, Mrs. Wanda Rutkiewicz. Ryszard Pawłowski, Bogdan Stefko, Mariusz Sprutta and me as leader, German Rüdiger Schleypen, Belgian Miss Ingrid Baeyens, Briton John Keska and Portuguese Gonçalo Velez. We hoped to climb the 1970 British route. We set up Base Camp at 4150 meters on September 11 and Advance Base at 4850 meters at the foot of the face. We cooperated with another Polish expedition led by Mieczysłav Jarosz. Camps I, II and III were established at 6100, 6800 and 7350 meters on September 20 and October 4 and 11. We fixed 2500 meters of rope on the exceedingly difficult route with numerous technical obstacles. To prepare and fix 700 vertical meters between Camps I and II, with ice gullies of 55° to 60°, took two weeks. The first summit attempt was thwarted by strong winds. Stefko and I reached the summit on October 21 at 11:30 A.M. In the top area, we found tracks made some hours earlier by the Belgian Gabi Denamur, a member of the other Polish party. He reached the summit by the British route and decided to descend the normal route. Unfortunately, he was never seen again. On October 22, Pawłowski, Rüdiger and Wanda Rutkiewicz got to the top, climbing separately. On the 23rd, Miss Baeyens, Sprutta and Velez were the third summit team. Base Camp was evacuated on October 26. Ours was the fourth expedition to climb the route. Velez was the first Portuguese to climb an 8000er. This was Ingrid's third 8000er and for both Wanda and me the eighth.

KRZYSZTOF WIELICKI, Klub Wysokogórski, Katowice, Poland

Annapurna South Face. Our expedition hoped to climb a direct route in the center of Annapurna's south face alpine-style. The team was made up of Valentin Ivanov, Dr. Valeri Karpenko, Vassili Elagin, Vladimir Bashirov, Vladimir Obichod, Sergei Isaev, Nikolai Petrov, Alexander Sheinov, Vladimir Yanochkin, Dmitri Egorov, radio operator Maria Klochko and me as leader. The first attempt of nine climbers reached 6500 meters. On September 30, rockfall broke Karpenko's leg and hit Egorov's back. The rescue operation took 60 hours. The pair was evacuated to Base Camp at 4100 meters and helicoptered to Kathmandu. The second attempt of seven climbers got to 7350 meters in a 12-day effort. They climbed extremely difficult ice and rock and never found a bivouac site except for artificial snow platforms. On October 17, Sheinov fell ill from high-altitude sickness and the team brought him down. We had almost no more food and all were fatigued. Andy Lapkass of the American Annapurna Dakshin expedition provided us with some food. After meeting with Krzysztof Wielicki of one of the Polish expeditions on the 1970 British (Bonington) route, Bashkirov, Obichod, Isaev and Petrov left Base Camp on October 22 and climbed that route, reaching the summit on October 26 from Camp III at 7350 meters.

VASSILI SENATOROV, *Periodicals Trading Service, Russia*

Varah Shikhar (Fang) Winter Attempt. South Koreans led by Yu Jae-Hyoung tried to climb the east face to the southeast ridge of Varah Shikhar, also called the Fang (7647 meters, 25,089 feet). They got to 6350 meters on January 1, 1992.

ELIZABETH HAWLEY

Annapurna Dakshin Attempt. New Zealander John Madgwick and a companion failed to climb Annapurna Dakshin by its south face. Their high point of 5500 meters was reached on March 28.

ELIZABETH HAWLEY

Annapurna Dakshin, Southeast Ridge Attempt. On October 14, only four days out from Kathmandu, Susan Diprima, Jim Jennings, John Lapkass, Geoff Radford, Dave Sullivan and I as leader reached Base Camp at 13,500 feet in the Annapurna Sanctuary. The next day we established Advance Base at 15,000 feet, partially up the Annapurna South Glacier. From October 16 to 19, we worked at finding a safe route through the icefall and into a snowy basin below the col on the southeast ridge of Annapurna Dakshin (South). Unfortunately, the icefall was either impassable or severely threatened by hanging séracs off Hiunchuli and the Fang. On the 21st, we called the climb off and spent until November 4 on one- to three-day climbs in the sanctuary. We burned and buried all garbage and carried out cans and bottles.

ANDREW LAPKASS, *Alpine Guides International*

Annapurna Dakshin. Six Japanese led by Yoshio Matsunaga climbed Annapurna Dakshin (South) by the southwest ridge. They established Base Camp and Camps I, II and III, at 4800, 5450, 5700 and 6400 meters on

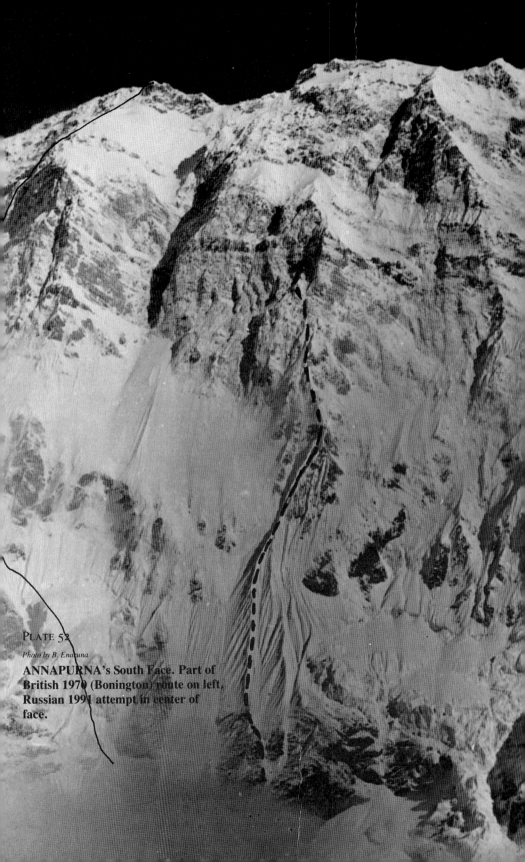

Photo by B. Enakuna

PLATE 52

ANNAPURNA's South Face. Part of British 1970 (Bonington) route on left, Russian 1991 attempt in center of face.

September 27, October 2, 9 and 19. On October 22, the leader Matsunaga, Yoshiyuki Shinji, Masayuki Yamamoto and Ngati Sherpa completed the 18th ascent of the peak (7219 meters, 23,684 feet).

ELIZABETH HAWLEY

Tilitso, Post-Monsoon. There were two successful expeditions to Tilitso (7134 meters, 23,406 feet) in the post-monsoon season. Fourteen Swiss and a Pole from the University of Bern, led by Karl Kobler, climbed the northeast spur to the north ridge. They set up Base Camp and Camps I and II at 4950, 5800 and 6200 meters. Rope was fixed between 5400 and 6200 meters. The summit was reached by the following: Kobler and Christoph Krell on September 29; Kobler (again), Henry Bartu, Fräulein Brigitte Huber, Christoph Pappa, Hanspeter Demund on September 30; Josef Faller, Alex Suter, Fräulein Marianne Jau, Stephan Aebersold, Pole Mirosław Matyja on October 1; and Manuel Gossauer, Martin Mast, Fräulein Mathilde Waser and Pasang Sherpa on October 2. A French expedition led by Christian Sounier was also successful on the same route. On October 8, Michel Feuillarade, Mlle Anne Rosa and Nima Kancha Sherpa reached the summit.

ELIZABETH HAWLEY

Tukuche and Dhampus Ascents. A French expedition led by Jean Moatti made the 16th authorized ascent of Tukuche (6920 meters, 22,703 feet). On September 28, Frédéric Buet and Lhakpa Norbu Sherpa reached the summit via the northwest ridge. This same group also made the 10th and 11th authorized ascents of Dhampus (6012 meters, 19,723 feet) via the southwest ridge. On September 21, Henri Coffy, Michel Huglin and Nawang Sherpa got to the top, followed on September 30 by Buet and Mrs. Nima Sange Sherpani. Japanese led by Takashi Ito also climbed the northwest ridge of Tukuche and on October 4, Ichita Ono and Yukito Ueno reached the summit.

ELIZABETH HAWLEY

Dhaulagiri, West Face. Our team from Kazakhstan sent ten members to the summit of Dhaulagiri by a difficult new route on the west face. They were climbing leader Yervand Ilinsky, Yuri Moiseev, Andrei Tselishchev, Anatoli Bukreev, Vladimir Sugiva, Renat Khaibullin, Valeri Khrishchaty, Artur Shegai, Alexandr Savin, Vladimir Prisyazhny, Zaurbek Mizambekov, Viktor Dedi and Dr. Valentin Makarov. They started up a rock spur of variable steepness. A rock wall of 75° between 5500 and 6000 meters was the most difficult part of the route. Difficulty up to UIAA VI+ and poor weather complicated efforts. Between 6000 and 6800 meters there was an ice slope followed by mixed ice and

PLATE 53

Photo by Jiří Novák

DHAULAGIRI's West Face. From left to right: Czechoslovak route, 1984; Kazakh route, 1990; Czechoslovak Attempt, 1985; Kazakh route, alpine-style 1991.

rock of 55°. Rope was fixed up to 7350 meters. Base Camp and Camps I, II, III, IV, V and VI were established at 3600, 4670, 5200, 5500, 6000, 6400 and 7400 on April 2, 6, 19, 15, 26, May 6 and 9. On May 10, Moiseev, Suviga, Bukreev, Tselishchev and Khaibullin reached the summit. On May 13, Khrishchaty, Shegai, Savin, Prisyazhny and Mizambekov climbed to the top. The eleventh member of the assault team, Dedi, broke a bone in his hand while moving a rock to set up Camp I and so could not climb higher.

KAZBEK VALIEV, *Kazakhstan*

Dhaulagiri. On May 14, a nine-member Danish team managed to place their leader Søren Smid on the summit of Dhaulagiri by the standard northeast ridge route. He became the first Dane to climb an 8000er. He climbed solo from their Camp II at 7200 meters, spent two nights alone at Camp II at 7700 meters and made his way to the top on a cold but clear and windless morning. He used no bottled oxygen.

ELIZABETH HAWLEY

Dhaulagiri, Post-Monsoon Northeast Ridge Ascents and Attempts. A party of five Spaniards to the normal northeast ridge was led by Xavier González. On October 2, Jordi Corominas completed the 51st ascent of the peak. Japanese under the leadership of Hitoshi Onodera were also successful when on October 11 Toshihiya Nakajima, Koji Yokoyama and Keepa Sherpa reached the top. Haruyuki Endo and his wife Yuka Endo had hoped to lead their group of five Japanese up the east face of Dhaulagiri, but they had to give up the attempt at 5750 meters on October 3. They then turned to the northeast ridge, getting as high as 8000 meters on October 15. Two French expeditions failed; the group led by Roger Laot at 7800 meters on October 2 and those with Philippe Le Balch at 8130 meters on October 6. Six Poles and an Austrian were to have climbed under the leadership of Wanda Rutkiewicz, but she arrived too late and they had as deputy leader Piotr Malinowski. The climbers reached 7100 meters on October 15 and 28. A Spaniard, Antonio Martínez, headed for Dhaulagiri without permission from the Nepalese authorities. He was stopped before he had climbed very high by the government-appointed liaison officer with an authorized expedition and was taken to Kathmandu, where he was fined about $1,750.

ELIZABETH HAWLEY

Putha Hiunchuli Attempt. German Heinrich Buhr and two Sherpas made an attempt on Putha Hiunchuli (7246 meters, 23,773 feet), hoping to climb the west ridge. They had serious problems on the approach. Their high point was 5300 meters, which they reached on October 20, after they had exhausted their supply of rope for fixing the route.

ELIZABETH HAWLEY

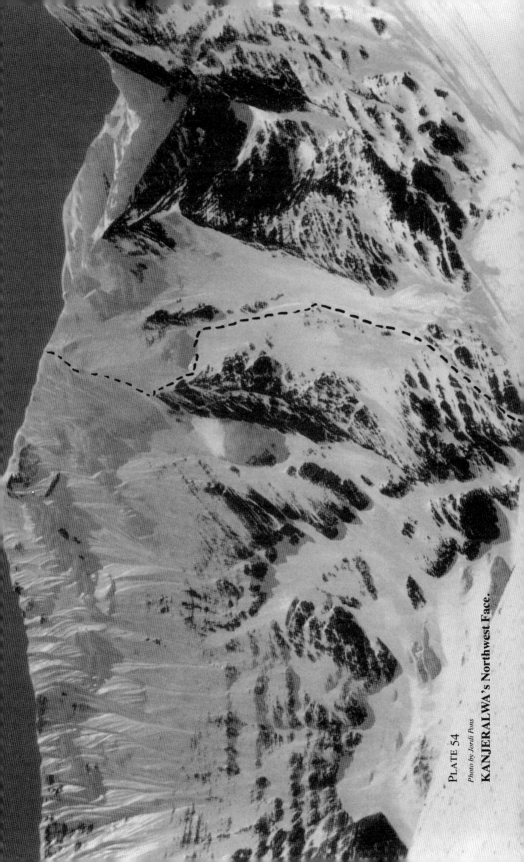

PLATE 54

Photo by Jordi Pons

KANJERALWA's Northwest Face.

Kanjeralwa Attempt. Our expedition was composed of Frenchmen Olivier Besson, leader, Guy Cousteix, Lukie Laurent and me from Spain. We were able to fly to the airstrip at Juphal, near Dunai. This lies only three or four days from Ringmo, the capital of Dolpo, situated on the most beautiful lake I have ever seen in the Himalaya. Kanjeralwa (6612 meters, 21,692 feet) lies in Phoksumdo National Park, east of the lake. We tried to reconnoiter the east face but found it inaccessible. We ascended the northwest face alpine-style on May 5. We set out at two A.M. with headlamps on a 40° slope. The slope is cut by a gigantic sérac barrier which obliged us to make a spectacular ascending traverse of some 200 meters. At five A.M. we made the exposed traverse on very hard ice. Once above the sérac, we could for a time follow a snow rib, which was the only place we could rest our feet. The rib then merged into the face. From there on, the slope steepened to 60° and 70° with pitches on transparent ice. There was not a single platform and changing leads was very uncomfortable. We continued up the face until we reached the ridge crest at 6400 meters. It was two P.M. Without going on to the summit, we descended the south face, bivouacking at 5100 meters. It was by the west face that Japanese led by Fumihito Watanable made the first and only other ascent of the mountain on April 23 and 24, 1973 after establishing five high camps.

JORDI PONS, *Centre Excursionista de Catalunya, Spain*

Tripura Hiunchuli IV (Hanging Glacier Peak IV), Kanjiroba Himal. After flying to Baglung, an international group led by Doug Scott began a long approach on September 30. They trekked via Beni, the Myagdi Khola, Darbanh, Dhorpatan, the Ghustang Khola, Tarakot on the Barbung Khola, Ringmo, over the Kagmara La, the Garpung Khola to the Jagdula Khola East, arriving at their Base Camp on October 25. They established Advance Base at 5200 meters below the start of the rocky ridge. On October 27, Britons Doug Scott, Nigel Porter and John Cullen and Indian Sharu Prabhu (f) made an abortive attempt on Tripura Hiunchuli IV (6294 meters, 20,650 feet), the southernmost of the Hanging Glacier Peaks, climbing from the west. On October 27, Scott, Porter and Prabhu completed the first ascent of the mountain. They had loose rock for 500 meters and then good ice and snow. They made an unplanned bivouac at 5500 meters on the descent. They returned to Jumla for a flight to Kathmandu on November 4. (Doug Scott has kindly provided this information.)

Api, Northwest Ridge. An expedition of five South Koreans was led by Lee Thea-Yeon. On May 27, Son Dong-Su, Pemba Tshering Sherpa and Pasang Gyalbo Sherpa completed the fifth ascent of Api (7132 meters, 23,399 feet), climbing the northwest ridge.

ELIZABETH HAWLEY

India—Kumaon and Garhwal

Panch Chuli II. An Indian army expedition from the Gorkha Rifles made the second ascent of the peak, 18 years after the first ascent. I led the 20-man team. We approached from the Darma valley in the east. Base Camp was at 3720 meters at Nyulpa and Camps I and II were at 5000 and 5740 meters on the Sona Glacier. Camp III at 6450 meters was on the north col. From there, on August 21, a first group composed of Riflemen Ram Bahadur Gurung, Kim Bahadur Puri, Krishna Bahadur Thapa and Lance Naik Ram Bahadur Bura and a second group comprising Majors A.K. Saxena and A.B. Goth, Subedar N.D. Sherpa and me headed along the northeast ridge toward the top. The first group reached the summit (6904 meters, 22,650 feet). When still 50 meters from the top, the second group was swept away by a massive avalanche. We were hurled down 80 meters but luckily could arrest our fall before plunging 1000 meters. W.H. Murray had intended to climb this route in 1950, but it took 41 years before it was done. The first ascent in 1973 was via the south ridge.

N.B. GURUNG, *Captain, Gorkha Rifles, Indian Army*

Panch Chuli II. A 24-man expedition of the Indian Army Kumaon and Naga Regiments was led by Lieutenant Suraj Bhan Dalal. In the post-monsoon, they climbed Panch Chuli II (6904 meters, 22,650 feet) from the east, which is said to be more difficult than the western approach. From a high camp on the east ridge, Dan Singh, Chandar Singh, Ranoder Singh and Captain Ganesh Pathak reached the summit on September 17.

KAMAL K. GUHA, *Editor, Himavanta, India*

Bamba Dhura. An Indo-Tibetan Border Police team led by Assistant Commandant Mahendra Singh climbed Bamba Dhura (6334 meters, 20,780 feet) in early September. It is situated at the head of the Kalabaland Glacier in eastern Kumaon.

HARISH KAPADIA, *Himalayan Club*

Hardeol and Tirsuli. A 43-member team from the Indian Border Security Force was led by S.C. Negi. On September 24, T.R. Angdoo, Jumma Khan, Jamuna Prasad, Naresh Singh and S.D. Thomas climbed over a 22,500-foot foresummit and reached the summit (7151 meters, 23,460 feet) of Hardeol. The following day, Angdoo, S. Gombu, Raymond Jacob, Jumma Khan and Nandan Singh climbed Tirsuli (7074 meters, 23,460 feet). [Though no routes were given, it is probable that since two men made the ascents in successive days, they must have climbed from the col between the two peaks. —*Editor.*]

KAMAL K. GUHA, *Editor, Himavanta, India*

Nanda Kot Attempt. We were Ajoy Mondal, Nishi Kanta Sen, Rakhal Ghosh, Naresh Rai, Amitabha Bhattacharya, Gopal Chakraborty, Dr. Amit Bhowmick and I as leader. After arriving at Munsiary on September 8, we had difficulty recruiting porters because the Indo-Ukrainian expedition to Nanda Devi East had engaged nearly all available local porters. We took five days to get through Martoli to Base Camp at 4150 meters. It was three hours from there to Advance Base, which we established on September 17. Despite wanting to pitch Camp I in the Kuchela-Nanda Kot col, we were first stopped by crevasses. We placed Camp I on the nearer side of the Kuchela Glacier at 5050 meters on the 19th. Rope was fixed on the rock buttress above Camp I. Altitude problems and incompetence of many high-altitude porters from Uttarkashi left Ghosh, high- altitude porter Gylzen and me alone to carry out the campaign above. Skirting an icefall on a spur coming down from the col, we pitched Camp II at 5700 meters on the spur and on September 24 placed Camp III at 6000 meters just below the col. The northeast ridge rises from the col to the summit. We hoped to make a summit bid from there, but a heavy snowfall began on September 25 and we gave up the attempt.

AMAR BISWAS, *Parvat Abhiyatri Sangha, India*

Nanda Devi East. The expedition which I led to Nanda Devi East was composed of 14 Indians and 14 Ukrainians. Because of the closure of the Nanda Devi Sanctuary, we approached from Kumaon to the east, making the second ascent of the peak from outside the Sanctuary. The first ascent was made by Poles in 1939. From the roadhead at Pithoragarh, we took five days to Base Camp at Badheli Gwar at 4425 meters, which we reached on September 7. We established four camps. Camp I was two hours above Base Camp. Climbing started there, ascending scree to a steep rock gully and up a narrow ridge to Longstaff's Col, where on September 11 we placed Camp II at 5950 meters. The route to Camp III began with two 125-meter-high gendarmes and then a narrow, exposed ridge. We fixed rope on all this section. Camp III was placed at 6250 meters on September 15. We fixed some of the route on the way to Camp IV, which we pitched at 6850 meters on September 20. The climb from Camp IV to the summit was first on a snow ridge and then on rock, where we fixed more rope. In all, we fixed 2750 meters of rope. On September 21, Matislav Gorbenko and Vladislav Terzeoul reached the summit (7434 meters, 24,390 feet). They were followed on the 22nd by Ibrahim Zade, Valentin Boiko, Aleksander Serpak, Aleksander Parkhomenko and Lobsang Sherpa. On September 23, Dr. Aleksander Vlasenko, Pavel Serenkov, Alexei Kharaldin and Yuri Zaverchinsky climbed to the top. On September 25, three Indians, Magan Bissa, Kusang Dorje Sherpa and Sanga Sherpa, also completed the ascent.

S. BHATTACHARJEE, *Climbers and Explorers Club, India*

Panwali Dwar. An Indian group from Bombay's Pinnacle Club, led by P.B. Bodhane, made the second ascent of Panwali Dwar (6663 meters, 21,860 feet)

They climbed the southeast ridge, joining the 1980 Japanese first-ascent route on the summit ridge. On September 23, Prasad Dhamal, Moreshwar Kulkarni, Surendra Chavan and Anil Sable reached the top.

HARISH KAPADIA, *Himalayan Club*

Bauljuri. On October 1, Lynne Wolfe, co-leader with me, William Porteous, Eric Hagerman, William Boerigter, Gordon Wilson, David Stevens, Chris Hovard and I climbed Bauljuri (5922 meters, 19,429 feet). The peak lies 12 kilometers south of Nanda Devi and is just outside the Nanda Devi Sanctuary. Although not a technical climb, it offers spectacular views of the surrounding peaks and is a good introduction to Himalayan climbing. It is popular with Indian climbers and was climbed just ahead of us by two Indian expeditions. The approach is up the Pindar River with Base Camp at 12,000 feet. We continued up grassy slopes to the Buria Glacier and on to the saddle between Bauljuri and beautiful Panwali Dwar. The summit is due south of the col. Most parties utilize two high camps.

TONY JEWELL, *National Outdoor Leadership School*

Baljauri. An Indian expedition of ten was led by Basanta Singha Roy. On September 24, the leader reached the summit (5922 meters, 19,429 feet).

KAMAL K. GUHA, *Editor, Himavanta, India*

Maiktoli, 1990. An Indian team led by Colonel J.C. Joshi ascended the Sundardunga valley and Dungia Dhong and set up Base Camp on the Maiktoli grazing grounds on September 16, 1990. They placed high camps on the 21st and 23rd. Anil Bisht, J.C. Bisht, Anil Sah and one other gained the summit (6803 meters, 22,320 feet) on September 25, 1990. This was the first Indian ascent by the difficult south face and ridge. They were caught by an avalanche on the descent but escaped unharmed.

KAMAL K. GUHA, *Editor, Himavanta, India*

Trisul Attempts and Tragedy. An 8-member Polish expedition led by Michał Kochańczak attempted to climb Trisul (7120 meters, 23,360 meters) from the west in August and September. In bad weather they got to 6700 meters. Mrs. Anna Bruzdowicz Dudek died from exhaustion on September 5 at Camp I (6000 meters). Germans led by Josef Gloggner attempted the Yugoslav route on the west face to the south ridge. They reached 6400 meters on October 19 but were turned back by the cold.

HARISH KAPADIA, *Himalayan Club*

Tribhuj. This small but fine peak, southwest of Trisul, was climbed by Britons Andrew Brett and Alexander Laird. They followed the southwest ridge to the summit (5055 meters, 16,584 feet) on May 17.

HARISH KAPADIA, *Himalayan Club*

Abi Gamin Ascent and Kamet Attempt. Our team consisted of Miss Maharookh Gowadia, Miss Medha Bapat, Dr. Suneel Vartak, Jitendra Hande, Prasad Mhatre, Rajesh Gadgil and me as leader. We established Base Camp on Vasudhava Tal at 15,400 feet on May 28. Camps I, II and III were placed on the East Kamet Glacier at 16,100, 17,200 and 18,200 feet on June 3, 5 and 10. We climbed a steep gully some 1500 feet to place Camp IV in a basin at 20,100 feet on June 14. Then a 1500-foot rock face, sometimes plastered with snow, and a 350-foot ice face led to Camp V, pitched at 21,600 feet on June 20. Camp VI was placed on Meade's Col at 23,100 feet on June 23. On June 22, Dr. Vartak and Hande climbed to the summit of Abi Gamin. Gadgil's attempt on Kamet on June 24 failed due to the sickness of a high-altitude porter who was with him. I was put out of action by a falling stone at Camp IV.

JAYANT DOFE, *India*

Abi Gamin, Women's Expedition. The 19-member, all-women, pre-Everest expedition was led by Bachendri Pal and Rita Marwah. Fourteen women left camp at 21,000 feet for Kamet, but on September 13, they were beaten back by a blizzard only 100 feet from the top. On September 15, some of the members climbed to the summit of Abi Gamin (7355 meters, 24,136 feet).

KAMAL K. GUHA, *Editor, Himavanta, India*

Rataban. A team from Calcutta led by Kala Chand Chatterjee approached the peak from the Valley of Flowers. On August 19, Rajat Mahalanobish, Ragban Singh Rawat and Jagat Singh Rana reached the summit (6166 meters, 20,230 feet).

HARISH KAPADIA, *Himalayan Club*

Satopanth. The members of our expedition were Santiago Arribas Pérez, leader, Dr. César Alfaro, Santiago Gómez, Francisco Soría, Alfonso Juez, Estaban López, Julio Fernández, Eduardo Fernández, Avelino Mora, Jesús Acaso, Pedro Exposito, Manuel Serrano and I. We established Base Camp and Camps I, II and III on May 5, 7, 8 and 14 at 4337, 4800, 5100 and 5950 meters, the latter in the col at the foot of the northeast ridge on the normal route. We had two periods of good weather with a total of nine days. It snowed and blew in the afternoons. The technical difficulties were between 6100 and 6400 meters. We fixed 400 meters of rope, using 17 snow pickets, 3 ice screws and 30 carabiners.

Deep snow over ice complicated the climbing. On May 17, Juez, Exposito, Eduardo Fernández and Mora completed the first Spanish ascent of the peak (7075 meters, 23,212 feet). On the summit day, it snowed and blew.

ANTONIO ANGEL CIPRÉS, *Grupo Militar de Alta Montaña, Jaca, Spain*

Bhagirathi II. A 26-member team from the Indian Special Frontier Force was led by Colonel H.B.S. Phokela. They set up Base Camp at Nandandan on May 11 and Advance Base in a bowl below Vasuki Parbat on May 17. Six members set out from there on May 20 and gained the summit. Another group, including a girl, summited on May 23.

KAMAL K. GUHA, *Editor, Himavanta, India*

Bhagirathi II. A Spanish expedition of eight was led by Conrad López. On June 12, López, Josep Lluis Sasot and Angel Casals reached the summit.

HARISH KAPADIA, *Himalayan Club*

Kedarnath, North Face Ascent and Tragedy. A joint Indo-Australian military expedition climbed Kedarnath (6940 meters, 22,770 feet) by a new route on the north face. It consisted of Australians Bob Killip, Nevin Agnew, Captain Brian Morrissey, Lieutenant Mike Kilcullen, Corporal Lance Einam and me as leader and Indians Captain M.S. Dhami, Subedars N.D. Sherpa, Binod Kumar, S.N. Singh, Naik Subedar Gurjant Singh, Havalders Chetram, Mohan Lal Kajuria, Shital Singh, Yadev, Major Arwind Shukla as doctor and Major Krishnan Kumar as co-leader. We set up Base Camp at Tapovan, Advance Base near the junction of the Gangotri and Kirti Glaciers and Camp I at the foot of Kedarnath's north face at 4460, 4750 and 5000 meters on September 25, 28 and October 3. We followed the glacier to a line of ice cliffs at 5800 meters, where Camp II was located. From Camp II, the only access to the broad upper slopes was a steep, avalanche-prone gully. A party of eight set out on a summit bid on October 7. Deep, loose snow made progress difficult. N.D. Sherpa achieved the summit in nine hours, the others reaching 6800 meters. On the descent N.D. Sherpa triggered a slab avalanche which carried him 300 meters down a steep gully. Luckily, both he and the avalanche stopped two meters short of Camp II. He was shaken but had only minor injuries. Yadev, Gurjant Singh and Kilcullen reached the summit on October 10 from their high camp at 6400 meters. After arriving at the summit at 5:20 P.M., they hurried down in the dark. They could not locate their camp. Singh and Kilcullen settled into a snow cave for the night, but Yadev continued on alone. He was never seen again and a search failed to find him. The other two in the morning crawled into their tent barely 100 meters away. Both Singh and Kilcullen suffered frozen hands and feet and it wasn't until the 12th that a ground party reached them to assist them down. They were eventually evacuated by helicopter along with Morrissey, who had also suffered during the first attempt.

ZAC ZAHARIAS, *Major, Australian Army Alpine Association*

Kedar Dome. A 13-member Indian team was led by Babban Prasad Singh. On September 7, four members and three high-altitude porters set out from Camp II at 6250 meters. Three of the members gave up but Sudhir Kumar Mahto and the porters continued on to the summit (6831 meters, 22,410 feet).

KAMAL K. GUHA, *Editor, Himavanta, India*

Dudh Ganga, 1989. From Kedarnath village, Dave Pollari and I carried heavy loads over a high pass to Vasuni Tal to make the first ascent of Dudh Ganga (5462 meters, 17,920 feet), which straddles the drainage to the north of the village. The peak rises prominently in the region. On September 30, 1989, we ascended tedious moraines and then a steep, frozen snow gully to rock. We climbed 5.7 in double boots. Fortunately we could protect with pitons and for the descent could set up a proper rappel. Pollari completed the final portion of the climb on ramps and moderate snow, while I waited a few hundred feet below the summit.

FRED BECKEY

Shivling. A three-man Norwegian expedition was led by Ole Haltvik. On September 12, the leader and Jore Keokk completed the ascent by the west ridge.

HARISH KAPADIA, *Himalayan Club*

Bhrigupath Attempt and Bhrigu Pathar. Britons Kevin O'Neale, Martin Welch, Ian Drigg and I were active in the Gangotri region in mid-September. The Bhagirathi Glacier and its encircling mountain faces had remained unexplored until our visit. Only two previous expeditions had recorded being in the area and they were restricted to the lower part of the glacier by the icefall. Neale and Welch climbed the 1000-meter-high, snow-and-ice, northeast face of Bhrigupanth (6772 meters, 22,220 feet) and reached the summit ridge some 150 meters below the summit, but they were stopped by poor snow conditions. Drigg and I started up a prow left of the blank white wall above the Bhrigupanth Glacier where we found an excellent free climb with sustained pitches of UIAA V, VI and VII with only short stretches of A1 to negotiate moss-choked cracks. The prow gave access to easier upper slabs and a shale-and-snow ridge leading to the summit of Bhrigu Pathar (6038 meters, 19,810 feet). We climbed the 26 pitches in capsule style over seven days, from September 8 to 14.

MARTIN MORAN, *Scottish Mountaineering Club*

Thalay Sagar, North Face. Berecz Gábor, Dékàny Peter, Kiszely György, Szikdzai Attila and I placed Base Camp near Kedar Tal at 4740 meters on August 24. Due to constant cloudy and rainy weather, we were not too active for the first two weeks. On August 30, we established Camp I at the bottom of the north face at 5600 meters. We then climbed unroped the 55° couloir leading to the Bhrigupanth-Thalay Sagar col, from which we originally had planned to climb the 1983 Polish-Norwegian route on the northeast ridge. On September 6, we set up Camp II on the col at 6000 meters. We spent two wet nights here in a crevasse and a snow cave. However, the tempting unclimbed north face seemed to be in suitable condition. Therefore, at dawn on the 12th, Dékàny and I set out from Camp I and climbed to 6200 meters on the north face. Afternoon and night snowfall caused a terribly uncomfortable bivouac. The next day, we ascended the objectively dangerous funnel below the vertical ice-chimneys. Ice-covered slabs and poor protection slowed progress. After a few pitches on varying ice, we bivouacked at 6400 meters. On the third day, we climbed a section of loose rock covered by thick, soft snow and spent the night on a tiny ledge on the steep face of the upper ice cirque at 6600 meters. From there, on the 15th, we climbed two pitches to the loose, rotten shale-and-limestone part of the summit cone, where fog and wet snowfall forced us to halt that day and the next. On the 16th, a traverse led to the right toward the northwest ridge. This 60 meters was the worst part of the route due to loose shale and soft snow. Continuing on the ridge, we joined the 1979 Anglo-American route at 6700 meters. Following this, we reached the summit (6904 meters, 22,650 feet) at one P.M. on September 17. Frequent snow avalanches caused difficulties on the upper part. The ice varied from 60° to 85°. This was the first ascent of the north face and the third line on the mountain. Descending the northwest couloir, we arrived at Kedar Tal the next evening. Meanwhile, the other three had set out for the northeast ridge on the 14th, but they abandoned the climb because of snowfall.

OZSVÀTH ATTILA, *Excelsior Mountain Club, Budapest, Hungary*

Thalay Sagar Attempt. A Japanese expedition led by Akira Kiuchi reached 6200 meters. Two members suffered from sickness and rockfall threatened.

HARISH KAPADIA, *Himalayan Club*

Matri. Thirteen climbers from Durgapur were led by Swapan Kumar Ghosh. They set up Base Camp near the snout of the Matri Glacier on August 14. On September 1, the leader and Arvind Patel climbed to the summit (6721 meters, 22,050 feet).

KAMAL K. GUHA, *Editor, Himavanta, India*

Shyamvarn and Yogeshwar. An Indian team from Bombay was led by Ramakant Mahadik. On June 20, seven completed the second ascent of Shyam-

6904 m

V+

IV–V

PLATE 55

Photo by Michael Kennedy

THALAY SAGAR's North Face.

III

V+

60° 65°

V

70°

80°

60°

80°

60°

45°

60°

30°

1. camp   5600 m

varn (6135 meters, 20,128 feet). The first ascent was in 1985, when the mountain claimed the life of one climber. On June 27, eight climbers made the first ascent of Yogeshwar (6678 meters, 21,910 feet), climbing the southeast ridge. This group had attempted the peak in 1989.

HARISH KAPADIA, *Himalayan Club*

Jogin I and II. A Japanese expedition climbed Jogin I (6465 meters, 21,210 feet) on August 19 when leader Jushichiro Otsubo, Mrs. Yachiyo Yamanaka, Mrs. Kimiko Yamashita, Yukio Shiozawa, Hideaki Nara and Mrs. Kieko Tezuka reached the top. On August 21, Kazutoshi Okuya and Tokuji Iida climbed to the summit of Jogin II (6342 meters, 20,807 feet).

Jaonli Attempt. From September 14 to November 6, we attempted the unclimbed east side of Jaonli (6632 meters, 21,760 feet). British members were Richard Brooke, Jim Milledge, Mike Westmacott and I, Irish members were Joss Lynam and Paddy O'Leary and our Indian member was C.P. Ravi Chandra. Our average age was 64 and we totalled 382 years! The outer defenses of Jaonli were formidable. It took three weeks to break through three major icefalls. The two strongest climbers, O'Leary and Milledge, were selected to make a summit bid via the long, snowy south ridge, starting from Camp III at 17,300 feet. They established Camp IV at 19,800 feet and the following day tried for the summit. They found the ice climbing more demanding than it had appeared from below but attained 21,000 feet before being forced to retreat by the onset of night. One more high camp would be needed. While the summit pair recuperated, Ravi Chandra and I climbed to 19,500 feet on the nearby east ridge. It did not offer a better route to the top. On October 19, five members were at Camp III. At 2:45 A.M. on the 20th, we were jerked into wakefulness. There was the roar of falling ice, snow and rocks. The glacier was shaking like jelly. Earthquake! Luckily the camp was well clear of avalanche danger. We had been caught in a major earthquake. The main destruction had struck the valley on the other side of Jaonli where one to two thousand people had been killed. It registered 6.1 on the Richter scale. Milledge and O'Leary immediately set off on a second summit attempt, supported to Camp IV by Westmacott and Brooke. The following day, we could see their figures climbing upwards. Suddenly, they stopped, cast left and right and came down. The earthquake had opened a huge cleft clean across the ridge. They faced an unclimbable ice wall topped with unstable ice blocks. The summit was unattainable.

MICHAEL BANKS, *Alpine Club*

Kalanag. Despite the fact that Kalanag was first climbed in 1957 and that there have been numerous ascents since, our group of Dartmouth students, with limited mountaineering experience, undertook its challenge. Inspired by Freshman Rupin Dang, son of Hari Dang, vice-president of the Indian Mountaineering Foundation, the expedition was finally limited to ten members, nine men and one woman, picked not on our climbing ability but based on the amount of time we were willing to commit to planning. In addition to Indian Rupin Dang, we were Americans James Ziobro, Tom Douglas, Ashley Campion, Matt Valentine, Joel Brenner, Jens Voges, Joe Bachman and I and Norwegian Odd-Even Bustnes. In India we were joined by several Indians. We were initiated to the terrors of Indian driving in the bus ride to the roadhead at Shankri. Finally on June 16, we were all together at Base Camp at Kiarkoti at 13,200 feet. A forward party had already established Advance Base at 15,500 feet. Our route traversed the bases of the Swargarohini peaks of the Banderpunch range, following the Kalanag Glacier west and then south. On June 18, we established Camp I, the first one on snow, at 16,500 feet. Fearing poor weather, we were forced to make our ascent more quickly than planned. Rather than ferrying loads to higher camps and descending to sleep, we spent only one day at each camp, allowing four days from Base Camp to summit. On June 19, Team 1 left Base Camp with Team 2 to follow a day behind. Camp II was occupied on June 21 at 18,500 feet, 1000 feet below the north col. June 22 was the first summit day. Ziobro, Bustnes, Douglas and I, led by Indians Kushal Singh Negi, Himraj Dang and Bachan Singh Pawar, left Camp II at 3:30 A.M., taking advantage of clear weather and hard snow. Although the 19,500-foot col was reached in two hours of steady walking up the 30° slope, the ascent to the summit (6387 meters, 20,956 feet) was delayed until nine A.M. by a difficult final pitch with a a 50° to 60° approach to the summit cornice. On June 23, Team 2 headed from Camp II for the summit. As the group tackled the final 1000 feet, the winds became fierce. Ashley Campion and Indian Bachan Singh Pawar climbed the final pitch unbelayed and reached the summit at eleven A.M. Rupin Dang, Joel Brenner and Jens Voges, suffering from altitude and fearing frostbite, descended. Joe Bachman and Indian D. Arun Kumar waited for the first rope to come down and then reached the summit at 11:30. On June 24, the entire expedition was again together at Base Camp.

HARRY MIDGLEY, *Dartmouth Outing Club*

Swagarohini I, South Face Attempt. An Indian team led by Arun Samant attempted the unclimbed south face of Swaragohini. Two separate attempts were made on the left ridge of the snow gully on the south face. Bad weather stopped the first try at 5500 meters while on the second attempt, Samant and two high-altitude porters reached 5900 meters. They were turned back from the summit ridge by an overhanging cornice.

HARISH KAPADIA, *Himalayan Club*

India—Himachal Pradesh
Gangchua, Kinnaur. An Indian army team led by Major R.J.S. Dhillon climbed Gangchua (6288 meters, 20,630 feet) in September.

HARISH KAPADIA, *Himalayan Club*

Sentinel, Devachan, Papsura Ascents and Tragedy. Base Camp was established by 17 New Zealanders on the west bank of the Tos Glacier at Sara on September 2. Over the next ten days, two camps were placed on the névé beneath the two principal objectives, Devachan (6200 meters, 20,342 feet) and Papsura (6451 meters, 21,560 feet). On September 9, Nick Brown and I bivouacked below the Sara Umga Pass. We climbed the impressive west ridge of Sentinel in 27 pitches. We spent a cold night on the summit before descending the eastern flank. We had believed the peak virgin but found a piton just below the summit. Roger Redmayne, Mike Peat, Chris Johnson and Robin Gurr left Camp I to attempt Papsura on September 12. They made good progress up the prominent gully to the northwest ridge. With good conditions, they moved unroped. At 6000 meters, Redmayne lost his footing and fell 400 meters to his death. He was aged 55 and an experienced climber. September 13 saw Rob McBrearty and Clinton Wadesworth ascend Devachan via a gully on its southern flank and the east ridge. All members withdrew from the mountain for two weeks while formalities were completed. Weather was unstable during a week of this time. On September 28, three parties left Camp I. Two were unsuccessful. Mike Peat, Nick Brown and I climbed the west face directly to Papsura's summit.

DONALD C. FRENCH, *New Zealand Alpine Club*

Kulu Pumori. A training expedition of the Western Himalayan Mountaineering Institute climbed this beautiful peak, which rises above Concordia in the center of the Bara Shigri Glacier. On August 15, three groups reached the peak, led by Instructor Rajeev Sharma. Seven trainees, a porter and three instructors got to the summit (6553 meters, 21,500 feet).

HARISH KAPADIA, *Himalayan Club*

Rubal Kang. Led by Dilip Kumar Bhattacharya, twelve Bengalis set up Base Camp at 4875 meters at Ratirang on July 30. Seven members and a Sherpa reached the summit (6188 meters, 20,300 feet) on August 3.

KAMAL K. GUHA, *Editor, Himavanta, India*

Karcha Parbat. An 11-member team from Calcutta was led by Satyajit Kar. They trekked from Batal and set up a transit camp at Grelu Thach and on August 30 established Base Camp at 4900 meters. Camps I, II and III were at 5180, 5640 and 5945 meters. On September 3, Sabyasachi Bose, Asim Kumar, Ghosh Chowdhury, Miss Minika Kar, Gopal Roy, and porters Alam Chand, Keshab Lal and Rup Lal reached the summit (6270 meters, 20,570 feet). This was the fourth ascent of the mountain.

KAMAL K. GUHA, *Editor, Himavanta, India*

Gangstang, South Ridge. Thirteen Bengalis were led by Amulya Sen. Base Camp was at 4490 meters. On August 17, Tushar Deb Tapadar, Goutam Ghosh,

Sandip Sarkar and Tapan Sarkar with high-altitude porters Jeevan Lal and Alam Chand Thakur left Camp II, fixed 30 meters of rope on steep rock and took a new route, the south ridge, which merged with the west ridge. On the west ridge, they found 150 meters of rope that a Japanese expedition on the west ridge had left. They got to the summit (6163 meters, 20,218 feet) at 12:30 P.M.

KAMAL K. GUHA, *Editor, Himavanta, India*

Mulkila IV. A five-member Japanese team was led by Yoshio Kondo. Masahiro Miyamoto and Indian Laxman Singh Rama reached the summit (6517 meters, 21,381 feet) on September 11.

HARISH KAPADIA, *Himalayan Club*

KR 5. A 12-member Indian expedition led by Miss Purnima Dutta climbed KR 5 (6258 meters, 20,532 feet) on July 2.

KAMAL K. GUHA, *Editor, Himavanta, India*

Phabrang. A 19-member team from the Indo-Tibetan Border Police was led by Kirpa Ram. On August 12, Company Commander Nirbhai Singh, Naiks Chholda Chhering, Harnam Singh, Ranjit Singh, Constables Raj Kishen, Vijay Kumar and Chhering Lobsang reached the summit (6172 meters, 20,250 feet).

KAMAL K. GUHA, *Editor, Himavanta, India*

India—Kashmir and Jammu

Cerro Kishtwar Attempt. Our team consisted of Andy Perkins, Brendan Murphy, David Cosford, Duncan Hornby, Jeremy Wilson, Kevin Dougherty and me. We managed the singular feat of never, before, during or after, actually being all in one place at the same time. We approached the Kishtwar from Leh via the Umasi La. Cosford, Wilson and Dougherty reached Base Camp at 4000 meters above the Haptal Glacier on September 15. Hornby, liaison officer Captain S.S. Mann and I followed a day later. Cosford had taken a fall on the walk in and Hornby had contracted hepetitis. Both left almost immediately. Perkins and Murphy arrived five days later. Murphy's sack had been lost by the airline and never found. On the 21st, we established Advance Base at 4400 meters below the northwest face of Cerro Kishtwar (6220 meters, 20,407 feet; the peak appears on some maps as Hattal. It lies 20 kilometers due east of Agysol). Perkins and Murphy attacked a direct line on this very steep and difficult face, setting out capsule-style on October 1. They spent 17 days on ground of considerable difficulty and regular spindrift avalanches. At 6100 meters, they moved onto the northeast face, only to find more very hard climbing. They managed only half a pitch before bailing out. Their food had run out that morning. Having been deprived of my original partner Hornby, I had to give up my main objective: the big ramp line on the left side of the wall. Instead, Wilson and I tried the right buttress, spending a day on it. Progress was poor. Wilson had to leave on October 1. While Perkins and Murphy were on the wall, I made a circumambulation around Cerro Kishtwar via the Muni La and Chomochar Glaciers. The peak is hard on all sides and the northeast face will give a superb mixed climb.

ANDREW MACNAE, *England*

Hagshu Attempt. Britons John Barry and John Romo set up their Base Camp on September 12 in bad weather. They attempted the peak by the north gully but bad weather defeated them. (Apparently, the first ascent of Hagshu was made by Poles several years ago.)

HARISH KAPADIA, *Himalayan Club*

Kun and Nun. An Italian expedition reached the summit of Kun (7087 meters, 23,252 feet) on August 16. Base Camp and Camps I, II and III were at 4000, 5500, 6100 and 6350 meters. The summit climbers were Santino Calegari, Battista Scanabessi, Mario Meli and Andrea Giovanzana. A French team led by Daniel Pertraud lost a member on Kun, Michela Cisotti, an Italian member of the team. She slipped and fell at about 6800 meters. The others reached the summit via the east ridge on August 17 and 18. An international expedition of police from India (Indo-Tibetan Border Police), Britain and New Zealand climbed Nun (7135 meters, 23,410 feet) by the east ridge. On August 23, New Zealander Steve Bruce, Britons Trevor Barnes, Jonathan Wakefield, Indians Pasang Lhakpa Sherpa, Nima Wangchuk, Khem Raj, Mohan Singh and two other Indians reached the summit. Germans under the leadership of Peter Metzger climbed Nun via the east ridge on September 9, 11 and 19. Nun was climbed on August 14 on the route from the west by three members of a Japanese expedition led by Hisashi Nakaoka: Yasuhiro Hashimoto, Masakatsu Tamura and Hiroaki Nakayama. An Indian team led by Harish Kumar Arya climbed Nun via the north face. Norwegians led by Aass Morten reached 7000 meters on July 19 from the west but were stopped by steep ice. A Spanish expedition led by Juan Orellana which attempted the western route of Nun also failed to get to the summit. A French group led by Michel Cormier was unsuccessful on the west ridge.

India—Eastern Karakoram

Chong Kumdan and Other Peaks. Our expedition consisted of Indians Muslim H. Contractor, Bhupesh Ashar, Vijay Kothari, Dhiren Pania, Ajay Tambe and me as leader, Britons David Wilkinson as British leader, Paul Nunn, Lindsay Griffin, John Porter, Neil McAdie and Dr. William Church, liaison officer Captain Arun Pandey and six porters. After completing preparations and

PLATE 56

Photo by Harish Kapadia

Mamostong Kangri's north face seen from Chong Kumdan group.

permissions, we left Leh on July 9 and started with 25 mules from Sasoma on the 12th. The approach to Base Camp was over the Saser La (5395 meters) and then north up the Shyok River. The Saser La was easy, but we crossed the Aq Tash and Thangman Nalas with some difficulty. Rock slabs below the Kumdam Plain were not fit for passage by loaded mules. We ferried loads and finally cajoled the mules up the Chong Kumdan Glacier moraine to within two-hours' walk of our proposed Base Camp. This we established at 5100 meters on July 18 on the only green spot beside the glacier near the junction with the Chogam I Glacier. This was as scheduled, which was remarkable as other expeditions have been delayed by bureaucratic and terrain hurdles. From July 19 to 21, loads were ferried to Base Camp. The main glacier was reconnoitered and above the junction of the Chogam II Glacier, Polu Camp was set up at 5450 meters. Contractor and I explored the western head of the glacier towards Nup Col (6250 meters). Porter and McAdie went up the Chogam III Glacier and explored the northwestern approaches to Chong Kumdam I. The early climbs completed the necessary knowledge of the region. Camps I and II were placed at 5900 and 6300 meters. The following first ascents were made. *Chong Kumdan V* (c. 6520 meters, 21,391 feet): This peak lies on the southeast ridge of Chong Kumdan I and rose above Base Camp. Wilkinson, Church, Griffin, Nunn, Porter, McAdie, Tambe and Ashar reached the summit in a two-day push on July 21 and 22 via the southeast ridge on ice and mixed terrain. *Chong Kumdan IV* (c. 6520 meters, 21,391 feet): Wilkinson and Church traversed the Chogam I Glacier to the foot of the peak on the northeast ridge of Chong Kumdan I on steep ice and mixed ground. They reached the summit on July 26. *Kichik Kumdan* (c. 6640 meters, 21,785 feet): This dome-shaped peak had a surprise in store for us. The peak was of hard ice and the north side had a continuous cornice. Nunn and Griffin climbed the steep south face to the east ridge on July 30. Keeping a few meters below the cornice, they had to traverse on ice constantly. After reaching the summit, they continued to the west but the difficulties did not cease. After six hours of ice work they got to the west col and returned to their bivouac exhausted. A second attempt on August 4 failed. *Chang Col* (c. 6500 meters, 21,326 feet): Contractor, porters Pasang Bodh and Tikam Ram, and I reached this high col between Chong Kumdan I and Kichik Kumdam on August 2. *Chong Kumdan I* (7071 meters, 23,200 feet): Wilkinson, Church, Porter and McAdie climbed this prized peak on August 4. It had been reconnoitered from all angles and finally the four were established near the Chang Col bergschrund. They left at three A.M. to climb the west face with head-torches in extreme cold. After sustained difficulties on ice and hard snow, they turned north onto a ramp where they had to guard against loose stones. They reached the northwest ridge at 6800 meters and climbed the ridge unroped to get to the top at ten A.M. The peak was later attempted on August 14 by Griffin and Nunn, but sickness of the latter stopped them at 6640 meters. The North and Central Kumdam Glaciers are major branches of the main glacier and lead to the northeast and northwest respectively. There was no history of visitors until we entered from August 8 to 16. We were stopped by two days of bad weather at Camp I North. Finally, from

Camp II North, *Laknis* (6235 meters, 20,456 feet) was climbed by the long southeast ridge. After many ups and downs and false summits, Wilkinson, Church, McAdie, Ashar, Contractor, Tambe, porter Pasang Bodh and I completed the ascent on the exposed ridge of rotten rock on August 12. *Chong Ibex Col* (c. 6000 meters, 19,685 feet): At the head of the Central Kumdan Glacier on the north ridge coming from Chong Kumdan II, it links the Kumdan Glacier system with the Terong Glacier, which we had explored in 1985. Ashar, Contractor and Pasang Bodh reached it on August 14 from Camp II North. *Kumdan Terong* (6456 meters, 21,182 feet): Situated on the watershed between the Central and North Kumdan Glaciers, it overlooks the Terong and Siachen Glacier peaks. Approaching from the south, Ashar, Contractor and Pasang Bodh reached the summit on August 15. *Landay* (6170 meters, 20,243 feet): On August 16, the last first ascent was made by McAdie and Church. They crossed the broken main glacier from Base Camp to a narrow valley to the southeast. The next day, they climbed the steep north ridge. *Chong Kumdan III* (6670 meters, 21,884 feet) was attempted unsuccessfully by Contractor, Pasang Bodh and Tikam Ram on August 3. From the col between the peak and Kichik Kumdan, they tried a route from the north first and then the northeast ridge. Loose powdery snow and two crevasses made the ascent too dangerous. Three second ascents were also made on the northern ridge of the Chogam I Glacier. All had been climbed by us in 1989. *Chogam* (6250 meters, 20,506 feet): August 4 by Kothari, Pania and porters Yog Raj Buruwa and Prakash Chand; August 7 by Captain Pandey, Tambe and Ashar; August 15 by Wilkinson, porters Tikam Ram Thakur, Tikam Ram and me; August 16 by Griffin. *Stos* (6005 meters, 19,702 feet): August 7 by Ashar: August 16 by Griffin. *Skyang* (5770 meters, 18,931 feet): August 17 by Wilkinson, Nunn, Griffin, porters Prakash Chand and Tikam Ram and me. By August 24, we were at Sasoma and were back at Leh on August 26. Excellent cooperation and friendship between all team members and porters made this the happiest international expedition in recent years.

HARISH KAPADIA, *Himalayan Club*

Saser Kangri II, West Peak. The second ascent of the west peak of Saser Kangri II (7518 meters, 24,766 feet) was made by an Indian expedition led by Heera Lohia. They climbed the west face, the first ascent having been made in 1985 by the northwest ridge. On October 6, Wangchuk Gyalchen and Pasang Sherpa reached the summit. On an earlier attempt, on October 1, Fateh Chand, an instructor at the Western Himalayan Mountaineering Institute in Manali, was taken ill with high-altitude sickness and died.

HARISH KAPADIA, *Himalayan Club*

Pakistan

K2. This remarkable climb made by Pierre Beghin and Christophe Profit, which began on the Pakistani side and continued up the northwest ridge and north face in China, is described in a complete article in this *Journal*.

K2 Attempt. Our expedition was composed of Bernd Arnold, Roland Mattle, Thomas Mügge, Steffen Otto, Dr. Walter Treibel, Thomas Türpe, and me as leader. We attempted the Abruzzi Ridge after arriving at Base Camp on May 23. The weather was bad in the whole Karakoram from May to July. Of the 58 days we had after getting to Base Camp, there were only 15 days of good weather. We reached the shoulder of K2 first on June 15 and left supplies for a later summit attempt. We were back on the shoulder on July 7 but had to leave immediately because the large amount of snow made avalanche danger too great. The mountain never gave us a chance.

SIGI HUPFAUER, *Deutscher Alpenverein*

K2 Attempt. Gary Ball and I received permission to climb the Abruzzi Spur of K2 in May due to the late cancellation of another team. We arrived at Base Camp in early July and established just one fixed camp at 6800 meters above House's Chimney. During the climb we benefited from fixed rope left by Sigi Hupfauer's German expedition, but also climbed on rope in the Black Pyramid which *we* had fixed three years earlier! The 1990 clean-up expedition, which did a marvelous job of tidying up Base Camp, did little to improve our safety as we encountered many ropes and anchors which had simply been cut and not removed. We climbed alone on the route for five weeks, indeed a rare pleasure despite the usual intermittent K2 weather. After bivouacking at 7300 and 7500 meters, we reached the edge of the shoulder at 7600 meters on August 15 but retreated in deep snow, concerned about the threat of avalanches from the unstable snow pack.

ROBERT HALL, *New Zealand Alpine Club*

Masherbrum Attempt. A British expedition led by David Hamilton attempted to climb Masherbrum but apparently was unsuccessful. Details are still missing.

Masherbrum II. Masherbrum II (c. 7200 meters, 23,622 feet) had previously been climbed only once, by Italians in 1988 on the southeast ridge. After approaching from Hushe, we established Base Camp on August 31 at the junction of the Bolux and Masherbrum Glaciers. We headed up the glacier until it bifurcated at a grassy knoll. We climbed the knoll and a rock valley and returned to the glacier where it dog-legged east into a wide couloir. On the top of the couloir in a rocky col, we placed Camp I at 5200 meters. We traversed east for 200 meters to an icy couloir where we were threatened by rockfall. The couloir widened into an icefield, which we climbed to the rim of a basin at 6000 meters. A 400-meter traverse due south brought us to a heavily corniced ridge which led to the foot of the summit pyramid, where we placed Camp II at 6400 meters. A shallow rib took us past two séracs on our right. We then climbed

PLATE 58

Photo by Mark Miller

Summit pitch on MASHERBRUM II.

directly to the summit, arriving on the east ridge, 50 meters from the top. A huge, overhanging mushroom surrounded the summit. This we surmounted with the use of aid. On September 11, Victor Radvills, Ewen Todd, Rob Spencer, Dave Little, Andy Mayers, Norman Croucher and I reached the summit, followed the next day by Argentine Miguel Helf, Graham Lipp and Ian Swarbrick. On the 12th, Dr. Christine Patterson took a 200-foot fall in the couloir above Camp I and suffered severe bruising. Nonetheless, on the 13th she accompanied Duncan Talbot, Mark Neave and Terressa Booth to the summit.

MARK MILLER, *Out There Trekking, England*

Great Trango Tower, Northeast Buttress. The northeast buttress of the Great Trango Tower was successfully climbed by Norwegians Hans Christian Doseth and Finn Doeli in 1984 but tragically they both died during the descent. Despite various tries, the climb was not repeated until the Japanese made a variant in 1990. Four Spaniards, Koldo Bayona, Miguel Berasaluce, Adolfo Madinabeitia and Antonio Miranda, approached the region, the first two having the Nameless Tower in mind and the latter two, the Norwegian route on the Great Trango Tower. The road is now complete as far as Askole, but in late July, it was cut and they had to complete the trek to Askole on foot with porters. From there, they continued on to establish Base Camp at 4000 meters on the Dunge Glacier. They carried loads up the threatened corridor to Camp I at the foot of both towers. Bayona decided to leave the expedition and so all three turned to the Great Trango Tower. On August 15, they began their attack on the buttress. After climbing ten pitches and 450 meters, they established Camp II. From there, they followed the 11-pitch Japanese variant. The cracks, dihedrals and vertical rock were as often as not encased in ice. On August 20 at the 18th pitch, the weather turned sour but they sat out a five-day storm in Camp II. By August 28, they had climbed 28 pitches and were 950 meters above the base of the buttress. They climbed another 150 meters and established Camp III, just below the formidable summit tower. A storm on September 1 again coated the tower with ice. They began the climb of the summit tower on the 2nd, finding extraordinarily difficult rock work. Despite leader falls and such, they persisted. Finally, on September 10, they completed the 41st pitch and arrived on the summit after 28 days on the mountain. The descent took them two more days. A full report with photos, map and topo appears on pages 35 to 45 of *Desnivel,* N° 68, December, 1991.

Broad Peak. Again this year there were a number of expeditions to Broad Peak (8047 meters, 26,400 feet), only three of which were successful. A Japanese expedition from Tokyo University led by Keijiro Hayasaka repeated the standard route. Leader Hayasaka, Toshimasa Yawata, Isao Ogasawara, Masanori Sato and Taro Tanikawa climbed to the summit on July 12. A 20-member international commercial expedition, organized by Himalayan Kingdoms and led by Stephen Bell, was formed of 13 Britons, two Finns, two

Venezuelans, a Spaniard, a Norwegian and an American. Having followed the standard route, guides Alan Hinkes and Robin Beadle and client Ramón Blanco, a Spaniard resident in Venezuela, reached the top on July 16. This was Hinkes' fourth 8000er, thus equalling the British record set by Doug Scott in 1983. At 58 years, Blanco becomes the oldest person to climb Broad Peak. Another Japanese expedition, led by Yasuyuki Kawashima, also managed to place Mrs. Taeko Nagao, Hirofumi Konishi, Tetsuaki Yoshimura, Masami Abe, and Yasushi Yamanoi on the summit on July 30. On the way back, Yamanoi and Atsushi Saito attempted the Trango Cathedral, but they had to give up low on the face because of Saito's mountain sickness. A joint expedition composed of 18 German doctors and six members of the Pakistani army, under the leadership of Dr. Thomas Alfred, failed at 7000 meters. A Japanese group of two men and two women led by Haruyuki Endo could not get higher than 7400 meters. A six-member French expedition was led by Jean-Marc Robert. Their attempt ended on August 15 when the leader and another member, with three Spaniards of the party led by Ramón Rodríguez, reached 7450 meters. A Spanish expedition, composed of leader Ramón Rodríguez, Pablo González, Ana and Jorge Sese, Juanjo Garro and Areceli Segarra, failed to repeat the standard route due to excessive snow. Their high point was reached on August 15 by Rodríguez, González, Ana Sese with two of the above-mentioned French. After losing a porter who fell into a crevasse while crossing the Ghandagoro La during the approach from Hushe, a nine-member Mexican expedition was the last group active on the Godwin Austen Glacier this season. They were led by Ricardo Torres, the first Mexican atop Everest. By August 26, they had set all camps to 7400 meters and were ready for the final assault. Unfortunately, the continuous bad weather during the first half of September prevented their getting to the summit.

XAVIER EGUSKITZA, *Pyrenaica, Bilbao, Spain*

Gasherbrum I (Hidden Peak) Attempt. A strong French group led by Jean-Jacques Prieur had originally planned an attempt on the southwest face of Gasherbrum I, a new line to the left of the Polish spur of 1983. Due to scarce snowfall in the spring, the access to the route was very slippery and they switched to the Yugoslav route on the west ridge. Continuous changeable weather with high winds from the west stopped the attempt at the end of July at 7400 meters.

XAVIER EGUSKITZA, *Pyrenaica, Bilbao, Spain*

Gasherbrum I Tragedy Correction. On page 261 of *AAJ 1991*, it stated that Grañó and Ibáñez last reported at 7400 meters. Their radio report was actually from 7900 meters.

Gasherbrum II. As in previous years, a large number of expeditions had Gasherbrum II (8035 meters, 26,362 feet) as their objective. Only three of them reached the summit. A six-member Swiss expedition was led by Nicole Niquille, the only woman of the group. Having followed the standard route, on June 28 Philippe Menu, Félix Thurlir, Christian Haymoz and Pakistani porter Ali Mohammad reached the summit. During the descent, Menu and Thurlir had a fall toward the Chinese slope, fortunately without serious consequences. A South Korean expedition succeeded in placing four on the summit by the standard route. On July 19, climbing-leader Kim Chang-Seon, ahead of his companions, got to the summit alone, followed a few hours later by three others. A second South Korean expedition, led by Han Sang-Kook, also made the ascent. On July 20, the summit was reached by five climbers. An eight-member American expedition was led by David Mention, who had to return home in the early stages of the expedition. The rest of the team left Base Camp on June 23 after two of their members had reached the site of Camp IV at 7500 meters. An eight-member international expedition led by Adrian Burgess (a Briton living in the United States) included his American sister-in-law Sarah Rogers, Briton Paul Moores, Swedes Mikael Reuterswärd, Oscar Kihlborg and Johan Lagne, and Catalan women Magda Nos and Mónica Verge. During the early stages of the attempt, Moores fell into a deep crevasse in the icefall and was held precariously at the end of the rope by Burgess; he suffered injuries to his leg. Later, on June 18, Kihlborg and Lagne reached a high point of 7800 meters. On June 28, Moores and an Austrian of Studer's group managed to get to 7700 meters. The expedition was left first by the three Swedes and then by Moores and Mónica Verge. A last attempt by Burgess ended at Camp II. The three remaining climbers left Base Camp on July 15. An Austrian expedition led by Wilfried Studer had to give up its attempt on July 13. As mentioned above, one of its members reached 7700 meters with Moores. Four Americans led by Dave McNally got to Camp III at 7000 meters. Eleven French climbers led by Jean-Pierre Fedèle had to give up their attempt at 7500 meters on August 18 because of bad weather conditions they had encountered since their arrival at Base Camp a month earlier.

XAVIER EGUSKITZA, *Pyrenaica, Bilbao, Spain*

Latok I North Ridge Attempt. Our objective was to make the first ascent, alpine-style, of the 2500-meter-high north ridge of Latok I (7145 meters, 23,452 feet), so nearly climbed in 1978 by Jim Donini, Mike Kennedy, Jeff Lowe and George Lowe. (See *AAJ, 1979,* pages 24-28.) We were New Zealander Andrew MacFarlane, Britons Carol McDermott, Andrew MacNae and me. We set up Base Camp at the junction of the Panmah and Choktoi Glaciers on June 5. After acclimatization trips and sitting out bad weather, we eventually set foot on Latok on July 10. The crest of the lower buttress was crowned with snow mushrooms and after a day of struggling up rotten slabs, we elected to retreat and tackle the ice gully just east of the buttress in order to expedite our objective of a rapid ascent. Unfortunately, during the retreat, MacFarlane was struck by a freak rockfall and we had to return with him to Base Camp. A storm began the next morning. We were back on the mountain on the 17th. At 5150 meters, MacNae became ill and so we descended to Advance Base. After a day's rest, McDermott and I returned to the mountain. By midday, we had topped out of the ice gully above the rock buttress but because of snow conditions had to stop for the night on a snow mushroom at 5350 meters. The next day, progress up the snowfield was made possible by cloud cover, We bivouacked in ice buckets at 5880 meters at the start of the main central buttress. By two A.M. a fresh storm had engulfed us. We made the decision to retreat. Fifteen hours and 32 abseils later, we reached safety. On July 25, we vacated Base Camp.

DAVID K. WILLS, *North London Mountaineering Club*

Snow Lake Peaks and Hispar Sar. New Zealanders Dave Bamford, Matt Comeskey, John Cocks, John Wild and I with liaison officer Major Arif Khan spent July and August climbing in the Lukpe Lawo (Snow Lake) region during a Biafo-Hispar traverse. We placed Base Camp at 4780 meters at the foot of the rock spur on the northern side of the junction of the Sim Gang Glacier with Lukpe Lawo. The voracious bears did visit us but proved more of an amusement than an inconvenience. This does, however, appear to be their furthest recorded incursion up the Biafo. From a camp at the northwestern head of the Sim Gang, an unnamed peak of about 5950 meters was climbed and another of about 6000 meters turned us back because of deep loose snow. We returned to Base Camp via a col leading to the most easterly feeder of Lukpe Lawo. We crossed the Khurdopin Pass and from a camp in the upper névé of the East Khurdopin Glacier all of us climbed via its southeast spur the highest and most elegant peak. It is about 6500 meters high and the height of 6858 meters on the new SFAR map is incorrect. On the return to Base Camp, a peak of about 5990 meters immediately south of Tahu Rutum was climbed from the Tahu Rutum Glacier. We visited a number of side glaciers and minor peaks and climbed Workman Peak (c. 5885 meters) by the west ridge. Skis were used to access all peaks. We then crossed into the upper Hispar and failed in two attempts to climb virgin Hispar Sar (c. 6400 meters). The first, via the north face from the Khani Basa Glacier, was turned back at 5850 meters by slab avalanche conditions. The second, from the glacier immediately down valley from the Khani Basa, was frustrated by a dangerous icefall. We continued down the Hispar to partake of the pleasures of Hunza.

JOHN NANKERVIS, *New Zealand Alpine Club*

Makrong Chhish Attempt and Tragedy. Steve Hillen, Mike Penlington, Dave Tyson and I traveled on June 16 with three jeeps along the Karakoram Highway from Gilgit to Nagar. At Nagar, 30 porters were hired. The jeeps continued to Huru, the furthest jeepable settlement along the road to Hispar. The walk-in began the following day and went past Hispar and on the north side of the Hispar Glacier to Bitenmal, where Base Camp was established in sight of unclimbed

Makrong Chhish (6608 meters, 21,680 feet). The walk-in took three days. With liaison officer Major Farooq, we established Advance Base in an ablation valley of the East Makrong Glacier, a tributary of the Hispar Glacier. We began the first attempt on July 27. The planned route was on the south face via a large gully leading to the east ridge about 300 meters below the summit. We made two bivouacs, the second just below our high point at 6000 meters. We abandoned the attempt as we were not sufficiently acclimatized. During a period of bad weather, Camp I was established at 4800 meters. The final attempt began on July 8, following the original route. We had some difficulty with crevasses which had opened up since the previous attempt. At eleven A.M. on July 9, we dug ledges at the previous high point in order to rest until evening. Shortly afterwards, a large avalanche swept down the gully over the ledges. No one was injured but we decided to abandon the attempt. At five P.M. on the descent whilst I was abseiling over two crevasses, a snow stake pulled out and I slid some 60 feet before stopping. This left Steve Hillen above the crevasses without a rope. He frontpointed down the slope to the second crevasse, which he jumped across, but he lost his footing and started to slide. Dave Tyson, who was below him, tried to stop him, but they became entangled and both slid down an avalanche runnel and over an ice cliff to their deaths. Penlington and I recovered the bodies and then arranged for an army helicopter to retrieve them and for them to be flown back to the United Kingdom.

DAVID LISTER, *Loughborough University Mountaineering Club, U.K.*

Hanispur. Our expedition was composed of Duncan Tunstall, Wiz Pasteur, Angus Atkinson and me. We had hoped to cross the Karakoram from Skardu to Shimhal via Snow Lake, ascending by the little known Nobande Sobande Glacier and descending by the Virjerab Glacier. With the help of nine porters, we established Base Camp on the Nobande Sobande Glacier at 4100 meters on July 16. The porters left. On the 21st, we set up Advance Base at 4600 meters seven miles up the glacier. Atkinson and Wiz Pasteur set off on July 29 and bivouacked at 5400 meters on the west ridge of Hanispur (5900+ meters, 19,357+ feet). The next morning they completed the ascent along a technically not difficult but long ridge with many false summits. On August 3 and 6, they made the ascents of two other smaller peaks. Meanwhile, Tunstall and I skied over the Skam La to Snow Lake. On August 8, we skied up the West Sim Gang Glacier to the Virjirab Pass, which we climbed by an easy 70° snow ramp. This is almost certainly the first ascent of the pass. We got only glimpses of the Virjerab Glacier because of poor visibility. We did not continue on to Shimshal but returned to Askole and Skardu by the Biafo Glacier.

CHRIS PASTEUR, *Scottish Mountaineering Club*

Diran. Two successful climbs of Diran (7257 meters, 23,810 feet) have been reported in 1991. An Italian expedition was led by Martino Moretti. Moretti, D. Deianna and P. Paglino took six days to ascend the north ridge. The ridge rises 2200 meters and is five kilometers long. Much of the ice is of 60° and some is vertical. Meanwhile, G. and T. Corbellini, M. Melacarne, D. Saettone and A. Zucchetti climbed the normal west ridge. A Spanish team under the leadership of Pere Gelis was also successful, but details are lacking. A French expedition led by Philippe Allibert failed.

Diran Attempt. Pole Aleksander Lwow, Americans Randy Rhodes, Ken Nolan, Steve Truitt, Clay McGann and I as leader attempted the standard west-ridge route on Diran. Extreme avalanche danger on the north face which led to the ridge prevented our climbing it. We had only three weeks for the ascent and ran out of time. We established Camp I at 5800 meters on the north face. We then climbed to 5950 meters but snow conditions prevented further progress. The face was a nightmare of avalanche conditions because of its northern exposure, huge size and ice séracs despite an angle of only 40°.

THOR KIESER

Distaghil Sar Attempt. Our members were Jean-François Lassalle, Jean-Claude Lefèbvre, Christophe Lefèbvre, Christian Mathieu and I as leader. We had hoped to climb Distaghil Sar (7885 meters, 25,870 feet) by its south face. We approached from Hispar via the Hispar and Distaghil Sar Glaciers. Base Camp and Camp I at 4200 and 4700 meters were set up on June 12 and 15. The latter was an hour from the foot of the face, reached after a very crevassed section. Much snow fell from June 17 to 24. A depot we had placed at 5800 meters was carried away by an avalanche on June 27. That was our high point. There are many dangerous séracs on the face and objective danger.

JEAN-LUC GINHOUX, *Club Alpin Français*

Momhil Sar Attempt. Our expedition, which attempted to climb Momhil Sar (7342 meters, 24,088 feet) by the northeast ridge, was composed of Michael Wärthl, leader, Volker Kron, Uli Schneider, Heiner Dehn, Dr. Alexandra Rothkopf, and me. We left Passu with 36 porters on June 29 and got to Base Camp at 4000 meters on July 2. We established Camps I and II at 4800 and 5600 meters on July 4 and 9. The route to Camp I was mostly easy glacier-walking. On the way to Camp II we fixed 150 meters of rope on easy mixed ice-and-rock climbing. On July 17, we reached a highpoint of 6200 meters. The attempt was unsuccessful because of bad weather conditions the whole time and avalanche danger.

TOM DAUER, *Deutscher Alpenverein*

Trivor Ascent and Momhil Sar Attempt. Masahiko Miyoshi, Morikatsu Hashimoto, Hidetoshi Nakama, Masahiro Izawa, Atsushi Endo, Hiroshi Kobayashi, Nabuaki Tuchizawa and I as leader reached Base Camp at 4300 meters on the Momhil Glacier on July 27. We continued up the broken glacier to Advance

Base at 4880 meters on a rocky hill. We then climbed the east ridge of Momhil Sar. We were on rotten rock until just below Camp I at 5480 meters, which we pitched on August 3. The route then changes to a 35° corniced snow ridge, which we followed to a snow shoulder, placing Camp II at 6050 meters on August 12. We continued up to the shoulder of Momhil Sar on gradually steepening, icy slopes. We pitched Camp III on August 15 at 6730 meters, where the Trivor and Momhil Sar ridges join. We descended toward Trivor to a col, over P 6880 and to another col, where we placed Camp IV. There were technical difficulties beyond Camp IV. Camp V was established at 6880 meters on August 29. Endo and I left camp at 3:30 A.M. the next morning and reached the summit of Trivor (7728 meters, 25,325 feet) at 1:50 P.M. despite unstable weather, completing the second ascent. [The first ascent had been made by Briton Wilfred Noyce and American Jack Sadler in 1960.] On September 5, Miyoshi, Hashimoto, Izawa, Endo, Tuchizawa and I climbed along the steep ridge toward Momhil Sar (7343 meters, 24,092 feet), but we were stopped by a steep ice gully at 7000 meters.

TOSHIFUMI ONUKI, *Waseda University Alpine Club, Japan*

Momhil Sar Attempt. Our expedition had as members Josep Cla, Joan Córdoba, Joaqim Cufí, Lluis Julià, Dr. Carlos de Mendoza, Francesc Xavier Miquel, Luis Olivas, Joan Ribas, Jordi Tosas and me as leader. We had hoped to climb Momhil Sar (7343 meters, 24,092 feet) by its east ridge. We established Base Camp at 4650 meters on the moraine of the Gharesa (Trivor) Glacier on August 5 after an approach of four days. We installed Camps I, II and III at 5150, 5650 and 6350 meters. We hoped to continue alpine-style with three climbers supported by four others. However, two suffered from the altitude and had to be helped down. We placed Camp IV at 6520 meters. On August 18, bad weather, deep snow and avalanche danger forced us to give up at 6700 meters.

SALVADOR BOIX, *Centre de Càlul Girona, Spain*

Bojohaghur Duanasir Attempt. Our expedition was composed of Austrian Günther Steinmair, American Dr. Michael Henry and Germans Hans Feith and me. Bojohaghur Duanasir (7329 meters, 24,045 feet) had first been climbed by Japanese by its west face and southwest ridge in 1984 and was attempted by British who got to 6800 meters by the south face and southwest ridge also in 1984. We traveled by bus from Gilgit to Karimabad. On June 12 we got to Base Camp on the Ultar Glacier at 4000 meters after a two-day approach with 30 porters. We had trouble in paying the porters as they demanded too much; we finally resolved this. The south face is very dangerous objectively with séracs and ice avalanches. We followed the British route on the left of the face. On June 20, we placed Camp I at 5000 meters after fixing rope on ice up to 90° and UIAA rock of VI- where there was rockfall and falling ice. As I rappelled, a rock the size of a football struck me in the head and left forearm, which put me out of action. My friends continued to the crest of the southwest ridge at 6000 meters, where they placed Camp II. Continuous bad weather and objective dangers compelled them to give up the attempt in mid July. This mountain has no safe route.

EDI BIRNBACHER, *Deutscher Alpenverein*

Ultar (Bojohagur Duanasir II) Attempt and Hunza Peak Ascent. Our expedition composed of Britons Victor Saunders, Crag Jones, Julian Freeman-Attwood and me and American Steve Sustad attempted to climb Ultar I (7388 meters, 24,240 feet) in July. Saunders and Sustad explored a remote valley difficult of access on the southeast side of Ultar. They decided against the southeast spur, finding that the conditions were not suitable. Instead they made an attempt slanting from left to right across the southeast face, heading for the upper section of the east ridge. After three days of climbing, a broken crampon and a broken ice axe forced a retreat. At the same time Jones and I attempted a line on the south ridge that the Japanese had tried in 1990. We climbed alpine-style and did not fix ropes or set up camps as the Japanese had. After five days, we reached a high point of 6500 meters on July 31 at the base of the summit buttress. Bad weather forced a retreat. Prior to this, Jones and I made the first ascent of Hunza Peak (6200 meters, 20,342 feet). We ascended from the Hasanabad Glacier to the col between Hunza Peak and Bublimoting and climbed the southwest ridge from there. We took three days for the climb. We also climbed Bublimoting from the col. This mountain had been climbed ten days earlier by a Swedish team.

MICK FOWLER, *Alpine Climbing Group*

Ultar (Bojohagur Duanasir II) Attempt and Tragedy. Our nine-member expedition was led by my husband Tsuneo Hasegawa, whose expedition last year attempted unclimbed Ultar (Bojohagur Duanasir II; 7388 meters, 24,240 feet) but had to give up 300 meters from the summit. We again in 1991 attempted the south ridge. Base Camp was established at 3300 meters on August 26 by Kiyotaka Hoshino, Hiroshi Yamaguchi, Mitsuru Shiraishi, Narimitsu Kawasaki, Tsutomu Sugisaka and me. We placed Camp I at 4900 meters on the 26th. My husband Tsuneo Hasegawa, Osamu Tagaya, Kenji Ota and liaison officer Nazir Sabir arrived at Base Camp on September 12. Above Camp I, the route entered a wide gully. Despite frequent rockfall and avalanches, we established Camp II on the ridge on September 15 at 5450 meters. We followed the ridge to 5900 meters and climbed steep ice above to place Camp III at 6000 meters on October 3. On October 6, my husband and Hoshino climbed to the site of Camp IV at 6500 meters and returned to Camp I for a rest. On the 10th, they started back up for Camp II and were overwhelmed by an avalanche and swept from 5350 to 4000 meters to their deaths. The expedition was abandoned.

(MRS.) MASAMI HASEGAWA, *U-Tan Club, Japan*

Sani Pakhush. German Hubert Bleicher led five Germans who climbed Sani Pakhush (6885 meters, 22,590 feet). Details are lacking.

Tirich Mir, Norwegian Attempt. Forty-one years after their compatriot, Arne Naess, made the first ascent of Tirich Mir, Jon Gangdal, leader, Halfdan Egeberg, Torstein Skacke, Sven Gangdal, Erik Johannessen and Erik Hankø hoped to traverse both peaks: Tirich Mir East (7692 meters, 25,236 feet) and Tirich Mir Main (7706 meters, 25,283 feet). Base Camp and Camps I, II, III, IV and V were placed at 3300, 4300, 4800, 5200, 6000 and 6900 meters. Unfortunately, bad weather frustrated their hopes. On July 12, the Gangdal brothers set out towards the top of Tirich Mir East but fierce winds stopped them on the 7620-meter foresummit. They had no political or security problems and recommend this beautiful area to other climbers.

JÓZEF NYKA, *Editor, Taternik, Poland*

Tirich Mir. Seven members of the Kyoto section of the Japanese Alpine Club led by Tateshi Sudoh joined with six Pakistanis. They placed Base Camp on the Upper Tirich Glacier and Camps I, II, III and IV at 4800, 5800, 6400, 6800 and 7300 meters on July 12, 16, 29, August 1 and 4. The climbing effort was interrupted on August 5 when they had to evacuate a Pakistani who had fallen. On August 10, Yoshiaki Horie and Osamu Funao were driven back by high winds. On the 14th, leader Sudoh, Kensuke Matsuda and Kiyoaki Miyagawa made an unsuccessful attempt but the next day Sudoh and Miyagawa were able to reach the summit (7706 meters, 25,283 feet).

Nanga Parbat, Rupal Face, Winter Attempt 1990-91. Our joint Anglo-Polish expedition flew to Gilgit on November 24, 1990. We were leader Maciej Berbeka, Jacek Berbeka, Andrzej Osika, Andrzej Samolewicz, Wojciech Szczerba, Zbigniew Terlikowski, Dr. Krzysztof Witkowski, *Poles*, and Sean Smith, Jon Tinker, Simon Yates and I, *British*. We hoped to make the first winter ascent of the direct Rupal route, first climbed in 1970 by the Messner brothers, Felix Kuen and Peter Scholz. Despite several attempts, no one has made a second ascent of the route. We arrived at the "Polish Base Camp" in the Rupal valley on November 29. With fine weather and experience from the 1988-9 Polish attempt made good progress. On December 1, we established Camp I at 4700 meters below the Wieland Rocks and fixed rope to a temporary camp at 5400 meters. We set that camp up on December 5. Soon the weather broke and progress to Camp II above the Wieland Icefield was slow. However, the climbing conditions were generally good with hard ice between 5500 and 6100 meters. On December 19, Base Camp was flattened by a pressure wave from an avalanche high on the Rupal Wall. Fortunately no one was hurt. We finally established Camp II in an ice cave at 6100 meters at the site of Camp II of the 1970 climb. The weather was then very unsettled and several feet of snow fell, confining all to Base Camp until January 3, 1991. We renewed our efforts to push the route to Camp III at 6800 meters below the Merkl Icefield. Repeated pairs extended the way up the Welzenbach Spur, struggling with increasingly high winds and deteriorating weather. By January 13, we ground to a halt at 6600 meters and made a general retreat from the mountain. With 14 days left of our planned 60 days at Base Camp, Maciej Berbeka suggested a radical change of plan. On January 17, we switched to the Schell route on the left side of the Rupal flank, planning to climb to 7000 meters alpine-style before making a summit bid. The Berbekas, Osika and Tinker climbed to 6600 meters, leaving 200 meters of fixed rope on the crux rock buttress, before descending in high winds. A summit attempt was not possible in the continuous bad weather and so Base Camp was quit on January 27. The journey back to Gilgit took six days as roads were blocked by rock slides. Whilst in Gilgit, we experienced an earthquake of 6 on the Richter scale which killed several hundred people in northern Pakistan and Afghanistan.

NIKOLA KEKUS, *Alpine Climbing Group*

Nanga Parbat, Ski Attempt. In 1990, under the sponsorship of the Deutsches Institut für Auslandsforschung, Josef and Marianne Walter reached the Diamir Col on skis but were unable to continue because of snow conditions. (*AAJ, 1991,* pp. 276-7.) The idea intrigued Peter Wörgotter, and so he and Austrian companions Christian Bogensperger, Fritz Hörhager, Herbert Rainer, Max Schneider and Dr. Joachim Zeitz arrived at Base Camp at 4000 meters below the Diamir Glacier, accompanied by 54 low-altitude porters. On June 24, Wörgötter, Bogensperger and Rainer climbed to 5000 meters on the Diamir Glacier, to where the 1961 and 1962 German expeditions had placed their Camp I. They traversed the glacier below the Sigi Löw Ice Couloir and on to 5600 meters where they placed their Camp I. After a long rest, the three climbed a steep gully after sundown and continued up a steep slope on the glacier where they set up a tent for Camp II at 5950 meters. Finally, the next day they found a way through the 150-meter-high step. After ascending a 30-meter-high ice cliff, they made a supply dump at 6170 meters. They skied back to Base Camp in only two hours. On July 4, after some bad weather, the same three climbed to Camp II and the next day to the supply depot. Clouds forced them back to Camp II, where they found Hörhager and Schneider. They all descended. On July 9, they returned to Camp II and the day after established Camp III at 6350 meters. On July 11, they ascended an 800-meter-high avalanche track since the snow beside it was knee-deep. They set up Camp IV at 7000 meters below a rock rib. Rainer climbed another 400 meters solo and left supplies to the north of the north summit. Bogensperger spent an uneasy night. Because of his condition, on the 12th they decided to descend. The snow in the avalanche track was full of humps and ridges; the snow beside it was heavy and covered with breakable crust. Eventually they reached Camp II. On June 13, they evacuated Camp II and descended to Base Camp. Depite bad weather, they had managed to open a new route which led nearly to the Bazhin Basin and the summit pyramid.

KARL MARIA HERRLIGKOFFER, *Deutsches Institut für Auslandsforschung**

---

*Dr. Herrligkoffer died on September 11, 1991. In his long career, he had led more than 20 mountain expeditions, particularly to Nanga Parbat. Well remembered are the first ascent by Hermann Buhl and the climb by Reinhold and Günther Messner, which ended with such dissension. He was also the author of many excellent mountain books.

Nanga Parbat, Diamir Face, Kinshofer Route, First British Ascent. Ours was a small expedition consisting of Ghazala Ahmad, my wife and expedition doctor, David Walsh and me. Also with us were Kevin Higgins and Ian Hilton during our acclimatization. We arrived at Base Camp on June 27 and almost immediately were deserted by our liaison officer, Najeeb Ahmad Khan. Najeeb had similarly abandoned a German expedition in 1989. Fortunately Ghazala's command of Urdu meant we were not hindered by his disappearance. We made several training climbs on the surrounding peaks. After three weeks at the foot of Nanga Parbat, on July 15 Walsh, Ghazala and I moved up to Advance Base at 5100 meters. On the 16th, Walsh and I set out alpine-style with six days of food and fuel and a bare minimum of equipment. We bivouacked at 5900 meters. We passed Koreans on the second morning at a camp littered with trash. On Day 3, we climbed through a snowstorm on ice as steep as the roof of a church. On Day 4, we made a long curving, sickle-shaped traverse which brought us onto easier ground in the Bazhin Basin. On the evening of Day 5, we had reached the base of the summit trapezoid at 7200 meters. Our previous bivouacs had been at 6150, 6400 and 6800 meters. On July 21, we set out at four A.M. enveloped in cloud. We plodded on endlessly. At noon the clouds parted to reveal the mouth of a narrow snow-filled gully cutting the final rocks and we could continue slow upward progress. Finally, at 4:30 P.M. we were on the summit, six days after crossing the bergschrund. In a little over two hours in the grey twilight we collapsed into our tent at the last bivouac site. We descended during the next days to 6900 meters, then to 6000 meters and arrived at Base Camp on July 24.

ROGER MEAR, *Alpine Climbing Group*

Nanga Parbat Attempts. There were several unsuccessful attempts on Nanga Parbat in 1991. Koreans led by Lee Dong-Won were unable to complete the climb via the l962 German Diamir route. Italians under the leadership of Stefano Righetti reached a highpoint of 7500 meters on the Rupal Face, while Japanese led by Seishi Wada had to give up at 7900 meters on the southeast buttress after spending 75 days in the attempt. Another Korean expedition led by Kim Hyoung-Joo also failed; we do not know which route they tried.

Naltar Valley, 1990. In August and September of 1990, Irish climbers Orla and Maurice Prendergast and Tomas Aylward visited the Naltar valley and climbed Snow Dome (5030 meters, 16,503 feet) by the north ridge, Sentinel (5260 meters, 17,257 feet) by the west ridge and a 5100-meter (16,733-foot) subsidiary of Shani by a gully on the north face, a new route.

JOSS LYNAM, *Federation of Mountaineering Clubs of Ireland*

Southeastern China

Gongga Shan Attempt. Our members were Masayoshi Matsudate, Kiyuharu Ito, Masaharu Moriya, Yasuhiko Matsuta, Yutaka Nakagawa, Kosuke Igawa,

Masaki Kawachi, Masaki Hayashi, Shinji Chiba, Seiji Takami, Suguru Kawakami and I as leader. We established Base Camp on September 15 at 3400 meters on the left side of the Hailuogou Glacier east of Gongga Shan (Minya Gongka). We placed Camps I and II at 4200 and 5000 meters on September 22 and 29. We fixed 16 rope lengths to reach the northeast ridge and establish Camp III at 5800 meters on October 13. We reached 6400 meters on the northeast ridge on October 30 but gave up because of heavy wind and bad snow-and-ice conditions.

KINICHI YAMAMORI, *Himalayan Association of Japan*

Namcha Barwa Attempt and Tragedy. What is doubtless the highest unclimbed main peak in the world, Namcha Barwa (7782 meters, 25,520 feet) was attempted by a joint Japanese-Chinese expedition from the Japanese Alpine Club and the Chinese Mountaineering Association with six climbers from each country. Base Camp was established at 3520 meters on September 28. They began to move over the south peak, Naipun (7043 meters, 24,107 feet), placing Camps I and II at 4300 and 4850 meters on October 2 and 13. As Hiroshi Onishi was pushing the route higher on October 16, he was killed by an avalanche. After a pause of ten days, they continued, harrassed by high winds and snowfall. Finally, Camps IV and V were established at 6150 and 6900 meters on November 2 and 15. They descended into the col between Naipun and the main peak and placed Camp VI at 6700 meters on the main peak on November 19. Ropes were fixed to 7200 meters. On November 20, Japanese Kazushige Takami, Satoshi Kimoto and another Japanese and two Chinese climbed to the base of the rock band at 7350 meters but turned back because of heavy snowfall and avalanche danger. On the 22nd, Takami and others climbed back, surmounted the rock band but gave up the attempt because of an avalanche-prone snow slope. Further details and a photograph are found in *Iwa To Yuki, 150,* February 1992.

Tibet

Everest Attempt, Ridge on Northern Edge of Kangshung Face. Our members were leader Shinichi Hirano, Ryouten Hasegawa, Fumio Sakamoto, Sadaki Matumura, Nobumi Nakazawa, Tetuya Sano, Manabu Hirose, Kozo Takeguchi, Hiroshi Aota and I. After a 12-day caravan from Kharta with 370 Tibetan porters, we made Base Camp on April 14 at 5400 meters on the Kangshung Glacier. We started up the ridge that borders the Kangshung Face on the northern (right) edge on April 14. We set up a preliminary Camp I on P 5900. We were delayed in getting higher because the ice blocks were unstable and the route was very long. On April 30, we established the real Camp I on P 6100. Above Camp I, the route was even more dangerous because of ice blocks and rockfall. We climbed to 6400 meters on May 5, but gave up the expedition at that point.

SHIN SAITO, *Meiji University Alpine Club*

Everest Attempt and Tragedy. Our expedition was composed of Austrians Wastl Wörgötter, Dr. Andreas Paul, Ingeborg Aufschnaiter, Harald Benzl, Johann Pree, Josef Inhöger, Martin Hornegger, Johann-Georg Bachmair, and me as leader, Germans Dr. Karl Wimmer, Reinhilde Natterer, Georg Wischmann, Peter Kowalzig, Otto Huber and Rüdiger Lang, Swiss Georges Piemontesi, Italian Teresa Zanol and Czechoslovak Dr. Margita Štěrbová. We hoped to climb Everest by the North Col without supplementary oxygen or high-altitude porters. We approached overland from Kathmandu. On April 7, Base Camp was set up at 5100 meters below the Rongbuk Glacier. Advance Base was established by mid-April on the East Rongbuk at 6400 meters. Strong winds destroyed numerous tents on the North Col and camps on the north ridge. On May 15, Hornegger, Kowalzik and Inhöger set out from Camp III at 8400 meters with a temperature of $-35°$ C. At 8570 meters they decided to turn back because of the excessive cold, luckily in time to avoid frostbite. Other groups were no more successful because of wind and cold. Rüdiger Lang, who in January had climbed a variant on the Vinson Massif in Antarctica, wanted to ascend a new route in the north face of the highest point of the north ridge. On May 1, he set out. He bivouacked at 7300 and 7700 meters. From May 3 to 7, the face was whipped by snow squalls and cloud. On May 8, he was found in an emergency bivouac at 7850 meters, where he had doubtless perished on the night of the 3rd. Saddened by the loss of a comrade, our group withdrew into Nepal on May 19.

MARCUS SCHMUCK, *Österreichischer Alpenverein*

Everest, Japanese and Hornbein Couloirs. A Swedish expedition led by Jack Berg made the ascent of Everest via the Japanese and Hornbein Couloirs. On May 15, two Sherpas, Mingma Norbu and Galbyu got to the top. They were followed on May 20 by Lars Cronlund, who was reported to have suffered quite severe frostbite. Other expeditions have spoken highly of medical care they received from the expedition's medical team.

ELIZABETH HAWLEY

Everest, Great Couloir. Our expedition was composed of Italians Graziano Bianchi, Battistino Bonali, Dr. Giuliano De Marchi, Fausto De Stefani, Sergio Salini, Wolfgang Thomaseth and me as leader and Czechoslovak Leopold Sulovsky. We set up Base Camp at Rongbuk on April 4 and, with the aid of yaks, Advance Base on the Central Rongbuk Glacier at 5500 meters on April 12. Salini left the expedition on the 14th. Camps I, II and III were at 6100, 6195 and 7600 meters. Much of our route was to the left of the Australian one. Camps II and III had only one tent each and room for two climbers. The first summit attempt was begun from Advance Base by De Marchi and De Stefani on April 30. They took three days to reach Camp III, where they were held up for a day by bad weather. On May 4, they bivouacked at 8000 meters and the next day at 8350 meters, below the rock barrier in the Great Couloir. They had hoped to climb to the summit on the 6th, but De Stefani was struck by cerebral edema. On the 7th a very difficult rescue began with the whole team involved. This lasted five days and De Stefani was sent back, by jeep, to Kathmandu on May 11. Thomaseth went with him. On May 14, De Marchi, who had suffered frostbite, was taken to Base Camp by Bianchi and me and also sent to Kathmandu. That same day, Bonali and Sulovsky started from Advance Base and got to Camp II. They reached Camps III and IV on the next two days. They climbed to the summit on May 17 at 3:30 P.M. and were back in Advance Base on the 19th. Our route reached the Great Couloir by climbing on the left of the big icefall, entered the couloir and followed it to the rock barrier of about 80 meters at 8400 meters. It took the summiters two hours to climb the barrier and was of Grade V difficulty. The Australians in 1984 avoided the barrier by climbing to the right before it begins. The last part of our route coincided with that of Messner. We used no supplementary oxygen. We had no porters. The only rope we fixed was on 70 meters of the rock barrier.

ORESTE FORNO, *Club Alpino Italiano*

Everest. Our expedition members consisted of Americans George Dunn, Larry Huntington, Charles Peck, Steven Potter, Scott Frantz, Dave Hahn, Curtis Fawley, Brent Okita, Paul Maier, Bob Sloezen, Andy Politz, Jason Edwards, Craig Van Hoy, Greg Wilson, medical researcher Jonas Pologe, Dr. Jean Ellis, video cameraman Markus Hutnak, geologist Dan Mann and me as leader, New Zealanders Michael Perry and Mark Whetu and Australian Michael Rhein- berger. We reached Xegar on March 10 in two groups. Ten members traveled via Lhasa and accompanied the six tons of food and equipment that had been shipped to China in November, 1990. The rest came from Kathmandu with the 13 Nepalese (two cooks and 11 Sherpa porters). Propane fuel, oxygen and additional food was also brought from Nepal. Base Camp was established on March 13 at 16,900 feet at the roadhead. Camp III (Advance Base) was established with 50 yak-loads a week later at 21,400 feet. Eventually, 130 yak loads reached Advance Base. Severe weather and heavy snow made it impossi- ble to establish Camp IV on the North Col at 23,000 feet until March 30. The route to the col was fixed. Camp IV consisted of eight tents, walled in and held down by nets. Extreme winds prevented Camp V at 25,600 feet from being established until April 21. Without the fixed ropes we put in on this part of the route, there would have been many days when we could not have climbed due to the extreme wind across the north ridge. Camp V was again an extremely windy site. Only four tents were able to withstand the beating here. Camp VI at 27,000 feet was established on May 7 after a long hard push that forced Wilson, Whetu, Okita, Edwards and Van Hoy all to spend the night in a tiny two-person tent. Every member who was healthy got a summit bid, as we had planned from the beginning. On May 15, the top was reached by Dunn, Politz, Sloezen, Lhakpa Dorje, Ang Dawa and me. On the 16th, Hahn, Rheinberger, Perry, Huntington,

COLOR PLATE 13

Photo by Kurt Diemberger

BROAD PEAK from North Gasherbrum Glacier in China. *Penitentes* rise to a height of 100 feet.

Ang Jangbo and Pasang Kami were turned back by wind. Perry stayed at Camp VI while the rest descended and made the summit solo on May 17. An attempt on May 21 by Wilson, Edwards, Van Hoy, Frantz, Whetu and Okita was partially stopped by the wind. Only Whetu and Okita were able to push on and reach the summit. Okita was forced to bivouac on the descent when he could not find the fixed ropes in the Yellow Band in the dark. Fortunately, he suffered no ill effects. Wilson remained at Camp VI for three more days and was joined by Mann for another attempt on May 24. Mann was forced to turn back, but Wilson reached the summit. All summiters used oxygen. After the climb, we removed all garbage from Advance Base to Base Camp. We sent approximately 8000 pounds of garbage to Xegar and left Base Camp spotless. The team left Base Camp on May 28 and all members returned home via Kathmandu.

ERIC SIMONSON

Everest, Northeast Ridge Attempt and North Ridge Ascent. Our co-leaders were Briton Harry Taylor and New Zealander Russell Brice. The other members were Britons Alan Hinkes, Bill Barker, Andy Parkin, Len Atkinson, Base Camp Manager Sam Roberts, Dr. John English, Norwegian Olav Ulvumd, Australian Mark Lemare, Frenchman Xavier Remond and I from the United States. We entered Tibet flying from Kathmandu to Lhasa and overland to the Rongbuk Base Camp, where we arrived on April 6. Already there were Americans, an elaborate Swedish expedition, a small but elite Italian group, a guided Austrian expedition and later two Japanese with Sherpa help. Yaks came, we bargained with greedy Chinese and in a three-day push got to Advance Base at the usual spot at 21,000 feet below the east side of the North Col. As usual, we went up too fast, and half our group went back down after the tents were erected. There were high winds on the mountain and even in Advance Base the temperatures were 0° F. We carried loads to Camp I on the North Col starting on April 12. Poor weather stymied us in our push for Camp II at 7800 meters for a long time and let us catch up to the Americans. More bad weather and fear of frostbite slowed our getting to Camp III at 8300 meters. The Americans were able to push on due to their use of oxygen. The Americans fixed most potentially dangerous spots and made retreats easy. Bill Barker established Camp III with a couple of Sherpas and kept on to 8400 meters on May 8 without supplementary oxygen. Two days later, I got to just below this height solo and decided it was too dangerous to continue; temperatures were about −40° and wind around 30 miles per hour. I had moved up from 7800 meters in three hours and a quarter. Sherpas Babu Tshering and Chuldin got to the summit on May 22. Taylor and Brice started up the northeast ridge on May 5 and bailed out on the north-ridge connection at Camp III on May 16 because of bad weather. Lemare suffered frostbitten toes and fingers. On May 25, we packed up for Base Camp, where the Swedes hosted one of the best parties ever given at 17,000 feet. Base Camp and Advance Base are free of garbage except for poor sanitary habits by most. We dug proper pit toilets. Most others are the behind-the-rock gang. All the expeditions did proper cleanup and used yaks to carry out all trash. However, the mountain itself is strewn with debris, especially above 7500 meters, especially in the spring due to the lack of snow. Oxygen bottles dating back to who knows when are everywhere with every imaginable article including dead bodies. Injuries were common: frostbite, edemas, death. If it weren't for the full field hospital of the Swedes, casualties would have been higher than the two I know about. The Swedes were very gracious and helped every expedition on the north side.

STEVEN UNTCH

Everest Solo Attempt. We established Base Camp and Advance Base on April 1 and 7. I had support from Margaret-Anne Seddon and Pasang Norbu and Kassang Tsering as far as Advance Base at 5500 meters on the Central Rongbuk Glacier. I ascended the glacier to 6100 meters at the base of the Japanese Couloir route. I then cut back to below the south face of Changtse, traversing below it into a basin at 6550 meters below the North Col. On April 11, I placed Camp I at the base of the extreme eastern side of the north face at 6700 meters. From there I angled up and left into a couloir on the extreme left of the north face and well to the west of the North Col. I reached the north ridge at 7470 meters. I made my first attempt on May 1, reaching 8100 meters, where I bivouacked before descending the next day with frostbitten feet. This was the same time that an Austrian soloist east of the north ridge remained high and froze to death during the second night. A second attempt on May 11 got to 7800 meters, but I descended the same day because of high winds. The third attempt from a high camp at 8200 meters reached 8300 meters on May 20, but I had to turn back because of cold and frostbite.

ROBERT ANDERSON, *Explorers Club*

Everest Ascent and Tragedy. Junichi Futagami and I were supported by six Sherpas. We climbed the normal North Col route of Everest. We established Base Camp, Camps I, II, III, IV, V and VI at 5154, 5500, 6000, 6500, 7028, 7790 and 8200 meters on April 29, May 1, 2, 3, 13, 14 and 26. On May 27, we two Japanese and Sherpas Nima Dorje and Finjo reached the summit at one P.M. Futagami was behind me on the descent. After we had descended some 150 meters, we noticed he was not following us. When we climbed back up, we saw scratches from his crampons as he fell to his death down the east-face side of the summit ridge.

MUNEO NUKITA, *Alpine Tour Service, Japan*

Everest Attempt. A Belgian expedition consisted of Alain Hubert, leader, Eugène Berger, Bertrand Borrey, Guido Cadoen, Jacques Collaer, Vincent Dewaele, Jean Philippe Perikel and Pierre Soeté. They had hoped to climb Everest's northwest face by the Japanese and Hornbein Couloirs. The climbers reached Advance Base at 5500 meters on August 2 and Camp I at 6000 meters on August 12. It was still two hours from Camp I to the base of the face. They were never able to establish Camp II at 7400 meters but did make a supply dump at 7200 meters. The monsoon hung on later than usual and prevented progress. They called off the attempt on September 7.

Everest Attempt. An Indian expedition led by Pranesh Chakraborty unsuccessfully attempted to climb Mount Everest via the Great Couloir. On September 22, they got to 7500 meters.

ELIZABETH HAWLEY

Everest Attempt. Our "Climb for Hope Expedition" was organized to get charity money to combat the Rett Syndrome. Our members, mostly from Canada, were Ernie Sniedzins, Dr. Mario Bilodeau, Dr. Dennis Brown, Jamie Clarke, Ross Cloutier, Jim Everard, Alan Hobson, Mike Kurth, John McIssac, James Nelson, Al Norquay, Hilda Reimer, Tim Rippel, Timo Saukko, I as leader and American Dr. Michael Sullivan. We fixed ropes up the North Col in early September. Monsoon snows buried them twice and so we had to dig them out. A huge sérac fall buried them a third time. It snowed continuously for the first three weeks of September. Then, after a week of fine weather, the jet-stream winds began. We established Camp V at 26,000 feet in late September. The whole camp was blown away in early October, a fact discovered by Brown, McIssac and Bilodeau. They encountered 60-mph winds and −30° C temperatures and were lucky to make it back alive. We performed a spectacular rescue from 25,000 feet when Rippel damaged leg ligaments and had to be lowered down the North Col. A summit attempt had been set for October 8, but jet-stream winds prevented any movement. Future expeditions may be well advised to camp above the North Col and at 24,500 and 26,500-27,000 feet and avoid a camp at 26,000 feet, where the winds funnel badly.

PETER AUSTEN, M.D., *Alpine Club of Canada*

Everest Attempt. We were Alfredo Bonini, Roberto Linsker, Kenvy Chung Ng, Ramis Tetu, Paulo and Helena Coelho, Dr. Eduardo Vinhaes, Sherpas Ang Rita, Ang Nima, Phuba and I as leader. We attempted the East Rongbuk-North Col route. We arrived at Base Camp on October 3 and with the help of yaks set up Camps I, II and III at 5600, 6000 and 6500 meters. On October 18, Ang Rita and I fixed rope to 6750 meters on the way to the North Col. This was the only day without hurricane winds; it took us then ten days to fix the route to the North Col. On October 28, Bonini, Ang Rita, Ang Nima and I established Camp IV at 7050 meters on the col. On the 30th, Ang Rita and I tried to advance to set up Camp V but had to retreat after gaining only 50 vertical meters. On November 11, we began another attempt but on the 16th, I made a last solo try but had to retreat from below the North Col because of wind and cold. Our team was 55 days on the mountain and except for two or three days it was clear and sunny but windy and cold. There was no avalanche danger.

THOMAZ A. BRANDOLIN, *Clube Alpino Paulista, Brazil*

Cho Oyu Southwest Ridge Attempt, 1990. An expedition of the Vysotnik Club of Leningrad was led by Aleksandr Glushkovski and consisted of Sergei Arsentiev, Nicolai Chorny, Dr. Valeri Karpenko, Aleksei Koren, Yuri Konovalov, Mikhail Mozhayev, Vladimir Moroz and Bulgarian Petko Totev. They had hoped to climb the still unclimbed southwest ridge of Cho Oyu, which had been unsuccessfully tried by three previous expeditions. Their club had lost 15 members in the tragic avalanche on Pik Lenina, including the initiator of this expedition, Leonid Troshchinenko. This caused them serious troubles and they were not able to establish Base Camp at 5050 meters until October 23. Despite the shortage of time, they surmounted subsummits of 6500, 7200 and 7400 meters and established four camps. Arsentiev, Chorny and Karpenko occupied Camp IV at 7450 meters. Chorny descended because of frostbitten toes, but the other two continued on November 14, 1990 to 7800 meters, where they bivouacked with a tent but no sleeping bags at the foot of the summit cone. Violent wind the next day forced them to retreat.

JÓZEF NYKA, *Editor, Taternik, Poland*

Cho Oyu, West Side, Pre-Monsoon. A number of ascents of Cho Oyu were made in the pre-monsoon period on the western side of the peak. Spaniard Andrés Ruiz, of an expedition led by Eloy Sánchez, completed the 83rd ascent of the peak on May 8. Swiss Peter Stadler led a group of 29 Swiss, Germans and Austrians. On May 8, Swiss Alfred Beetschen and Mario Rizzi reached the summit, while the next day Germans Matthias Respondek, Wolfgang Maier, Austrians Ewald Eder, Theo Pichler and Swiss Frédéric Pantillon, Niklaus von Schumacher, Elizabeth and Peter Wullschleger also got to the top. The expedition was, however, marred by the death of a German member in a fall. Three of six Greeks climbed to the summit on May 8. They were leader Ioannis Konstantinou, Petros Kapsomenakis, Konstaninos Tsivelekas, accompanied by Nepalese Tirtha Tamang. South Tirolean Hermann Tauber was the leader of nine Germans and seven Italians (mostly South Tiroleans). On May 27, Germans Andi Wiedemann, Adelbert Albrecht, Ottmar Fangauer, Frau Monika Kumpf, Josef Weissenberger, Helmuth Bauer, Horst Conrad and Italians leader Tauber, Roland Erardi, Josef Pallhuber, Konrad Renzler, Frau Karoline Wolfsgruber and Robert Gasser reached the summit.

ELIZABETH HAWLEY

Cho Oyu, West side from the North, Ascents and Attempts, Post-Monsoon. An international expedition that climbed Cho Oyu's western side from Tibet was led by Frenchman (Corsican) Hughes Griscelli. There were 2 French, 4 Italian, 2 Spanish and 1 Polish climbers. On September 25, the summit was reached by South Tirolean Christian Kutner, who had been joined by Swiss Jacob Reichen. The latter approached from Nepal and made the climb illegally. On September 26, Pole Wanda Rutkiewicz climbed to the top. This was the seventh 8000er for this remarkable Polish woman. On September 28, Spaniard Bartolomé Quetglas also completed the climb. David Lam from Hong Kong had hoped to make the ascent on a one-man expedition. Tsindin Temba Sherpa, who accompanied him, alone got to the summit on September 28. Japanese led by Tadao Kanzaki were also successful. On September 28, Tomiyasu Ishikawa, Miss Tamae Watanabe, Yoshikazu Nezu, Nima Temba Sherpa and Mingma Norbu Sherpa reached the summit, followed on September 29 by Kaneshige Ikeda and Pemba Norbu Sherpa. French leader Philippe Grenier and Guy Borrel completed the ascent of September 28. Americans led by Jerry Kennedy were on the summit on September 29. They were Kent Groninger, Miss Cathleen Richards, Cleve Armstrong and Miss Karen Young. Others were less successful. Climbers from Taiwan led by Gau Ming Ho failed at 7800 meters on September 4. South Koreans under the leadership of Oh In-Hwan failed at 8100 meters on October 23. Other South Koreans led by Kim Myong-Soo got to 7400 meters on October 29.

ELIZABETH HAWLEY

Cho Oyu Ascent and Shisha Pangma Attempt. Spaniards Bartolomé Quetglas and Ramón Alfredo arrived at the Cho Oyu Base Camp on September 5. They placed Camps I and II at 6400 and 6900 meters. On September 28, Quetglas climbed to the summit. Alfredo with porter Tirta Tamang established Camp III at 7500 meters and on the 29th headed toward the summit but this pair was driven back by high winds. Feeling well acclimatized, they moved to Shisha Panga, which they hoped to climb in only two days from the base. However, high winds prevented their completing the climb after they reached 7400 meters.

Shisha Pangma Correction. On page 296 of *AAJ 1991,* it should have stated that Jean-Pierre Bernard's party got to the *central* summit of Shisha Pangma, not the *main* one. Regarding the many groups that fail to climb the main summit of Shisha Pangma (8027 meters, 26,336 feet) in favor of the subsidiary central summit (8008 meters, 26,274 feet), it is worth noting that in 1990 only eight climbers (two in the spring and six in the autumn) managed to reach the main summit, whereas as many as 59 (40 in the spring and 19 in the autumn) ended at the more conspicuous central summit.

XAVIER EGUSKITZA, *Pyrenaica, Bilbao, Spain.*

Shisha Pangma Central Summit. A Belgian expedition included leader Mark Baruffa, his wife Gille Pille, Reginald Roels, Kris Doom, Jan De Boe, Wouter

PLATE 58

Photo by Kurt Diemberger

Camels on Aghil Pass on approach to Broad Peak from the north.

Bebusscher, two doctors and a TV team. Like many groups before them (see item above), they declined to undertake the Chinese traverse toward the main summit but followed instead the north ridge that leads to the central summit. This was reached on May 14 by Baruffa and his wife with Tibetans Ceran Doje, Qimi and Khtun. In view of the dangerous cornices, they did not attempt to follow the connecting ridge to the main summit.

XAVIER EGUSKITZA, *Pyrenaica, Bilbao, Spain*

Shisha Pangma Ascent and Tragedy. Our Austro-German party was composed of Germans Günther Semmler, Werner Braun, Frau Ottilie Dörrich, Dieter Porsche, Werner Meichsner, Karl Heinz and Helmut Thiele, Johann Obermaier, Dr. Karl-Wilhelm Dehn, Wilhelm Kummer, Max Stückl, Theo Zunterer, Thomas Krempl and Klaus-Dieter Scheld, and Austrians Theo Fritsche, Herwig Schnutt, Dr. Kurt Hecher and Johann Poell. We established Base Camp and Camps I, II, III and IV at 5100, 5900, 6400, 6900 and 7400 meters on May 5, 9, 10, 12 and 19. On May 20, we continued to follow the Chinese route up the north ridge with a traverse to the left at 7900 meters. There was much snow and avalanche danger on the traverse. The main summit was reached by Fritsche, Schnutt, Dörrich, Porsche, Hecher and me (my fourth 8000er and Porsche's and Hecher's second). Frau Dörrich at 54 years was the oldest woman to have reached the summit of an 8000er. Two days later, a second summit party composed of Semmler, Braun, Meichsner and Karl Heinz Thiele left Camp IV, intending to reach the central summit in view of the dangerous conditions on the traverse. They established radio contact with me at eleven A.M. and reported that they were at 7800 meters on the north ridge. After that there were no more radio contacts and the four climbers disappeared, presumably engulfed by an avalanche. The three Sherpas tried unsuccessfully to reach Camp IV to search, but deep snow and avalanche risk turned them back.

GÜNTHER HÄRTER, *Deutscher Alpenverein*

Western China

Broad Peak Central Attempt from the North. Our expedition was composed of four Catalan Spaniards, Oscar Cadiach, Lluis Rafols, Joan Gelabert and me, Austrian Kurt Diemberger, Italian Alberto Soncini and Sherpas Sakipa, Pemba and Pasang. The problem of the Shaksgam valley is that it is flooded from the end of June until nearly the end of August. We crossed the border from Pakistan into Xinjiang, China on August 16. We got to Mazardara, a small military post, on August 16. With camels, we ascended the Surukwat valley on August 22, 23 and 24 and the Shaksgam on August 25, 26 and 27. River crossings were a real problem for the camels, but we finally got to the tongue of the North Gasherbrum Glacier. We had hoped to set up Base Camp on the east bank of the glacier, but 30-meter-high *penitentes* and torrents prevented it. We set up Base Camp about an hour up the side of the glacier on the west bank. The glacier was a labyrinth

PLATE 59

Photo by Kurt Diemberger

BROAD PEAK CENTRAL from the north. Camp III at 6500 meters was at the top of the terrace at the bottom center.

of ice, where you had to get by one *penitente* to see your way past the next. It took us five days to get a route up the 25 kilometers. Once marked, it took seven or eight hours. We could not see the east face of Broad Peak until we were at Advance Base, which was on a moraine at 4500 meters. From there, we ascended two or three hours towards Gasherbrum IV over hidden crevasses. This placed us in a cirque below Broad Peak. We spent four days observing the peak to plan routes and to scan possible avalanche tracks. We then decided to attack a spur on the right side that led over a 6400-meter foresummit, beyond which we placed Camp II. The climbing on the spur was difficult. We placed our Camp I at 5400 meters. We then traversed left and climbed ice up to 55° to a nearly vertical, 10-meter-high sérac. We traversed below the top of the forepeak on ice up to 80° and another traverse to Camp II at 6400 meters. A rather easy ridge section led to a last sérac barrier where we set up two small tents as Camp III. We climbed up the séracs to about 7000 meters on ice that varied from 60° to 80°. The route to the summit seemed clear. The temperatures were frigid and another storm kept us tent-bound from September 22 to October 10. We gave up the attempt. Diemberger did a considerable amount of reconnaissance in the region. He investigated the approaches to Windy Gap (Skyang La), ascending the Southeast Skyang Glacier, and the Urdok Glacier.

JORDI MAGRINYÀ, *AAEET de Valls, Tarragona, Spain*

Xuebao Ding, Sichuan. The first ascent of Xuebao Ding (5588 meters, 18,334 feet) was made by an expedition of the Himalayan Association of Japan led by Kunimitsu Sakai. After reaching Base Camp on August 5, they climbed the south ridge. On August 12, Hitoshi Kubo, Yasuji Moriyama, Hideo Tobe, Hidekatsu Kashiwakura and Mrs. Hiroko Hirakawa reached the summit. They were followed the next day by the leader, Mitsunori Naka and Yasuke Gouda. A Himalayan Association of Japan expedition in 1986 did not reach the top.

Former USSR

Kamchatka Volcanoes. One pleasant benefit from the improving relations between what was the USSR and the United States is that previously closed areas are becoming open for exploration and climbing. One of these is the Kamchatka peninsula with its 29 active and 300 dormant volcanoes. It had been closed to foreigners from 1917 to 1990. Our group of Americans organized by REI Adventures and of Russians from the Alpinklub Kutq of Petropavlovsk climbed several of these volcanoes in late August and early September. The Americans were Frith Maier, Chuck and Judy Demarest, David Koester, Chuck Wolf and I.

RICK JALI

Khan Tengri and Pik Pobedy. Our expedition was composed of Roger Payne, Iain Peter and Allen Fyffe from the UK and me from New Zealand. Our trip was

PLATE 60

Photo by Roger Payne

PIK POBEDY.

arranged through the International Mountaineering Camp Khan Tengri based in Alma Ata. We were flown from Moscow to Alma Ata and transported by van to Camp Karkara in the foothills. We were flown by helicopter to Base Camp on the South Inylichek Glacier at 4100 meters. After a week of acclimatization, we left on July 23 for an attempt on Khan Tengri. The first afternoon, we traveled to an Advance Base on the glacier at 4300 meters. After a night there, we continued up the avalanche-prone Semenovsky Glacier to camp at 5400 meters. On July 25, we ascended to snow caves beneath the west col at 5800 meters and rested a few hours before going onto the west ridge itself. Payne and I bivouacked at 6200 meters while the other two continued on to 6400 meters. There are few campsites on the ridge and they are small and exposed. On the 26th, Peter and Fyffe climbed to the summit but Payne and I, feeling the altitude, descended to Base Camp. We two set out again on July 28 and reached the summit of Khan Tengri on the 30th. Peter and Fyffe headed for Pik Pobedy but were turned back by bad weather. All four of us moved to Advance Base on the Zvezdozhka Glacier at the foot of Pik Pobedy on August 5. On the 6th, we climbed up to the Dickey Pass and up the north ridge of the west peak to snow caves at 5800 meters. Two nights were spent there due to bad weather. On August 8, it dawned clear and in a very long day we climbed the west peak (6918 meters, 22,698 feet) and traversed a short distance along the west ridge of Pik Pobedy to snow caves at 6900 meters. The next day, Fyffe and Peter climbed to the summit (7439 meters, 24,276 feet). Payne and I followed a day later on August 10. These were the first New Zealand ascents of both peaks and the first UK ascent of Pik Pobedy and the second of Khan Tengri. Prior to our arrival, another British team (Rick Allen, Simon Yates and Shaun Smith) had made the first British ascent of Khan Tengri, also by the normal west ridge. Their attempt on Pik Pobedy was turned back by illness and bad weather.

JULIE-ANN CLYMA, *New Zealand Alpine Club*

Granitic Peaks of Kirgizia. An informative article describing this comparatively unknown region, many ascents there and climbing opportunities appears earlier in this *Journal*.

Piramidalny. In the summer of 1991, five climbers from the United Kingdom visited the Ak-Su massif. After a delay caused by a mud slide on a road, we were finally helicoptered to the Asan Base Camp on August 2 from the Ak-Su International Base Camp. We spent the rest of the day ascending Point Holland, a rock gendarme of perfect granite. The following day, we made a fine climb on the Yellow Wall. After bad weather, time began to run out. We established an advance base in hopes that the clouds would lift. Miraculously, the next morning dawned clear. The first day saw us gain the west ridge at 4500 meters. The next day, we climbed over a subsidiary peak and descended to a 5000-meter col. The final day of the ascent took us to the summit (5507 meters, 18,068 feet) of

Piramidalny. The major obstacle was four sustained pitches of ice cliffs. We returned to the col that night. It took a further day to descend to Base Camp via easy slopes at the head of the glacier formed by the west ridge.

TREVOR MARTIN, *England*

Piramidalny and Other Peaks, Pamir Alai. It was not difficult to get to the region. The Russians tooks us in a helicopter. The cirque of towers was lovely with great possibilites of new routes, although the granite was not always of the best quality. Up to 4000 meters lichen and dirt in the cracks were a nuisance. Paolo Tamagnini and I climbed some new routes on "Little Asan," some 4000-meters-high. On P 4810 (15,781 feet), the highest tower in the immediate valley, we climbed the west pillar, crossing at times a route done in 1990 by Russians when they traversed Asan-Usan-P 4810. The climbing was complicated by ice in the cracks. Tamagnini made a fine solo route on the north face of Piramidalny (5507 meters, 18,068 feet).

GIACOMO BARONI, *Club Alpino Italiano*

Pamir Alai. A French group led by Pierre Faivre was composed of talented young alpinists: Frédéric Gentet, Robin Givet and Zébulon Roche. They made some excellent new rock routes, particularly on P 4240 and P 3850. They gave up their attempt on Piramidalny because of potential avalanche danger.

Korzhenevskaya, Pamirs. After three storm-bound weeks on Pik Lenin, our joint REI-Crimea Alpine Club expedition was helicoptered to the 4500-meter Moskvina Base Camp on August 12. After a rest day, we stormed the mountain by the Suloyeva Ridge in sunny weather, climbing through 700 meters of mud cliffs, scree and crossing a rock-spitting hanging glacier. The next day, with the weather still holding, we arrived after traversing under cliffs atop a steep glacier at the 6100-meter upper camp perched on a thin ridge. On the morning of August 16, Sergey Bershov, Michael Firth, Matt Hyde, Ansel Wall, Michael Young and I set out for the summit. Rapid ascent took its toll and we found the steep winding snow ridge and a short rock pitch difficult going. By three P.M. we were on the summit (7105 meters, 23,310 feet). On the descent, we were surprised to see Gennady Vasilenko on his way up, setting a personal speed record of 11 hours from Base Camp to summit.

DANIEL MAZUR, *REI*

Mongolia

Munkhairkhan. The British Mongolian Altai Expedition consisted of Richard Wojtaszewski, Helen Sweet, Alan Hughes and me with Mongolian guides T. Byraa and Balto and cook Chegme. Our objective was the first ascent by

Westerners of Munkhairkhan (4204 meters, 13,803 feet), whose massif lies about 80 miles southwest of Hovd in the far western part of the Mongolian People's Republic. Though previously reported as the highest in the country, it appears to be third after 4374-meter Huithen in the Taban Bogdo massif and 4208-meter Tsast Uul just north of Hovd. After arriving in Ulan Bator on July 16, we flew to Hovd on the 18th and reached Base Camp in the Doolon Nuur (Seven Lakes) valley by lorry on the 19th. We established a high camp at 12,500 feet on a boulder field lying above a prominent outcrop to the southeast of the Doloon Nuur cwm. On the 22nd, the British members of the team and Balto climbed straightforward glaciated slopes to the summit. Balto and I later crossed a high pass to explore the upper Shurkhe valley, descending 14 miles to meet the others who had established a second Base Camp by lorry. On July 28, we five climbed the shapely Malchin (c. 4150 meters, 13,616 feet), the second peak in the group, last climbed in 1974.

JOHN TOWN, *Alpine Club*

Taven Bogd. The mountains near Mongolia's border with both Siberia and China are little known. Mongolia's highest mountain, Taven Bogd (4374 meters, 14,350 feet) lies on the country's western border. It was climbed in 1991 by Netherlanders Ronald Naar, Bas Gresnigt and two others. From the summit, they skied across the frontier to the Chinese summit. They also climbed Burged (4068 meters, 13,347 feet), which lies to the east.

The Seven Summits in Seven Months, 1990. New Zealanders Rob Hall and Gary Ball reached the summits of the seven continents in just seven months of 1990. (It must be stated that they consider Mount Kosciusko in Australia and not Carstensz Pyramid in Australasia as one of these. The Editor takes no sides in this dispute.) They made the following ascents: Everest, May 10; McKinley, June 28; Elbrus, August 8; Kilimanjaro, August 17; Kosciusko, August 26; Aconcagua, November 21; Vinson Massif, December 12.

Book Reviews

Edited by John Thackray

Mount McKinley: The Conquest of Denali. Bradford Washburn and David Roberts. Preface by Ansel Adams. Photographs mostly by Bradford Washburn (more than 120 illustrations, including 77 photographs in duotone, 41 in full color). Text by Bradford Washburn and David Roberts. Relief map by Dee Molenaar. Index and Bibliography. Harry N. Abrams, Inc., New York, 1991. Printed and bound in Japan. Price $60.

Mount McKinley is the American mountain book of the year, possibly the century. Its black-and-white and color photographs are the cream of the many pictures of Mount McKinley taken by Bradford Washburn in over half a century. They are largely full page (12x10¼ inches with no border), and sometimes spread across both pages. They show America's greatest mountain from every side, clarifying the difficulties thwarting explorers who tried to reach it from the coast, and showing in great detail routes on the mountain made by climbers in recent decades. The late Ansel Adams, writing about Brad Washburn in his preface, remarked, "It is astounding to realize what tremendous physical risks he took to get these shots—many, for instance, were taken from unpressurized airplanes or helicopters often at temperatures far below zero, with the door removed and Brad tethered to the opposite side of the cabin."

Though the book is large and heavy, great beauty and much information lie between its covers. Washburn and Roberts both write well. The text, beginning with the experiences of the early explorers, concludes with the situation today, when even a thousand may try to climb the peak in a given year. Each new route is described, including David Roberts' modest tale of how he and six other college students climbed the long-thought-impossible Wickersham Wall in 1963. Dee Molenaar's maps are helpful in understanding the complicated geography of the McKinley area, but the extraordinary feature at the end of the book is the nearly 14-page bibliography, with about half a thousand references to books and articles about McKinley, including first ascents on neighboring Huntington, Hunter and Foraker.

Washburn's foreword states, "This book has been nearly a lifetime in the making;" yet his fascination with the world's greatest northern mountain remains undiminished, for he declares, "Just being in its presence is still as exciting to me as it was the first time I saw it." That excitement is in no way limited to the mountain's climbing opportunities, for many of the photographs have great artistic beauty, especially when he focuses on patterns of crevasses, wind-swept snow slopes or details of sheer rock walls.

Washburn had read books by Belmore Browne and Hudson Stuck before his first expedition to Alaska in 1930, and by the time Gilbert Grosvenor, head of the National Geographic Society, in 1936 asked him to suggest future northern exploration objectives, he had already led five expeditions to Alaska and the Yukon Territory. One, for the National Geographic Society in 1935, spent a winter in the St. Elias Mountains travelling by dog team and mapping that then virgin area of sub-Arctic Canada. In January, 1936, Washburn suggested to Grosvenor flights to photograph then little known Mount McKinley. So that summer he made a highly successful photographic survey for the N.G.S. at a cost of slightly less than $1000! That began his love of McKinley.

In early 1942 when the Quartermaster General's Office and the Army Air Force were seeking a place to test cold-weather clothing and equipment that spring, Brad strongly recommended Mount McKinley, and this became the region where the Alaskan Test Expedition in May, 1942 tried out 30 prototype items for mountain and winter warfare. Representing the Army Air Force on this expedition, Brad was very active, leading the first rope up Karstens Ridge, and along with others, all of whom wore different test clothing and footwear, making the third ascent of Mount McKinley.

After the war he climbed McKinley by the Muldrow route again, this time to film for RKO and to help make cosmic-ray studies. Barbara, his wife, who was with him, became the first woman to climb McKinley. Their team constantly used igloos instead of tents. Though they spent 90 days on the mountain and climbed the north summit as well, he was not finished. Four years later he persuaded Terris Moore to use his plane on skis to land him and other climbers on the Kahiltna Glacier. From there they made a new route up the West Buttress. Since then, this flight-assisted route has become the favorite way to climb the mountain. In fact, in 1991, in a single season, nearly 600 climbers reached the summit, most of them on this route.

Washburn did not climb to the summit again, but year after year he took new aerial photographs, many while making his outstanding map of Mount McKinley. Regularly publishing superb pictures of the mountain in the *American Alpine Journal* and elsewhere, he kept pointing out new route prospects. These pictures and articles more than anything else have led to the tremendous national and international interest in climbing our highest mountain. Some of the world's most famous climbers have been attracted by them, men such as Riccardo Cassin, whose party made the first ascent of a difficult route up the middle of the South Face, now known as the Cassin Ridge. Famous mountaineers who have climbed McKinley or its surrounding peaks, tempted by Washburn's prodding, include Lionel Terray, Reinhold Messner, Dougal Haston, Doug Scott, and the famous Japanese, Naomi Uemura, who lost his life while descending from the south summit after a successful winter solo climb. By now McKinley has been climbed solo winter and summer. It has even been climbed by the West Buttress route up and back in one day, but none of these extreme achievements take away from the challenges of the early climbs or the majesty of a mountain that at times endangers everybody on its slopes. More than fifty have already died there. Despite this book's subtitle, McKinley will never be permanently "conquered." Instead it will accede to human ambitions when it wishes or crush them violently when it does not.

This book is sure to be a cherished item in mountain libraries far, far into the future.

ROBERT H. BATES

Surviving Denali: A Study of Accidents on Mount McKinley 1903-1990. Jonathan Waterman, with an Introduction and chapter on Mountain Medicine by Peter H. Hackett, M.D. Second Edition, Revised. American Alpine Club Press, New York, 1991. 67 pages of black-and-white pictures, plus appendices and short bibliography. Soft cover.

Surviving Denali should be required reading for people climbing Mount McKinley. The first edition was published in 1983 and this edition brings it up to date. Accidents on the mountain are still common and the death toll continues to rise. This does not mean that climbing Mount McKinley should be discouraged, but that before climbers commit themselves, they should know what can happen. The book describes a series of accidents, most of which could have been avoided.

Chapters discuss high altitude, pulmonary and cerebral edema, frostbite, climbing falls, crevasse falls, avalanches, unusual accidents, preparations for Denali, and the use of drugs at high altitude. There are summaries of each type of accident.

Nobody is better prepared to write about the danger of climbing McKinley than Jonathan Waterman, who from 1976 to 1987 has been closely involved with the mountain as climber, ranger, guide and rescuer. He has risked his life to help others on various occasions, and knows well the highest northern mountain in the world and McKinley's unique conditions and dangers.

ROBERT H. BATES

The Endless Knot: K2, Mountain of Dreams and Destiny. Kurt Diemberger. Translated by Audrey Salkeld. Grafton Books, London, 1991. 308 pages, profusely illustrated; diagrams and tables, necrology and bibliography. $32.

This is not so much a mountaineering book as a love story. A story of the love between a man and a woman and their passion for mountains. A soliloquy rather than a narrative, a story of death and disaster with few heroes.

At 60, Kurt Diemberger is a grand veteran of climbs around the world. Mountains are not the main part of his life—they are, he writes, "what we are living for". Since his youth he has been devoted to mountains as climber, photographer, writer and lecturer. Julie Tullis became his acolyte and partner and her memory permeates this entire book. She was 47 when she died. Both were happily married—she in Britain, he in Italy—and both had children.

They met in 1975 but climbed together for only five years. The Karakoram became their dream, and the summit of K2 their obsession. It is consoling to know they had reached their goal before Julie died, overcome on the descent. Most of the book is devoted to K2 but Diemberger tells brief, taut stories of Herman Buhl and himself on Chogolisa, and of how Julie and he almost died during their climb of Broad Peak. Many vivid flashbacks illuminate the central figure—Julie.

In June, 1986, the encampment of the world's greatest climbers from nine countries was happy and convivial; there was friendship without much competition. Then the weather window narrowed. The deaths began. The mood changed. The struggle for the summit was on. The book focuses on the polyglot team which Kurt and Julie of necessity had joined.

Exactly what happened to Julie and others who died high on K2 in the awful weeks can never be fully known. In this book the horror has been softened by time and the search for healing, as it was at the time by lack of oxygen, food and water and by the sapping cold. Many others have recounted the triumphs and tragedies of that summer and the deaths of 13 of the 90 men and women who watched and yearned for the great mountain. It is easy to find inconsistencies and discrepancies. Many facts are disputed. Memories have faded. There have been sharp disagreements and bitter recriminations. To his credit Diemberger points no finger, assesses little blame except on himself.

There's no stiff upper lip here, emotions are laid out and wept over. One feels that the author is seeking absolution, relief by catharsis for intolerably sad memories. Yet through his pain comes the awe and wonder which envelop the greatest peaks. It is an enthralling book, and beautifully illustrated.

Still, I found the book hard reading. Many flashbacks and digressions disorder the course of the mountaineering narrative. I found it difficult to keep track of who was where and what was happening much of the summer, especially during the climactic week. For those who need the chronology, the long list of the dead is helpful.

It was hard for me too because 33 years before, to the very week, my friends and I lived through a similar storm in the same place; we also lost our friend. Diemberger opened memories I thought safely locked away.

It is saddening, too, to realize how few of the lessons of the past had been remembered in 1986—or have been learned today. The sharp thrust of ambition, the quest for fame and fortune continue to spur some climbers. The mind-numbing effect of too little oxygen which blunts judgment, even will, high on these great and beautiful and deadly mountains was surely a major cause of most of the deaths.

Is this what mountaineering has become? Must great risks be taken for great rewards? Does death somehow enlarge and render heroic the venture, flawed though it may have been? Are the great mountains a battlefield—or a shrine?

CHARLES S. HOUSTON, M.D.

Reinhold Messner Free Spirit: A Climber's Life. Reinhold Messner. Translated by Jill Neate. The Mountaineers, Seattle, 1991. 250 pages, illustrated. $32.00.

Although he is still well under 50, perhaps Messner has already accomplished too much for an autobiography. Too much, certainly, for *this* autobiography: not just the fourteen 8000-meter peaks (some of them more than once), but the highest points on all the continents, a sledge crossing of Antarctica, the Kilimanjaro icicle, numberless new routes in Europe, some solo or in foul conditions. Not to mention a medieval castle converted into a private residence, a divorce, a baby, and two brothers killed in the mountains. He has only two pages, for instance, for an ascent of K2; only two paragraphs for the traverse of Gasherbrum I and II. Much of the material may be found in greater detail in his many other books.

As so often when climbers tell their stories, the personal life barely exists. Some passages are introspective, but we learn little of Messner's wife, who meets him at the Munich airport on his return from Dhaulagiri "to say adieu to me;" Messner merely observes that "marriage was perhaps not the best way of living together; at least, not when more time was spent in the Himalayas than at home." Later we read of the birth of his daughter by another woman, whereupon mother and child virtually vanish from the book. The omissions extend to climbing relationships: only a photo caption alludes to the end of Messner's famous partnership with Peter Habeler.

But if a lot is slighted or left out, plenty remains. Many of the accounts, especially the early ones of the Alps and Dolomites, remain exciting despite their brevity. And Messner does leave more room (though still less than the reader wishes) for some crucial climbs, particularly on Nanga Parbat. His first ascent, with the loss of his brother Günther, was a major episode in his life, as was his remarkable solo climb eight years later. The sheer profusion of achievements is astonishing. Far from content with seizing the likeliest summits and routes, Messner has sought out truly remote places: the Tibetan plateau, the New Guinea highlands, Antarctica. And he has never settled for the obvious or become complacent about his accomplishments. One famous instance: having reached the top of Everest without oxygen, he repeats the achievement by a different route—this time, solo.

Messner has firm and, to my mind, admirable views on the mountain environment. He rejects the drilling of bolts and is particularly harsh about their use on climbs that had been established without them. "For a pure climb on extreme rock a sporting spirit is a prerequisite . . . it is not climbing 'by fair means' to carry on using all available aids." He has initiated "a small agricultural project in South Tyrol" that is run on ecological principles. "It is important that we leave all areas which we visit as we find them," he writes near the end. "Deserts and mountains are a catalyst for our humanity." He concludes with a strongly-urged tribute to Tomo Česan, whose solo first ascent of Lhotse's South Face embodies what Messner most admires: a solitary achievement, accomplished with great risk and in fine style.

Adding to the book's attraction is its excellent production by The Mountaineers. The text, like the many photographs, both black-and-white and color, is on glossy paper, and the signatures are sewn. This volume is meant to last on your shelves.

STEVEN JERVIS

Un Pionero de Bariloche: Otto Meiling. Vojslav Arko. Bavaria y Cía., Bariloche, Argentina, 1991. 125 pages, 58 black-and-white illustrations, 6 sketch-maps. Paperback.

Sitting at the gates of Argentinian Patagonia, Bariloche (population: 100,000) is the only important town in the entire Andes that lives for winter and mountain sports. Its Club Andino Bariloche (4000 members) is by far the largest in Latin America. It was founded in August 1931 by four residents of the town, of which the German Otto Meiling (1902-1989) was one. This book is his biography. While containing at the same time a parallel story of the Club Andino Bariloche itself, the work also covers a good part of Patagonian mountaineering history. Meiling and club members took part in the first ascents of San Valentín (3876 meters), highest in the southern Andes, of Balmaceda (2035 meters), attempted Paine in 1957, explored the valleys of northeastern Patagonia and pioneered rock routes around Bariloche itself. Author Arko portrays him as a rather eccentric person, a hermit and a thinker, who in the last years of his life chose to live in isolation in a hut perched on a high place. Having been besides a youth leader and one of the founders of Argentinian skiing, he left an imprint on the succeeding generations. The biography, well illustrated and straightforwardly narrated, represents a unique book in South American mountaineering: it is the very first biography of an *andinista,* and a good one at that.

EVELIO ECHEVARRÍA

Shawangunk Rock Climbs. Dick Williams. The American Alpine Club Press. New York, 1991. Volume One: *The Trapps.* 346 pages. 55 black-and-white photos. $25.00. Volume Two: *The Near Trapps.* 218 pages. 28 black-and-white photos. $20.00. Volume Three: *Sky Top.* 196 pages. 38 black-and-white photos. $20.00.

Much has changed in the Gunks since Williams' last guide appeared in 1980. For one thing, there have been two editions of another guide to the area. For another, the crowds that throng the Trapps on any given weekend dwarf the relatively small population of climbers who used the region twelve years ago. And of course, there are a few more routes; well over a thousand now.

The Gunks lend themselves to verbal description rather than topo format, and because of their detail and explicitness, the guide comes in three volumes:

One volume covers the Trapps, another Millbrook and the Near Trapps and the third Sky Top. This feature makes the chosen volume less of a hassle to cart around on climbs, or stuff in the top pocket of your pack, but will empty your wallet a bit more than one condensed book. If you are visiting the area with any frequency or for a prolonged stay, you'll need all three volumes.

There are a lot of things to like about this guide. First and foremost, *it guides.* Williams spent much time doing his homework on route descriptions, eliciting details from first ascentionists and avoiding the trap so many guide book authors fall into of relying on just a few people to offer information and opinions. The result is the most complete and detailed guide the region has ever seen. All three volumes give the details on the current rules and regulations of the area, which everyone should read thoroughly to assure future access to sensitive areas. The Trapps volume also gives a lengthy history lesson, beginning with the dark ages of hemp rope and Wiessner/Kraus classics, up to the more recent days of bolt wars and Franklin desperates. There is plenty of fuel for rainy days reading and debate. As Williams has been around for more than half the time climbers have been cragging here, his perspective has merit. Another very useful feature is a topo of the base of the cliffs, which correlates with the photos of the routes. This visual information, along with the written descriptions, will make it an effort to get lost. Well, most of the time.

My criticisms of the guide are few, and mostly personal. The starring system is ultra-conservative and will keep visitors away from many excellent climbs if they use it as a guide, especially in the upper grades. The photos of Millbrook are less than perfect, and for some reason, this cliff always hosts the largest amount of description errors in the various guides. In the guide of this part, there are starting pitches omitted from several routes, but at least the descriptions are accurate for the pitches described. Since Millbrook is so rarely visited, few will worry about missing out on several rope-lengths of climbing. A final personal gripe is the lack of a recommended route list. Maybe it's because I've grown sick of listing the same old routes for hundreds of visitors over the years. In any case, it's a minor point.

So buy the guide and have fun in the Gunks. Buy your button or day pass, be nice to the rangers and they will be nice to you. Carry a little plastic bag and pick up trash left by others as you wander down the carriage road; if you smoke, quit. If you choose not to quit, please carry your butts out with you. Climbing at the Gunks is a privilege; the rules are few and simple, the pleasures immense.

RUSS CLUNE

The Basic Essentials of Hypothermia. William W. Forgey. ICS Books, Merrill-
    ville, Indiana, 1991. 68 pages, many diagrams and tables.

This book is one of the Basic Essentials Series of 24 outdoor volumes, written to provide the average outdoor person with all one needs to know about problems likely to be encountered. The style is serious, the writing terse. Case histories

illustrate more important points. Numerous charts and diagrams provide technical data in an understandable way. The information is up to date. The author
manages to avoid medical jargon and to speak to the average reader without
condescension. This is an inexpensive, valuable addition to any outdoor library.

CHARLES S. HOUSTON, M.D.

Peaks and Passes of the Garhwal Himalaya. Jan Babicz. Alpinistyczny Klub
   Eksploracyjny, ul Armii Krajowej 12, Sopot, Poland, 1991. 246 pages,
   ridgeline maps, numerous drawings of peaks with routes marked, topos.
   Available postpaid from Jan Babicz, ul Grottgera 24/2, 80-311 Gdańsk,
   Poland, $14.00 (US). (Better to send banknotes than a check.)

This very valuable book, written in English, begins with general information
about Garhwal. Part two deals with the 7000-meter peaks of the region,
including Nanda Devi, Trisul, Kamet, Mana, Chaukhamba, Satopanth and
others. Part Three has data on the peaks of the western part of the Gangotri
region, such as Thalay Sagar, Shivling, the Bhagirathi peaks and many others.
These two sections give a detailed history, in most cases up to 1989, of the
individual mountains, the routes by which they were climbed and by whom.
There are skillful drawings of the peaks with the routes shown, plus topos of
some routes, maps locating the mountains and other important information. The
final section describes high treks.
   This reviewer, who has made several expeditions in the region, finds the
book accurate and a great reference tool. It should be consulted by anyone
planning to visit the region. The author believes that the book will soon be
available from Chessler in the United States and from Cordee in England, but it
may be ordered directly from him.

H. ADAMS CARTER

Trekking Mount Everest. Ryohei Uchida. Chronicle Books, San Francisco,
   1991. 128 pages, 257 color photographs, 3 sketch maps. $16.95.

Ryohei Uchida is a master photographer. He has been a professional for 21 years
and has visited Nepal thirty times. While preparing the present volume, he made
six trips to Nepal during four years. The photographs are stunning. There are
lovely scenes of the landscape taken along the route between Jiri to Everest Base
Camp, photographs of the local people at home and at work, shots of festivals
and art objects.
   This is more than just a trekker's guide, thanks to the gorgeous photographs
and information it gives. Eight of the well-illustrated chapters are devoted to the
trekker routes to approach the Base Camp of Everest: for instance from Jiri to
Lukla, from Lukla to Namche Bazar, etc. There are also two side trips: from

Khumjung to Gokya and to Chhukung. A final photographic section contains beautiful Himalayan flowers. The book ends with fifteen pages of practical text about lodging, food, appropriate clothing, porters, climate, required permits, mountain sickness and the people of the region. There is also a glossary of Nepali words and phrases.

Trekking Mount Everest is valuable for anyone planning a visit to Everest Base Camp, a book to evoke memories for those who have already been there and a splendid presentation for the armchair traveler—in short a book for everyone.

H. ADAMS CARTER

Green Cognac: The Education of a Mountain Fighter. William Lowell Putnam. American Alpine Club Press. New York, 1991. 288 pages, 52 black-and-white photographs, 9 maps. $35.00.

Most books and articles about the 10th Mountain Division in World War II have been written in the third-person, in a style varying from the formal to the pretentious. Bill Putnam's book, *Green Cognac: The Education of a Mountain Fighter,* is relaxed, informal and written in the first-person without becoming an "I did this, and I did that" narrative. In the early chapters he tells a story of coming of age, combat in Italy, being wounded, winning a Silver Star and developing his own life-time philosophy.

As an undergraduate at Harvard, Putnam was very active in the Harvard Mountaineering Club, which he credits with giving him a start in mountaineering and blames for keeping him in a happy and almost perpetual state of "on probation." This all culminated later in mountaineering activities at Camp Hale, Colorado, on the Aleutian Island of Kiska and in the Italian Apennines.

There are many hilarious happenings here. One involves Christmas leave following his return from Kiska when he was too short on money to phone his family to say that he would be arriving on Christmas Day. When he arrived and the doorbell was answered by his little brother, the youngster took one look and retreated, shrieking, "A ghost!, A ghost!"

Not so amusing is his account of Company L's first action in which he played host to a German shell fragment which is still a nuisance when modern airport security devices cause bells to ring and lights to flash.

Bill Putnam recounts his experiences on Monte Belvedere during the Po Valley pursuit, fighting along Lake Garda and the move into Venezia-Giulia to checkmate Marshall Tito. Throughout these engagements, the chronic mountaineer continued to find opportunities to enjoy his hobby and, best of all, to make it possible for the climbers of his company to do so.

Finally, Bill Putnam summarizes the roles the 10th Mountain veterans have played in developing our American winter and alpine recreation industry as well as what happened to those who returned to more conventional activities. In any event, there seems to be agreement among 10th Mountain veterans that their time with the Division in Italy was among their finest moments. By all means, read *Green Cognac* and enjoy the account of how a young man became a veteran mountain trooper and achieved an education in life.

ALBERT H. JACKMAN

Antarctica: Both Heaven and Hell, Reinhold Messner. Translated by Jill Neate. The Mountaineers, Seattle. 1991. 375 pages. $35.00

Some of the glory attached to Scott, Shackleton, Herzog and Shipton is owed to their unsung language teachers. In adventuring, one has not only to do the deed but tell it well. Reading Reinhold Messner is like contemplating an unwrought sculpture and imagining the form that might lie inside. Not that Messner is short on words or, as Steve Jervis points out in the accompanying review, shy about going into print. Not that his literary persona is uninteresting: quite the contrary, Messner's obsessive quest for identity through the overcoming of extreme obstacles has led to magnificent achievements. What's more, he is a man of considerable charm and verve.

So why then is *Antarctica: Both Heaven and Hell* such a mind-glazer? Why is it that halfway into what should be a ripping yarn one cares so little?

This book actually starts out well. Messner is wracked by existential doubt. His South Tyrol neighbors urge him to stay home and tend to his castle, while his soul cries out with wanderlust. A bit melodramatic, but okay.

Then the story begins and we launch into the preparations, accompanied by copious historical snippets and photos from the Antarctic library. Here, too, we learn a little about his companion, Arved Fuchs, who has walked to the North Pole. Messner's friends warn that Fuchs may be a phoney. En passant, Messner confesses to a little phoneyness of his own: when he got sucked into a "childish game . . . to impress the media public," which is what he now calls the Seven Summits on Seven Continents caper that got him to climb the Vinson Massif in 1986.

Once on the ice in December 1989, Messner has a row with Adventure Network International, who provide less air support than promised, and he makes an effort to get acquainted with the enigmatic Arved. Meanwhile, who should breeze through the camp but another trans-Antarctic expedition, the Steiger-Etienne six-man dog sled team bent upon a 6000-kilometer traverse of the continent, from the Palmer Peninsula to Queen Maud Land. What a break for the little press corps that Messner had lured to the scene. And when they tag along with the dog-sledders for a few days, and file thousands of words back to their editors, the becalmed Messner tries not to feel too miffed.

Finally, Messner and Fuchs set off from a somewhat arbitrary coordinate, 500 kilometers south of the Ronne ice shelf and Shackleton's proposed jumping off point for his 1914 trans-Antarctic trip. Very soon Fuchs has a case of chronic blisters from boots that are too small. (Shucks, we all make mistakes sometimes.) Also Fuchs is much less fit than Messner. Both pull sledges with 80-kilo loads, reprovision from an airdrop in the Thiel Mountains, arrive at the South Pole for a resupply and party with the USARP (U.S. Antarctic Research Program) crew there, and then make an exciting dash for McMurdo, more or less along Scott's route. A total of 2800 kilometers in 90 days.

From time to time Messner's writing about the journey communicates. And one suspects that some South Tyrolean high school teacher really made an impression. A random sample: "Arved and I were travelling without any scientific pretension and yet we endeavoured to grasp this white infinity, to assess it, to find a relationship with it. For the time being it held us fast, nevertheless we were not yet fully conscious of its significance."

But then comes an unconvincing passage about his feeling like a primitive man at the dawn of time. And so once again the sculpture inside the stone recedes from view. As with his mountaineering tales, only the most determined reader is going to be alert for the Messnerian gems amidst the dross. But they *are* gems, of sensibility more than close observation.

A satisfying account of this journey would need a more coherent narrative. There are deep flaws in its logic, chiefly because there are no rules of play, no clean "ethic." And the achievement itself is beset with a mass of contradictions, as well as false comparisons with other Antarctic crossings. For instance, Messner puts down the high tech, all-tractor Fuchs-Hillary trans-Antarctic venture of 1957, but himself uses planes for resupply. True, not nearly as frequently, he insists, as the Steger-Etienne crew, who had many more dumps and also a constant supply of fresh flown-in dogs. Nor did he have their lavish corporate sponsorship. But he did have one crucial corporate backer to defray the million Deutschmark cost.

In the end Messner's claims to have used only "fair means" don't hold up very well. While his boast to a better manhauling speed than Shackleton's on his run for the Pole—who had no air support, no satellite tracking, no freeze-dried foods, no high-tech skis—is ridiculous. As to the trip's other motive—to express personal commitment to an Antarctic World Park—it remains throughout an abstraction, a slogan.

To be sure, nearly all adventure raises tricky ethical questions of appropriate risk, the fairness of the contest, the utility of the quest. These existed even when there were some blank spaces on the map. But the flaws, inconsistencies, presumption and even serious mistakes of a venture get excused when there's good writing, as Scott's last journey demonstrated.

Following the show-and-tell to newspapers and TV, the two explorers rift. Apparently a pattern with Messner. He is caught off guard and cannot believe the stories given out by Arvid Fuchs—or maybe just his handlers—the unkindest being that Fuchs, who Messner says took the lead only once, for a paltry 10 kilometers, was the trailbreaker throughout the march. Messner is hurt. One by the betrayal. Two by the fact that Arvid—such a nice quiet boy on the ice—seems to have bested him in the media.

Alas, Messner's letting-it-all-hang-out style destroys his effort to identify his epic with the Antarctic Greats. *They* never blabbed. Yet one cannot help but root for him, and his ingenuous determination to be honest at all costs. On page 267 he declares that "just because I write openly about fears, egotism and aggression, I have frequently been called an *all-consuming* (kilometers, summits, successes, people) *Super-Neandertaler*. My claim to be sincere *vis-à-vis* myself and my readers was construed continually as me showing off." And then just as one feels this guy really is too much, in the next sentence he says something Goethe might have written: "I know only that the word you have torn out of your soul has power."

JOHN THACKRAY

Second Ascent, The Story of Hugh Herr. Alison Osius. Stackpole Books, Harrisburg, PA, 1991. 240 pages. Black-and-white photographs. $19.95.

I knew Hugh Herr. First, as a teen-age prodigy smoking his way through Shawangunk test-pieces. (He soloed "P.R.", 5.11+, when he was sixteen.) Then, after the event which cost him both legs, I knew him during his remarkable recovery and spectacular comeback as the Mechanical Boy, a prodigious feat of an altogether higher order of magnitude. We weren't close, not even casual friends, barely acquaintances. But I had a strong sense of Hugh Herr. And I can tell you that the portrait Alison Osius paints in her stunning biography, *Second Ascent, The Story of Hugh Herr,* captures his likeness with total accuracy.

Osius has honed her literary skills on numerous articles for outdoor periodicals and now is Senior Editor at *Climbing* magazine. To my knowledge, this is her first full-length work. Hugh's story has all the ingredients for soap-opera tragedy which could be easily told with saccharine sympathy, recrimination and other pseudo-literary conceits. However, Osius resists every pitfall and does more than justice to her material, telling Hugh's story with a forthright directness worthy of and no doubt inspired by those very qualities embodied in her subject.

Osius starts the book with a discussion of Hugh's Mennonite ancestors who settled in eastern Pennsylvania in the early 18th century. Examining the values which shaped that culture, she puts Hugh into a context that informs his personality and nature in terms of the ongoing and unbroken tradition from which he springs. She speaks of the extremely close-knit family whose summer trips out West first introduced Hugh to the mountains. The non-climbing reader then learns about technical rock climbing as Hugh and his older brother, Tony, first learn about it themselves, as young boys reading instructional manuals and then putting their information about these techniques into practice on the local crags and outcrops near their home farm.

What becomes clear early in the story and runs as a leitmotif throughout the book is Hugh's passion for climbing. He is driven! Virtually every other aspect of his life is subsumed in his obsession with climbing. (He even gets involved with gymnastics at school to improve his climbing.) Hugh discovers as a boy what most great climbers learn only later in their careers: it's all in the mind. Physical strength was never an issue for Hugh. The strength of the mind is the only limiting factor. Osius points out again and again, albeit with a light touch, that Hugh devoted an enormous amount of time and effort developing and cultivating his ability to control his mind. His efforts are rewarded as he discovers that he can virtually eliminate fear while climbing through the intensity of his focus and concentration. It is perhaps this quality and characteristic more than any other that enables and empowers him not only to recover from the loss of both legs but to re-learn to climb at the very highest standard.

Osius has done all the meticulous research, speaking to virtually any and everybody involved in the events of Hugh's life. It's all here; Hugh's one-fall ascent of "Super Crack," and the vision of his potential to become one of the world's elite rock climbers. Then the "accident" on Mt. Washington intervenes and claims not only his legs, but also the life of one of his would-be rescuers, Albert Dow. Osius devotes an appropriate portion of the book to Hugh's struggle to come to terms with his sense of responsibility for this man's death. We see how his iron will and phenomenal mental disclipline, nurtured on the crags of his youth, help him forge a resolution to the conflicts raging within him.

The book functions on many levels. It is both biography and inspiration. Problems and setbacks that loom in one's own life tend to retreat into perspective when reading about the obstacles Hugh encounters and how he triumphs over them. After his recovery and time spent in New Hampshire confronting his demons and re-integrating into the community that previously resented him, he enters college near his home in Pennsylvania. He spends a couple of years working on innovative ideas for prosthetic devices and ends up in a graduate program in engineering at MIT. Hugh feels that people are not handicapped, it is rather technology that suffers this shortcoming. As he says himself, if someone would invent sufficiently sophisticated mechanical legs he could run a marathon. He would probably win!

JON ROSS

LEIGH N. ORTENBURGER
1929-1991

In Memoriam

LEIGH N. ORTENBURGER
1929-1991

On October 19, 1991, Leigh N. Ortenburger, who had survived over 40 years of active mountaineering in the world's greatest mountain ranges, died in the firestorm that swept the Oakland, California hills and destroyed 3000 houses and apartments and killed 25 people. Leigh didn't even live there. He just happened to pick that day when disaster struck to make a rare visit to his friends and fellow mountaineers, Al and Gail Baxter. Gail also died in the fire and Al was severely burned. Leigh is survived by his daughters Carolyn and Teresa and his brothers Robert and Arthur Ortenburger.

Leigh was born in Norman, Oklahoma, on February 14, 1929. At an early age he demonstrated an instinctive interest in climbing by falling out of a tree and breaking his arm. In 1948, he first went to the Tetons and soon became a guide with the Exum Guide Service. He was in fast company with the likes of Glenn Exum, Bob Merriam, Dick Pownall, Willi Unsoeld, Art Gilkey and others at the guide shack and Dick Emerson at Park Headquarters. But even in that group, Leigh could hold his own. He might not have had the flair of an Unsoeld, the technique of an Emerson nor the strength of a Pownall, but he was a highly capable, competent and determined climber, always a reassuring presence on a rope. No matter how bad the situation became, Leigh was one person you never had to worry about. He was always part of the solution and not the problem.

Leigh was also interested in the history of mountaineering. Once in 1951, he was persuaded by friends into climbing the regular route on Cloudveil Dome in the Tetons. It turned out the real reason Leigh wanted to climb the mountain was that it still had the original register from the first ascent in 1931. It was a typical Ortenburger con job, skillfully performed and when it was over, the "victims" were glad to have done it. The culmination of this interest was his *Climber's Guide to the Teton Range,* which first appeared in 1956. Comprehensive, meticulously researched, it became a standard against which guidebooks were judged. Moreover, Leigh personally had done most of the climbs himself. He had just completed his most recent two-volume update of the guidebook and had published it in preliminary form when he died.

Besides being an historian, researcher and guidebook writer, Leigh was also an outstanding photographer. In an era of the teensy Kodak Flash Bantams, he didn't haul that big Speed Graphic camera around just as an excuse for his companions to carry the pack. He used it, as evidenced by the many superb pictures that grace his books. His friends always made sure to send him a Christmas card, because Leigh's card would have another one of his marvelous pictures.

He was also doing the hardest climbs in the Tetons, such as the North Face Direct on the Grand Teton and the Direct South Buttress on Mount Moran.

What was significant was not that his companions were the likes of Willi Unsoeld and Dick Emerson but that he belonged to that crowd. The man could climb!

Leigh graduated from the University of Oklahoma in 1952 with a degree in mathematics and got a master's degree from the University of California in Berkeley in 1953. While in the San Francisco Bay Area, he frequently climbed in Yosemite, often with members of the Stanford Alpine Club. It was there that he met and in 1956 married Irene Beardsley, a member of the club who shared his determination, dedication and love of the mountains. They proceeded to climb all over the Tetons and then the Andes, especially the Cordillera Blanca—like the Tetons, a good-weather area. He made ten expeditions to the region and accomplished such difficult climbs as Huantsán and in 1964 the second ascent of Chacraraju by the unclimbed north ridge.

Although one associates Leigh with the Tetons and the Andes, the ultimate test of his courage, skill and dedication to his fellow climber occurred on Makalu in 1961. Leigh was a member of Ed Hillary's 1961 expedition to that mountain. When Tom Nevison and New Zealander Peter Mulgrew were making their summit assault from Camp VII without artifical oxygen, Mulgrew collapsed at 27,400 feet with a pulmonary embolism. After two nights above 26,000 feet, Nevison as well as Mulgrew was severely dehydrated and could barely move. It was left to a few Sherpas and Leigh Ortenburger, who had climbed up in support, to get Peter Mulgrew down to Camp V. At one point, Leigh had to spend the night out alone with Mulgrew between Camps VII and VI. But Leigh not only survived; he persevered and eventually Peter Mulgrew was saved. It was one of those great selfless moments in the history of mountaineering.

Besides rearing a family and climbing mountains, Leigh worked for over thirty years at Sylvania in Sunnydale, California, as a statistician specializing in the propagation of radio waves. He obviously was a valuable man because Sylvania always allowed him to take several months off each summer to go climbing.

Leigh joined the American Alpine Club in 1952 and was active in the affairs of the Club, especially on the Expeditions Committee. He was Western Vice President of the Club from 1965 until 1967.

Like many mountaineers of his era, Leigh was a man of firm convictions, some of which might even be considered eccentric by his eccentric friends. For instance, he had distinct tastes in food, which once led him to turn down most of the offerings of his friends when he had left his entire food supply, five jelly sandwiches, at the base of a climb and was in danger of starvation. But this interest in food also led to such immortal comments as his remark about one companion, "He is the kind of man who will pick all the cashews out of a can of mixed nuts."

Leigh was an original. It was only after his death that his friends realized that they probably had more Ortenburger stories than stories about even more famous climbers. For many years, when asked about what is the most important quality in a mountaineer, I always liked to quote what I call Ortenburger's law.

"A strong man who won't get out of the sack in the morning is useless." Leigh always got out of the sack in the morning.

My favorite story, one that illustrates his love of climbing, his enthusiasm, his ability to con others and his imperturbability in the face of circumstance and human disdain, occurred in the Tetons in the early 1950s. At six in the morning at Jenny Lake Campground, Leigh was shaking the tent, trying to get his companions to do a new route on the south face of Symmetry Spire. Ugly black streamers were scudding off the summits. When this was called to his attention, he pointed to a small hole in the clouds that was rapidly disappearing east over the Gros Ventre Range and shouted, "Look, Blue Sky! Blue Sky!" We went for a picnic on the Snake River instead. But Leigh did not give up. He finally got some innocents to join him. They were about 500 feet up the face when the inevitable happened. The skies opened and they were deluged in rain and hail. It was so heavy that they couldn't even rappel. His three companions huddled miserably on one end of the ledge and Ortenburger sat on the other. As his victims glowered at him under their leaking parkas, Leigh glanced up and said, "Who talked me into this?"

We shall miss him!

NICHOLAS B. CLINCH

DANIEL A. REID
1941-1991

On September 10, 1991, Dan Reid, M.D., an AAC member since 1971, and his wife Barbara were killed in a climbing accident on Mount Kenya. Their death left a void in many lives which can never be filled.

Dan was an extraordinary mountaineer. His climbing accomplishments include the first ascent of the Kangshung Face of Mount Everest and one of the earliest ascents of the North America Wall on El Capitan. He made the first ascent of South Taku Tower in Alaska's Coast Range and the first solo ascent of the University Wall on Squamish Chief. He was the leader of the Juneau Icefield Expedition and the British-American Torre Egger Expedition. His determination and belief in himself was infectious, and his attitude often gave others the inspiration they needed to carry on in adverse circumstances.

More than an extraordinary mountaineer, however, Dan was truly an extraordinary man. He was a highly regarded cardiothoracic surgeon, practicing at the Mount Diablo Medical Center in Concord, California. After growing up in Birmingham, Michigan, Dan attended Michigan State University and then Medical School at the University of Michigan. He received his surgery training in Seattle and thoracic training at the Albany Medical Center in New York.

In Dan's many avocations, he was an athlete, a fisherman, a bagpiper, a soldier and a charitable and public-minded citizen. He was a member of the U.S. Polo Association, the Diablo Valley Fly Fisherman's Society, the Saint Andrew's Society of San Francisco, the Clan Donnachaidh Society and the

Board of Directors of the American Himalayan Foundation. He often spoke to local children about his adventures and about drug-abuse prevention.

Dan's military career included three tours of duty in Vietnam as a Green Beret surgeon. He held the rank of Lieutenant Colonel in the Army Reserve and served a tour of active duty during Operation Desert Storm.

Dan loved life and lived it as few people do. His enthusiasm, approachable demeanor and sparkling wit made him widely loved and respected by everyone he met. Barbara, who probably was the only woman who could have kept up with Dan, was his ideal companion and was equally capable in the myriad of activities in which the couple participated. To say Dan and Barbara will be missed seems totally inadequate. Perhaps the words of the great Scottish bard, Robert Burns, are more appropriate:

> *We saw thee shine in youth and beauty's pride,*
> *And virtue's light that beams beyond the spheres;*
> *But, like the sun eclipsed at morning tide,*
> *Thou left'st us darkling in a world of tears.*

J. BRUCE McCUBBREY

LEWIS FROTHINGHAM CLARK
1900-1991

Lewis Frothingham Clark was born in Boston on October 29, 1900 and died on March 8, 1991 at the age of 90. The family moved to California when he was four years old. He was a member of the American Alpine Club for well over a half a century, having joined the Club in 1933.

He graduated from the University of California at Berkeley in 1922, having majored in electrical engineering. He then took an advanced degree at the Massachusetts Institute of Technology. He worked as a staff engineer with the American Telephone and Telegraph Company until he retired in 1965. A bachelor, he lived in the beautiful house his father built in 1908 in Alameda, California

Lewis was very active in environmental work in the Sierra Club, which he joined in 1928. He served for 36 years on the Board of Directors. He was President from 1949 to 1951 and Honorary Vice-President from 1968 until his death. He and his brother Nathan were the only brothers both to have served as presidents of the Sierra Club. He was a pioneer in the construction of Sierra Club huts.

He led many trips not only in California but also to Canada, Europe and Japan. He did much for the early development of long-distance ski mountaineering to remote summits at moderately high elevations, such as the first winter ascent of Mount Lyell, at 13,000 feet, fifty years ago. He climbed Fujiyama in his 70s and Greece's Mount Olympus when he was 80. Recently he went with Lindblad to Antarctica.

We are grateful to Lewis that he gave so much time and energy to preserve our wilderness areas. The burden is now on us.

RICHARD M. LEONARD

LYDIA LYMAN HALL
1899-1991

Two years ago, when she became so terribly ill, although she knew exactly what was going on, her optimism and courage never flagged for a moment. Her patience was thrilling. Her marvelous and oft-subtle sense of humor was ever-present.

A beautiful, thoughtful, warm and gallant friend has left us, and we can all be thankful that we've been able to share even a tiny part of our lives with Lydia Lyman Hall.

Mountains and exploration were, of course, the catalyst that brought us together at the beginning—but, as the years went by, the real roots of our relationship ran much deeper than that: countless teas and dinners at 154 Coolidge Hill, weeks together at the Hôtel Couttet et du Parc in Chamonix, sumptuous meals together at Zürich's Baur au Lac, and winter holidays at the Glen House with Bob and Miriam Underhill, and Carl and Dorothy Fuller.

I met Henry and Lydia Hall for the first time in New York on January 9, 1926. That was also the first time I had ever worn a tuxedo, borrowed frantically from someone at the very last moment. Our distinguished mutual friend and former president of the American Alpine Club, Dr. Harry Pierce Nichols, had invited me, age 15, to attend the annual meeting of the American Alpine Club. At that moment, a wonderful 66-year-long friendship with Lydia as well as with Henry Hall began.

Ever since Lydia was a little girl, she always had animals: her pig Lemuel, the turkey Pyramus, a pony Tom Thumb, ducks, hens, geese. But horses were the most important. For years, she was involved with the Millwood Hunt. As Whip, she trained the hound puppies, helped with the trails and rode and showed her own horses. She became Master of Fox Hounds after World War II, a position she held for twenty years. This was a full-time job—planning the "runs," (it was a drag hunt), directing operations and most important, being a good public-relations person. She had to talk with and soothe land-owners, over whose land the hunt would go. She was hospitable to the members and staff at the hunt teas and was a wonderful hostess, making people feel welcome.

I vividly remember meeting Lydia and Henry late in the afternoon at the Museum of Science four and a half years ago. We drove together to Coolidge Hill. It was a beautiful early-spring afternoon, and I shall always cherish the vivid memory of those last extremely happy moments with both of them at the end of a long, long friendship. Above all else, it was in that lovely living room at Coolidge Hill that Lydia's grace and warmth and delightful sense of humor captivated us all. Those red-hot cups of tea on chilly winter afternoon, scrumptious cookies and sandwiches, and conversations with endless scores of friends from every corner of the earth. Lydia was always at the helm, full of fun, ever the perfect hostess, ever saying exactly the right thing at the right moment—and always keeping Henry on a rather tight leash.

BRADFORD WASHBURN, *with assistance from* EDITH HALL OVERLY

FRANCES ANDREWS MULLEN
1902-1991

Frances Mullen died on April 14 in Sherman Oaks, California of Alzheimer's disease. She had been a member of the AAC since 1967 and was also an active member of the Chicago Mountaineering Club and the Sierra Club.

She received her Ph.B in mathematics in 1925, her M.A. in Education in 1929 and her Ph.D in Psychology in 1937, all from the University of Chicago. She joined the Chicago public schools in 1925 as a teacher and became a grammar school principal. She was Assistant Superintendent of the Schools for Special Education from 1953 to 1966. Thereafter, she had a private practice for psychological counseling, was editor of *International Pychologist* and President of the International Council of Psychologists.

Already in her childhood, Frances loved mountains, and with her father had climbed all of the Presidential Range of the White Mountains in New Hampshire by the time she was ten years old. As an adult, whenever possible, with her husband and children, she hiked and camped in the mountains. Family responsibilities and a demanding career frustrated her desires for greater involvement in these outdoor activities. In 1953, Frances with some reluctance attended a Chicago Mountaineering Club outing to the Wind River Range. The joys of mountaineering that she experienced on that outing fulfilled latent desires and life took on a new meaning for her.

From 1953 until she moved to California in 1975, she was a regular attendant at local weekend outings, summer and winter. In 1956, she attended the Alpine Club of Canada Golden Jubilee outing at Glacier Park, British Columbia. In 1957, she climbed in the Alps. In 1958, she assisted the leader of the Sierra Club in scouting for a base near Huascarán in Peru. In various years, she scrambled over the Julian Alps of Slovenia, hiked around the Piz Bernina, hut-hopped in Norway above the fjords out of Stavanger and in 1971 traveled to Hunza and the Karakoram. For her, the greatest adventure was in 1965 when she made a five-week trek from Kathmandu to the Thyangboche Lamasery under Mount Everest.

In 1968, Frances purchased a Chevrolet van and starting in August drove with two friends from Le Havre, France overland to Calcutta, India by way of the mountains of Europe, Turkey, Iraq, Iran and Nepal. The following year, she drove the van along the Pan American Highway from Chicago to Lima, Peru and then to Huaraz to join the Iowa Mountaineers outing in the Cordillera Blanca.

She had an enormous appeal for all who met her and especially the young climbers who adored this lady of the mountains. Her van was more often than not filled to capacity with young people on outings to Devils Lake, Wisconsin or to some western outing. She had a distinguished professional career and achieved much in the field of special education programs. Her wisdom and influence have left the world a better place for many. Her friendship will be missed by all and in particular the mountaineering community.

GEORGE POKORNY

CHARLES HAROLD WILTS
1920-1991

Charles (Chuck) Harold Wilts, a 26-year member of the American Alpine Club, died of a heart attack on March 12 while hiking on Echo Mountain in the San Gabriel Mountains, north of Pasadena, California. He was born on January 30, 1920 in Los Angeles, the son of Charles H. and Rose Goldberg Wilts. At the time of his death, he was Professor Emeritus of Electrical Engineering and Applied Physics at the California Institute of Technology. He is survived by me, his wife, his son Charles and daughters Gail and Janet.

Chuck received his B.S. (1940), M.S. (1941) and Ph.D (1948) at the California Institute of Technology. He joined the faculty in 1947. During World War II, he was appointed assistant supervisor in Aircraft Ballistics on the Rocket Project for both the Army and Navy. He worked on retrorockets and on fuses for igniting solid propellant.

Early in Chuck's career at Caltech, his work focused on the development and application of large-scale analog computers. In 1960, he began research in ferromagnetism in metal alloys and garnets, with emphasis on the use of thin films as research medium. He studied structure and surface properties, spin wave resonance and magnetization dynamics. He was a member of the Institute of Electrical and Electronic Engineering, the American Association for Advancement of Science and Sigma Xi. He wrote numerous scientific papers and authored *Principles of Feedback Control*. After retirement, he continued his research projects in magnetism.

Chuck began his relationship with the mountain world early in his life. From the age of six months until his mid twenties, he spent his summers with his family in the Sierra Nevada Mountains of California, camping in the Tuolumne Meadows and Yosemite Valley. With his father, he hiked, backpacked and fished, gaining his first experience in mountaineering. That early life endowed him with his lifelong love of wild places, rugged terrain, silent mountain splendor, beautiful landscape, the thrill of high-country exposure and challenges.

We met in June of 1941 in Tuolumne Meadows. In the fall of 1941, on a Sierra Club outing, Les Grossman introduced Chuck to the greatest love of his outdoor adventures, rock climbing. I was an initiate at the same time. Chuck became a Sierra Club member in 1942. Soon after joining the Sierra Club Rock Climbing Section, he discovered another lifetime outdoor activity, skiing, and he joined the Sierra Club Ski Mountaineering Section. He served as chairman of both sections. In 1945, he was a founding member of a skiers folk-dance group, "The Mountain Dancers," which is still active today. After the war, we mountaineered, rock climbed, skied and folk danced together and then married in 1947.

During the war years, he and climbing buddies made trips to local climbing areas. After the war, he spent much time in Yosemite Valley and at Tahquitz Rock, making many first ascents and attempts. He and Spencer Austin competed with Salathé and Nelson to make the first ascent of the Lost Arrow Chimney in

1946 and 1947. They bivouacked on the climb several times and, although they lost the competition, they helped make big-face climbs popular in Yosemite. Other Yosemite climbs included the first free ascent of the Higher Cathedral Spire, first ascents on the classic east face of Cathedral Peak in Tuolumne Meadows, the north ridge of Half Dome, the Leaning Tower Traverse and the south face of Rixon's Pinnacle. First ascents in the Sierra Nevada included three minarets: the east face of Starr, the south ridge of Ken and Jensen Minaret. Other ascents were the southeast face of Banner Peak, the northeast ridge of Mount Darwin, the northeast wall of Mount Morrison and the south arête of Matthes Crest. In the Canadian Rockies, first ascents included Mounts Symthe, Gec and Nelson. Some of the other climbing areas he enjoyed were the Needles in South Dakota, the Tetons, the Pinnacles and Joshua Tree National Monument.

At Tahquitz Rock, Chuck made too many first ascents to list. He also published in the 1956 second edition of the *Guide to Tahquitz Rock* the first official "decimal system" used for classifying and comparing climbing routes. Climbers originally called it the "Sierra-Wilts Decimal System." Chuck objected to the original name and finally it came to be known as the "Yosemite Decimal System." Throughout the years, he updated and published the guide five times. In 1964, he became a member of the American Alpine Club, which published the fourth, fifth and sixth edition of the *Guide to Tahquitz and Suicide Rocks*. He donated the book's proceeds to the Club. During Chuck's many years of climbing, he wrote articles for climbing magazines, Sierra Club publications and journals on safety concerns, rope durability and climbing hardware. He invented the knife-blade piton. He also built a device to test the strength of climbing ropes.

In Chuck's lifetime, he saw a revolutionary change in the sport of rock climbing. He began climbing with manila rope and heavy, bulky European climbing hardware. His footwear included tennis shoes, hiking boots and even, on occasion, nailed boots. His clothing consisted of army-surplus full-cut climbing pants, a pullover parka and a brimmed shade hat. Climbing was confined to weekends or vacations.

For several years, Chuck enthusiastically shared his interest by teaching a rock-climbing class to Caltech students. He also encouraged and joined the students in ascending campus buildings at night when they could not be seen by campus security. Needless to say, the Administration frowned on such "dangerous shenanigans." A Caltech climbers' guide for routes on the campus buildings was written by the students and dedicated to Chuck.

During the winter months, Chuck took to his skis. He earned the special "Big Badge" membership in the Ski Mountaineering Section of the Sierra Club for outstanding knowledge in mountaineering and snow craft. The Sierra Club honored him with the "Leadership Award" in 1980. He was on the Mount Waterman Ski Patrol for many years. He enjoyed downhill skiing, but ski mountaineering was a top priority. He went on many winter trips to the Sierra Nevada. Just a year before his death, he was in the Selkirks in Canada for the fourth time, snowcat skiing for a week in beautiful powder snow.

Chuck had many interests. He loved classical music and played the piano with great skill. He traveled for business and pleasure to Russia, Japan, many European countries and Mexico. His projects at home included the skills of carpenter, mason, plumber, cabinet maker, tool designer. He became a family genealogist and had just completed his book on his maternal line three days before his death. He researched and recorded information on the computer on the Mayan and Hebrew calendars. He was concerned about environmental and social problems facing the country and the world. He had a joy of living, a ready smile, a contagious laugh and displayed great enthusiasm for all the activities he undertook. Chuck leaves a record of many achievements and interests, but the one that remained to the end was a lifelong love affair with the wilderness of mountains.

ELLEN BEAUMONT WILTS

KENT ALAN JAMESON
1958-1991

Kent Alan Jameson of Oxnard, California, was killed on July 7 in a rappelling accident while descending Thunderbird Peak in the Sierra Nevada. Kent's loss will be deeply felt by many. He left behind a substantial climbing record, excelling equally at rock, ice and mountaineering. His love for the high peaks took him to the tops of Denali, Alpamayo and the Mexican volcanoes. His list of climbs in the Tetons was formidable and included ascents of the north face and north ridge of the Grand Teton, the south buttress of Moran, the Snaz and a winter ascent of the Black Ice Couloir. He was a leading figure of the climbing scene around Salt Lake City in the early 1980s as a part of a small group of climbers responsible for repeating hard routes and pioneering new ones.

Kent was a truly unique and outstanding character. Blessed as he was with a combination of intense drive, a volatile temper and a flare for the unusual, he gave color and texture to otherwise mundane climbing experiences. There were many times when I belayed him long after dark as he refused to give up on a lead, even several hundred feet up a frozen waterfall. Yes, he was a driven dude for sure. One of my last memories of Kent is of a changed person. With a different perspective derived from an enforced layoff from climbing and a change of jobs, it was a mellower Kent that met me at Joshua Tree. A small group of us listened as Kent spoke eloquently about problems of the world while we passed a long, cold New Year's Eve stuffed in the back of a van. What a simple pleasure good friends, good conversation, good music and a fine Joshua Tree night added up to. Kent was one of us. Though he had been removed by distance for some years, his presence was felt. Our early years of climbing together were magical. Propelled by his drive, we pushed our personal limits and felt as if we were making our mark, however tiny it may have been. Much like John Long and the Stonemasters of the 1970s, we felt important, courageous and vital. Kent will be missed.

KEN GYGI

HAZEL BRILL JACKSON
1894-1991

Hazel Brill Jackson died on May 22, 1991 at her home in Newburgh, New York at the age of 96. She was the daughter of William Henry and Lizabeth Lee Stone Jackson. She studied at the Museum School of the Museum of Fine Arts in Boston, at the Scuola Rosatti in Florence and with Angelo Zanelli in Rome. She was a prize-winning sculptress and also won acclaim for her drawing and wood engravings. Her bronze portrait busts received praise, but it was for her animal sculptures that she was most famous. The National Academy of Design awarded her the Altman Prise in 1945 and the Ellen P. Speyer Prise in 1947 for a bronze called "Indian Antelope." Her work was exhibited internationally and is in the permanent collections of museums in the United States and Canada.

Miss Jackson joined the American Alpine Club in 1935. In the 1920s and 1930s she climbed extensively in the Alps and the Dolomites. In 1932, she went to the Caucasus. A long-time member of the Ladies Alpine Club of London, which she joined in 1936, she had several articles published in its journal. Among these were "Rock Climbing on the Coast of Maine" (1943) and "South Wall of the Cir (Tschierspitze)" (1946).

FREDERICK C. WING
1915-1991

Fred Wing was born in Brooklyn and reared in Montclair, New Jersey. He graduated from Oberlin College and Harvard Law School. A life-long distance runner, he was captain of his high school and college track and cross-country teams and at one time ran a 4:29 mile. In 1986, he finished second in the over-70 age category in the New York City Marathon.

Fred began his law career serving with the Judge Advocate General of the U.S. Army during World War II. After the war, he worked for his family's New York law firm, Wing & Wing, and then as an attorney and business affairs executive for National Sugar, manufacturer of the Jack Frost brand. In 1959, Fred joined the Columbia Broadcasting System as an attorney. For several years, he was responsible for protecting CBS's copyrights and trademarks. He moved to Los Angeles in 1965 after his promotion to Senior Attorney at CBS Television City, where he concentrated on entertainment law. Fred became General Attorney for the network in 1969 and Broadcast Counsel in 1983 before retiring in 1985.

Few of his climbing friends knew that Fred had a beautiful singing voice. He sang professionally for most of his adult life, performing as soloist for the Harvard Glee Club, in New York's Dessoff Choirs and with the Pacifica and Neo-Renaissance Singers in Los Angeles.

Fred took up mountaineering relatively late in life. Following his move to Los Angeles, he became actively involved in the Sierra Club and soon found himself on the sharp end of the rope with the Angeles Chapter's Rock Climbing

Section. After his retirement, he was elected to the Angeles Chapter's Executive Committee. It will long remember his keen legal and business mind, as well as his generosity, kindness and wit.

Fred Wing is survived by his wife Helena Bessie, his son and daughter Michael and Rachel and his brother Sherman.

I saw Fred last December at the American Alpine Club's annual meeting in San Diego. As I approached his table, I knew what he was going to mention, indirectly, of course: the new route he had pioneered on the north face of Mount Williamson in the Sierra Nevada with the late John Mendenhall and Tim Ryan. He was never boastful about this new route but it was obvious to his climbing friends that Fred was very proud of his first ascent. He even mentioned it in his background statement that appeared on the ballot for the Executive Committee election. I never saw his *curriculum vitae*, but I often assumed that this ascent would appear between the lines of television programming and theatrical film production. At his request, there was no memorial service, but I know that he would have appreciated this being mentioned in any written memorial. So here it is, Fred.

ROBERT J. SECOR

HARRIET TRUMBULL PARSONS
1901-1991

Harriet Trumbull Parsons died on May 11 in Pacific Grove, California. She was born on October 26, 1901 in San Mateo, California, the daughter of the Right Reverend Edward L. Parsons, bishop of the Episcopal Diocese of California. She was a graduate of Wellesley College.

She climbed in the Cascade Mountains of Washington and the Sierra Nevada. In the latter, she made the first ascent of the northwest face of the Hermit in 1939 and did a new route on Mount LeConte in 1946. She joined the American Alpine Club in 1946.

A memorial service was held at St. Mary's-by-the-Sea Episcopal Church in Pacific Grove. She is survived by a niece and a great-niece.

RICHARD LEONARD

ROBERT DUSCHINSKY
1900-1991

Robert Duschinsky was born in Vienna on October 25, 1900. He studied chemistry at the University of Vienna.

He became a devoted mountain climber while still a student. He climbed the mountains in the surroundings of Vienna, which he got to know very well. On June 29, 1924, he had a tragic experience; he lost five of his closest climbing companions in a snowstorm on the Tamischbachhorn. That was always a day of mourning for him. The mountains of the South Tirol, especially the Sella and Marmolada groups, were the goals of his longer vacations. He was a pioneer of ski mountaineering.

After completing his studies with a Doctorate in Chemistry in 1926, he was employed as a research chemical engineer. He joined Hoffmann-La Roche in Paris in 1930 and spent the rest of his career with them. He engaged in research for that institute and discovered numerous significant medicaments, which brought him world-wide fame. It was his life-long passion to do what he could to alleviate human suffering.

He joined the French Alpine Club in 1927 and spent nearly every weekend in his favorite areas, the Mont Blanc range or in the Alps of the Valais in Switzerland.

In 1932, he married an American, Marian Wyman. In 1940, they moved to the United States, where he continued to work for Hoffmann-La Roche. They lived very happily together until her death in 1975. He made a great many outstanding climbs in the United States and Canada, being enchanted by the expansiveness and wilderness of America's mountain world. He often proudly told me how pleased he was when in 1949 he was accepted for membership in the American Alpine Club.

After World War II, he made regular trips to Zermatt and made a number of ascents of the Matterhorn by various routes. He was particularly pleased to have been invited to the 125th anniversary of the first ascent of the Matterhorn and was awarded a gold medal at that time. Zermatt guides still talk of his climbs. He made his last ascent of the Matterhorn at the age of 66. He climbed all the 4000-meter peaks of the Alps, the last being the 4165-meter Breithorn, which he ascended at the age of 81! After he retired from Hoffmann-La Roche, to be close to his beloved Alps he moved to Lausanne, Switzerland, where he continued work at the Swiss Institute for Experimental Cancer Research. In complete harmony, he completed his long and fruitful life, the last fifteen years of which I was privileged to share.

SUSANNE BARTA, *Austria*

Club Activities

EDITED BY FREDERICK O. JOHNSON

A.A.C., New York Section. The year 1991 was a busy and productive one for the Section. *Alpinfilm '91*, a festival of prize-winning mountain films from all over the world, attracted another large and enthusiastic audience to Manhattan's Florence Gould Hall on March 21. Thanks to the success of last year's festival and sponsor support, *Alpinfilm* now offers cash awards to outstanding film-makers. Prize winners were "E Pericoloso Sporgersi" by Robert Nicod, "Moj Mahly Everest" by Poland's Miroslaw Dembinski, "To Climb A Mountain" by Rick Ridgeway and Diane Baker, and "Le Skieur du Vide" by Alan Tixier. Among the celebrities in attendance was Sir Edmund Hillary, who received a standing ovation. This year's festival was run as a fund-raiser for the Mohonk Preserve, which is engaged in ongoing conservation efforts in the Shawangunks. A special tribute was paid to the Smiley family for their years of enlightened custodianship of the East's premier rock climbing area.

Our lecture series featured Ian Wade, climbing team leader of Jim Whittaker's successful 1990 Everest Peace Climb, and Larry Huntington, a member of the 1991 American Everest North Face Expedition. Larry, a bank chairman in real life, narrowly missed making the summit and beating Dick Bass's age record. These slide shows are followed by a social hour.

June was another successful Adirondack climbing outing with approximately 35 members and guests in attendance. After a busy day on the rocks, members and guests attended a Saturday evening banquet in Lake Placid followed by an absorbing slide show on climbing in the Pamirs by Nola Royce.

Finally, Bill Putnam, former A.A.C. President and its newest honorary member, was the special guest speaker at the Section's Annual Dinner. This year's gala black tie event commemorated the 50th anniversary of the formation of the 10th Mountain Division, America's mountain troops in World War II. Bill, a twice decorated veteran of the illustrious unit, recounted its history from the early days of training at Camp Hale to the final, decisive Italian campaign of 1945. A special tribute to the 10th was paid by the West Point Cadet Drill Team. Robert Anderson, leader of the 1988 Everest East Face Expedition, gave a short preview of his attempt to be the first to solo the Seven Summits, thus rounding out the evening's program. Twelve new members were introduced and presented their membership pins. The evening benefited the American Alpine Journal Publishing Fund.

With membership rolls reaching a new high of 250, the Section looks forward in 1992 to continued membership growth, fun and camaraderie for its members and constructive support of climbing-related causes. Out-of-town A.A.C. members who wish to receive invitations to New York events should write to: NY Section A.A.C., Box 5475, Rockefeller Station, New York, NY 10185.

PHILIP ERARD, *Chairman*

A.A.C., Oregon Section. After six years of planning and construction, Silcox Hut on Mount Hood's upper slope is 95% complete. The restoration group, "Friends of Silcox Hut," include A.A.C. members Dick Pooly, Lew McArthur, Neil Cramer and myself. The majestic mini-lodge was rescued from ruin by "The Friends." The completed hut will be operated by Timberline Lodge as a bed-and-breakfast for skiers, climbers and hikers. It features 24 bunks, a shower room, commercial kitchen, 400-amp electrical service fed under a glacier, and a one-mile high-pressure waterline from Timberline Lodge. The construction has been an uphill battle.

In the Portland area, climbing access on the local crags has repeatedly been a precarious situation. Much maneuvering has taken place to keep these areas from being lost altogether. Daryl Nakahira, Tim Olsen, Laura Potter, Gary Rall and John Sprecher have been instrumental in negotiating for continued access. Access to some local areas remains in delicate balance.

BOB MCGOWN, *Chairman*

A.A.C., Southern California Section. Section members gathered in July for a meeting at the Malibu branch of the Los Angeles County Library, home of one of the Club's five branch libraries. The core consists of over 3000 volumes of mountaineering literature donated by Ruth Erb, in memory of her husband, Club member Arkel Erb, who was killed in an accident in the Himalaya in 1977. Members browsed through the library with the assistance of Madelena Bastos-Connelly, a library official who serves, in effect, as curator of the A.A.C. collection. The County Library has added recently published volumes and maintained subscriptions of interest to climbers.

William Lowell Putnam addressed the Section's annual dinner November 1 on his experiences in the Army's 10th Mountain Division during World War II. Copies of Putnam's book, *Green Cognac,* newly published by the A.A.C., arrived just in time to be available for purchase at the dinner. More than 30 members and guests attended the affair at the Quiet Cannon Restaurant in Montebello.

Section leaders are planning a series of regional events in an effort to make Club activities more available to the widely dispersed membership, which ranges from Fresno and Mammoth Lakes in central California southward to San Diego and eastward to Tucson and Phoenix. The first regional program is being planned for the Eastern Sierra.

BILL STALL, *Chairman*

The Alpine Club of Canada. The major highlights of 1991 in the facilities area were the renovation and re-opening of Fay Hut and the Water, Energy and Waste Management Symposium (WEWMS). The first hut built by the A.C.C. (1927), the Fay Hut, was fully renovated during the summer with the assistance of the Rocky Mountain Section and Kootenay National Park. The renovations included a new roof and windows and a completely new interior. The popularity of this hut was evident by the number of reservations that were received almost immediately after the renovations were complete. The WEWMS, held in late October and the first of its kind in North America, attracted over 100 delegates and speakers. Attendees included National Parks personnel, private chalet operators and others concerned with the management of waste in the backcountry. The proceedings are expected to be published in early 1992. An extensive five-year renovation plan for the A.C.C's backcountry huts was completed in 1991.

The expanded summer and winter activities schedule was very successful, and a number of international camps have been added to our schedule. Although the location of the General Mountaineering Camp had to be changed at the last minute, the new location at Farnham Creek proved popular, and all four weeks were full.

The Environment Fund has been well supported with pledge donations totalling almost $30,000. The Mountain Guides' Ball and charity auction in October netted over $10,000 for the Fund. The Fund will provide financial support for environmental initiatives by the club.

The Mountaineering Course Syllabus was completed and distributed for comment. It is hoped that the Syllabus will be widely used to standardize mountaineering course content in Canada. The A.C.C. continues to support its National Sport Climbing Team, and a successful national competition took place in Edmonton, Alberta, in January. The Expeditions Committee continues to support international expeditions through letters of endorsement.

The Silver Rope for Leadership was awarded to Mike Haden (Canmore, AB) and Roger Wallis (Weston, ON), and Distinguished Service Awards went to David Brown (Toronto, ON) and David Gillespie (Montreal, PQ). Special awards were presented to Leslie DeMarsh, Brad Harrison and Chic Scott at the Annual General Meeting at Lake Louise in October.

Membership remains steady, and a membership drive aimed at section-only members was moderately successful. The existing membership structure is being analyzed and some changes are expected in 1992 to meet the needs of the mountaineering and hiking communities.

The Canadian Alpine Journal had a number of full-colour pages added to it, making it the best *C.A.J.* yet. As always, more material was received than could be published. Continued changes to the newsletter have resulted in positive feedback from the membership.

Over $10,000 was allocated to eight projects including publications, youth scholarships, a portable climbing wall, the Kluane Lake Shelter and a waste-management project.

The Canadian Alpine Centre and International Hostel at Lake Louise was completed in December. This marks the successful completion of a long-time dream of the club. The facility provides low-cost accommodation for 100 in Lake Louise and is bound to be popular. The official opening will take place in January 1992. Reservations can be made by calling (403) 522-2200.

BEVERLEY BENDELL, *Activities Manager*

Arizona Mountaineering Club. The club conducted two basic schools for beginning rock climbers and a lead school for advanced climbers. There were also courses on anchors and advanced ropework as well as orienteering and a seminar in Flagstaff on winter survival.

We maintained the summit trail on Camelback Mountain, rebuilding and revegetating the area around it. In November, at the request of Grand Canyon National Park, we staged a two-day cleanup, hauling out a ton of garbage.

The access committee was formed to help deal with the access to local and national climbing areas. It has worked with park officials to educate them about bolting in the Supersitions. A decision about climbing there is now being awaited. We also have worked with the City of Scottsdale on access to Pinnacle Peak and Svens Slab.

KIM HUENECKE

Dartmouth Mountaineering Club. Our club has concluded another safe, productive year. While others waited for the winter snows to melt in New England, three members went to the Mealy Mountains in Labrador for a two-week ski trek. Spring brought the usual trips to the White Mountains, northern Massachusetts and the Shawangunks in New York for rock-climbing instruction. In the fall the club continued its commitment to introductory climbing and ran first-year, rock-climbing trips to Artist's Bluff at the northern end of Franconia Notch. Climbing went into late November, taking advantage either of unusually warm days or of aid climbing under protective overhangs. In December, six members went to their first climbing competition in upstate New York, with some placing successfully and all having a great time. Ice climbing on the small formations of western New Hampshire provided weekend entertainment for a few of our members.

KEITH RAINVILLE, *Activities Director*

Iowa Mountaineers. With another active year, club membership has grown to 5100. Members live in 38 states, and over 4,750 people participated in the club's many instructional courses, mountaineering camps and foreign expeditions.

Under Jim Ebert's instruction, the club taught over 500 members how to cross-country ski at Devils Lake State Park, Wisconsin, during January and February. Winter survival skills, emergency shelters, proper dress, hypothermia, frostbite and avalanche awareness and precautions were included in the program. Also at Devils Lake the club taught 37 three-day courses in basic rock climbing and in hiking. Over 60 members from nine states took one of the club's four one-week basic rock-climbing courses offered during May, June and August.

In March, 65 members hiked for four days in the Havasu Canyon in Arizona's Grand Canyon. Over the Memorial Day weekend 30 members took a four-day intermediate rock-climbing course at Devils Tower, Wyoming. Following bad weather, 26 climbers climbed the Tower in one day. The other four made their climbs the next day.

John and Jim Ebert took 32 members to Tanzania and Kenya in June-July. Eighteen climbed Kilimanjaro, and in the course of a trek on Mount Kenya, eight ascended 16,000-foot Point Lenana.

The annual summer mountaineering camp was held July 29-August 7 in Mount Assiniboine Provincial Park, Canada. Twenty-seven members attended the Base Camp at O'Brien Meadows, and numerous ascents were made on six peaks in the area.

The Iowa Mountaineers held their 51st annual banquet in May in Iowa City with 112 in attendance. John Ebert presented his African film on the club's past 10 mountaineering trips to Uganda, Tanzania and Kenya.

As a final note, two of the club's climbing leaders, who met in a club rock-climbing course, became on September 28 the second couple to get married on top of Wyoming's Devils Tower.

JIM EBERT, *President*

Idaho Alpine Club. The club became increasingly active during 1991 in climbing access issues. Friends of City of Rocks, which is operated primarily by club members, published several newsletters funded by both the Access Fund and T-shirt sales. The City of Rocks climbing ranger formed a climbing-management planning team that included 11 regional climbers. This is an effort to preserve climbing at the National Reserve, with the primary goal of achieving greater access than would be allowed by the general management plans proposed by the National Park Service.

Several groups made winter ascents of the Grand Teton by both the Exum and Owen-Spaulding routes, inspired by the greater challenge of winter conditions and the solitude which is rare during the busy summer season. Ascents were made of "The Snaz" in Death Canyon and the southeast buttress of Mount Moran.

This year's club president, Chuck Odette, climbed the Cassin Ridge on Denali and led winter ascents of the Grand Teton. In addition he has pushed local sport climbing to the edge of 5.12d/13a and placed second in the men's local competition in the Pocatello Pump. He has developed several local sport-climbing rocks in response to the increased popularity of difficult sport climbing.

The club continued its rock, snow and knot schools. Topics covered include proper harness use, leader protection, belaying, ice axe self-arrest, glacier travel, avalanche awareness and ice-climbing techniques.

Those interested in contacting us, please write to: Idaho Alphine Club, Box 2885, Idaho Falls, ID 83403. For access issues, please contact: Friends of City of Rocks, Box 2053, Idaho Falls, ID 83403 or call (208) 745-9094.

STEVEN REISER

The Mazamas: Following is our report for the fiscal year starting October 1, 1990: The Banquet Committee staged the 98th Annual Mazama Banquet at the Airport Holiday Inn, attended by 240 people on November 2. Master of Ceremonies, Dr. Christine Mackert, supervised the traditional passing of the Sholes ice axe from Lis Cooper to Ray Sheldon, our new president. The Climbing Committee presented 34 awards, and the Trail Trips Committee presented 11, including the Hardesty Cup to Don Fournier. Elinor Levin received the Montague Cup for her contribution to conservation, and Jeff Thomas was recognized by the Margaret Griffin Redman Cup for outstanding literary work on his *Oregon High,* a new climbing guide to the Oregon Cascades. Jim Whittaker, the first American to ascend Mount Everest, was declared an honorary member of the Mazamas. Scott Woolums highlighted the evening with slides of awe-inspiring western scenery by himself and Galen Rowell.

The 12-member Climbing Committee ran 283 scheduled mountain climbs and 26 summer rock climbs. The Basic Climbing School returned to Whitaker Middle School in northeast Portland with enrollment of 270 students. Rock sessions were staged at Horsethief Butte in the Columbia River Gorge, and snow-practice sessions at Mount Hood. Forty students entered Intermediate School and 23 Advanced School.

Mike DeLaune chaired the Expedition Committee, which extends Mazama climbing to distant ranges and other continents. It encourages and trains climbers in expedition techniques; assists non-Mazama expeditions through endorsement, sponsorship and funding; and promotes Mazamas as a world-class climbing organization to those outside the club. In November the committee brought Galen Rowell to Portland with his highly acclaimed *Mountain Light* photography seminar. This highly successful event drew 170 participants and netted $4,000 to help support expedition climbing. In January, Edwin Bernbaum presented his *Sacred Mountains of the World* show to an audience of 165. In February, the Executive Council approved a committee recommendation for endorsement, sponsorship and funding to the 1991 Mazama Ecuador Expedition, which left Portland in December, 1991 for attempts on six Ecuadorean summits. The fifth annual Mazamas Expeditions Biathlon, held in April, drew 242 individuals and 30 teams to net $3,100 for the Expedition Reserve Account.

The 19 members of the Climb Explorer Post 936, under Mazama supervision, attended a snow bivouac at Mount Hood, rock practice at Horsethief Butte, nine mountain climbs and an outing to Smith Rocks. Four members attended the Mazama outing to the Tetons. The post's only girl, Amy Martens, was consistent in attendance and one of the toughest members.

The Nordic Committee continued to focus its activity on the annual Nordic Ski School, which drew 250 participants. This year the Nordic Committee was able to complement its ski school training with ski tours in February and March. Ski Mountaineering became an official program this year.

The Outing Committee sponsored eight events, with hiking and backpacking the most popular. There were two of these in Washington's Olympic Peninsula and one in Grand Teton National Park. A group of 44 climbers and hikers were in the Banff/Jasper area of Canada, where Mount Athabaska, Mount Temple, Castle Mountain and Crowfoot were climbed. In Europe smaller groups hiked and climbed in Norway, Austria's Dachstein Alps, the Swiss Alps (with climbs of the Matterhorn, Breithorn, Jungfrau and Mönch), and a group of six skiers found lots of snow at Chamonix and Les Menuires, France, in March.

The Trail Trips Committee scheduled 306 diverse events, including Tuesday evening street rambles, A, B and C hikes each weekend, Wednesday hikes, snowshoe hikes and clinics, backpacks, snow bivouacs, car camps and work trips. A total of 3646 participated. The Trail Tending program was initiated to train new work-trip leaders and interface with government agencies in a long established practice of maintaining trails.

The Conservation Committee keeps the club alert on policies of the U.S. Forest Service, Fish and Wildlife Service, and our National Parks. Developing federal interest in sustained forest yield, soil conservation and other new policies has been heartening, though slow to be implemented. Development of the management plan for the Columbia Gorge National Scenic Area has been another area of key interest. The club made a modest donation to the Public Forest Foundation, whose professional foresters have assumed leadership roles in educating federal land managers in less destructive forestry practices. We have also continued to work with the Friends of Mount Hood in expressing disapproval of the development of a destination resort proposed by Mount Hood Meadows on U.S.F.S. land.

JACK GRAUER, *Past President*

Memphis Mountaineers. Despite the lack of local climbing resources, the Memphis Mountaineers enjoyed a productive year. The 1991 membership of 51 included 33 regular members residing in the Memphis, Tennessee, area, six honorary members and 12 associate members scattered throughout the United States.

In addition to numerous rock-climbing trips to the local crags of the Mid-South, individual members were active afield in areas ranging from France (Mont Blanc) to South America (Roraima, Pico Bolívar, San Tigro) to Canada (Mount Athabasca) and Colorado. The climbing year ended with several members teaching mountain-rescue techniques to park rangers in Venezuela.

Most of the administrative activities included basic rock-climbing instruction, but primarily dealt with petitioning the state of Mississippi to re-open access to Tishomingo State Park to climbing. We worked closely with the Access Fund to develop a permit system for use at Tishomingo which the park is currently reviewing. As a result of this work, the club was invited to select a delegate to serve on the National Advisory Council of the Access Fund.

The Memphis Mountaineers meet on the second Sunday of the month at seven P.M. in the Highland Branch of the Memphis Public Library. Members are informed of club activities through the monthly newsletter, the *Memphis Moun-*

tain News. Club officers for 1991 were Barbara Knowles, president; Robin Daniels, vice-president; Ted Burkey, treasurer; and Suzy Ferrenbach, secretary.

Anyone interested in climbing in the Mid-South is encouraged to join the club. For more information write: Memphis Mountaineers, Inc., Box 11124, Memphis, TN 38111.

BARBARA KNOWLES, *President*

The Mountaineers. In 1991, we saw our membership top the 12,000 mark! Our Basic and Intermediate Climbing Courses were as popular as ever. At our headquarters in Seattle, over 200 enrolled in our Basic Climbing course and 70 students graduated; 70 students entered the Intermediate Climbing Program and 15 completed graduation requirements. Our Olympia Branch started the 1991 season with 38 climbing and five alpine scrambling students. Nine 1st-year and eight 2nd-year climbing students, and four alpine scramblers graduated. Fifty-two students entered the Everett Branch's Basic Course and 37 graduated; one person finished Everett's Intermediate Course in 1991. Eleven Basic students graduated from our Bellingham Branch's Basic Climbing Course; 66 students took the Tacoma Branch Basic Course and 18 entered Tacoma's Intermediate Course last year.

Demand was also high for our Mountaineering Oriented First Aid (MOFA) courses. This course, developed by The Mountaineers in 1968 with the American Red Cross, meets the requirements of Red Cross Standard First Aid with an additional 22 hours of training using simulated mountain accident scenarios. It is designed for those who venture where medical assistance can be hours or days away, and is a requirement for graduation from our Basic, Intermediate, or Alpine Scrambling Courses. In 1991, 519 people completed The Mountaineers' MOFA courses.

A campaign begun in 1990 reached success in April of this year when the Peshastin Pinnacles were reopened to climbers. These 200-foot sandstone spires in Eastern Washington had been closed in 1986 because of the owner's liability concerns. The Mountaineers, working primarily with the American Alpine Club, the Trust for Public Land and Recreational Equipment, Inc. (REI), raised public interest and support for state acquisition of the property. In all, The Mountaineers and its members contributed $18,000 of the $60,000 in private funds needed to acquire and open the Pinnacles as a State Park. Sixty-five members participated in work parties to build trails and clear and grade the parking lot and restroom areas. This popular climbing area, with over 90 established routes, is excellent for teaching and practicing.

We were fortunate to have some interesting speakers address the club in 1991. Geoffrey Tabin, the fourth person in the world to reach the "Seven Summits," spoke at the annual banquet, and Carlos Buhler, the most accomplished North American climber in the Himalaya, spoke at our Tacoma Branch banquet. As in 1990, we again sponsored and organized local showings of the Best of the Banff Festival of Mountain Films.

The Mountaineers continued to work for natural resource conservation, and increased efforts to promote a wilderness ethic among members in all club activities. As the year closed, Mountaineers Books had sent the fifth edition of *Mountaineering: The Freedom of the Hills* to the printer, for distribution by January, 1992.

Although there were over 300 climbs organized by The Mountaineers in 1991, this may have been our most exciting: Under the auspices of The Mountaineers International Exchange Committee, 10 climbers departed for the Pamir Mountains of the Soviet Union in July. Upon arrival in Osh the team was treated like royalty with a five-course breakfast and police escort as it departed toward Achik-Tash Base Camp, situated at 12,140 feet. While acclimatizing at Base Camp, all members climbed nearby Pik Petrosky (15,421 feet). A couple of days later the team's climbing equipment was flown to Camp I at 13,860 feet on Pik Lenina while team members hiked eight miles of moraine and glacier. Two more camps were established as the team progressed up the mountain, the highest at 20,400 feet. Just as the climbers were preparing for the summit bid, a storm descended which stopped all movement and left the group waiting impatiently for several days. On August 10, five of the group made a summit bid, which Bob St. Clair alone made in that attempt. The following day Dave Gordon, Dan Luchtel and Howard Weaver also successfully climbed the peak. With a feeling of accomplishment, all members cleared the mountain of equipment and returned to Achik-Tash on August 13. Many difficult goodbyes were said to new acquaintances as the team departed. Deep gratitude was expressed to Soviet friends for providing an "experience of a lifetime" in the Pamirs. The Mountaineers look forward to hosting their Soviet counterparts in the Northwest in 1993.

DIANNE M. HOFF, *President*

AAC BOOKS

THE AMERICAN ALPINE JOURNAL, edited by H. Adams Carter.

THE AMERICAN ALPINE JOURNAL INDEX
1929-1976, Edited by Earlyn Church.
1977-1986, Edited by Patricia A. Fletcher.

ACCIDENTS IN NORTH AMERICAN MOUNTAINEERING, edited by John E. Williamson.

CLIMBING IN NORTH AMERICA, by Chris Jones.

THE COLUMBIA MOUNTAINS OF CANADA—CENTRAL (The Interior Ranges of B.C.), by Earle R. Whipple, John Kevin Fox, Roger Laurilla and William L. Putnam.

THE COLUMBIA MOUNTAINS OF CANADA—WEST & SOUTH (The Interior Ranges of B.C.), Earle R. Whipple and William L. Putnam.

THE GREAT GLACIER AND ITS HOUSE, by William L. Putnam.

GREEN COGNAC: The Education of a Mountain Fighter, by William Lowell Putnam.

HIGH ALASKA, by Jonathan Waterman.

MOUNTAIN SICKNESS, by Peter Hackett, M.D.

THE MOUNTAINS OF NORTH AMERICA, by Fred Beckey.

THE RED ROCKS OF SOUTHERN NEVADA, by Joanne Urioste.

THE ROCKY MOUNTAINS OF CANADA—NORTH, by Robert Kruszyna and William L. Putnam.

THE ROCKY MOUNTAINS OF CANADA—SOUTH, by Glen W. Boles, with Robert Kruszyna and William L. Putnam.

SHAWANGUNK ROCK CLIMBS: The Third Edition, by Dick Williams.

SURVIVING DENALI, The Second Edition, by Jonathan Waterman.

TAHQUITZ AND SUICIDE ROCKS, by Chuck Wilts.

TOUCH THE SKY: The Needles in the Black Hills of South Dakota, by Paul Piana.

TRAPROCK: Rock Climbing in Central Connecticut, by Ken Nichols.

A WALK IN THE SKY, by Nicholas Clinch.

WASATCH ROCK CLIMBS, by Les Ellison and Brian Smoot.

WHERE THE CLOUDS CAN GO, by Conrad Kain.

THE WORST WEATHER ON EARTH: A History of the Mount Washington Observatory, by William Lowell Putnam.

YURAQ JANKA: The Cordilleras Blanca and Rosko, by John Ricker.

Maps

ACONCAGUA, by Jerzy Wala; text by Carles Capellas and Josep Paytubi.

ANTARCTICA: McMurdo Sound Area, by Dee Molenaar. (Includes history and information.)

Prices and order information on request from The American Alpine Club, 113 East 90th Street, New York, NY 10128-1589.

INDEX

Volume 34 ● Issue 66 ● 1992

Compiled by Patricia A. Fletcher

This issue comprises all of Volume 34

Mountains are listed by their official names and ranges; quotation marks indicate unofficial names. Ranges and geographic locations are also indexed. Unnamed peaks (e.g., P 2037) are listed following the range or country in which they are located.

All expedition members cited in major articles are included, whereas only the leaders and persons supplying information in the **Climbs and Expeditions** section are listed.

Titles of books reviewed in this issue are grouped as a single entry under **Book Reviews**.

Abbreviations used: Article: *art.*; Bibliography: *bibl.*; Obituary: *obit.*

INDEX